THE MAKING OF THE GREEK GENOCIDE

War and Genocide

General Editors: Omer Bartov, Brown University; A. Dirk Moses, European University Institute, Florence, Italy / University of Sydney

In recent years there has been a growing interest in the study of war and genocide, not from a traditional military history perspective, but within the framework of social and cultural history. This series offers a forum for scholarly works that reflect these new approaches.

"The Berghahn series Studies on War and Genocide *has immeasurably enriched the English-language scholarship available to scholars and students of genocide and, in particular, the Holocaust."* —**Totalitarian Movements and Political Religions**

For a full volume listing, please see back matter

THE MAKING OF THE GREEK GENOCIDE

Contested Memories of the Ottoman Greek Catastrophe

Erik Sjöberg

berghahn
NEW YORK · OXFORD
www.berghahnbooks.com

Published in 2017 by
Berghahn Books
www.berghahnbooks.com

© 2017, 2019 Erik Sjöberg
First paperback edition published in 2019

Library of Congress Cataloging-in-Publication Data

A C.I.P. cataloging record is available from the Library of Congress

British Library Cataloguing in Publication Data

A catalogue record for this book is available
from the British Library

ISBN 978-1-78533-325-5 hardback
ISBN 978-1-78920-063-8 paperback
ISBN 978-1-78533-326-2 ebook

CONTENTS

ACKNOWLEDGMENTS

This study was made possible by the support of various institutions and individuals in different countries. The Swedish Research Council (Vetenskapsrådet) provided me with the funding that enabled me to carry out this project. I am grateful to Sam Wineburg, who welcomed me as a postdoctoral fellow to Stanford University between 2013 and 2015, where much of this book was written. I am also indebted to several other colleagues (in no particular order of hierarchy) for their advice, encouragement and helpful assistance in matters large and small: Taner Akçam, Peter Balakian, Cecilie Stokholm Banke, Petter Bergner, Magdalena Gross, Antonis Liakos, Norman Naimark, Christian Axboe Nielsen, Mogens Pelt, Catharina Raudvere, Doyle Stevick, Eric Weitz, and Trine Stauning Willert. At Berghahn Books I would like to thank Chris Chappell and the anonymous reviewers of the proposal for this book as well as for the final manuscript. Any remaining errors in the text are, of course, my own.

Finally, I would like to thank my wife, Elisabeth Hallgren Sjöberg, for her love and encouragement over the years, and to acknowledge the support of our respective families and friends: Gunnel and Johan Sjöberg, Gunnar and Birgit Hallgren, Anna Sjöberg-Smith, Monica Bergman, Torbjörn Hallgren, Kristina Blombäck, Annika Rubinstein, Jacob Stridsman, AnnaSara Hammar, Linn Holmberg, Robert Eckeryd, Olivia Ekman, Annette and Johan Nilsson, Tomas Karlsson, and Per-Olof Grönberg. Without you this book might never have come into being.

Umeå, May 2016

ABBREVIATIONS

⟨ɷ§§ઽ⟩

AHIF	American Hellenic Institute Foundation
AKP	Adalet ve Kalkinma Partisi (Justice and Development Party)
ANCA	Armenian National Committee of America
ANEL	Anexartitoi Ellines (Independent Greeks)
ASALA	Armenian Secret Army for the Liberation of Armenia
CUP	Committee of Union and Progress
DIMAR	Dimokratiki Aristera (Democratic Left)
EDA	Eniaia Dimokratiki Aristera (Unified Democratic Left)
EEE	Ethniki Enosis tis Ellados (National Union of Greece)
IAGS	International Association of Genocide Scholars
ICTY	International Criminal Tribunal for the Former Yugoslavia
KEPOME	Kentro Pontiakon Meleton (Center for Pontian Studies)
KKE	Kommounistiko Komma tis Elladas (Communist Party of Greece)
KMS	Kentro Mikrasiatikon Spoudon (Center for Asia Minor Studies)
LAOS	Laïkos Orthodoxos Synagermos (Popular Orthodox Rally)
ND	Nea Dimokratia (New Democracy)
OPSE	Omospondia Prosfygikon Somateion tis Elladas (Federation of Refugee Associations of Greece)
OPSVE	Omospondia Pontiakon Somateion Voreiou Ellados (Federation of Pontian Associations of Northern Greece)

PASOK	Panellinio Sosialistiko Kinevma (Panhellenic Socialist Movement)
PKK	Partiya Karkerên Kurdistan (Kurdistan Workers' Party)
POE	Pampontiaki Omospondia Ellados (Pan-Pontian Federation of Greece)
POPS	Panellinia Omospondia Pontiakon Somateion (Panhellenic Federation of Pontian Associations)
SAE	Symvoulio Apodimou Ellinismou (World Council of Hellenes Abroad)
SEKE	Sosialistiko Ergatiko Komma tis Ellados (Socialist Labor Party of Greece)
SYN	Synaspismos tis Aristeras kai tis Proodou (Coalition of the Left and Progress)
SYRIZA	Synaspismos tis Rizospastikis Aristeras (Coalition of the Radical Left)

INTRODUCTION
COSMOPOLITAN MEMORY AND THE GREEK GENOCIDE NARRATIVE

On 11 March 2010, the Parliament of Sweden voted to endorse a motion calling for recognition of the "1915 genocide of Armenians, Assyrians/Syriacs/Chaldaeans and Pontic Greeks" as a historical fact.[1] The motion, which passed the vote by narrow majority, stirred an emotionally charged debate, with allegations on the one hand of history being politicized, and on the other hand accusations of genocide denial for the sake of good relations with Turkey, the successor state to the crumbling empire of 1915's perpetrators. Sweden's government, for which the Parliament's resolution was a source of diplomatic embarrassment, maintained that history should be left to the historians, not to legislative assemblies. Those who supported the recognition of the atrocities committed against Ottoman Christians as an act of genocide argued that the historians had already established the facts. The genocide was a reality and it was now the politicians' duty to urge Turkey to face its own history. But while the plight of the Armenians and of other Christians in Eastern Anatolia was never disputed in the debate, the Pontic (or Pontian) Greeks mentioned among the victims seemed to raise a few eyebrows. One commentator claimed that there had never been a genocide of the Greeks once inhabiting the region of Pontos in northern Turkey, and that the Swedish Parliament and certain historians had bestowed an "inaccurate historiography with legitimacy."[2] Few seemed to recall ever having heard of this community and an event

that nonetheless was recognized as true. Responses to this assertion ranged from awkward uncertainty among those who had voted in favor of the resolution and outrage from Sweden's Pontian Greek community. "What makes him an expert of our history?" stated a representative of that community. "We just want recognition and in the end an apology from the Turkish people."[3]

This book examines the distinctive forms that collective memories take and the ways in which they find acceptance as facts, in an age of human rights and an emerging cosmopolitan culture of remembrance. More specifically, it examines how the notion of the Greek genocide has come into being, and how different forces, circumstances and debates have shaped this "memory" over the course of the past three decades. Memories do not arise from a void. Whether they stem from lived experience or are constructed for a purpose, they always reflect a certain historical, cultural and political setting. Although a configuration of recent vintage, the "Greek genocide" refers to an event, or series of events, which, known as the Asia Minor Catastrophe, had lived for more than half a century before in the collective remembrance and national imagination of Greeks. Some of the Swedish MPs might have been aware of the population exchange between Greece and Turkey in 1923, through which around 1.2 million Anatolian Greeks and 400,000 Balkan Muslims were forcibly expelled from their homelands. Perhaps they also knew that this event had been the precedent of the ethnic cleansing carried out on a much grander scale in Central and Eastern Europe during and after World War II. But what the petitioners of the motion asked for was political recognition of a new interpretation of these events, which sought to make sense of them not just within the context of a national past, or Greek-Turkish relations, but within a broader framework of crimes against humanity. According to the advocates of this interpretation, the catastrophe of the Greek inhabitants of the Ottoman Empire must not be understood in isolation from but rather as a parallel to the (internationally much better known) Armenian genocide.

In order to understand why this redefinition of national experience, or collective remembrance, came about, we need to consider the intricate set of processes that is globalization and its impact on local contexts. The preoccupation of Swedish politicians with the tragic fate of the Ottoman Empire's Christian minorities nearly a century ago signals the coming of transnational history-cultural concerns into a society unaffected by (and largely unaware of) the historical event in question. These concerns are the outcome of intertwined and mutually reinforcing processes—globalization, transnational and institutionalized remembrance of the Holocaust as a new form of "cosmopolitan memory," and growing attention to human rights issues—which all gained momentum at the end of the Cold War.[4] While it is all too easy to assume that state boundaries erode as the result of the nation state's decline, or that all aspects of human life necessarily mirror the economic transactions that take place on a global level, there is much to be said for the observation that transnational migration, new technologies and other processes influence how a growing number of people around the world perceive themselves and others. Even those who resist globalization must find ways to come to terms with it. Its influence is, among other things, to be found in the ways in which the Holocaust has been reconfigured as a sort of "cosmopolitan" past that transcends national boundaries, as an event of European, if not global, significance. Attention to the Nazis' destruction of European Jewry has shifted from debates about its origins and nature to a broader emphasis on its public remembrance; how it was remembered, how it should have been remembered, and, consequently, how it can and ought to be remembered in the future. This is not merely an academic debate. Films, speeches, commemorative dates, museum exhibits and other media highlight these issues. Educators look to the Holocaust to teach their students the values of democracy and tolerance, while political leaders across the Western world evoke it to reaffirm the state's commitment to these values, using the event as a negative example to tell its citizens precisely what their society is not.

From being treated as a mere side effect of World War II, the Holocaust has taken center stage as the "absolute evil" of the modern age.[5] This and the increasing willingness of states to admit guilt for their own part in this and other events in the past, sometimes mending wrongs by making reparations to victims of earlier state policies,[6] have contributed to change common views about history as something that imbues the present with meaning. No longer is the progress or heroic exploits of nations the dominant sort of history from which meaningful lessons are drawn, or ideas about the human condition are nurtured, in the Western world, but more so the moral collapse that from time to time has marked the twentieth century: the two world wars, the totalitarian ideologies and the phenomenon of genocide, the "crime of all crimes" known to mankind. States are neither the only parties involved in memory politics. Public Holocaust remembrance has opened, in the words of David B. MacDonald, a window of opportunity for substate actors to draw attention to their own historical or current predicaments.[7] Meanwhile, the human rights challenge to state sovereignty and the renewed significance of the genocide concept as perpetrators of atrocities face trial in international courts of law at the dawn of the new millennium pave the way for the, more or less, forgotten tragedies of the past. The most notable example is the Armenian genocide, carried out by the Young Turks in the shadow of World War I, which in itself is considered by many the original disaster that spawned Europe's "dark" century, the "age of extremes," the "century of camps and genocides." As a Swedish historian has put it, the Swedish Parliament's recognition of the 1915 genocide in 2010 is "a good illustration of the force history can possess when Sweden, a country which for decades praised itself for having had no part in the great tragedies of modern European history, now has entered World War I, on the side of the victims and the injured."[8]

Purpose, Aims and Argument of the Book

It is against this backdrop that activists in Greece and the Greek diaspora set their claim for the national and international recognition of their community's experience as genocide. Though the Greek state recognizes two dates that commemorate the "genocide of the Greeks of Pontos" and the "genocide of the Greeks of Asia Minor by the Turkish state" respectively, the claim is mostly advanced by nonstate actors. Commemoration thereof is, despite the occasional lip service of political leaders and government officials in Greece, mainly the concern of dedicated individuals and nongovernmental organizations. Meanwhile, despite the predictable Turkish efforts to discredit it, Greek mainstream historians, educators and influential commentators oppose this claim as founded upon "ahistorical and anti-scientific opinion."[9] An important objective of this book is to understand why the notion of the Greek genocide, or the Pontian and Anatolian Greek genocides, has become so contested. What are the reasons for what I call the Greek genocide narrative's impact on debates on the Greek past as well as the difficulties encountered in finding acceptance as true history and a valid "national memory"? An important analytical perspective is therefore political, which means paying attention to how the claim has been lobbied in political assemblies, as well as understanding the particular political context in which debates occur, and the cultural and historical circumstances that underpin them.

As the appearance of the Greek genocide issue in Swedish politics demonstrates, this is not a debate or a memory-political phenomenon that is confined to one national context. An important second category of analysis is transnational or comparative, which is understood as the examination of links between the Greek activists and similar memory-political initiatives among other ethnic groups. What is the relation between the Greek genocide narrative and other histories of atrocity? Connected to this is a third category that might be called a science-sociological perspective, which analyzes the various academic responses to this claim, both in Greece and in the international community of scholars that encounter it. Finally, there is also a fourth perspective, which has to do with education and historical sense-making. How is remembrance of the Greek genocide constructed, taught and made sense of by activists, scholars, educators, and others concerned with it?

It is not entirely possible to separate one perspective from another among those mentioned here. When a politician argues that the memory of genocide is paramount to national self-understanding, and of equal significance to internationally recognized cases, such as the Holocaust, he or she is using ideas about a cosmopolitan past to make sense of a national or ethnic experience. In a similar way, historians that take part in this debate do so not strictly as scholars weighing the evidence for or against a certain interpretation of history, but also as citizens concerned with how the past is used and what lessons should be handed down to society. Nonetheless, the reader of this book may find the distinctions useful.

The debates explored here occur at a national as well as international level, and this has consequences for how remembrance of Greek suffering in Anatolia is represented, as the claims that fuel it move between different settings. In this way, this study brings attention to the making of a modern memory, in this case that of the Greek genocide, in its transition from a narrative of ethnic distinctiveness to transnational or cosmopolitan history, recognized as carrying universally valid experiences and values. A word is due about the concepts of cosmopolitanism and cosmopolitan memory. According to sociologist Ulrich Beck, cosmopolitanism refers to a process of "internal globalization" through which global concerns become part of the local (or national) experience of an increasing number of people.[10] This notion has been elaborated by fellow sociologists Daniel Levy and Natan Sznaider, who have traced the emergence of "cosmopolitan memory" through the examination of how the Holocaust has been remembered and imbued with new meanings in different national societies. By cosmopolitanization they understand a sort of collective memory that has been "de-territorialized," removed from its original historical and geographic context and made a universal concern for people in places far away. Remembrance of the event today known as the Holocaust is not the sole concern of Jewish victims and German perpetrators, and their descendants, as we have seen.

What was once considered local concerns can in the age of globalization thus be made global concerns, as the quest for international recognition of atrocities so aptly illustrates. Efforts to study, recognize and teach genocide are premised on the belief that knowledge about past atrocities will prevent similar crimes from happening in the future. The rise of the transnational human rights regime, which since the end of the Cold War has grown more prominent, enables local (ethnic or national) experiences to become part of a universally shared past and thus to matter to others than those immediately involved. According to Levy and Sznaider, rather than being erased in the age of globalization, national and ethnic memories are transformed and subjected to a common patterning. "But in each case, the common elements combine with preexisting elements to form something new. In each case, the new global narrative has to be reconciled with the old national narratives, and the result is always distinctive."[11]

I argue that the emergence of the notion of the Greek genocide offers a case in which this interplay between the global and the local, between universalism and particularism, can be studied and better understood. Remarkably little has been written about this phenomenon among scholars of modern Greece, who, to the extent that they attend to it, tend to dismiss it as a mere expression of nationalism resting on an unsubstantiated claim that is unworthy of scholarly inquiry.[12] We know little of how the claim has been lobbied, its reception and the forces, interests and circumstances that have shaped its underpinning narrative. The quest for recognition is a dual process of nationalization and cosmopolitanization of memory, or a certain interpretation of history. This means that activists strive to convince a national audience that the experience of genocide is paramount to the community's self-understanding and merits a special place within the nation's canon of memories. At the same time, they strive to make sense of this perceived genocidal experience, and remembrance thereof, within a larger transnational context, with regard to audiences usually skeptical of nationalism. This is a process fraught with contradictions, which is why it is sometimes difficult to speak of one narrative of genocide, in the singular. Fierce controversies over definitions, historical interpretation and representation, and whom to include or exclude from the circle of victims divide activists among themselves and challenge the idea of a unified memory of genocide. Often, this discord results in part from exposure to the influence of cosmopolitan memory and contacts with other ethnic communities with similar agendas. The relations with similar memory-political projects offer a key toward understanding how "ethnic memories" are cosmopolitanized in a broader transnational perspective.

Historical culture in Greece—that is, the totality of discourses through which a society understands itself, the present and the future through interpreting the past—has often been described in terms of ethnocentrism. Ever since scholars like Konstantinos Paparrigopoulos and Spyridon Zambelios stressed in the nineteenth century the continuity of Hellenic culture as a way to bridge the gap between the classical civilization admired by Philhellenes and Westernizing Greeks, and the traditions of Orthodox Byzantium, the Greek school system has stressed the unique features of the nation's historical experience. According to critics of this history education, this comes at the expense of broader European or world history perspectives, which might expand the mental horizons of students.[13] Scholars of modern Greece have discussed the tendency toward what they call Greek exceptionalism, "an approach to Greek history focusing on its singularity that refuses to situate historical events in a broader comparative framework."[14] It is precisely this notion of exceptionalism—by no means exceptional to Greece—that makes relations to other memory communities important to study, as the idea of common fate may force Greek activists to re-conceptualize their notions of uniqueness. Sometimes this memory-work has other outcomes than what activists might have anticipated in the first place. These processes are little known and little studied. In that respect this book contributes to our understanding of a contemporary political as well as history-cultural phenomenon that is both national and transnational.

Terms and Theoretical Considerations: Genocide, Remembrance, Trauma

Before presenting the outline of this book, some recurring concepts need to be clarified. The first is that of genocide, which plays a central role in the activism and debates that are analyzed throughout the book. The term was coined by Polish-Jewish lawyer Raphael Lemkin in his work *Axis Rule in Occupied Europe*, in 1944, to describe the ongoing Nazi annihilation of European Jewry, but reflected over two decades of Lemkin's thinking on the "crime of barbarity."[15] It was subsequently adopted and codified in the United Nations Convention on the Prevention and Punishment of the Crime of Genocide of 1948, whose Article 2 defines genocide as follows.

> In the present Convention, genocide means any of the following acts committed with intent to destroy, in whole or in part, a national, ethnical, racial or religious group, as such:
> a. Killing members of the group;
> b. Causing serious bodily or mental harm to members of the group;

    c. Deliberately inflicting on the group conditions of life calculated to bring about its physical destruction in whole or in part;

    d. Imposing measures intended to prevent births within the group;

    e. Forcibly transferring children of the group to another group.[16]

Originally conceived of as a legal term to be used in the prosecution of individuals suspected of any of these acts, genocide has changed the way mass violence, in the past as well as in the present, is understood by scholars and laymen alike. It is, however, a concept that gives rise to inevitable controversies, political as well as academic. Its definition relies upon the intention of the perpetrator to "destroy, in whole or in part," a certain group "as such." It can be argued that an act of mass killing or policies that led to the mass death of a certain group was not genocide, because the perpetrators had some other "intent," or because they intended to kill someone, but not any specified group "as such." Another problem arises from the way in which the Soviets, contrary to Lemkin's intentions, were able to compromise the definition by excluding political and social groups, for obvious reasons.[17] Academics argue about whether the UN's definition is too narrow, excluding virtually any atrocity that is not the Holocaust out of a misguided interpretation of the criteria and the original context in which it was conceived, or too broad, making the term vulnerable to rhetorical overuse, or as Frank Chalk and Kurt Jonassohn put it "devoid of all cognitive content," communicating "nothing but the author's disapproval."[18] Others still question the term's value as a guide to historical interpretation. "In the end," as Timothy Snyder puts it, "historians who discuss genocide find themselves answering the question as to whether a given event qualifies, and so classifying rather than explaining."[19] Snyder may be right in that a simple classification cannot substitute for an explanation of the complexities of each case, but his own preferred term "mass killing" raises more questions than it answers. Even though it is not the purpose of this book to determine whether the violence against Ottoman Greeks was genocidal or not, it is perhaps inevitable to discuss the evidence supporting such an interpretation; something which I briefly do in Chapter 1. In any case, the disagreements and confusion surrounding the term suggests attention to how participants in debates about Greek genocide remembrance understand the concept itself.

Genocide is not a term confined to courtrooms and scholarly debates. As the case of the Holocaust's legacies demonstrates, it also has a profound impact on what Levy and Sznaider call the modern memory-scape, meaning that it has given a name to events that many people find important and deeply meaningful to remember. This relation between genocide and remembrance brings us to the thorny topic of collective memory, which has generated a vast literature in the humanities and the social sciences. The term collective memory was suggested by Maurice Halbwachs in his seminal work, *Les cadres sociaux de la mémoire*, in 1925, by which he understood the process in which different collectives, from groups of two individuals to groups in their thousands, come together to remember. When such people lose interest, or move away, or die, or for any other reason cease to engage in these acts of shared remembrance, the collective dissolves, and so does the collective memory that bound the individuals together.[20] Memory is thus a social as much as an individual process, something that continues to evolve, and is subject to changing circumstances. Often, memory is taken to be the opposite of history, understood as the scientific study of the past.[21] Several historians have lamented the influence of the so-called memory boom, which they see as a perversion of historical knowledge in the service of identity politics, nostalgia, and other subjective truths.[22] While there are differences between history—as a profession with rules about evidence, publication, and peer review—and memory as a process ungoverned by such rules, the distinction is not clear-cut. All historians are in a sense the children of their own time and place, which means that they are hardly isolated from the concerns and convictions about the past of their social settings. It is useful to keep the distinction between the historian's work and more general "memory-work" in mind, but this should not blind us to the many overlaps that exist between the two. Jay Winter has suggested the term "historical remembrance" to overcome the binary opposition between history and memory in the analysis of how people make sense of the past. By insisting on such sense-making as acts of remembrance, he argues for avoiding "the pitfalls of referring to memory as some vague cloud which exists without agency, and to history as an objective story which exists outside of the people whose lives it describes."[23] I agree with his critique of the concept of collective memory as vague; something that also can be said for Levy's and Sznaider's concept of cosmopolitan memory, which is not always clear on who it is that remembers, but which I nonetheless find useful for my analytical purposes. Memories of events exist but they do not acquire meaning before someone actively remembers them. In this study I refer to public or other forms of remembrance, and historical culture. By the latter term, I understand the set of discourses through which broader collectivities, such as national, religious or political communities, or individuals claiming to speak for such communities, make sense of themselves, their present and expectations of the future, by interpreting the past. Historical culture is the communicative context in which history, or the narration of past events, is produced, mediated, discussed, and consumed. Dominant "grand" or "master" narratives provide a framework of interpretation through which individuals and collectivities remember, but the historical culture of any living society is also subject to change, as new political and cultural concerns, and demands from certain groups and international developments, challenge old certainties.[24] This suggests attention to how domestic concerns of national historical culture interact with those of other societies and a broader international community.

The concepts of genocide and memory come together in the notion of trauma, commonly understood as the (often involuntary) remembrance of dramatic events with disastrous consequences. Of specific interest to a study like this is Jeffrey C. Alexander's notion of cultural trauma, or trauma drama. While traumas certainly haunt individuals with first-hand experience of such events, and often their immediate relations, collective traumas do not exist in and of themselves; rather than being found they are made, in response to different political, cultural and personal needs, which often change over time. Such collective trauma constructions, or cultural traumas, occur "when members of a collectivity feel they have been subjected to a horrendous event that leaves indelible marks upon their group consciousness, marking their memories forever and changing their future identity in fundamental and irrevocable ways."[25] Seen from this perspective, it is important to ask why and under what circumstances such cultural traumas emerge— or fail to develop and gain a wider acceptance. Alexander argues that every trauma claim faces certain challenges, if it is to be recognized as a wound to a broader collectivity than those who experienced the injury first hand. "It begins with defining, symbolizing, and dramatizing what 'happened'. In the course of this narration, the identity of the victims must be established, and so must the identity of the perpetrators ... Finally, a solution appropriate to these three 'facts' must be proposed."[26] Certainly, material resources, such as media access, and demographic strength of a given "trauma community" matter, but the crucial element in the process is the making of a powerful narrative, a "cultural script" or drama, that tells the story of who did what to whom, and how society must respond if a collective identity is to be sustained. The truth of a cultural script depends, in Alexander's view, not on its empirical accuracy, but its symbolic power and enactment, framed against the background expectations of the audiences the claim must convince. Often it is the already established cosmopolitan trauma drama of the Holocaust that provides the templates into which activists inscribe their drama. "[Turkish leader Kemal Atatürk] was the Hitler of our peoples," a leading Pontian Greek lobbyist states in a letter addressed to Armenian activists, calling upon them to join forces in response to the European Holocaust Remembrance Day. "The European peoples, but also the Jewish people as well as the people of Israel ... are obliged to say that Hitler was their Kemal."[27]

The material used for this study is texts found in books, press coverage, websites, blogs, public speeches, articles, and writings by activists and their opponents on the subject of genocide remembrance. I analyze these texts with particular attention to the ways that people interpret historical events and use them to frame their arguments, and also to the historical, political and cultural contexts in which these debates occur. All translations from the Greek and other languages are my own, unless stated otherwise.

How this Book is Structured

Apart from the introduction, this book is divided into six chapters and a concluding discussion. Chapter 1, "Ottoman Twilight: The Background in Anatolia," describes the chain of events leading up to the compulsory population exchange between Greece and Turkey, set against the backdrop of Ottoman reform, war and collapse, and competing national aspirations. Although not a primary purpose of the study, it also discusses possible interpretations of the violence that unfolded, so as to provide the reader with a basic understanding of the often complex historical issues evoked by later activists and others struggling to make sense of this past.

Chapter 2, "'Right to Memory': From Catastrophe to the Politics of Identity," examines the history of the Anatolian refugees in Greece and public remembrance of the expulsion, from the interwar years to the decade following the democratic breakthrough in 1974, and the coming of identity politics of the refugee descendants, notably the Pontian Greek community. In this chapter, I argue that the transition from the traditional authoritarian society to cultural and political pluralism had profound repercussions in national historical culture, as the dominant state narrative was challenged by alternative readings of the past. This development provides the immediate context in which a trauma narrative of Pontian Greeks as the victims of genocide emerged in the 1980s, framed as a demand for the "right to memory."

In the following Chapter 3, "Nationalizing Genocide: The Recognition Process in Greece," I examine the attempts to have the remembrance of this Pontian genocide, as well as a corresponding narrative about the

Catastrophe of the Greeks of Western Anatolia as genocide, acknowledged as a national trauma. Separate remembrance days of these events
were established by the Hellenic Parliament between 1994 and 1998, but
a thaw in Greek-Turkish relations would change the preconditions for
the recognition process. The core of the chapter is an analysis of the
public controversy that erupted in 2001, when predominantly left wing
intellectuals called the interpretation of the Asia Minor Catastrophe into
question, leading to a significant backlash for the genocide narrative.
The skepticism toward this trauma claim, or rather resistance from a
competing trauma narrative, is analyzed as responding to a perceived
attempt to exculpate Greek right wing nationalism from the charge of
having caused the Asia Minor Catastrophe, thereby reintroducing a
nationalist agenda into mainstream debate and history education. The
deeper causes of opposition to recognition of this tragedy as genocide,
often framed as a defense of genuine collective memory and "national
self-knowledge," are found in the history of the political Left's relation to
the Asia Minor question, as well as in the scholarly ideals of the "new historians." Both opponents to and, to some degree, supporters of the genocide narrative sought to frame their arguments in an anti-nationalist,
antiestablishment discourse. Nonetheless, ethnocentrism was at the
heart of these arguments, as both the former and the latter revealed little
in terms of familiarity with international scholarly debates on genocide.

However, the relation between the notion of national suffering and
histories of victimhood perceived as non-Greek would acquire a growing significance in debates concerning the Greek genocide(s) under the
impact of official Holocaust commemoration. Chapter 4, "The Pain of
Others: Empathy and the Problematic Comparison," overlaps in some
respects with the previous Chapter 3 but examines in greater depth the
role played by the Holocaust and the Armenian genocide in these debates.
These were not only the cases that activists of the Greek genocide narrative turned to for historical analogies or inspiration, but also histories
of victimhood where Greeks had been involved as either co-victims or
bystanders. Thus the pain of Others became a mirror for national concerns, making comparison an increasingly crucial part of arguments for
and against the Greek genocide narrative. However, these comparisons
involve their own set of ethical conundrums, which I argue might lead
even well-intentioned debaters toward morally untenable positions. The
official efforts to nationalize the Holocaust made it a contender for the
sort of public commemoration that activists felt was being denied their
own trauma, which played into the hands of right wing extremists,
bent on pitting remembrance of Greek suffering against the cosmopolitan memory allegedly imposed from abroad. However, this tainted

association with xenophobia could also work as an incentive to address more universal concerns previously neglected in the trauma narrative.

Chapter 5, "Becoming Cosmopolitan? The Americanized Genocide Narrative in the Diaspora," broadens the perspective by examining how the Greek genocide narrative plays into diaspora concerns about Greek ethnicity in the United States. Seen against the backdrop of ongoing assimilation, the genocide narrative is analyzed as responding to a need for orientation in time and a reaffirmation of a Greek identity perceived to be in peril. It pays particular attention to the role played by a successful Greek American novelist in popularizing the Pontian trauma drama, and also analyzes attempts to teach the Greek genocide narrative in an American school setting, while discussing factors involved in its international reception.

Chapter 6, "Three Genocides, One Recognition: The Christian Holocaust," examines the politics of international academic recognition and the sometimes uneasy relationship between Greek activists and their Armenian and Assyrian counterparts. This is done through the analysis of the controversy that erupted within the International Association of Genocide Scholars (IAGS), in 2007, over a resolution that called upon the organization to extend its previous recognition of the Armenian genocide to the Greek and Assyrian tragedies as well. While accusing Armenian scholars and their supporters of denying victim status to the Ottoman Greeks, the advocates of the Greek genocide narrative also sought to enroll the Armenians as allies in the struggle for international recognition, by presenting the Greek, Assyrian and Armenian genocides as one, a "holocaust" targeting all Ottoman Christians. The strategy of placing one's own community within an expanded circle of victims meant that elements in the trauma narrative that seem too ethnically peculiar came under attack from within activist circles. The consequences of the Greek genocide narrative opening toward identification with suffering Others are discussed toward the end of the chapter, before the book's concluding part summarizes the findings of the study, and discusses the dangers involved in this sort of meaning-making memory.

Notes

1. Motion 2008/09: U332. Folkmordet 1915 på armenier, assyrier/syrianer/kaldéer och pontiska greker. http://www.riksdagen.se/sv/Dokument-Lagar/Forslag/Motioner/Folkmordet-1915-pa-armenier-a_GW02U332/. Last accessed 3 May 2011.
2. Ingmar Karlsson, "Folkmordet som aldrig ägde rum" ["The Genocide that Never Happened"], *Svenska Dagbladet*, 3 April, 2010.
3. http://www.svd.se/nyheter/inrikes/fortsatt-strid-om-folkmordsbeslut_4520091.svd. Last accessed 3 May 2011.

4. Daniel Levy and Natan Sznaider, *The Holocaust and Memory in the Global Age*, trans. Assenka Oksiloff (Philadelphia, 2006); Daniel Levy and Natan Sznaider, *Human Rights and Memory* (University Park, PA, 2010).

5. J.C. Alexander, "On the Social Construction of Moral Universals: The 'Holocaust' from War Crime to Trauma Drama," *European Journal of Social Theory* 5, no. 1 (February 2002): 5–85.

6. Elazar Barkan, *The Guilt of Nations: Restitution and Negotiating Historical Injustices* (New York and London, 2000); Jeffrey K. Olick, *The Politics of Regret: On Collective Memory and Historical Responsibility* (New York, 2007).

7. David B. MacDonald, *Identity Politics in the Age of Genocide: The Holocaust and Historical Representation* (London and New York, 2008).

8. Klas-Göran Karlsson, *"De som är oskyldiga idag kan bli skyldiga imorgon": Det armeniska folkmordet och dess efterbörd* ["Those Who Are Innocent Today Might Become Guilty Tomorrow": The Armenian Genocide and its Aftermath] (Stockholm, 2012), 10.

9. N. Filis, "To sch. P. D. gia ti 'genoktonia' anapempetai gia meleti" ["The Plan for Presidential Decree on the 'Genocide' is Referred Back for Examination"], *Avgi*, 25 February, 2001, 5.

10. U. Beck, "The Cosmopolitan Society and its Enemies," *Theory, Culture and Society* 19, No. 1–2 (2002): 17–44.

11. Levy and Sznaider, *Holocaust and Memory*, 3–4.

12. Among the few Greek scholars who have addressed the issue as a history-cultural problem, see, especially, Ch. Exertzoglou, "Mnimi kai genoktonia: I anagnorisi tis 'Genoktonias tou Pontiakou kai Mikrasiatikou Ellinismou' apo to Elliniko Koinovoulio" ["Memory and Genocide: The Recognition of the 'Genocide of Pontian and Asia Minor Hellenism' by the Hellenic Parliament"], *Historein* 4, 2003–2004, CD-ROM edition.

13. E. Avdela, "The Teaching of History in Greece," *Journal of Modern Greek Studies* 18 (2000): 239–53. Anna Frangoudaki and Thalia Dragona, eds., *Ti ein' i patrida mas? Ethnokentrismos stin ekpaideusi* [What is our Fatherland? Ethnocentrism in Education] (Athens, 1997).

14. Loring M. Danforth and Riki Van Boeschoten, *Children of the Greek Civil War: Refugees and the Politics of Memory* (Chicago and London, 2012), 264. See also Roderick Beaton, "Introduction," in *The Making of Modern Greece: Nationalism, Romanticism and the Uses of the Past (1797-1896)*, ed. R. Beaton and D. Ricks (Farnham and London, 2009), 6. Martin Conway, "The Greek Civil War: Greek Exceptionalism, or Mirror of a European Civil War?" in *The Greek Civil War: Essays on a Conflict of Exceptionalism and Silences*, ed. P. Carabott and Th. Sfikas (Aldershot, 2004), 17–40. T. Gallant, "Greek Exceptionalism and Contemporary Historiography: New Pitfalls and Old Debates," *Journal of Modern Greek Studies* 15, no. 2 (1997): 209–16.

15. Raphael Lemkin, *Axis Rule in Occupied Europe: Laws of occupation, analysis of government, proposals for redress* (Washington, 1944).

16. Convention on the Prevention and Punishment of the Crime of Genocide. http://www.hrweb.org/legal/genocide.html. Last accessed 28 November 2015.

17. Norman M. Naimark, *Stalin's Genocides* (Princeton and Oxford, 2010), 15–29.

18. Frank Chalk and Kurt Jonassohn, "Introduction," in *The History and Sociology of Genocide: Analysis and Case Studies*, ed. Frank Chalk and Kurt Jonassohn (New Haven, CT, 1990), 3. For a discussion of the term genocide and alternative definitions, see Mark Levene, *Genocide in the Age of the Nation-State. Volume I: The Meaning of Genocide*, 2nd ed. (London and New York, 2008). Cf. Martin Shaw, *What is Genocide?* (Cambridge and Malden, 2007).

19. Timothy Snyder, *Bloodlands: Europe between Hitler and Stalin*, 2nd ed. (New York, 2012), 413.

20. Maurice Halbwachs, *On Collective Memory*, trans. Lewis A. Coser (Chicago, 1992).

21. Pierre Nora, "General Introduction: Between Memory and History," in *Realms of Memory: Rethinking the French Past*, vol. 1, ed. P. Nora and L.D. Kritzman, trans. Arthur Goldhammer (New York, 1996), 1–20.

22. For a critical discussion of the memory concept's impact upon historical discourse in academia, see Kerwin Lee Klein, "On the Emergence of Memory in Historical Discourse," *Representations* 69 (2000): 127–50.

23. Jay Winter, *Remembering War: The Great War between Memory and History in the Twentieth Century* (New Haven and London, 2006), 11.

24. For a discussion of historical culture, see Klas-Göran Karlsson, "The Holocaust as a Problem of Historical Culture: Theoretical and Analytical Challenges," in *Echoes of the Holocaust: Historical Cultures in Contemporary Europe*, ed. K-G. Karlsson and U. Zander (Lund, 2003), 9–57.

25. Jeffrey C. Alexander, *Trauma: A Social Theory* (Cambridge and Malden, 2012), 6.

26. Alexander, *Trauma*, 119.

27. Michalis Charalambidis, "I 19i Maïou Imera Mnimis olon ton laon enantia sto ratsismo" ["May 19 as Memorial Day of All Peoples Against Racism"], in *Pontioi: Dikaioma sti mnimi* [Pontians: Right to memory], ed. M. Charalambidis and K. Fotiadis, 4th ed. (Athens, 2003), 143.

CHAPTER 1

OTTOMAN TWILIGHT

THE BACKGROUND IN ANATOLIA

"1922. The East was as sweet as ever—right for a sonnet, that sort of thing."[1] Thus reads the opening paragraph of Greek author Ilias Venezis' *To noumero 31328* (Number 31,328) about his harrowing experience as a prisoner in a Turkish labor battalion. The late summer of 1922 saw the sudden collapse of the Greek army in Asia Minor at the onslaught of Mustafa Kemal's Turkish nationalist forces. Within days of the military defeat, the westward roads of Ionia were crammed with fleeing Orthodox Christians, who, fearing the revenge of the victorious Turks, sought to make their way to safety across the Aegean Sea.[2] The year 1922 stands out as a fatal year in modern Greek history and has acquired the status of a *lieu de memoire*, a "realm of memory," to use the terminology made famous by Pierre Nora, in popular historical imagination; epitomized by pictures and stories of the great fire that ravaged the port of Smyrna, as desperate civilians waited in the harbor to be evacuated by ship.

The Asia Minor Catastrophe and the Smyrna fire, as these events came to be known as, spelled the doom of a Greek presence east of the Aegean that dated centuries back, creating a humanitarian tragedy that was to leave its imprint on the social fabric of the countries involved for years to come. For both Greece and Turkey, these events and the subsequent peace settlement at Lausanne in 1923 mark the end of the old dreams of empire, characterized by religious and linguistic diversity, and the emergence of the respective countries as modern nation-states, built on the notion of national homogeneity. Thus, the events of 1922 also mark the end of the Ottoman Empire's long disintegration and a series of simultaneous processes that had been set in motion almost exactly a century before, by the outbreak of the Greek War of Independence in 1821.

This book is only indirectly about these events. Nevertheless, since its topic is the ways they are interpreted and made sense of in the present, it is necessary, indeed inevitable, to address them, if only in an incomplete fashion. Since the history of the region is not a matter of general knowledge, the events need to be put into a broader historical context. This entails a longer chronological perspective than the years of World War I and its aftermath, and attention to the interwoven processes of modernization, reform, revolution, and the emergence of rivaling national movements in the late Ottoman Empire.

Christians and Muslims in the Age of Ottoman Reform

As of old, the subjects of the Ottoman sultans were categorized according to religion. This order of things had been established even before the conquest of Constantinople in 1453 and meant that the various religious communities of the Empire formed semiautonomous entities, whose leaders were held accountable before the sultan for the doings of their members. Such an entity was called a *millet*, an Arabic term that originally denoted a "flock of believers" but later in the nineteenth century acquired the meaning of "nation," under the impact of the Western notion of national self-determination. Save for the dominant Sunni Muslim community, there were a number of such millets for the Jews and for each of the various Christian denominations, from the large Greek-Orthodox one, headed by the Ecumenical Patriarch of Constantinople, to the Armenian Apostolic Church and the considerably smaller Catholic millet (and the one made up of Protestant converts). In 1914, the year the Empire entered the Great War, fourteen millets co-existed on Ottoman soil.

The millet system allowed for a certain degree of self-governance by the non-Muslim subject populations, as long as the sultan's authority was not challenged or the legal disputes handled by religious judges did not involve Muslims, in which case Islamic law reigned supreme. The legacy of this premodern institution in historiography has varied greatly depending on the point of perspective. While historians writing about the Ottoman Empire in general terms have emphasized the positive aspects of the millet system, such as the centuries-long peaceful coexistence and religious tolerance, other historians describing imperial history from the viewpoint of one or several of the minorities tend to highlight the inequity inherent in the system, the arbitrary ways in which the Ottomans wielded power, and recurring persecutions. Without doubt the millet system fares well in a comparison with the religious bigotry of early modern Europe, but this harmony came with the price of systematic discrimination against non-Muslim subject populations. Eventually, this order would be challenged by external pressure as well as forces within the Empire.

By the early nineteenth century, the once mighty Ottoman Empire had entered a state of decline, which in due time would render it the infamous nickname "the sick man of Europe." The reasons for this decline can be traced to a set of factors that had made their presence felt in the two preceding centuries; the loss of the Empire's privileged position in world trade to the Europeans, the halt of Ottoman expansion, and the subsequent reversal of military fortunes, to name but a few. The emergence of Russia as a great power, in part at the expense of the Ottomans, raised expectations among Orthodox Christians of liberation from the sultan's rule, or at least improvement of their lot. The French Revolution and the Napoleonic Wars were to have repercussions in the Ottoman Empire, as the notions of constitutionalism and national self-determination found fertile soil within the mostly Greek-speaking merchant class that had emerged there in the eighteenth century. Successive rebellions in the Balkans paved the way for Serbian autonomy and later independence in the early years of the nineteenth century. In 1821, the Greek-Orthodox subjects of present-day southern Greece rose up in arms against the Ottomans and eventually gained their independence after the intervention of the European great powers. In a similar way, Russian intervention on behalf of Bulgarian insurgents in the 1870s, who were able to establish a nation-state of their own, further undermined the Ottoman hold in the Balkans. At the same time, Russia's advance in the Caucasus pushed back the Ottoman boundaries there and raised hopes in the emerging Armenian national movement for some kind of autonomy under Russian protection. In the second half of the nineteenth century, the gradual diminishment of the Empire was a fact and its final demise seemed only a matter of time to contemporary observers, if nothing was done to reverse the process.

A series of setbacks suffered in the 1830s, beginning with Greek independence and culminating in the de facto defection of Egypt, initiated an era of reform from above in the Ottoman Empire known as Tanzimat, the "Reorganization,"[3] The Tanzimat proclaimed in 1839, followed by a second reform in 1856 at the request of the Empire's European allies at the time, aimed to restore Ottoman strength and to modernize the armed forces. An important step in this process was to reorganize the tax system and the relations between the Muslim and Christian millets. Non-Muslims were traditionally exempt from military service and forbidden to carry weapons. Instead they had been subjected to a certain tax of exemption. The Tanzimat reforms meant to impose equal obligations on all, thus rendering the military power more effective and avoiding bankruptcy, but they also raised the issue of equal rights for all subjects; by extension also the issue of constitutional government. Many of the promises initially held out by the reform decrees were never implemented, but seeds of change had been sown. From that time onward, the sultans had to face not only the military threats posed by Russia and the European powers, but increasing domestic opposition as well.

The intellectual currents of Europe such as nationalism and constitutionalism not only spread to the Christian subject populations but also to members of the ruling Muslim millet. The independent press that emerged in the 1860s introduced the Turks to debates about these issues and the problems of the Ottoman state. Writers like Namik Kemal propagated the use of the Turkish language as a means of liberating education from the stifling grip of Arabic. He also advocated an Ottoman nationalism, known as Ottomanism, departing from the notion that all who lived in the Empire, regardless of tongue or creed, were Ottomans with equal rights and obligations toward their Ottoman fatherland. This notion of "the unity of nationalities" challenged the traditional understanding of Muslim-Christian relations and offered an alternative to the national aspirations of the various minorities. Namik Kemal's writings were an important inspiration for the movement of the Young Ottomans, which called for constitutional monarchy as the only means to resolve the Empire's problems. Muslim Turks were the core of the movement's adherents, but the promises held out by Ottomanism at least initially attracted intellectuals and activists from the Christian populations. What united liberal Muslims and Christians alike was the discontent with the sultan's autocracy and the demand for political representation.[4]

Hamidian Rule, Economic Growth, and the Rise of the Young Turks

Financial bankruptcy and a subsequent crisis in the succession to the throne in the 1870s paved the way for a brief political success for the Young Ottoman cause. In order to secure support for his claim to the throne, heir apparent Abdülhamit (later Abdul Hamid II) promised constitutional reform. A constitution was proclaimed in December 1876 and the following year an elected parliament, made up of both Muslim and Christian deputies, convened under the umbrella of Ottoman patriotism. This first experiment with constitutional government did not last long. The Russo-Turkish War of 1877–78 proved to be disastrous for the Empire, which saw its dominion in the Balkans further diminished through the Austro-Hungarian occupation of Bosnia and Herzegovina, and the emergence of a Bulgarian state under Russian protection, although Great Power intervention restored Ottoman reign in Macedonia, Albania, and Thrace. Further to the east, Russia annexed the regions of Kars, Ardahan, and Batum. Having already secured the throne, Abdul Hamid II used the external threat as a pretext to suspend parliament in 1878, although acting under the pretense that constitutional government would one day be restored.[5]

During the three decades that the so-called Hamidian era lasted, the sultan's regime evolved into an increasingly repressive and reactionary police state. Abdul Hamid turned his back on many of the reforms initiated by his predecessors and viewed with growing suspicion all calls for the restoration of the political liberties heralded by the 1876 constitution. Complaints advanced by religious minorities against ill-treatment and addresses to international opinion on the subject of civil rights for these groups were viewed as a direct challenge against his rule and the unity of the Empire. The Armenians, in particular, bore the brunt of Abdul Hamid's wrath, as their political demands were met with a series of massacres in the years 1894–96, which in scholarship on the subject are viewed as the forerunner of the genocide carried out during World War I.[6] The mass violence against the fellow Christian Armenians aroused a public outcry in the Western press of the time, which made Abdul Hamid even more determined to stamp out domestic opposition and end what he saw as foreign interference in Ottoman affairs. Politically, the language of Ottomanism was replaced with Pan-Islamism as the Empire's unifying ideology, emphasizing the common creed of the Turkish- and Arabic-speaking peoples and the loyalty to the sultan as caliph of the faithful.

Although the Hamidian era represented a backlash against liberal reform, other aspects of modernization were embraced. The bankruptcy crisis of the 1870s was overcome and foreign capital became available for various projects, after the confidence in the financial stability of the Empire had been restored. German capital financed the railroad works crucial to economic modernization, which served to tie the Empire closer to the interests of Germany, forging an alliance that would survive the downfall of Abdul Hamid and later determine the fate of the Ottoman state in the Great War.

Rapid economic growth also paved way for an emerging Ottoman bourgeoisie, largely made up of elites within the Greek-Orthodox and Armenian millets. With trade as the venue traditionally left open to them and with international networks and know-how, they were able to take advantage of the generous capitulation agreements, which opened up the Ottoman economy to foreign investments, and to a large extent bypass the Ottoman state as middleman, by placing themselves directly under the protection of foreign consulates. A Greek-speaking merchant class had evolved already in the late eighteenth and early nineteenth century as a new force rivaling the old elite of the Greek-Orthodox Patriarchate's higher echelons, which fearing the diminishment of the clergy's traditional authority tended to side with the Sublime Porte in its effort to preserve status quo.[7] Similar developments occurred within the Armenian millet, which among its ranks saw the emergence of a wealthy class of traders, bankers, bureaucrats and other white-collar professions within the public and private sector. Together, members of the two mentioned Christian groups owned more than half of the private banks in Constantinople in 1912, while none was owned by Muslims, as Charles Issawi has noted.[8] That year, at the eve of the Balkan Wars and, later, World War I, Ottoman Greeks alone controlled around 49% of the Empire's firms in industry and crafts, while Armenians accounted for roughly 30% and Muslim Turks for a mere 12%.[9]

This new commercial and administrative elite, with its acquired "Frankish" tastes and manners, was a driving force in the modernization of the Empire, sending their children to European-oriented schools in the capital and the larger cities. Although the last decades of the nineteenth century witnessed progress in Muslims' access to nontraditional education, this did not match the achievements of the Christians in that field.[10] What the Christians lacked in political clout, they thus made up for in terms of economic strength. This socioeconomic development was an important factor behind the competing national aspirations and the ethnic-religious tensions that were to characterize late Ottoman society. Even though far from all Christians were beneficiaries of this economic boom—the Greek-Orthodox peasantry of Cappadocia, in the Anatolian interior, or its counterpart among the Armenians of the border provinces further to the east had little or no share in the accumulated wealth of their coreligionists in Constantinople or Smyrna—the common image of them among the Muslims left out from lucrative business was that of an enriched group, agents of foreign interests in the Empire. These issues will be addressed further below.

Hamidian rule came to an end in a series of crucial events in 1908–9 that were to have dramatic repercussions both inside and outside of the Empire, and to set the stage for its final demise. The force behind the coup d'état that eventually deposed Sultan Abdul Hamid II, after first having forced him to restore constitutional government, was a group of officers known as the Young Turks. Founded as a secret society in the 1890s, and eventually known as Ittihad ve Terakki Cemiyeti, the Committee of Union and Progress (CUP), the Young Turks had made common cause with other illegalized organizations, such as the revolutionary Armenian Dashnak Party, in order to overthrow absolutism and set the Empire back on the course of reform. The movement found its adherents mostly in the army, especially among graduates of the military academy and the military medical school in Constantinople, who were exposed to the influence of contemporary European debates but also the writings of Namik Kemal and the positivist Ahmed Riza. Support for the Young Turks was particularly strong in the European parts of the Empire, among officers serving in the Ottoman Balkan army; the headquarters of the movement was, before transferring to the capital, located in Salonica, where the rebellion against the sultan was first proclaimed in 1908.

The Young Turks are perhaps best understood as a movement consisting of factions with different ideas of how the Empire might be reformed and salvaged, rather than a political party united around a coherent ideology. A liberal faction, with the aristocratic and cosmopolitan Prince Sabahattin as its figurehead, favored the idea of Ottomanism and worked closely with the Christian parties in the newly restored parliament. The faction that came to dominate the CUP, however, was under the strong influence of more narrowly Turkish nationalism, which rejected Ottomanism and Pan-Islamism alike in favor of an ideology that proclaimed the Turkish-speaking nation as the first among equals. This ideology envisioned a return to a mythical tribal genesis of the Turks, uncorrupted by later cultural contacts with Arabs and the Christian world. In this vision, the Empire would be reorganized so as to include all Turkish-speaking peoples in Central Asia and the Caucasus, which would ensure a solid Turkish demographic majority.[11]

The existence of these ideas has led some scholars to conclude that national homogeneity, which inevitably would entail the destruction or expulsion of the Christian minorities, had been on the CUP's agenda already in 1908, or at the latest in 1911, when the idea of population transfers within the Empire came under discussion.[12] Another way of looking at it is that CUP was increasingly radicalized by having to respond to a number of crises and challenges toward the Empire's cohesion in the years following the coup.[13] An attempt at restoring Hamidian rule through counterrevolution in 1909, which also led to renewed massacres against Armenians in the Adana region, as well as the rebellion and subsequent secession of the predominantly Muslim Albanians in 1912, served to undermine the relevance of Pan-Islamism. Whether initially hostile toward the notion of Ottomanism or not, the CUP soon found itself pitted against its former Christian allies, whose demands for further autonomy ran contrary to its goal of a centralized state, on a par with the Young Turks' chosen role models, Imperial Germany and Japan.[14]

Apart from these "inner threats" to the realm's cohesion, the Empire was threatened by external enemies with imperialist designs. Austria-Hungary took advantage of the political crisis in 1908 by annexing Bosnia and Herzegovina, while Italy declared war in 1911, in pursuit of the Ottoman provinces in present Libya. To the east, the Russian Empire seemed ever ready to continue its advance into Ottoman lands. What worried, or alternatively angered, the predominantly military men at the helm of the CUP was that the Christian subject populations might place themselves under the protection of fellow Christian powers, thus providing the latter with a pretext for intervention in Ottoman affairs. The largest Christian population to the east was the Armenians, who did not have an established nation- state of their own to "protect" them, but nevertheless could be expected to harbor pro-Russian sympathies, as many of their brethren were already living under Russian dominion in the Caucasus. The other large Christian population of the Empire, mostly concentrated in its western parts, was the Greeks. Representatives of both these groups had called for greater political and cultural rights at every major crisis in the previous decades; thus, in the eyes of many Young Turks, undermining the prospect of Ottoman unity.

It should be stressed that the Ottomanism of Namik Kemal, the Pan-Islamism of Abdul Hamid and the Pan-Turkism articulated chiefly by Ziya Gökalp, an intellectual of Kurdish origins who became the leading ideologue of CUP, all shared the features of a state nationalism that sought to preserve the Empire in one way or another, even if their agendas seemed to differ radically from each other. To many Young Turks and others concerned with the survival of the realm, they may not have seemed mutually exclusive.[15] It is difficult to predict what might have happened if the outbreak of war in 1912 had not sharpened tensions between the communities. Before turning to these events and their interpretation, I will to some extent explore the situation of the Ottoman Greeks in the age of nationalism, since their experience lies at the heart of present-day memory-political concerns.

The Ottoman Greeks and the Great Idea

Among the various Christian subject populations of the Ottoman sultans, the Greek-Orthodox community was undoubtedly the most significant, both in terms of numbers and of influence. As mentioned above, a wealthy and well-connected Greek-speaking merchant class had emerged already in the eighteenth century, which came to dominate the naval trade of the Empire. This success story had come to an abrupt end in the 1820s, as Orthodox Christians across the Aegean basin were targeted for widespread massacres in retaliation for the Greek uprising, and atrocities done to Muslims in the Peloponnese. In the course of the eighteenth century, they managed to reassert themselves, and by 1912 they once again occupied the prosperous position held before 1821.

It should be stressed that the term "Greeks" with reference to these Ottoman Christians is misleading, and often invites anachronism and essentialist notions of national belonging. To most of them, terms like "Hellenes," or "Greeks" (in Modern Greek, *Ellines*), denoted a very distant, pagan past, which few would relate to before the coming of Western Romanticism's idealized perceptions of their putative ancestors. Well into the twentieth century, *Romioi*, "Christian Romans," was the term preferred by Orthodox Christians, especially those of the Ottoman lands, to denote themselves, which reflected the Byzantine Emperors' claim to be legitimate heirs in unbroken succession to the Caesars of Rome. This past was also reflected in the way the Turks referred to their community as the *Millet-i Rum*; the "Roman flock."

It does however make sense to use the term Ottoman Greeks with reference to this group in the late nineteenth and early twentieth centuries; not only because the subtleties of Byzantine and Ottoman terminologies would be lost on the general reader, but more so because the group in the eyes of the Turks became associated with the new Kingdom of Greece (which in name adopted the neo-Hellenic identity conjured up by Enlightenment and early Romantic intellectuals). The nationalism of Independent Greece also came to exert its influence upon the Orthodox intelligentsia of the Ottoman lands; not in the least because it offered a modern alternative to the traditional religious identity fostered by the Church. The revival, or construction, of a Hellenic identity, which emphasized a perceived continuity with a glorious past, stretching back to the dawn of Western civilization, had initially been brought about by intellectuals from the merchant class, who in many cases had spent their formative years in Western Europe. Receptive toward the French Enlightenment's and later the Revolution's ideas, as well as neoclassicist ideals, they reacted against what they perceived as the obscurantism of the Orthodox Church, which only served to keep their countrymen under the yoke of the sultan, by rejecting the Byzantine heritage and instead turning toward classical antiquity, with its more "European" characteristics. How far-reaching this secularization really was is debatable. The result of this intellectual orientation toward the more remote past, boosted by the enthusiasm of Western philhellenes, was nevertheless that alternative self-conceptions, rather than just a sense of religious belonging, were opened up to Orthodox Christians.

The Greek-Orthodox of the Ottoman Empire (far from all of which chose to become or ended up becoming Greeks) lived scattered across a vast territory. Unlike their Serbian and Bulgarian coreligionists (the latter of which drove a wedge into the Greek Orthodox community by breaking with the Patriarchate and establishing their own national church, known as the Exarchate, in 1870), who populated lands in the Balkans in which they were the majority, the presence of the Greeks spanned from Southeast Europe and Thrace, over the Aegean Islands and Cyprus, to the Anatolian peninsula. In Asia Minor, large Greek-Orthodox populations were to be found in the imperial capital, around the shores of the Marmara Sea and further south in the administrative region (*vilayet*) of Aydin and the port of Smyrna. In Cappadocia, a largely Turkish-speaking group of Orthodox Christians, known as the karamanlides, dwelled more or less untouched by the modernization process experienced by the Ottoman Greeks in the western parts of the Empire; as did a few Arabic-speaking villages in Cilicia. Further to the northeast, in the mountains and along the coast of the Black Sea known as the Pontos, lived a Greek-Orthodox community, which largely cut off from the rest of the Greek-speaking world had developed a peculiar dialect scarcely intelligible even to other Ottoman Greeks. What united these communities across the Empire was not so much language as their belonging to the flock of the Ecumenical Patriarch of Constantinople. However, this was a notion that was increasingly being challenged by the spirit of reform heralded by Tanzimat as well as the adherents of the neo-Hellenic nationalist creed of newly independent Greece.

The Hellenic kingdom, which came into statehood in the wake of the 1821 uprising and the eventual intervention of the European Great Powers, was far smaller in size than what some revolutionaries, envisioning a resurrected Byzantium, had hoped for; consisting merely of the Peloponnese, the region of Attica around the new capital, Athens, and the lands immediately to the north of the Corinthian Gulf in what is now central Greece. None of the prosperous centers of commerce in the Greek-speaking world—Salonica, Smyrna, and Constantinople—had fallen into the hands of the Kingdom of Greece, which meant that the large majority of the Christian population thought to be Greek was still living outside the nation-state. To some of the intellectuals oriented toward a classical, European definition of Hellenic identity this had mattered little, since the territories of the kingdom were considered more or less identical to the heartland of classical Greece. To those oriented toward a more traditional Greek-Orthodox conception of "Greekness," the meagre outcome of the War of Independence was a call for continuous struggle.

The theme that came to dominate the political aspirations of the young nation-state for much of the nineteenth and early twentieth centuries was that of the Megali Idea, the Great Idea. It was an irredentist vision of a Greater Greece, consisting of all of the Byzantine lands still inhabited by Greeks and with Constantinople—in Greek vernacular simply known as "the City"—as its resurrected capital. "The Greek kingdom is not the whole of Greece, but only a part, the smallest and poorest part," the politician Ioannis Kolettis stated in a later much cited address to the newly convened Hellenic Parliament in 1844. "A native of Greece is not only someone who lives within this kingdom, but also one who lives … in any land associated with Greek history or the Greek race."[16] In this vision, old Messianic beliefs in time became entwined with the Social Darwinian notions of modern nationalism, which held the fulfillment of this national project to be the sole way of redeeming Greek society from all the problems that had plagued it since independence.

The Great Idea had emerged in response to sharpened social and political tensions in the newly independent Kingdom of the 1830s and 1840s. These expressed themselves in a bitter competition for political influence between the autochthones, the indigenous population of the Peloponnese, Attica and present-day central Greece, and the heterochthones, Greeks from Constantinople and other parts of the Ottoman Empire, and/or from the diaspora communities in Western Europe. Since the latter in many cases were both wealthier and better educated than the former, they tended to be favored by the Bavarian authorities imposed upon Greece by the European Protecting Powers, to the dismay of the old local elites and veterans who had fought in the War of Independence; they felt themselves pushed aside and the spoils of their revolution usurped by outsiders. When fortune favored the autochthons in the domestic struggle for power, they passed legislation aimed at preventing their outside rivals from holding office in the Kingdom.

It is against this backdrop of internal strife that the dreams of national aggrandizement were formulated, chiefly by heterochthon Greeks, like Kolettis. The Great Idea, which favored the interests of those who saw

Constantinople, not Athens, as the true center of the Greek world, would in a couple of decades emerge as the dominant national ideology, unifying the various components of Greek society with a common cause. In historiography, a reorientation from the initial emphasis on the classical past toward the inclusion of the medieval Empire of Byzantium into what was considered national history paved the way for a geographically much broader definition of Greece and of Greekness. The idea of Greek history as a continuum spanning millennia—championed by the Constantinople-born Konstantinos Paparrigopoulos in a work of paradigmatic importance in Greek national historiography—reconciled the competing conceptions of Greek culture and identity, achieving a synthesis of classical Hellenism with the *Romiosyni* ("Romanness") of Byzantium and later centuries.

The underlying tensions between Greeks of what would become present-day southern Greece and those of the exterior nevertheless persisted. Ion Dragoumis (1878–1920), a leading advocate of the Greek nationalist cause in his native Macedonia at the beginning of the twentieth century, but also a staunch critic of the Westernizing Greek nation-state, wrote accusingly that the "Greeks of Greece [*Elladites*, "Helladic" as opposed to *Ellines*, "Hellenes"], identified in their minds the Greek state, the Greek Kingdom, the small Greece, with the Greek nation. They forgot the [wider] Greek nation, Romiosyni and Hellenism."[17] In his view, it was among the rural populations in Macedonia and Greek diaspora communities elsewhere in the Ottoman Empire, still unaffected by the modern state and foreign contamination, that a genuine national consciousness had been preserved.[18] As we shall see, this tension between the indigenous "Helladic" element of Greece and that of the "lost homelands" in Asia Minor still echoes in the writings and discourse of today's activists concerned with genocide recognition.

The Great Idea was thus a project that had been developed largely by Greeks deriving from or with strong ties to territories still under Ottoman control. It is, however, important to stress that Greek nationalism, as formulated in Athens, was not the only option left open to Ottoman Greeks in search of a cultural or political identity. For many members of the ascendant and increasingly prosperous Ottoman bourgeoisie, the Empire offered better opportunities than the debt-ridden national economy of Greece or the in many ways rather provincial capital of Athens. Contrary to what some might have expected, the second half of the nineteenth century actually witnessed labor migration from Independent Greece to the Ottoman lands. For many of these prosperous Greeks, the Ottomanism espoused by Namik Kemal and, at least initially, the Young Turks, with its promises of civic rights regardless of religion, seemed to hold out a more promising future than Greek irredentism. Even a fervent supporter of Greek expansionism like Ion Dragoumis, considered to be one of the leading theoreticians of Greek nationalism in the early twentieth century, at times toyed with the idea of a combined Byzantine-Ottoman Empire, in which the Ottoman Greeks would be invited to share power with the ruling Turks. In his eyes, it was not the Turks that constituted the gravest threat against Greek national aspirations. Rather, the nation's enemies were to be found in the Bulgarians; Slavs who had rejected Hellenism by forming an apostate Orthodox Church of their own, and now had emerged as the main rivals of the Greeks in the struggle for influence in, and eventually dominion of, his native Macedonia.[19]

However, the choice of national belonging was in the end not the Ottoman Greeks' to make. The main reason was that the Great Idea of Independent Greece in effect held them hostage. Adherence to the fledgling idea of Ottomanism could not avert the suspicions of the ruling Turks with regard to their loyalty and the stigma of treason. The Greek-Orthodox community had already once paid a heavy price for the doings of the Greek insurgents in 1821. Recurrent flare-ups over the course of the nineteenth century, as the Greeks of Ottoman Crete rebelled in favor of unification with mainland Greece, and attempts from the Kingdom to lay claims to Ottoman territories contributed to this perception. The arrival of several waves of Muslim refugees from Thessaly, annexed by Greece in 1881 with the blessing of the European powers, and other lands lost to Russia in the Caucasus and the newly established Christian states in the Balkans furthermore soured inter-communal relations in the Empire. As far as the Ottoman Greek subjects were concerned, the threat of retaliation was less imminent, as long as the ambitions of the young Hellenic nation-state were not matched by military capability or diplomatic clout. As late as 1897, the Ottoman army was able to fend off an ill-conceived attack from Greece with relative ease, effectively humiliating the Kingdom in the eyes of domestic and international opinion. However, the coming of the new century, the downfall of the Hamidian regime and geopolitical developments in the wake of the Young Turks' coup would bring about a reversal of fortunes, with dire consequences for the Empire's Christian populations.

The Balkan Wars, the Great War, and the Armenian Genocide

The Young Turks' coup in the Ottoman Empire was mirrored in a coup staged by malcontent officers at Goudi on the outskirts of Athens, in

1909. This military takeover without bloodshed led to a series of events that propelled Eleftherios Venizelos' rise to power. Venizelos, a former Cretan revolutionary turned liberal politician, was brought to Athens as head of a government of national salvation. Within a short space of time, he managed to secure stability in state finances and domestic politics. Eventually acknowledged and internationally acclaimed as one of the great statesmen of his time, Venizelos dominated Greek political life for a quarter of a century, creating a bitterly divisive legacy; revered with a quasi-religious fervor by his supporters and vilified as a diabolic mastermind by his opponents.

Venizelos' initial claim to greatness lay in the skillful way he exploited the situation created by the Italian-Ottoman war, 1911–12, and forged alliances with the other Christian Balkan states, which radically improved the preconditions for Greek expansion. In the fall of 1912, Greece, Bulgaria, and Serbia joined Montenegro in a declaration of war against the Ottoman Empire, whose army in the European provinces was outnumbered by the combined forces of the Balkan allies. The result was the most disastrous defeat in the history of the Empire, which at the peace conference in London in May 1913 was forced to accept the loss of all the lands west of the Dardanelles that it had held since the fourteenth century, with the exception of Eastern Thrace. Only the second Balkan War in 1913, as Greece and Serbia turned on Bulgaria for the spoils, gave the Ottomans some respite, which enabled them to restore the city of Edirne (Adrianople)—occupied by the Bulgarians in the first war—to the Empire. For Greece, the Balkan Wars of 1912–13 were a defining moment in the fulfillment of an almost century-old dream of national prowess. The country doubled in size and population, while the conquest of Thessaloniki and most of the Aegean Islands established Greece as a significant naval power in the Eastern Mediterranean. However, this leap toward the realization of the Great Idea also put the remaining "unredeemed" Ottoman Greeks in a position of peril.

The disasters of 1912–13 created an atmosphere of impending doom among the ruling circles in Constantinople and among Turks elsewhere in the Empire. Almost all of the leading Young Turks (and many in the future elite of Republican Turkey, including the Salonica-born Mustafa Kemal) were men born in, or with ties to, the lost provinces in the Balkans; the psychological effects of which must be taken into account when trying to understand their determination to save the remains of the Empire at any cost.[20] Worse was that the war had set large groups of Muslims, fleeing the advance of the Christian armies, in motion. Their arrival in the imperial capital and to regions around the Sea of Marmara and the Aegean coast of Asia Minor—territories populated by large groups of Greek Orthodox Christians—brought further strain to the already troubled relations between the ethnic and religious communities living there. Traumatized and embittered by the uprooting from their native Balkan lands, the *muhacirs* (refugees) found themselves on a course of collision with the native Ottoman Greeks of their new homeland. Along with them came also the descendants of Muslim refugees from earlier expulsions, who had settled in these regions, and others who had felt marginalized by the economic success of the Greek and Armenian merchant classes; all adding up to an explosive mix, and creating the local preconditions for the violence that was to unfold.[21]

One of the immediate effects of the First Balkan War was the coming to power of a triumvirate in Constantinople, bent on securing the survival of the Empire, apparently at any means. The military coup, which in January 1913 elevated the Young Turkish hard-liners Ismail Enver, minister of war, Mehmet Talaat, minister of the interior, and Ahmet Djemal, minister of the navy (the so-called "three Pashas"), to dictatorial power, effectively put an end to the spirit of reform and experiments with equal rights for all Ottoman citizens. Even though opposition to CUP—largely coming from liberal Young Turks, non-Turkish Muslims, and Christian deputies—survived in the Ottoman Parliament, which even after the coup continued to convene, power was effectively in the hands of the triumvirs, which went about solving the Empire's predicament the way they saw fit.

The chain of events transpiring in the few years and months leading up to World War I and the deportations of chiefly the Armenians in 1915 is at the center of dispute in scholarship and propaganda, which seek to either support or reject the charge of genocide. At the heart of the matter is the question of intent; that is, to what extent the killings afflicting Christians—once again chiefly the Armenians—were part of a carefully planned and executed extermination. The scholars who interpret the events as an indeed deliberate act of murder—that is, genocide according to the definition established by the UN Convention from 1948—seek to demonstrate that the decision to physically annihilate the undesired populations was taken at central level by the triumvirate, under the influence of the CUP's exclusivist Turkish nationalism.[22] In support of that argument, they have pointed to the vast amount of wartime testimonies by diplomats from countries either neutral or allied to the Ottoman Empire and other foreigners present in the realm at the time; survivors' accounts as well as testimonies given during the 1919 Ottoman trials against CUP officials charged with wartime crimes, and also the minutes of the Ottoman Parliament, where inquiries into the fate of the deported Christians and their stolen properties were made in the wake of the 1918 defeat and the triumvirate's fall from grace.[23] Other sources are the so-called Naim-Andonian documents, which is a series of telegrams claimed to have been issued secretly by Talaat to various CUP function-aries in the provinces involved in the deportations of Armenians.[24] The purpose of these unofficial wires, supplementing the official commands for the removal of Armenians, was to instruct these functionaries and the Special Organization—the militia set up by the CUP—to kill off the deportees while they were en route to their designated destinations, often in the Syrian deserts. Even though the details of the chain of command remain obscure, either because the Ottoman archives have been purged or the fact that foreign or independent scholars have been denied access to them, the surviving documentation point in the direction of murder, premeditated by the ruling elite.

The opposing view, which can be described as the official Turkish version, as presented by the Turkish Foreign Ministry and various other government branches, including textbooks,[25] and reproduced by advocates of its cause in Turkey and abroad, dismisses this evidence as either forgeries or based on biased and therefore unreliable sources of information. To the extent that the issue is not avoided or glossed over entirely, this branch of historiography tends to view the deporta-tions as motivated by a justifiable wish to remove population elements with a history of disloyalty toward the realm from the scene of combat, with the view of resettling them in areas where they would not pose a threat to national security. Measures were allegedly taken to protect the deportees from harm, and whatever violence done to them is attributed to unlawful elements among the Kurdish tribes of Eastern Anatolia or vengeful acts committed by muhacirs, Muslim refugees who were themselves the victims of persecutions by Christian armies. Sometimes this violence is contextualized as part of an ongoing civil war between Ottoman Muslims and Christians, where the former allegedly were forced to defend themselves against armed Armenian revolutionaries, such as those who resisted the deportation orders and rebelled in Van in the spring of 1915. Whatever acts of injustice or unnecessary cru-elty committed against the Armenians and other Christians, according to this line of argument, happened without the knowledge or approval of the central government. A proof of this is allegedly seen in the lack of existing, authentic documentation demonstrating any intention of annihilating the Empire's Christian minorities, in whole or in part. The losses suffered by said populations are attributed to the general car-nage and harsh conditions during wartime, which saw staggering death tolls among the overall Ottoman population, regardless of ethnic or reli-gious belonging. As a result of this, the argument implies, the Ottoman leadership—and by extension the Turkish nation—cannot be arraigned with the culpability for genocide.[26]

The issue of the lacking documentation incriminating the Young Turkish leadership—the "smoking gun" that once and for all would determine the question of guilt—does not mean that there never was any such evidence, or that the truth cannot be ascertained. The deportations and killings were on such a scale that it could not be concealed from the world entirely, even though they were carried out under the cover of the Great War. The judgment of international opinion fell hard upon the Ottoman leadership and the entente powers at war with the Empire and its allies Germany and Austria-Hungary, stated in public their intention to bring those responsible of the Armenian massacres to justice, once the war was over. This was the first time that the expression "crime against humanity" was used in international relations, anticipating its usage much later in international law and human rights discourse.[27] Faced with these charges, it seems likely that the CUP leadership saw to the destruction of incriminating documents already during the war, especially toward the end of it when it became evident that defeat was imminent. Much evidence suggests that this was really the case.[28] Taner Akçam, one of the few Turkish scholars who openly recognizes the Armenian genocide, has furthermore demonstrated in a recent publication that even given the destruction—willful or through neglect—of certain documents, enough traces of the decision-making process have survived in Ottoman and other archives that either directly or indirectly shed light on the intentions of the CUP leaders and functionaries.[29] Together with the testimonies mentioned above they paint a grim and convincing picture. In fact, with regard to the Armenians there is a fairly general consensus among scholars not aligned with the Turkish state that their fate indeed reads like a classic case of genocide.

I will not address the debates about the Armenian genocide in detail, as these have been discussed extensively in a vast body of scholarship, and also because they do not always relate directly to the case under scrutiny here. The reason for addressing them at all is that they nevertheless constitute a point of departure, in some respects, to discussions regarding the fate of the other Christian communities of the Empire, notably the Ottoman Greeks (but also the Assyrians). Already contemporary observers of Ottoman policies toward the Christians noted similarities in the methods of forcible migration used against Greeks in the Aegean region in 1913–14 with those used against the Armenians in 1915; circumstances that have led some present-day scholars to discuss to which degree the two campaigns, though carried out separately, were connected to each other.[30]

The Anti-Greek Persecutions during World War I and the Aftermath in Pontos: A Case of Genocide?

As noted above, the existence of Greek irredentism championed by the Kingdom of Greece put the Ottoman Greeks in a perilous position, as Turks held them accountable for the doings of their kinsmen. It was no secret that local Christian militias had paved the way for and fought alongside the invading armies in Ottoman Macedonia. Furthermore, accusations that wealthy Ottoman Greeks had aided Greece's military armament financially cemented the impression that treason was at the heart of the imperial defeat. Beginning in the Balkan Wars and continuing throughout 1913 and 1914, an economic boycott targeted Greek business in the Empire, with the support of the CUP. Furthermore, Greek villages in the Aegean region of Asia Minor were raided and looted on subsequent occasions, allegedly by Muslim refugees from the Balkans seeking vengeance for their losses at the hands of Christians during the recent wars there. The Ottoman government denied all charges of involvement in these attacks, but even though some of them might very well have been spontaneous, carried out by embittered refugees taking matters into their own hands, much evidence points in the direction of covert encouragement by the authorities.

The persecutions against the Aegean and Thracian Greeks initiated in 1913 and brought to a halt in November 1914 can be seen against the backdrop of the refugee crisis caused by the Balkan Wars and ongoing negotiations between Athens and the Sublime Porte regarding a partial population exchange. The CUP wished to resettle the newcomers from the Balkans into certain areas in Anatolia in the hope that their arrival would alter local demographic conditions in favor of a secure Turkish population majority. A part of that policy was to compel the Christian inhabitants of those areas to leave. In May 1914, contacts were made with Venizelos' government in which an exchange of the Greeks of the Aydin vilayet in Ionia for the Muslims of Greek Macedonia was proposed. This exchange was said to be "mutual and voluntary," and was initially met with Venizelos' principal approval. However, persecutions against Ottoman Greeks were already in progress before a joint agreement on the conditions for the "exchange" could be made. Apart from what appear as systematic raids on Greek villages and occasional massacres,[31] of which the Porte claimed no knowledge or responsibility for, Ottoman Greek men were conscripted in large numbers into labor battalions (the so-called *amele taburlari*) and marched into the Anatolian interior to work under often harsh conditions, in which many perished. The wide scale of terror

and intimidation, serving to force Greeks to leave their homes and properties "voluntarily," caused hundreds of thousands to flee to Greece and
led the two countries to the brink of war in the summer of 1914.[32]

Only the outbreak of World War I seems to have spared the remaining Ottoman Greeks from a worse fate, at least for a few more years. In
November 1914, Talaat ordered a halt to the persecutions of the Greeks
in Thrace and the Aegean littoral. The reasons for this change of policy
were first and foremost strategic. Greece had proclaimed neutrality in
the Great War and Germany, which did not wish to push that country
into the entente camp, exercised pressure on its Ottoman ally to cease
all activities that might provoke Athens.[33] As a result of this, Ottoman
Greeks were largely left undisturbed in 1915, when the Armenians were
deported en masse. Greeks would, however, be subjected to deportations
and, on occasions, massacres later on in the Great War; most notably
at the end of 1916 and throughout 1917.[34] What seems to have brought
about this new turn toward more repressive policies was the Russian
offensive into Eastern Anatolia, which saw the occupation of the important port of Trabzon (Trebizond) on the Black Sea coast, along with the
entente's military presence at Lesbos and other Aegean islands just
off the coast of Ionia, and the increasing likelihood that Greece would
finally enter the Great War on the side of the Ottoman Empire's enemies. Whether these population transfers were motivated by military
concerns to move elements deemed unreliable from the borderlands
on an ad hoc basis or formed part of an overarching policy toward the
Empire's Greek population as a whole is open to question.

In a collective work on aspects of the Armenian genocide published
in 1992, the Greek historian Ioannis K. Hassiotis brought attention to
the persecutions of Greeks in Thrace and on the Aegean coasts of Asia
Minor in the wake of the Balkan Wars. In his view, it was strange that
Greek and Armenian historians alike thitherto had treated "the first
persecutions of the Greeks in 1913–14 and the Armenian Genocide of
1915 as two separate phenomena."[35] Citing the work of a prominent
Pontian Greek activist, Hassiotis pointed to the persecution of Greeks
as "the first systematic phase of the unified plan for the elimination
of the foreign elements in the Ottoman Empire," while the Armenian
genocide "in its turn set the pattern for the extermination of the Greeks
of the Pontus in 1919–21."[36] The similarities in methods led him to
conclude that the purpose was "the biological annihilation of both elements," meaning that "despite quantitative differences, the Greek persecutions and the Armenian Genocide were but two sides of the same
coin." The Armenian historians, he argued, had been too weighed down
by the significance of their own genocide to discuss the connections.

Hassiotis' comparative approach has in recent years been picked up by some scholars of the Armenian genocide interested in broadening the lens through which it has been studied.[37] The "cleansing operations" in 1914 against Ottoman Greeks in Western Anatolia undoubtedly seem to have a lot in common with the subsequent "cleansing" of the Armenians that began in the following year. In both the Greek and Armenian cases, expulsions and deportations were carried out ostensibly under the legal umbrella of Ottoman population policy and military necessity, while an unofficial plan was implemented by paramilitary units that terrorized the Ottoman Christians, in keeping with what Taner Akçam has called a dual-track mechanism. Another striking parallel is the conscription of both Greek and Armenian men of military age into labor battalions, in which they were either worked or put to death. These similarities have led Akçam, in particular, to discuss the Greek persecutions as a "trial run," foreshadowing the Armenian deportations.[38]

However, Hassiotis reserved the term "genocide" for the Armenians. Although referring to a policy of extermination against the Greeks of Pontos in the early postwar years (carried out by the Young Turks' Kemalist successors), and a sense of shared fate between the two Christian groups, Hassiotis was not concerned with recognition for a particular Pontian or in any other sense Greek genocide. Rather than depicting the Greeks of Asia Minor as co-victims, his angle was to present them as witnesses of the unfolding Armenian genocide, or to use a term more associated with Holocaust terminology, "bystanders," who in some cases tried to help, "sometimes sharing the fate of their persecuted fellows."[39] The losses of the Greek community dwarfed in comparison with the Armenians, while the mass flight and subsequent "exchange" of populations agreement in 1923 ipso facto averted a repetition of the Armenian genocide.[40] In a similar fashion, prominent scholars such as Akçam tend to avoid the term "genocide" in their references to the Greek case, preferring instead the less problematic term "ethnic cleansing."[41] "Despite the increasingly severe wartime policies," Akçam writes, "the government's treatment of the Greeks—although comparable in some ways to the measures against the Armenians— differed in scope, intent and motivation."[42] Although local CUP functionaries involved in the Armenian deportations might not always have cared to distinguish between the various Christian groups, the killings of Greeks were more limited. Rouben Paul Adalian, a director of the Armenian National Institute in Washington D.C., puts the difference in even starker words. Whereas the Ottoman Greeks were protected by their association to a country that the Young Turks did not wish to provoke, the Armenians, a stateless nation with no given protector, bore the full brunt of annihilation. "The Greeks were exchanged," Adalian concludes, "The Armenians were disposed. That is the difference that makes a genocide."[43]

Activists, who are dissatisfied with the designation of the Anatolian Greeks as mere bystanders and call for the recognition of a Greek genocide alongside the Armenian, protest this view as an attempt to establish a hierarchy of victims.[44] This sort of memory politics will be further explored in the later chapters of this book. As for the scholarly discussion on the similarities and the differences of the two cases, one might also mention regional differences as to the experience of the various Greek Orthodox communities of the Empire. Whereas the Greeks of Western Anatolia and the Turkish-speaking Orthodox Christians of Cappadocia were largely spared from wide-scale violence and deportations for most of the war years, the Greeks of Pontos were situated closer to what Mark Levene has called the "zone of genocide" in Eastern Anatolia.[45] That may have made them more vulnerable to the sort of spill-over effects emanating from the Armenian genocide that the Assyrian Christians fell prey to, even if they were not the primary targets for elimination. More importantly, the eastern parts of Pontos became a war theater as the Russian army advanced into Anatolia and occupied huge swaths of territory, making it a "military necessity" for the CUP to remove Orthodox Christians from the front lines. No doubt the existence of armed bands of Pontian Christians, who having avoided conscription were involved in some of the fighting, contributed to retaliatory massacres and deportations in that area.[46] However, this violence varied greatly from one vilayet to another, and the reason for this is partly to be found in local circumstances and the differing approaches toward cooperation between Ottoman authorities and Christian community leaders (ethnarchs).

In the western Pontian province of Sivas (Sebasteia), the newly appointed Metropolitan Germanos Karavangelis of Amasya, a well-known supporter of the Greek nationalist cause, took advantage of the Russian offensive and organized secret Orthodox Christian militias. These guerrillas would at the time of the armistice in 1918 amount to roughly 3,000 men, who would remain at arms in the postwar years and eventually engage in heavy fighting with the Kemalists. It was chiefly the areas where they were active that experienced the gruesome "cleansing" actions undertaken by military authorities, supported by Muslim irregulars commanded by the notorious mayor of Giresun, Osman Agha, aka Topal Osman.

In the east, the Metropolitan Chrysanthos Filippidis of Trebizond chose the opposite course. Suspicious of secular nationalist overtures and determined to save his flock from the Armenians' fate, Chrysanthos avoided any public statements or actions that might provoke Ottoman charges of treason, and worked to alleviate the lot of the Muslim population during the Russian occupation of Trebizond 1916–18. This policy seems at least initially to have paid off. Despite Chrysanthos' later advocacy for an independent Greek state in Pontos at the Paris Peace Conference in 1919, the Greek-Orthodox of Trebizond remained under the local Ottoman governor's protection for the larger part of the period from the Russian withdrawal in the wake of the Bolshevik takeover to the final expulsion in 1923.[47]

It should however be stressed that the escalation of violence and anti-Greek persecution in Pontos largely occurred after the Great War and the 1918 downfall of the Young Turkish regime, culminating in the summer and fall of 1921. Policies adopted toward the Greek-Orthodox population there need therefore not have reflected CUP planning, although the individuals carrying out these were often the same that had served in leading positions during the triumvirate.[48] The collapse of central authority in the chaotic months and years following the armistice, before Kemal and his nationalists were able to assume control throughout Anatolia, enabled local elites to work out their own arrangements. Thus, some Greek communities were protected from persecution by Turkish notables, who mistrusted the Kemalist warlord Topal Osman and refused his militia to enter their fiefdoms. In other places in the mountainous Pontos, Orthodox Christian guerrillas were able to stand their ground thanks to local agreements with either Ottoman officials or Muslim leaders, who left them alone up until the compulsory "population exchange" in 1923.

Nevertheless, there were decisions and incidents that seemed to forebode worse things to come.[49] On 2 March, 1921, an order was issued to transfer newly conscripted members of minorities (Christians and Jews) to labor battalions, which no doubt roused fears among those concerned, since the killing of Armenians in similar units had marked the beginning of their extermination in 1915.[50] The arrival of Hellenic warships off the coast of Pontos in June 1921, as part of the build-up to the Greek royal army's summer offensive further to the west, triggered the deportation of potentially disloyal Christian populations from the littoral in view of an enemy landing that never came. On some notable occasions, Greek Christians from towns like Bafra and Mersivan were attacked and massacred by the irregulars of Topal Osman in a way that echoed practices developed in 1915, with the nationalist government at Ankara washing its hands from these excesses.[51] The terror culminated in the autumn of 1921 when almost the entire Greek-Orthodox elite of Pontos was either annihilated or condemned to death in absentia, on the charge of treason, by the Independence Court at Amasya. This event could with some plausibility be interpreted as part of a genocidal scheme; something that modern-day Pontian Greek scholarly activists also conclude.[52] However, the Kemalist campaign of repression in the Pontos seems to have cooled down once the Greek military threat against Ankara had been effectively thwarted.[53] Although the Kemalists shared the Young Turks' overall aim of a Turkified Anatolia, "liberated" from "alien" or otherwise hostile minorities, the long term plans they might have had for the Pontian Greeks are at best subject to speculation.

While some massacres involving Greek victims in certain parts of Anatolia thus may be characterized as genocidal—drawing on the distinction made by Levene between "total genocide" and "partial," or (near) genocidal episodes[54]—there is (as of yet) little in the way of evidence suggesting them to be part of a uniform, overall plan for the physical annihilation of the Ottoman Greek community as a whole. Scholars of the Armenian genocide, such as Fuat Dündar, Uğur Ümit Üngör, and Taner Akçam, have in recent years pointed to the demographic policies of the CUP, according to which no non-Turkish ethnic group— be they Muslim Albanian refugees, unruly Kurds or "treacherous" Armenians— must exceed 5 to 10% of the total population of a given region.[55] Since the transfer of large population groups from one end of the Empire to another—as in the case of the Muslims, aimed at the dissolution of old tribal loyalties and assimilation into the Turkish majority, unlike the "unassimilable" Armenians—one is bound to ask how the percentage rule affected the Ottoman Greek population. Were the Orthodox Christians slated for death or expulsion in their entirety, or could the new, secular Turkey have tolerated a docile Christian minority in its midst? Could these Orthodox Christians, in the mind of the CUP and later Kemalist leadership, be turned into Turks without having to abandon their religion? Not all clerics of the Greek-Orthodox Church in the Empire were willing to exchange their traditionally "ecumenical" ideals for the more narrow interests of Greek nationalism. Attempts to put a supporter of Venizelos on the Patriarch's throne in 1921 led some of them to declare their allegiance to the Kemalists.[56] An interesting case in question is the plans to proclaim a Turkish Orthodox church as late as in the fall of 1922, shortly after the end of the Greco-Turkish war (see below). The purpose was to wrest the Turkish-speaking Christians of Cappadocia away from the flock of the Greek Patriarch in Constantinople. The idea was nonetheless scrapped, with the result that the bewildered karamanlides were in the last hour included in the 1923 "population exchange" with Greece.[57]

It seems, in the end, unlikely that the Turkish nationalist leaders, though secular in name, ever had any intention of allowing any sizeable non-Muslim minority to remain. Riza Nur, one of the Turkish delegates to Lausanne, writes in his memoirs that he struggled hard to avert recognition of any linguistic, racial or religious minorities in the terms of the peace treaty (though Turkey eventually made an exception for the Christians of Istanbul). "The lesson to be drawn from this: disposing of people of different races, languages and religions in our country is the most ... vital issue."[58] For those who wish to make a case for the Ottoman Greek experience as genocide, as either premeditated or "cumulative," arising from a process of events and decisions leading up to a "genocidal moment," such statements seem to demonstrate intent to destroy the minorities as such. However, it is far from obvious that the "disposing of people" literally meant the physical annihilation of all non-Turkish communities, as the different policies that were adopted toward each of these groups suggest.

In understanding the motivation for exterminating the Ottoman Armenians but not the Greeks, despite the irredentist policies of Greece, the existence of that country as a state entity that the Turkish state would have to come to terms with in the future seems, along with wartime German pressure, to have played a pivotal role. There was also the issue of the still sizeable Muslim minority in Greece that had come into being as a result of the Balkan Wars' border revisions. As long as Greece refrained from persecuting its Muslim citizens, the CUP could not use that as an excuse for retaliating against the Ottoman Greeks with wholesale massacre. Uğur Ümit Üngör has suggested that the Greek minority was spared from the Armenians' fate during the Great War because the wartime CUP leaders wished to use it as a bargaining chip in future negotiations with Greece.[59] If scruples did not hold the Young Turks back, geopolitical concerns did. Neutral or not, a Greek state already existed on former Ottoman soil in the Balkans, and the Turkish nationalists did not mean to change that. The Armenians appear to have posed a more existential threat in the minds of the CUP leaders; both they and their Kemalist successors were determined to prevent an Armenian nation-state in Eastern Anatolia from ever coming into existence. It is nevertheless difficult to determine, based on the available sources, whether the policies toward the Ottoman Greek population were made up ad hoc, answering to temporary diplomatic and military needs, or whether there really was a more long-term plan for its fate once the war was over. The changing fortunes of the Great War also changed the preconditions for such policies, especially toward 1917 when Greece finally entered the war on the side of the entente.

Prelude to Disaster: The National Schism in Greece and the Greek Occupation of Western Anatolia

Greece declared war on the Ottoman Empire and the Central Powers in the summer of 1917, after a murderous split that had divided the country for the two previous years. The root of the split, known as the "National Schism," was the disagreement between King Constantine I and his premier Venizelos as to the country's position in the ongoing European conflict. While the former, often accused of pro-German leanings, favored neutrality, the latter called for joining the cause of the entente for fear that Greece otherwise would miss out on the spoils from a future carve-up of Ottoman lands. Venizelos, ever the pragmatic, was to this end willing to cede territories gained in the Balkan Wars in return for a sphere of influence in Asia Minor promised by Great Britain and France. His dismissal as prime minister in 1915 led to the de facto division of the state into two entities; a northern part of Greece, where Venizelos headed a provisional government in Salonica hosting an Anglo-French expeditionary force, and a southern part loyal to the king and under the naval blockade of the entente. With Constantine I finally forced into exile and domestic opposition temporarily subdued in the summer of 1917, Venizelos was able to take the helm of a reunited country committed to the war effort.[60]

The defeat of the Central Powers brought about a reversal of fortunes for the parties involved in the Ottoman drama. The separate armistice agreement of Modros in October 1918 and the subsequent flight of Enver, Talaat and Djemal from the country spelled the end of CUP rule. Several concessions were made by the new government in Constantinople, which, in addition to the establishment of a tribunal with the task of indicting CUP officials for wartime atrocities against the Armenians, enabled deported Christians to return to their homes and reclaim seized property. Meanwhile, foreign troops would occupy strategic locations throughout the defeated Empire, in accordance with armistice regulations and interest spheres of the entente powers; the French in Cilicia, the Italians in southwestern Anatolia, and the British in and around the imperial capital, with control of the Straits.

For Greece, the Ottoman defeat had opened up the prospect of the further realization of the Great Idea. The landing of a Greek expeditionary force at Smyrna in May 1919, where the victorious Allies had granted the kingdom an occupation zone, seemed to herald the dawn of a new era, sealed one year later by the Treaty of Sèvres, which recognized Greek claims in Eastern Thrace and Ionia. Venizelos was credited by his supporters for having created a Greater Greece of "the two continents and the five seas." Problems were, however, mounting even before the treaty was signed, making it a hollow triumph. In Asia Minor, the Greek military presence enabled native Orthodox Christians to exact revenge on Muslim neighbors, which reignited the vicious cycle of violence. Soon after the landing at Smyrna, Greece found itself caught up in guerrilla warfare with Turkish nationalists paying heed to Mustafa Kemal's call to resist the foreign invaders and the Ottoman "puppet" government in the capital. Atrocities carried out in retaliation by Greek troops and irregulars against Muslim civilians created much negative publicity in international opinion.[61] Developments in the domestic politics of Greece did further damage to the morale of Greek troops. The unexpected death of King Alexander I, the puppet of Venizelos, in October 1920 caused a constitutional crisis in the month leading up to the parliament elections. Since no obvious heir to the throne was left but the deposed Constantine, the National Schism returned to divide public opinion. The November elections self-confidently proclaimed by Venizelos turned into a crushing defeat for his party, as a war-weary electorate ousted his government from power. Royalists embittered by their humiliation in 1917 assumed power, paving the way for the exiled King Constantine's return while in the process removing many of Venizelos' supporters from key positions in the military, including the command of the Anatolian expeditionary force.

The royalists had come to power on the promise of ending the war in Asia Minor, rallying support for the notion of a "small but honorable Greece," which was also why Muslim and Jewish voters in the new lands acquired in the Balkan Wars, never enthusiastic for Venizelos, had supported them. Once in government, this policy was abandoned in favor of continued warfare; in part because they, after all, did not wish to see the spoils of Venizelos go to waste, but also in part because it had become increasingly difficult to disentangle Greece from its Anatolian venture. The new Turkish nationalist movement of Kemal was growing stronger by the day. In Eastern Anatolia, it had pushed back the forces of the fledgling Armenian state that had proclaimed its short-lived independence, and made peace with Bolshevik Russia. France, preferring to reach an agreement with the Kemalists over military confrontation, withdrew its forces from Cilicia, while the Italians renounced all claims in their part of Anatolia.

This meant that the Turkish nationalists could turn their full attention to their Greek adversary in Western Anatolia. The French openly used the return of the "anti-entente" Constantine I as a pretext for terminating their commitment to Greece and declared neutrality in the Greco-Turkish conflict, while the British, despite some Philhellenic statements by Lloyd George, proved unwilling to aid their Greek ally. With no friends left and in view of the Kemalists' military build-up, the Greek high command launched a major offensive in the summer of 1921, hoping to strike a decisive blow to the new Turkish nationalist stronghold at Ankara, and force a peace settlement on favorable terms. Despite initial success, the offensive met with fierce resistance at the Sakarya River in the early fall that year, and was subsequently stalled in the Anatolian interior, leaving dangerously exposed supply routes. For the larger part of the following year, the Greek political and military leadership found itself in "a maze with no exit"; [62] unable to defeat the Kemalists and unable to end the war in a way that would allow it to save face. A British compromise proposal for a Greek retreat and the establishment of League of Nations protectorate in Ionia was considered in the spring of 1922, but negotiations with the Kemalists led nowhere. Such was the situation when Mustafa Kemal launched his counteroffensive at the end of August 1922.

Catastrophe and Aftermath

Just as 1912 had been a disastrous year for the Ottoman Empire, so was 1922 for Greece. Unable to hold their line of defense in the Anatolian interior, the Greek forces withdrew in disarray and were evacuated from Smyrna on 8 September. The Kemalist capture of said city a few days later, known in Turkish vernacular as "infidel Izmir," and the subsequent fire that turned the Christian and Jewish quarters of this once flourishing port into ashes marked the end of the war. Hundreds of thousands of Anatolian Christian refugees flooded the Greek islands and the ports of mainland Greece, while others remained at the victors' mercy. While women and children were belatedly evacuated from the Quay of Smyrna, thousands of Christian men of military age—among them the young Ilias Venezis from Aivalik—were taken prisoner and marched inland to forced labor and in many cases death, before the International Red Cross intervened.

In Greece, a group of disenchanted officers belonging to Venizelos' camp seized power in a military coup and took their revenge upon their royalist opponents, making them scapegoats for the military defeat. In the infamous Trial of the Six, a group of royalist politicians and high-ranking officers were court-martialed on the trumped up charge of high treason and subsequently executed. Even if this move seemed to satisfy a substantial part of Greek opinion, including the newly arrived refugees, it also ensured a bitterly divisive legacy associated with the Asia Minor Catastrophe for decades to come.

The Treaty of Lausanne signed by Venizelos and his counterpart Ismet Pasha (later Ismet Inönü) on behalf of their governments in 1923 brought a formal end to the Greco-Turkish war. Almost all Greek gains at Sèvres in 1920 were lost (though not those of the Balkan Wars from ten years before). A central tenet of the peace agreement was the compulsory exchange of minority populations between Greece and Turkey. Religion was the criterion that determined who would stay or go; thus some 400,000 Muslims (many of whom native Greek-speakers) were expelled from Greece to make room for approximately 1.2 million Orthodox Christians from Anatolia and Eastern Thrace, of which many knew only Turkish. For the Greeks, the exchange agreement merely formalized a fait accompli, since a majority was already refugees in an unfamiliar homeland. For the Orthodox of Cappadocia, who had lived in relative peace with their Muslim neighbors before 1923, the expulsion came unexpectedly. For their coreligionists in Pontos, far beyond the front lines even at the height of Greek power in Asia Minor, the treaty put an end to a state of terror, including forced marches and sometimes massacres. In their case, the population exchange might thus have saved them from the Armenians' fate; the latter of which, following Turkish demands, went unmentioned in the final treaty.

The Lausanne treaty set a terrifying precedent in "demographic engi-neering" by pointing to a way of solving national minority issues that would be implemented on a much grander scale in Eastern Europe after 1945. Yet the swap of populations in 1923 was not as complete as one would believe, since the Turkish negotiators grudgingly agreed to make an exception for the Greek community of Constantinople, henceforth Istanbul, which compelled Greece to exempt a fairly substantial Muslim minority in Greek Thrace from the exchange. These two groups would in essence remain hostages caught up on the wrong side of the new border; targets of popular and sometimes state-incited rage at every crisis in Greek-Turkish relations throughout the twentieth century. Nevertheless, with the bulk of Muslim and Christian populations dis-entangled from each other, the main casus belli had been removed and the two states could embark on their separate nation-building processes undisturbed. For Greece, the departure of the Muslims and the arrival of the Anatolian refugees provided an opportunity to repopulate the lands won in the Balkan Wars, thereby forging a Greek demographic majority in territories bordering Bulgaria, the main rival in the recent scramble for Macedonia. In a similar fashion, the peace allowed for Kemal, later named Atatürk, to rid himself of all domestic opposition and to forge a new and homogenous Turkish nation of the diverse Muslim populations left in the lands emptied by the Christians. With the Sultanate abolished and the Young Turkish as well as the neo-Byzantine dreams of empire buried, a new narrative came to dominate national ideology in Turkey. According to this story, engraved in school books and monuments across the country, Atatürk had single-handedly saved the Turkish nation from a corrupted and disgraced Ottoman Sultanate and its foreign masters, punished the Christians for their treason, restored national security through their removal, and finally made peace with the former enemies. The Greco-Turkish war was commemorated as the War of Independence, which paved the way for the modern Turkish Republic.

For obvious reasons, this narrative was unparalleled on the other side of the Aegean. The invasion of Asia Minor could never be turned into a heroic tale as the 1821 Uprising or the recent Balkan Wars had been. Yet the outcome of that war, catastrophic as it was, could with some good-will be construed as a happy ending, since the national project of the nineteenth century in the end had been fulfilled. The Ottoman Greeks had by and large been brought "home" to Greece, if not in the manner originally envisioned. The passing of the Great Idea also enabled a fresh start between the two newly established republics, symbolized through the Ankara Convention of 1930, whereby the leaders of Turkey and Greece, Atatürk and Venizelos—who having been out of office at the time of the Catastrophe was never held accountable for it—sealed their countries' reconciliation by dropping the claims of compensation for lost properties, which had been a burning issue ever since Lausanne. If not cordial, Greek-Turkish friendship would remain a cornerstone in the foreign policy of the two nations; at least until the second half of the twentieth century.

Figures and Morals

An issue that has come to preoccupy latter-day scholars and activists is the question of how many victims the Catastrophe and the persecutions of the decade that preceded it claimed. For those who wish to make a case for the recognition of genocide against Greeks, a high toll of casualties serves to highlight the magnitude of the crime, though skeptics tend to push estimates toward the lower end of the scale. The estimated deaths among Greek-Orthodox Christians during the period 1912–22 range from between 200,000 and 300,000 at the lowest to 1.5 million or even more in some accounts.[63] The reasons, among others, for this discrepancy are to be found in the difficulty of determining how many Ottoman Greeks lived in the various parts of the Empire before and after the Great War. The question boils down to a disagreement regarding the assessment of partially contradicting statistics. While Turkish or pro-Turkish scholars of Ottoman historical demography put faith in the accuracy of late Ottoman census data, which sets the total population of Anatolia in 1914 (excluding other territories still in the Empire by that time) somewhere between 15 and 17.5 million in 1914, with a comfortable Muslim majority,[64] some Greek scholars have criticized them for underestimating the numbers of the Christian minorities; especially the Ottoman Greeks.[65] Instead they point to higher figures provided by the Orthodox Patriarchate's own 1912 census, along with data collected for the Foreign Ministry of Greece, which pro-Turkish scholars such as Justin McCarthy dismissed as propaganda for Greek territorial claims.[66] Dimitri Pentzopoulos, a Greek diplomat writing in 1962 about the impact of the refugee crisis on Greece, saw no major disagreement between the Ottoman census data and the Patriarchate's numbers, which put the Anatolian Greeks alone at over 1.7 million in 1912 and which together with the roughly 700,000 Greeks of Thrace and Constantinople amounted to a total of some 2.5 million (excluding the Ottoman Greeks in the lands annexed by Greece in the Balkan Wars).[67] In an essay, often cited by both activists for genocide recognition and their critics in Greece, the scholars Paschalis Kitromilides and Alexis Alexandris put the toll of dead and vanished Ottoman Greeks at almost 700,000. They reached this estimate by comparing the number of people registered as refugees in the 1928 Greek census (1.1 million), subtracting the Greeks of Constantinople, who were exempt from the population exchange, and those of Eastern Thrace (evacuated without bloodshed) from a perceived total population of 1,547,952 Asia Minor Greeks in 1912, and adding that only around 848,000 had survived and managed to take refuge in Greece and other countries by 1923.[68]

However, these statistics—assuming that they are accurate—reveal little about the circumstances in which people died or disappeared. Even advocates of a genocide interpretation have difficulties estimating how many died as a direct consequence of violence as opposed to indirect causes of death that were beyond human calculation and control. Nevertheless, there is a temptation for such advocates to put the death toll in the higher numbers, as it adds clout to their claim that "their" genocide merits equal attention to better known cases. "A comparison of victim tolls," claims Tessa Hofmann, "illustrates that the cumulative genocide against the Ottoman Greeks was equally fatal as that of the Armenians."[69]

An illuminating example of this practice is to be found in the case of Pontos. In 1925, a total of 353,000 Greek casualties in Pontos was established by the refugee scholar Georgios Valavanis.[70] This figure stuck, as latter-day activists for genocide recognition faithfully reproduced it until it achieved official status, mentioned on virtually all occasions of commemoration. However, as the journalist Tasos Kostopoulos has demonstrated, Valavanis had reached this figure by simply adding a rough estimate of 50,000 "neo-martyrs" to the figure 303,238, which had been presented in a pamphlet from May 1922 that sought to draw the world's attention to the ongoing drama in Pontos. This figure had in its turn been arrived at through listing the estimated number of deported Greeks from various towns and villages of the region as "exterminated," prior to any verification. Kostopoulos' own estimate of dead is considerably lower; between 100,000 and 150,000 in Pontos during the years 1912–24.[71] The lure of death toll inflation is also present in estimates made for Asia Minor as a whole. One leading activist thus attributes a figure of "more than 800,000" casualties to Kitromilides and Alexandris (their actual estimate is 699,998), and then adds another 500,000 dead for the period 1915–18 alone (although these were already accounted for in Kitromilides' and Alexandris' total); in this fashion ending up with a total of 1.3 million Ottoman Greek victims.[72]

Behind contemporary controversies concerning population statistics and a seemingly cold-hearted body count looms a larger moral issue. The interpretation of the Ottoman Greeks' ordeal as genocide entails a moral vindication of these victims and possibly recognition of their descendants' right to compensation. It is an interpretation that highlights the agency and intentions of the Empire's ruling Turkish elite, the Young Turks and the Kemalists, who stand accused for the planning and execution of a crime against humanity. The other understanding of the process leading up to the Catastrophe emphasizes the suffering of Christian and Muslim populations alike and how the violence unleashed by both sides of the Greco-Turkish conflict escalated it until a point where the forced exchange of minorities seemed the only option left. The events would thus be better described in terms of "ethnic cleansing"—that is, a gruesome act of expulsion along the line of ethnic and/ or religious belonging, but not necessarily with the intent to physically annihilate the victim group.[73] Although condemned by international law and ethics, ethnic cleansing is less controversial as a label than genocide and seemingly neutral, as both Greeks and Turks were the victims of such acts. This interpretation, with its emphasis on competing national ambitions and mutual complicity in war crimes, harks back to the time of the war itself and the writings of British historian Arnold Toynbee, who appalled by the atrocities of Greeks and Turks alike saw the arrival of Western-style nationalist doctrine into the Near East as the ultimate cause of the tragedy.[74]

It is, however, a reading of the events that can be criticized on moral grounds since it seems to suggest that both sides were equally at fault and that no one therefore can be charged with culpability. Such a reading seems to de-emphasize the role of the Turkish leaders, who due to asymmetric power relations were able to carry out atrocities on a much grander scale during the period 1914–18 and after August 1922, when no military force remained to oppose them, and allow their latter day defenders to submerge the losses of the victim population within the general carnage of the wars, which indeed saw staggering death tolls even among the Turks.[75]

This is, however, a debate that tends to emerge not so much in scholarly environments as in the public arena, where issues of morality and victimhood play an important part in contemporary identity politics. The following chapter will explore how memories of the Catastrophe emerged from obscurity to the center of such politics at the end of the twentieth century.

Notes

1. Ilias Venezis (1931), quoted and translated in Roderick Beaton, *An Introduction to Modern Greek Literature*, 2nd ed. (Oxford, 1999), 140.
2. Richard Clogg, *A Concise History of Greece*, 2nd ed. (Cambridge, 2002), 98.
3. Erik J. Zürcher, *Turkey: A Modern History*, 3rd ed. (London, 2009), 50–70.
4. Sina Akşin, *Turkey – From Empire to Revolutionary Republic: The Emergence of the Turkish Nation from 1789 to the Present*, trans. Dexter H. Mursaloglu (New York, 2007), 32–36; Behlül Özkan, *From the Abode of Islam to the Turkish Vatan: The Making of a National Homeland in Turkey* (New Haven and London, 2012), 12–55.
5. Akşin, *Turkey*, 37–42.
6. For example, Vahakn N. Dadrian, *The History of the Armenian Genocide: Ethnic Conflict from the Balkans to Anatolia to the Caucasus* (Providence, RI, 1995), 113–76.
7. Richard Clogg, "The Greek *Millet* in the Ottoman Empire," in *Christians and Jews in the Ottoman Empire. The Functioning of a Plural Society. Volume 1. The Central Lands*, ed. B. Braude and B. Lewis (London, 1982), 191–92.
8. Charles Issawi, "The Transformation of the Economic Positions of the Millets in the Nineteenth Century," in *Christians and Jews in the Ottoman Empire. The Functioning of a Plural Society. Volume 1. The Central Lands*, ed. B. Braude and B. Lewis (London, 1982), 262–63.
9. Issawi, "The Transformation", 263; Charles Issawi, "Introduction," in *Ottoman Greeks in the Age of Nationalism: Politics, Economy, and Society in the Nineteenth Century*, ed. D. Gondicas and C. Issawi (Princeton, NJ, 1999), 5.
10. Akşin, *Turkey*, 44; Issawi, "Introduction," 8.
11. Zürcher, *Turkey: A Modern History*, 85–103, 127–32.
12. Dadrian, *History of Armenian Genocide*, 179–84. Tessa Hofmann, "Genoktonia en Roi – Cumulative Genocide: The Massacres and Deportations of the Greek Population of the Ottoman Empire (1912–1923)," in *The Genocide of the Ottoman Greeks: Studies*

on the *State-Sponsored Campaign of Extermination of the Christians of Asia Minor, 1912–1922 and Its Aftermath: History, Law, Memory*, ed. T. Hofmann, M. Bjørnlund and V. Meichanetsidis (New York and Athens, 2011), 39–49, 101.

13. For this alternative view, see Donald Bloxham, *The Great Game of Genocide: Imperialism, Nationalism, and the Destruction of the Ottoman Armenians* (Oxford, 2005), 62–68.

14. Feroz Ahmad, "Unionist Relations with the Greek, Armenian, and Jewish Communities of the Ottoman Empire," in *Christians and Jews in the Ottoman Empire. The Functioning of a Plural Society. Volume 1. The Central Lands*, ed. B. Braude and B. Lewis (London, 1982), 401–34; Catherine Boura, "The Greek Millet in Turkish Politics: Greeks in the Ottoman Parliament (1908–1914)," in *Ottoman Greeks in the Age of Nationalism: Politics, Economy, and Society in the Nineteenth Century*, ed. D. Gondicas and C. Issawi (Princeton, NJ, 1999), 193–206.

15. Zürcher, *Turkey: A Modern History*, 127–28.

16. Ioannis Kolettis (1844), quoted and translated in Clogg, *Concise History of Greece*, 47.

17. Ion Dragoumis, translated and quoted in Robert Shannan Peckham, *National Histories, Natural States: Nationalism and the Politics of Place in Greece* (London and New York, 2001), 40.

18. Peckham, *National Histories*, 83.

19. Thanos Veremis, "The Hellenic Kingdom and the Ottoman Greeks: The Experiment of the 'Society of Constantinople,'" in *Ottoman Greeks in the Age of Nationalism: Politics, Economy, and Society in the Nineteenth Century*, ed. D. Gondicas and C. Issawi (Princeton, NJ, 1999), 181–91.

20. Erik J. Zürcher, *The Young Turk Legacy and Nation Building: From the Ottoman Empire to Atatürk's Turkey* (London, 2010), 196, 220–21.

21. See, especially, Ryan Gingeras, *Sorrowful Shores: Violence, Ethnicity, and the End of the Ottoman Empire, 1912–1923* (Oxford, 2009).

22. Taner Akçam, *From Empire to Republic: Turkish Nationalism and the Armenian Genocide*, trans. Paul Bassemer (London, 2004); Taner Akçam, *A Shameful Act: The Armenian Genocide and the Question of Turkish Responsibility*, trans. Paul Bessemer (New York, 2006).

23. Akçam, *Shameful Act*, 4–8; Taner Akçam, *The Young Turks' Crime against Humanity: The Armenian Genocide and Ethnic Cleansing in the Ottoman Empire*, trans. Paul Bassemer (Princeton, NJ and Oxford, 2012), 1–9. Vahakn N. Dadrian, "Documentation of the Armenian Genocide in German and Austrian Sources," in *Genocide: A Critical Bibliographical Review*, vol. 2, ed. I.W. Charny and A.L. Berger (New York, 1991), 77–125.

24. V.N. Dadrian, "The Naim-Andonian Documents on the World War I Destruction of Ottoman Armenians: The Anatomy of a Genocide," *International Journal of Middle East Studies* 18, no. 3 (August 1986): 311–36.

25. J.M. Dixon, "Education and National Narratives: Changing Representations of the Armenian Genocide in History Textbooks in Turkey," *The International Journal for Education, Law and Policy*, Special Issue on "Legitimation and Stability of Political Systems: The Contribution of National Narratives" (2010): 103–26.

26. For recent representations of this position, see Guenter Lewy, *The Armenian Massacres in Ottoman Turkey: A Disputed Genocide* (Salt Lake City, 2005); Michael M. Gunter, *Armenian History and the Question of Genocide* (New York, 2011).

27. Dadrian, *History of Armenian Genocide*, 216–18.

28. Akçam, *Young Turks' Crime*, 9–20.

29. Akçam, *Young Turks' Crime*, 25–27.

30. Henry Morgenthau, *Ambassador Morgenthau's Story* (Garden City, NY, 1918),
     323–25; Arnold Toynbee, *The Western Question in Greece and Turkey: A Study
     in the Contact of Civilisations* (Boston and New York, 1922), 140–142, 280. Cf.
     Akçam, *Young Turks' Crime*, 95–96; D.J. Schaller and J. Zimmerer, "Late Ottoman
     Genocides: The Dissolution of the Ottoman Empire and Young Turkish Population
     and Extermination Policies – Introduction," *Journal of Genocide Research* 10, no. 1
     (2008): 7–14.
31. The most notorious of these massacres occurred on June 12, 1914, in the Aegean town
     of Foça (Phokaia), where about 100 Greek-Orthodox residents were killed. Michael
     Llewellyn Smith, *Ionian Vision: Greece in Asia Minor 1919–1922*, 2nd ed. (London,
     1998), 31–32. See also Matthias Bjørnlund, "Danish Sources on the Destruction of
     the Ottoman Greeks, 1914–1916," in *The Genocide of the Ottoman Greeks: Studies
     on the State-Sponsored Campaign of Extermination of the Christians of Asia Minor,
     1912–1922 and Its Aftermath: History, Law, Memory*, ed. T. Hofmann et al. (New York
     and Athens, 2011), 152–55.
32. J. Mourelos, "The 1914 Persecutions and the First Attempt at an Exchange of
     Minorities between Greece and Turkey," *Balkan Studies* 26, no. 2 (1986): 389–413.
33. Akçam, *Young Turks' Crime*, 74–75, 99–105.
34. In March 1917, the entire Greek population of Ayvali was thus deported to Balikesir
     and other inland regions, while Muslim refugees from the Balkans were settled in
     the town. The desecration of Greek churches, schools and hospitals suggest that
     the expulsion was intended to be permanent. Similar expulsions targeted the Greek
     inhabitants of Dikili, Bergama and other towns near the coast, while those of Manisa
     (Magnesia), Aydin and Smyrna further south were largely spared from deportations
     during this period. Toynbee noted the brutality of such events, but stressed the dif-
     ference between these expulsions and those of the Armenians in 1915. The Greeks
     of Ayvali, he contended, "were not massacred on the road, or driven on and on until
     they dropped, or marooned in deadly swamps or deserts, like the still more unfortu-
     nate Armenians. The extent of their loss and suffering largely depended upon the
     behaviour of their Moslem neighbours." Toynbee, *Western Question*, 143–44. See also
     Smith, *Ionian Vision*, 34.
35. Ioannis K. Hassiotis, "The Armenian Genocide and the Greeks: Response and Records
     (1915–23)," in *The Armenian Genocide: History, Politics, Ethics*, ed. R. Hovannisian
     (London, 1992), 135.
36. Hassiotis, "Armenian Genocide and Greeks," 135–36. The reference cited by Hassiotis
     is Kostas Fotiadis (1987), "Oi diogmoi ton Ellinon tou Pontou" ["The Persecutions
     Against the Greeks of Pontos"], in *Pontioi: Dikaioma sti mnimi* [Pontians: Right to
     Memory], ed. M. Charalambidis and K. Fotiadis, 4th ed. (Athens, 2003), 39–114.
37. See M. Bjørnlund, "The 1914 Cleansing of Aegean Greeks as a Case of Violent
     Turkification," *Journal of Genocide Research* 10, no. 1 (2008): 41–57; H. Georgelin,
     "Perception of the Other's Fate: What Greek Orthodox Refugees from the Ottoman
     Empire Reported about the Destruction of Ottoman Armenians," *Journal of Genocide
     Research* 10, no. 1 (2008): 59–76; Akçam, *Young Turks' Crime*, 63–123.
38. Akçam, *Young Turks' Crime*, 94–96.
39. Hassiotis, "Armenian Genocide and Greeks," 140.
40. Hassiotis, "Armenian Genocide and Greeks," 132, 139.
41. Akçam, *Young Turks' Crime*, xvii, 55, 97. Cf. Norman M. Naimark, *Fires of Hatred:
     Ethnic Cleansing in Twentieth-Century Europe* (Cambridge, MA, 2001), 42–44.
42. Akçam, *Young Turks' Crime*, 123. The author even mentions occasions when Greeks
     mistakenly included in the Armenian deportations were allowed to return once their
     true ethnicity was established by Ottoman authorities.

43. R.P. Adalian, "Comparative Policy and Differential Practice in the Treatment of Minorities in Wartime: The United States Archival Evidence on the Armenians and Greeks in the Ottoman Empire," *Journal of Genocide Research* 3, no. 1 (2001): 45. See also Vahakn Dadrian's discussion of the "German factor" and the threat of retaliation against Muslims in Greece as elements of constraint in the CUP's treatment of the Ottoman Greeks. Vahakn N. Dadrian, *German Responsibility in the Armenian Genocide: A Review of the Historical Evidence of German Complicity* (Cambridge, MA, 1996), 223–31.

44. "Review of Rouben Adalian's Paper on Comparative Treatment of Ottoman Armenians and Greeks," dated 21 June, 2008: http://www.greek-genocide.org/review_adalian.html (site discontinued). Last accessed 17 June 2011.

45. M. Levene, "Creating a Modern 'Zone of Genocide': The Impact of Nation- and State-Formation on Eastern Anatolia, 1878–1923," *Holocaust and Genocide Studies* 12, no. 3 (Winter 1998): 393–433. Levene does not discuss the Pontian Greek or the Assyrian experience, yet claims that his treatment of the "genocidal sequence affecting Armenians and Kurds" would also be pertinent to the study of these cases.

46. In his speech to the deputies and representatives of his Republican Party at Ankara, 15–20 October 1927, Kemal played up the threat posed by these bands to justify his actions in the Pontos during the Greco-Turkish war. He claimed that as many as 25, 000 Greek "brigands" had infiltrated the region by the end of 1919 in preparation of a Pontian declaration of independence and a "general massacre" of the Turkish population. Though these claims are clearly exaggerated, the prospect of an enemy landing on the Black Sea coast that might link up with local guerrillas was perceived as enough of a military threat to keep two army corps preoccupied in counterinsurgency operations, aimed at the annihilation of the bands and their perceived supply networks among the Christian civilian population. Kemal Atatürk, *A Speech Delivered by Mustafa Kemal Atatürk 1927* (Istanbul, 1963), 526–29. See also Nikos Marantzidis, *Yasasin Millet/Zito to Ethnos. Prosfygia, katochi kai emfylios: Ethnotiki tautotita kai politiki symperifora stous tourkofonous ellinorthodoxous tou dytikou kosmou* [Long Live the Nation. Refugeehood, Occupation and Civil War: Ethnic Identity and Political Behavior among Greek-Orthodox Turkish-Speakers of the Western World] (Iraklio, 2001), 39–83.

47. Alexis Alexandris, *The Greek Minority of Istanbul and Greek-Turkish Relations 1918–1974* (Athens, 1983), 59–60; Bruce Clark, *Twice a Stranger: The Mass Expulsions that Forged Modern Greece and Turkey* (Cambridge, MA, 2006), 110–12; Tasos Kostopoulos, *Polemos kai ethnokatharsi: I xechasmeni pleura mias dekaetous ethnikis exormisis (1912–1922)* [War and Ethnic Cleansing: The Forgotten Side of a Ten Years Long National Campaign (1912–1922)], 4th ed. (Athens, 2008), 227–33.

48. On the continuity between the Young Turkish and the Kemalist movements, see Zürcher, *Turkey: A Modern History*, 3–4.

49. Kostopoulos, *Polemos*, 238–39. Clark, *Twice a Stranger*, 113.

50. Corinna Görgü Guttstadt, "Depriving Non-Muslims of Citizenship as Part of the Turkification Policy in the Early Years of the Turkish Republic: The Case of Turkish Jews and its Consequences during the Holocaust," in *Turkey beyond Nationalism: Towards Post-National Identities*, ed. H-L Kieser. 2nd ed. (London and New York, 2013), 51–52.

51. Kostopoulos, *Polemos*, 237–41. Greek historian Dimitris Stamatopoulos has, along with Arnold Toynbee, interpreted the atrocities in Pontos as acts of retaliation for massacres against Muslim civilians, carried out by Greek troops, aided by Ottoman Christian and Circassian irregulars in the eastern Marmara region between May and June 1921. Dimitris Stamatopoulos, "I mikrasiatiki ekstrateia: I anthropogeografia

tis katastrofis" ["The Asia Minor Campaign: The Human Geography of the Disaster"], in *To 1922 kai oi prosfyges: Mia nea matia* [1922 and The Refugees: A New Perspective], ed. A. Liakos (Athens, 2011), 74–75. Cf. Toynbee, *Western Question*, 289–92.

52. For example, Theofanis Malkidis, *I genoktonia ton Ellinon tou Pontou: Istoria, politiki kai anagnorisi* [The Genocide of the Greeks of Pontos: History, Politics and Recognition] (Athens, 2008) 123–53. See also Hofmann, "Cumulative Genocide," 71–84.

53. Kostopoulos, *Polemos*, 245.

54. By "total" genocide, Levene denotes the overall annihilation of an entire community. The three examples of total genocide identified by him are the Armenian genocide in 1915–16, the Holocaust and the 1994 Rwandan genocide. The new round of Armenian massacres carried out after 1918 by the Kemalists, which some have regarded as a direct continuation of the 1915 genocide, is according to the distinction rather to be understood as of (near) genocidal nature than a genocide per se, since the scope of the killings was more limited. Levene, "Zone of Genocide," 395–97. The distinction was originally made in Leo Kuper, *Genocide: Its Political Use in the Twentieth Century* (London, 1981).

55. Fuat Dündar, *Crime of Numbers: The Role of Statistics in the Armenian Question (1878–1918)* (New Brunswick and London, 2010); Uğur Ümit Üngör, *The Making of Modern Turkey: Nation and State in Eastern Anatolia, 1913–1950* (Oxford, 2011); Akçam, *Young Turks' Crime*.

56. The Venizelist cleric Meletios Metaxakis, formerly Archbishop of Athens, was elected Ecumenical Patriarch of Constantinople in late 1921, despite vehement opposition from the royalist government of Greece. He abdicated from the throne in November 1923, at the request of Turkey's new nationalist government. Smith, *Ionian Vision*, 339–40. Stamatopoulos, "Mikrasiatiki ekstrateia," 75–78.

57. Clark, *Twice a Stranger*, 101–7.

58. Riza Nur, quoted and translated in Umut Özkirimli and Spyros A. Sofos, *Tormented by History: Nationalism in Greece and Turkey* (London, 2008), 161–62.

59. Uğur Ümit Üngör, "Paramilitary Violence in the Collapsing Ottoman Empire," in *War in Peace: Paramilitary Violence in Europe after the Great War*, ed. R. Gerwarth and J. Horne (Oxford, 2012), 174–75. Cf. Dadrian, *German Responsibility*, 223–31.

60. Smith, *Ionian Vision*, 35–61.

61. For example, Toynbee, *Western Question*, 293–99.

62. Smith, *Ionian Vision*, 266.

63. Leonidas Kallivretakis, cited in Panagis Galiatsatos, "Erotimatika apo aima gia Mikrasiatiki Katastrofi" ["Question Marks in Blood Concerning Asia Minor Catastrophe"], *Ta Nea*, 24 February 2001, 10–11. Justin McCarthy puts the Anatolian Greek death toll at 313,491, or 25% out of an estimated prewar population total of 1, 229, 491. Justin McCarthy, *Muslims and Minorities: The Population of Anatolia and the End of the Empire* (New York, 1983), 130–133. For the considerably higher estimate of between 1.3 and 1.5 million dead, see Charis Tsirkinidis, *Synoptiki istoria tis genoktonias ton Ellinon tis Anatolis* [Concise History of the Genocide against the Greeks of the East] (Thessaloniki, 2009). Cf. Hofmann, "Cumulative Genocide," 104–5.

64. Kemal Karpat, *Ottoman Population, 1830–1914: Demographic and Social Characteristics* (Madison, 1985), 190; McCarthy, *Muslims and Minorities*, 110. Cf. Akçam, *Young Turks' Crime*, 30–31.

65. P. Kitromilides and A. Alexandris, "Ethnic Survival, Nationalism and Forced Migration: The Historical Demography of the Greek Community of Asia Minor at the

Close of the Ottoman Era," *Deltio Kentrou Mikrasiatikon Spoudon* 5 (1984–1985): 21–30.

66. J. McCarthy, "Greek Statistics on the Ottoman Greek Population," *International Journal of Turkish Studies* 1, no. 2 (1980): 66–76. McCarthy, *Muslims and Minorities*, 89–99.

67. Dimitri Pentzopoulos, *The Balkan Exchange of Minorities and Its Impact Upon Greece* (Paris and The Hague, 1962), 29–34.

68. Kitromilides and Alexandris, "Ethnic Survival," 34.

69. Hofmann, "Cumulative Genocide," 101.

70. Georgios Valavanis, *Sygchronos geniki istoria tou Pontou* [Modern General History of Pontos] (Athens, 1925).

71. Kostopoulos, *Polemos*, 252–65. Cf. Kitromilides and Alexandris, "Ethnic Survival," 28, 34.

72. V. Agtzidis, "Mikra Asia kai amfisvitisi tis Istorias" ["Asia Minor and Contestation of History"], *Kathimerini*, 16 September 2001. Cf. Kitromilides and Alexandris, "Ethnic Survival," 34.

73. For this view, see Naimark, *Fires of Hatred*.

74. Toynbee, *Western Question*.

75. See Zürcher, *Young Turk Legacy*, 139, 186–87.

CHAPTER 2

"RIGHT TO MEMORY"

FROM CATASTROPHE TO THE POLITICS
OF IDENTITY

⟡⟡⟡

The Early Afterlife of the Catastrophe, 1923 to the 1980s

At a congress commemorating Hellenism in Asia Minor held in the "ref-ugee capital" of Thessaloniki in 1990, the president of the local Society of Macedonian studies, Konstantinos Vavouskos, addressed the dele-gates with a speech on how the Anatolian Greeks had contributed to forge modern Hellenism in Macedonia.[1] In the address, sprinkled with references to the conflict over Macedonia with Skopje looming on the horizon, he praised the diligence of the refugees and "their love for their new fatherland." With their arrival they had strengthened the Greek character of the Macedonian lands, and by mixing their blood with the local inhabitants they had given birth to a new type of Hellenism that would guarantee the "Greek future" of the northern borderlands.[2]

What was conspicuously absent in the address was attention to the refugees themselves and their history before their forced "repatriation." Vavouskos' speech was in that sense rather characteristic of the tradi-tional role assigned to them in national ideology and historiography—that of human raw material, with whose help the new lands to the north had been populated and secured for Greece. There were other, less appreciative accounts of the refugees' impact upon Greek society as well. The newcomers from Asia Minor had entered into an already polarized political atmosphere, marked by the previous National Schism between the royalists and the followers of Venizelos. It was well known that the Ottoman Greeks in general had been staunch supporters of the latter, their would-be savior, and that the leaders of the royalist camp had been executed to placate them. The supporters of the abolished monarchy, with their strongholds in the Peloponnese and other parts of "Old Greece" from before 1912, were resentful of the way their Venizelist opponents exploited the newcomers for electoral purposes. As a result of that, much of their rage and the blame for the Catastrophe were directed at the refugees themselves. Yet, the sheer numbers of the Greeks from Asia Minor and Eastern Thrace—they constituted one fourth of the total population in Greece after 1923—made them too powerful to ignore even for royalist politicians. The resettlement policy, whereby refugees were settled and employed in agriculture on lands vacated by expelled Muslims, made them the dominant population element in strategic areas in northern Greece; whereas densely populated "refugee neighborhoods" altered the urban landscapes of Salonica, Piraeus, and Athens. Realizing the potential of the refugee vote, associations representing refugee interests were able to influence the agendas of the political parties in their new homeland. Issues of refugee settlement and integration were of central concern to all of the five governments that came to power between 1924 and 1928, whether through military coups or democratic elections.

The refugee vote largely favored Venizelos and his party, at least until the signing of the Ankara agreement in 1930. After that final blow to the hope of future return to Anatolia and the recovery of lost property, the loyalties of the refugee electorate became more diverse. While some made their peace with the royalists, others—most notably the refugee proletariat in the shanty towns, which had sprung up around the major urban centers—veered toward the third emerging force in Greek politics: the Communist Party of Greece (KKE). Founded in 1918 (as SEKE), the communists had opposed the campaign in Asia Minor from its onset. While this initially may have deterred the Anatolian Greeks from supporting it, the Party's antiestablishment rhetoric, which blamed bourgeois machinations for their misfortunes, would in time find willing listeners among refugees, who felt betrayed by Venizelos and royalists alike.[3] However, although many of the leading members of KKE—including its most well-known Secretary General in the twentieth century, Nikos Zahariadis—were of Anatolian origins, the fact that the Party adhered to the Communist International, which forced it to propagate its policy of an autonomous Slav-dominated Macedonia, which was to include the parts of northern Greece where the bulk of refugees had settled, had a hampering effect on the communist appeal among the newcomers for most of the interwar years.[4] Nevertheless, their proneness toward political radicalism, along with their Eastern mores, made them somewhat suspect in the eyes of indigenous Greeks with right wing sympathies.

While the attitudes of the right wing establishment toward the refugees were for a long time ambiguous, the National Schism between royalists and Venizelist republicans eventually gave way to a greater ideological chasm in Greek society—that between Left and Right. With Venizelos gone from national politics, and his supporters cowed by the Metaxas regime, the whole issue of blame for the policies that had led Greece toward the disaster faded from public view. Whatever ethnocultural or regional grievances that once existed between Greeks of indigenous stock and those of the "lost homelands" in the East seemed to have lost their relevance during the ordeals of World War II, the Axis occupation of Greece, 1941–44, and the subsequent Greek civil war, 1946–49, between communist rebels and the Anglo-American-backed government. In the atmosphere of the early Cold War, and in the national ideology of the prevailing Right, the refugees performed a vital function as a bulwark of Hellenism against the nation's Slavic and communist foes; guardians of the north whose loyalty toward the fatherland was seldom publicly disputed.[5] The stigma of treason, in the form of collaboration with the Axis Powers during the occupation or with the communists during the civil war, was reserved for minorities perceived as non-Greek, such as the Slav Macedonians or the Albanian-speaking Chams of Epirus. Gradually, as a new generation with no personal recollections of the Catastrophe grew up, the divide between indigenous Greeks and refugees seemed to be disappearing, as urbanization and economic growth reshaped postwar Greek society. Writing in 1962, forty years after the Catastrophe, the scholar and diplomat Dimitri Pentzopoulos noted that the influx of refugees had caused some social problems that still remained to be solved—most notably housing—before the integration was complete, but nevertheless ended his study on an optimistic note on its role in "the transformation of Greece from a backward and parochial country to a forward-looking and dynamic one."[6] In the postwar reality, the memory of the expulsion seemed to be fading, long ago replaced by more urgent concerns related to future prosperity—the 1950s and 1960s saw new waves of migrants, many of them of Asia Minor origins, bound for labor in Germany, Sweden, and the New World—or current threats in the shape of international communism.

If the Greek state paid little attention to the commemoration of the Eastern world that had been lost in 1922, various refugee associations took it upon themselves to keep the memory alive. Commemoration was not the original purpose of these associations, which, mostly founded in the 1920s, functioned as guilds that helped their members out in matters of housing and employment. The long-term effect was nevertheless a recreated attachment to the various regions and places of origins throughout Anatolia and Eastern Thrace, and by way of nostalgia an interest in the history of those locations. Among demands forwarded by refugee organizations to the government in the 1950s was, in addition to claims for improved housing and titles to the "exchangeable property" left behind by the Muslims and now controlled by the state, the call for the establishment of academic centers, which would collect and preserve artifacts demonstrating "the miracles that were accomplished by the formerly unredeemed Greeks."[7] Such work had already been undertaken by association-founded centers and journals such as the Commission of Pontian Studies (1927), Archeion Pontou (Pontos Archive, 1928), Mikrasiatika Chronika (Asia Minor Chronicles, 1936), Mikrasiatiki Estia (Hearth of Asia Minor, 1946), and Pontiaki Estia (Hearth of Pontos, 1950), to name but a few.[8] The most important mediator of this semi-official memory of Anatolia, although not founded by refugees, was the Center for Asia Minor Studies (1930), headed by Octave and Melpo Merlier. Beginning in the late 1940s, the Center collected a vast array of oral testimonies from Anatolian refugees, which eventually were published in the voluminous and often cited tomes entitled *The Exodus*, whose very name invoked the biblical vocabulary used already in the 1920s to convey the magnitude of the population exchange.[9]

However, while the folklore of the Greek East was being studied in great detail and attention was given to the "uprooting" of Hellenism in Asia Minor, this body of scholarship, let alone public discussion, rarely addressed the history of violence preceding the "exchange." To be sure, gruesome details of the atrocities abounded in the various "black books" issued by the warring parties during the conflict and in its immediate aftermath, but this body of literature was made obsolete by the peace agreement, which terminated the prospects of a return to the lost homeland as well as hopes for material reimbursement for the suffering described in these works. There was little to be gained from continued attention to the massacres and persecution, to which the "population exchange" had put an end.

The topic of violence was mostly dealt with in stories of individual survival and narrow escape by authors, such as Ilias Venezis, who had endured the ordeals of the labor battalions in the wake of the Catastrophe, or Stratis Doukas, who in a partly fictionalized account narrated the story of an Anatolian informant taken captive by the

Turks.[10] These eventually bestselling accounts, written in the immediate aftermath of the events they portrayed, did not concern themselves with historical interpretation or any attempt to make sense of the suffering in a larger political context; rather they focused on the experience of pain, fear, and survival against all odds. Despite the brutality suffered at the hands of Turks, the authors displayed little interest in accusing and condemning the former enemies. Those writers who did attempt to identify the forces responsible for the victimization of the Anatolian Greeks, usually belonging to a later generation with the experience of the 1940s in recent memory, tended to avoid too overt emphasis on inter-communal enmities in the Ottoman Empire, choosing instead to blame foreign influences. This was the case with the 1962 novel *Bloodied Earth*—translated and published in English as *Farewell Anatolia*—by Dido Sotiriou, who in a left wing fashion interpreted the war and catastrophe as caused by international capitalism, which had pitted the Greek and Turkish peoples against each other after years of peaceful coexistence.[11] "So much suffering ... If it could only all be a lie, if only we could go back to our land, to our gardens," the narrator of the novel extols as he bids farewell to the Anatolian soil that gave birth to Greeks and Turks alike. "Hold it not against us that we drenched you with blood ... A curse on the guilty ones!"[12]

Latter-day activists for genocide recognition as well as scholars of collective memory have grappled with the question of why the Asia Minor Catastrophe, despite its vast impact upon Greek society, remained largely absent from public debates and official manifestations of remembrance. The former seek to explain the perceived silence as emanating from a repressive political climate, in which dictatorial or otherwise authoritarian regimes imposed censorship on scholarly or artistic work that was deemed harmful to Greek-Turkish relations, as well as a particular malevolence toward the refugees displayed by the Greek Right that dominated politics well into the 1970s. According to this interpretation, various Greek governments, indifferent to the suffering of the Anatolian refugees, had deliberately concealed the true dimensions of the Catastrophe by underestimating the loss of lives and obscuring the role played by the political establishment of Greece in the defeat.[13] The scholar of literature Thomas Doulis noted similar explications made by resentful refugee intellectuals in his 1977 study on the impact of the Asia Minor disaster upon Modern Greek prose fiction, but reached a different conclusion. Departing from the question of why the "trauma of the Disaster" seemingly had not inspired any major work of fiction that explored the full width of this historical watershed event before the "resurrection of the Asia Minor theme" heralded by Sotiriou's 1962 novel, Doulis addressed the most common interpretations among his Greek peers; "the tendency of the Greek people to forget unpleasant things," the "anti-refugee spirit," the imposition of censorship during the Metaxas regime of the late 1930s, and the lack of chronological and thus emotional distance to the event.[14] Of these, only the last two were found to have merit. Doulis did account for a few occasions when concerns for diplomatic relations with Turkey had stopped the distribution of certain works,[15] but the main reason for the silence that he stressed was in the end the lack of time elapsed since 1922. For refugees struggling to make a living in a new land in the aftermath of expulsion, there were more urgent matters than finding ways to express their pain in writing or in art.

Although primarily a scholar of literature, unfamiliar with the sociological theories on collective memory and trauma that would later rise to prominence in academia, Doulis addressed the same sort of questions that this study attempts to answer, and made several astute observations. One, although not articulated by himself, is the issue of intergenerational and cultural trauma. Doulis, a second-generation Asia Minor Greek influenced by the growing international attention to the trauma of the Holocaust of the 1970s, sought to make sense of a perceived absence of memory in the generation of his parents. In this, he himself becomes an illustration of cultural trauma, something that occurs "when members of a collectivity feel they have been subjected to a horrendous event that leave indelible marks upon their group consciousness, marking their memories forever and changing their future identity in fundamental and irrevocable ways."[16] Inherent in this notion of trauma as cultural is the idea that traumatic experience is not constricted to those individuals who suffered them firsthand, but that their pain is shared by a larger collectivity, and that the sorrow and sense of injustice can be inherited. The roles of different generations have been identified as being of central importance by scholars studying such trauma processes, whereby collectives either remember or forget.[17] In such research, a differentiation is made between the first generation, for which silence and forced oblivion during postwar reconstruction often have served as survival strategies, and a second generation, which although aware of the ordeals suffered by the parents has felt compelled to look forward, and finally the third generation, which plays a key role in the formation of a coherent and meaningful interpretation of the event; a temporally distant but emotionally close "cultural memory" tied to an articulated identity. Seen in this longer perspective, the delayed response to the Asia Minor Catastrophe in the historical culture of Greece does not appear as surprising. It took a long time before the scattered memories of the mass murders of the Jews and the Armenians evolved into the powerful symbols of evil they are known as today. This analysis of intergenerational trauma is largely shared by Greek genocide activists, who early on made sense of themselves as belonging to the "third generation," which rejected the passive resignation of their elders and set out to recover historical truth.

But collective traumas do not exist in and of themselves, sociologist Jeffrey Alexander argues in opposition to the common view that events are inherently traumatic.[18] Individuals do not respond to traumas but to trauma constructions; rather than being found they are made, in response to different political, cultural and personal needs, which often change over time. Without making this point explicitly, Doulis identified the coming of a second trauma, the occupation and the civil war, which overshadowed the events of 1922 and further delayed their absorption into the cultural concerns of Greek society and its intellectuals.[19] It is significant that the first call for international recognition of a genocide against Greek victims that Greece addressed to the UN already in 1948, even before the Genocide Convention was signed and ratified, made no mention of Greek suffering at the hands of the Turks. Rather, the demand arraigned the communists in the ongoing civil war with a plan to exterminate the Greek race by abducting children en masse from villages in guerrilla-held territory, and sending them to indoctrination camps in Eastern Europe.[20] Turkey was at that time an ally in the struggle against world communism; present concerns therefore had primacy over past grievances. The Greek state could, in spite of its ethnic nationalism, relate to Turkey's concern for national security, to which "alien" minorities constituted a threat, since Greece was perceived to face similar problems in its northern borderlands, where especially Macedonian or "pro-Bulgarian" Slavs, allied to the communist rebels, accounted for a separatist threat until the end of the civil war. Furthermore, seen against the turmoil of the 1940s, the Asia Minor Catastrophe was just one out of several possible "trauma dramas," "suppressed memories" or "unmastered pasts." To this observation should be added that the renewed experience of war promoted a more heroic self-image for the national collectivity that could not be easily reconciled with the defeatist temperament associated with 1922. Greece had in the past referred to the suffering of Anatolian Greeks to gather international support for its cause in Asia Minor,[21] and later on humanitarian aid, but victimhood was not considered a virtue in itself in the 1950s. For a nation that cherished heroism, the memory of massacres and expulsions was an uncomfortable reminder of national weakness. This view was indicated in a negative review of Ilias Venezis' childhood nostalgic novel

Aeolian Earth, published in the midst of German occupation. "In the hands of a worthy writer," the critic Vasilis Laourdas wrote, "the never-ending struggle of the 'cultivated' Greek spirit with Eastern irrationality could have provided material for a very substantial work ... Asia Minor Hellenism was and will remain for us ... a world of Greek moral values; this is how we would have wanted it to live in the art of the Greeks of Asia Minor."[22]

Nevertheless, the experience of new national traumas also had the effect of adding new meanings to older wounds. Doulis noted in passing how the Catastrophe attracted the interest of the left wing opposition in the 1950s, which, intimidated from discussing issues of the recent past such as wartime collaboration with the Axis and the civil war, turned to the topic of the Greco-Turkish war. In this earlier national disaster, they saw evidence of the bourgeois Greek state's subservience to its powerful Western allies and its inability to represent what they considered the true interests of the Greek people.[23] This was also a theme developed in historiography by Nikos Psyroukis, whose work on the Asia Minor Catastrophe came to exert great influence on interpretations of this event, especially among left wing intellectuals.[24] Psyroukis' interest lay in the contests between the imperialist great powers, chiefly France and Britain, for control of the oilfields in Mosul and Kirkuk, in which Greece had been used as a pawn for British interests in Anatolia and abandoned as soon as fortunes favored the Kemalists. In this scheme, the threat of an alliance between Kemal and Bolshevik Russia prompted Whitehall to reconsider its claims toward the defeated Ottoman Empire, and to sacrifice the interests of its Greek ally. It was an interpretative framework, which, with its emphasis on imperialist designs and the interplay with Greek foreign policy concerns, paid little attention to Ottoman domestic affairs in the years before the Greek expedition to Smyrna and Young Turkish policies toward the Christian minorities.[25]

The coming of the Cyprus question in the mid-1950s would however alter the picture of unproblematic Greek-Turkish relations to some extent. The left wing opposition in Greece, with the United Democratic Left (EDA) standing in for the outlawed KKE, skillfully stirred the nationalist sentiments of public opinion to expose the flatness displayed by the conservative government toward the demands of the "unredeemed" Greeks of the British crown colony for unification with the "motherland." The prospect of *enosis* (uniting) with Cyprus and the anti-Greek riots in Istanbul, in September 1955, brought reminiscences of the Great Idea, long thought buried, as well as earlier persecutions, which opened a public venue for anti-Turkish publications.[26] However, the conservative government of the time sought to contain expressions that might provoke Turkey and cause friction within NATO, which was a policy that even the junta of the late 1960s initially adhered to, for all its nationalist rhetoric. This order of things ended abruptly with the failed Greek military coup in Nicosia and the subsequent Turkish invasion of Cyprus in 1974, which with the resulting mass flight of Greeks from the northern part of the island, seemed to many a re-enactment of the 1922 disaster, albeit on a smaller scale. The downfall of the dictatorship and the transition to parliamentarian democracy it prompted enabled a wider array of participants in public debates; especially after the landslide electoral victory of Andreas Papandreou's Panhellenic Socialist Movement (PASOK) in 1982, which promised to exorcize the ghosts of civil war and social injustice.

For the refugees and their descendants, the democratization of Greek society coincided with and overlapped with a revived interest in Greek folk culture. Along with this broader revival, which began in the emergent liberal climate of the 1960s and exploded after 1974, came a reappraisal of the Anatolian Greeks' cultural features. The years after the downfall of the junta witnessed an avalanche of newly founded cultural associations among refugee descendants. The aspects in focus were primarily music and dances, folk art and cuisine, but a perhaps inevitable offspring to this general interest was the renewed attention given to the historical experience of the Asia Minor refugees, which surfaced in popular TV series and cinema, such as Kostas Ferris' *Rebetiko* and Nikos Koundouros' *1922*; the latter loosely based on Venezis' *Number 31,328*. Although much of this artistic work dealt with the hardships of the refugees after their arrival to Greece, the history of violence loomed in the background, readily exploitable in the new climate of openness and continuously deteriorating Greek-Turkish relations. Ironically, it was at this moment that rifts regarding the commemoration of the expulsion became manifest in the wider community of refugees.

"63 Years Away from Asia Minor": Pontian Identity Politics and the Narrative of Genocide

The story of how a new memory of what would later be termed "the Greek genocide" has several possible beginnings. One is the general preconditions brought about by the political transition in Greece after 1974, which enabled public confrontation with certain aspects of the past; indeed, held it to be a desirable undertaking. Another is the international developments of the 1980s and 1990s, which became manifest in the memory boom well under way even before the end of the Cold War and were further reinforced by the passing of political certainties and taboos born out of its bipolar world order. Yet another beginning, for those more inclined to pinpoint exact moments in history, is found in commemorative events of symbolic significance, or in landmark publications thought to have changed the overall public discourse on the subject matter.

One such beginning is the ceremony that took place in downtown Athens on 22 September, 1985, in honor of the dead of the Asia Minor Catastrophe. Unlike similar ceremonies held at the 60th anniversary of Smyrna's fall, this one was presented as the first of an annually reoccurring "Day of National Memory," in remembrance of the "holocaust of two million Greeks." The initiative for the national memorial day had come from the Federation of Refugee Associations of Greece (OPSE), with the support of the PASOK minister Giannis Kapsis, himself a descendant of one of Smyrna's more prominent families. Reading contemporary press coverage of the ceremony, one is left with the impression that it responded to a need for a unifying formula, a common trauma memory that would unite the various organizations of the refugee community in a time when their relations had grown critical, due to the massive increase of associations in the past ten years. Although the president of OPSE in an interview with the press sought to downplay the disagreements between refugee organizations in different parts of Greece, he stressed the importance of reaching out to the Pontian Greeks in particular, who "seem to prefer their own congresses and their own declarations, without any cooperation with the Federation [of Refugee Associations of Greece]."[27]

As noted earlier, the Greeks of the former Ottoman lands had not been a homogenous group, and even in exile their descendants continued to cultivate their attachment to the regions, towns and villages of their ancestors. This meant that, save for the generic term "refugee," there was no strong sense of a shared Anatolian Greek identity. Even the term *Mikrasiates*, Asia Minor Greeks, most commonly in use with reference to the large refugee community, was often also used to denote people from Ionia on the Aegean coast of Anatolia, in a geographically more narrow definition of Asia Minor. The various degrees of integration into Greek society had often corresponded to the geographic location of origin and the extent of linguistic affinity to the form of Modern Greek spoken in Greece. Being Eastern Anatolians, who spoke either Turkish or the peculiar Pontian dialect of Greek, the Christians from Pontos had belonged to the category most exposed to social marginalization in the new country. Like other refugee groups, they had set out to recreate their community life through associations that commemorated their distant homelands as well as reconstructed their principal monasteries, once they had settled in Greece.[28] Also like their fellow refugee descendants they had been caught up in the movement for cultural revival, which for them expressed itself in a quest to preserve and revitalize the dialect and the mores of Pontos.

However, unlike most other groups involved in the Greek folk culture revival and the rediscovery of Eastern exotica, the Pontian intellectuals who rose to prominence in the 1980s aimed to halt or even reverse the process of assimilation into the national majority culture, which they perceived as the major threat toward the particular Pontian identity. This "re-Pontianization" of the younger generations gradually took the shape of a de facto ethnification of the Pontian community, albeit within the wider framework of Greek national identity. Maria Vergeti, the Greek sociologist who studied this process in the early 1990s, insists upon defining it as a case of ethno-regional identity, which also reinforced the broader national one, as opposed to ethnic identity, which in her understanding of the term would indicate an alien national consciousness, bordering on separatism.[29] The analytical distinction is not altogether convincing, but it has to be taken into account that Vergeti and her Pontian informants had an interest in stressing the national credentials of their community in the nationalist climate of the Macedonian name controversy of that time, during which expressions of ethnocultural distinctiveness were viewed with suspicion by state and society. The Pontians were not the only ones demanding group rights and reparation for past injustice by the state in the whirlpool of populist sentiments during the decade of PASOK rule in the 1980s; also human rights activists within the Slav Macedonian minority pursued similar agendas, which served to fuel the alarmism about foreign irredentist designs against Greece in which the conflict with Yugoslav Macedonia evolved. Regardless of the specifics of the Greek context, the Pontian cultural movement shared similar characteristics and concerns with other previously marginalized groups involved in identity politics around the world in the 1970s and 1980s. In this process, dances and folksongs were deemed insufficient means by leading advocates of a specific Pontian identity. From the mid-1980s and onward, the Pontian revival became more explicitly oriented toward the cultivation of collective remembrance; not of the nostalgic kind or of the sort that stressed the refugees' gratitude toward and contributions to their new Greek fatherland, but one that emphasized trauma and called for justice.

The birth of the new Pontian trauma drama can, in a symbolic sense, be dated to 17 and 18 September 1986, when its manifesto appeared in one of the prominent national dailies of Greece, *Eleftherotypia*.[30] Its author was Michalis Charalambidis, an original member of PASOK's

Central Committee who in the previous year had founded a new Center for Pontian Studies (KEPOME). As stated in his text, with the telltale title *Pontians: Right to Memory*, later published as a book, the aim of KEPOME's work was to restore the collective memory of the Pontian Greeks through the recognition of their past sufferings as genocide; a deliberate attempt at wiping out their entire community from the surface of the earth, on a par with the great crimes against humanity over the course of the twentieth century. The "right to memory," defined as knowledge of one's own history and the political causes behind the present reality for Pontians all over the world, was presented as the first "basic precondition for Pontian existence and continuity," while the second was international recognition of the genocide and the Turkish state's responsibility for it.

The struggle for vindication was also presented as a fight against historical oblivion in Greece, due to decades of governmental neglect and "the violent logic of states," which paid no attention to the history and interests of peoples. In this oblivion, the right wing and left wing forces of Greece were equally at fault; the former for sacrificing refugee interests for the sake of Greek-Turkish friendship, the latter for treating the refugee problem as solely class-based, thereby ignoring the dimension of cultural identity. It was however not only within the confines of the Greek nation state that the Pontian experience was made sense of. Charalambidis portrayed the struggle for recognition as having "liberating dynamics," which would go beyond the Pontian dimension and affect the entire Eastern Mediterranean, assisting also Kurds and Armenians in their struggles as well as the democratic forces in Turkey. The policy of states and great powers, as the perpetrators of crimes and sponsors of oblivion, was effectively contrasted with the popular quest for truth and justice, as expressed in the demand for history written from the perspective of "peoples" instead of governments. "The Pontian people were stripped of the right to existence, the right to keep and possess their territory peacefully, the right to respect for their national and cultural identity," Charalambidis wrote.

> The greatest crime, however, committed against the Pontian people with the Turkish state as perpetrator and which admits neither prescription nor oblivion,—and even less—neither forgiveness nor excuse, is that of the genocide. If the logic of states, geostrategic and geopolitical dogmas and expediency downgraded, hid, pursued the oblivion of the events, the injustices that were committed against the Pontian people, today—even more because of these reasons—the wish and the demand for their recognition intensify. All peoples have the right to insistently demand the official recognition of the crimes and injustices committed against them.[31]

The cultivation of Pontian identity and remembrance would thus be synonymous with the trauma of genocide. As Charalambidis confidently put it in a later edition of the book, it was "the beginning of the awakening and the rebirth of a people, the Pontians, the beginning of their return to history, politics and geography."[32] While he and his fellow memory-political activists were not the first to address the history of violence against the Greeks of Pontos during and after the Great War,[33] they were the first to place it in a larger framework of historical interpretation, beyond the traditional emphasis on the Greco-Turkish war 1919–22 and the population exchange. As a crime against humanity, on a par with the Armenian genocide and the Jewish Holocaust, it was to acquire a new meaning, which would also serve to rally the Pontians for a common cause.

The timing of this identity-political movement, with genocide commemoration at its core, is important. The early 1980s had seen an ever-growing attention in North America and Western Europe to the horrors of the Jewish tragedy, in what Peter Novick has termed the Americanization of Holocaust memory, which entailed a spill-over effect, as the phenomenon brought about an upsurge in interest and sensibility toward genocide in general, which other victim groups in turn could capitalize on. Of particular importance to Charalambidis and his associates were the efforts of the Armenian diaspora, which gained momentum in 1986 and 1987, when the UN Commission of Human Rights and the European Parliament respectively recognized the Armenian genocide. One year later, the book *A Crime of Silence: The Armenian Genocide* by the NGO Permanent Peoples' Tribunal appeared in Greek translation, with an introduction that stressed the common fate of Greeks and Armenians, as well as the genocide's topicality for contemporary Greek-Turkish relations.[34] Also the "right to memory" manifesto contained passages that connected the Pontian cause with the Armenian, although Charalambidis never went into detail of how the two cases linked up with each other. For him, the Armenian case was more of an example to be followed in the struggle for international recognition. "Nobody can deny that our psychological and moral condition would be completely different, had the genocide been recognized [just as] the psychological condition of the Jews and the Armenians would be different if the international community and public opinion did not recognize the genocides committed against them."[35]

This ambition was to wield an ever growing influence on the activities of Pontian cultural associations in the years that followed. Apart from Charalambidis' own group of people, sometimes nicknamed "the Italians," since several of them had spent their formative years during the dictatorship in exile in Italy, a newly founded association in Athens called Argo took the lead in spreading the gospel of genocide recognition, through a steady flow of pamphlets and street banners. Argo's most active members were young people in their twenties at the time, often with their political background in radical student politics, who had grown disenchanted with traditional left wing ideology and instead turned to ethnocultural identity politics. They perceived themselves as spokespersons of the "third generation" of Pontians who demanded to know the truth of what had happened in the years before the expulsion.

The main venue for this activism would be the global congresses of Pontian Hellenism, which from 1985 and onward were held in Thessaloniki, the second city of Greece and home to a substantial part of Greeks originating from the Black Sea region. The genocide issue was presented to the Second Global Congress in 1988 by Charalambidis, who called for the delegates' support for the demand to have the alleged genocide recognized by the international community. To this end, he also proposed the establishment of 19 May as a "memorial day for the victims of the Pontian genocide." The proposed date was the day when Mustafa Kemal had arrived in Samsun at the Anatolian Black Sea coast to take charge of the nationalist resistance against the Greek-entente occupation. Ever since 1927, when Kemal mentioned it in the opening sentence of *Nutuk*, "the Speech," which was to provide the guidelines for the Turkish state narrative on the foundation of the Republic, this date has acquired a mythical aura in Turkish nationalist historiography and is celebrated as a national holiday.[36] The very same date and event of Kemal's coming to the Pontos allegedly marked the beginning of a new, intense phase in the persecutions against the Pontian Greeks, and was therefore bound to draw Turkish attention. The commemoration of this date, Charalambidis argued, would give the benefit of a "fixed day of the year when Pontians all over the world—in Greece, in the Soviet republics of Georgia, Russia, Ukraine, Kazakhstan, Armenia, in the United States, Canada, Argentina, West Germany, Sweden, Australia— will honor the hundreds of thousands of our unjustly lost relatives and countrymen with petitions, protestations and marches."[37]

What Charalambidis offered to the delegates at the congress was, in other words, a common memory and an annual ritual that would unite the Pontians of Greece and the diaspora, while strengthening their Pontian consciousness. The support of the organizing committee of the Second Global Congress proved to be the first major breakthrough for the "right to memory" campaign. Not all Pontian Greek delegates present at the congress shared this enthusiasm for the genocide narrative, however. In the press, Pontian intellectuals who belonged to an older generation with more conservative political leanings expressed their dismay at how the demand for international recognition had been imposed upon the congress, amidst clamor and applaud in an "explosive atmosphere." The critics claimed that the organizing committee had been hijacked by a small group of radicals who demanded support for a new interpretation of Pontian history, in which the "genocide against the Pontian people" was presented, without a shred of scholarly evidence, as an established fact. By pursuing this, these activists were sowing discord and confusion within the Pontian community, as well as driving a wedge between it and the rest of the Anatolian refugees, let alone the rest of the Greek nation. One of the critics, Stathis Eustathiadis, who supported the cultivation of ties with the refugee federation OPSE, pointed out that neither the Asia Minor refugees from Western Anatolia or those from Thrace had ever made any such demands, nor had the Greek Parliament, and yet the Pontians now turned to other states for recognition of "their" genocide. Eustathiadis pointed to the danger of the rhetoric of shared martyrdom with other diaspora peoples victimized by the Turks and expressed his skepticism with regard to the course that Pontian identity politics had taken.

> The complete identification of the Pontians with the Armenians, Kurds etc., is a dangerous step. The Pontians are part of the Greek nation. Whatever injuries they suffered are injuries against the nation. The separation from the national body leads our community into the position of a minority! The Pontians are not in search of a homeland. Mother Greece is their homeland, to which they returned after their uprooting on the ground of international treaties and which they manned, especially in the borderlands.[38]

The critics clearly viewed the emphasis on an historical experience that distinguished the Pontians from the rest of the national community as a leap away from traditional Greek patriotism, which would only serve to alienate them from the nation and play into the hands of those "enemies of Hellenism" who denied the Greek character of Macedonia. The threat of being a minority was seen within the prism of the state's national ideology, which in the Balkans as well as in Turkey views minorities as agents of competing national movements and thus a threat against the territorial integrity of the state. It was therefore, according to one of the critics, Gavriil Lampsidis, "a crime and a calamity ... to make reference to the 'Pontian people' and to claim ... that the trials the Pontians suffered from the Young Turks justify the characterization of genocide."[39]

A response to this critique came from Vlasis Agtzidis, vice president of Argo and a member of the organizing committee, a young mathematician and PhD student of history, who would in time emerge as one of the most vociferous advocates of genocide recognition in Greece. He presented the issue as essentially a clash between the "third genera- tion of Pontian refugees," to which he belonged, and the second gener- ation, which clung to an outmoded historical interpretation that only served the state establishment that had kept the Pontians in the dark about their past. "If something became clear during the Second Global Congress of Pontian Hellenism, it was precisely the emergence of *a new discourse* on modern Pontian history and prospects, and *the coming to the foreground of the new Pontian generation* ... which neither wishes to forget nor to compromise, and above all, nor to find excuses for anyone." The real problem that the modern Pontian community was facing was, in Agtzidis' view, the silence surrounding the genocide issue and the history of mistreatment of its members in Greece and the Stalinist repression suffered by Pontian Greeks in the Soviet Union. "The fear in the face of the new that emerges and the desperate efforts to extend the period of silence" had led some prominent Pontians to belittle the significance of the genocide, and *"to turn a blind eye to this fact in the name of elucidating the concepts of* 'genocide,' 'extermination,' 'holo- caust,' 'annihilation.'"[40]

The process of "re-Pontianization" seemed irreversible, and with that the process for the recognition of genocide as an experience cen- tral to Pontian self-understanding. Delegates from the Pontian Greek diaspora in North America, in particular, came out in strong support of the demand for international recognition of the alleged genocide, and even launched an unsuccessful proposal to have the next world congress convene in New York, with this goal in mind.[41] The genocide issue was to be revisited at the Third Global Congress of Pontian Hellenism in 1992, which in turn would pave the way for broader political acceptance of the activists' demand. Nevertheless, the marginalized critics within the Pontian community had pointed to a substantial problem, which in one way or another would continue to mar the identity politics, in which the demand for recognition of the alleged genocide played such an import- ant role. In order to make this an issue for the international community, one would first have to make it a national issue. Eustathiadis had unwit- tingly identified a strategic objective for the activists when he pointed to the absurd in turning to other states for recognition without having secured the support of the Hellenic Parliament. In order to get this sup- port, the activists would have to convince a broader audience outside the Pontian community that the trauma the Pontian Greeks had suffered was the Greek nation's trauma as well. If pushed too far, Pontian iden- tity politics would only have the effect of alienating non-Pontian Greeks, most notably the West Anatolian refugees, by denying them their sense of victimhood at the hands of the same Turkish perpetrators. The road to the cosmopolitanization of the "genocide trauma" thus lay in its nationalization. The following chapter will further explore how the notion of the Pontian Greek genocide left the confines of ethnocultural identity politics and entered the agenda of national policymakers, as well as inspired similar demands among other Asia Minor Greeks, bent on claiming a place at the center of national historical remembrance.

Notes

1. Parts of this chapter are a revised version of Chapter 4, in Erik Sjöberg, *Battlefields of Memory: The Macedonian Conflict and Greek Historical Culture* (Umeå, 2011).
2. K. Vavouskos, "I prosfora tou Mikrasiatikou Ellinismou eis tin diamorfosin tou syg-chronou Makedonikou Ellinismou" ["The Asia Minor Greeks' Contribution to the Formation of Macedonian Hellenism"], *Annales*, vol. 5 – *Meletai Konstantinou An. Vavoskou* [Studies of Konstantinos A. Vavouskos] (Thessaloniki, 1993), 1779–83, cited in Sjöberg, *Battlefields*, 115.
3. Dimitri Pentzopoulos, *The Balkan Exchange of Minorities and Its Impact Upon Greece* (Paris and The Hague, 1962), 190–92.
4. Richard Clogg, *A Concise History of Greece*, 2nd ed. (Cambridge, 2002), 104.
5. For illuminating examples of this view, see Pentzopoulos, *Balkan Exchange*, 125–40.
6. Pentzopoulos, *Balkan Exchange*, 254.
7. Kentriki Epitropeia Prosfygon, *To prosfygikon zitima kata tin parousan fasin tou* [The Refugee Question in its Present Phase] (Athens, 1957), 13, cited in Pentzopoulos, *Balkan Exchange*, 235.
8. A.S. Alpan, "But the Memory Remains: History, Memory and the 1923 Greco-Turkish Population Exchange," *The Historical Review/La Revue Historique* 9 (2012): 213–14, 219–21; Charis Exertzoglou, "I istoria tis prosfygikis mnimis" ["The History of Refugee Memory"], in *To 1922 kai oi prosfyges: Mia nea matia* [1922 and The Refugees: A New Perspective], ed. A. Liakos (Athens, 2011), 192–93.
9. Fotis D. Apostolopoulos and Giannis Mourelos, eds., *I Exodos* [The Exodus], 2 vols. (Athens, 1980–82).
10. See Ilias Venezis, *To noumero 31328* [Number 31328] (Athens: 1931); Stratis Doukas, *Istoria enos aichmalotou* [A War Captive's Story], 44th ed. (Athens, 2008).
11. Thomas Doulis, *Disaster and Fiction: Modern Greek Fiction and the Asia Minor Disaster of 1922* (Berkeley and Los Angeles, 1977), 202–8; Roderick Beaton, *An Introduction to Modern Greek Literature*, 2nd ed. (Oxford, 1999), 241–42.
12. Dido Sotiriou, *Farewell Anatolia*, trans. Fred A. Reed (Athens, 1991), 298.
13. For example, Vlasis Agtzidis, "Mnimi, tautotita kai ideologia ston pontiako ellinismo" ["Memory, Identity and Ideology among Pontian Greeks"], in G. Kokkinos, E. Lemonidou and V. Agtzidis, *To trauma kai oi politikes tis mnimis: Endeiktikes opseis ton symvolikon polemon gia tin Istoria kai ti Mnimi* [The Trauma and the Politics of Memory: Indicative Aspects of the Symbolic Wars for History and Memory] (Athens, 2010), 223–51; Theofanis Malkidis, *Ethnikes kai diethneis diastaseis tou Pontiakou Zitimatos* [National and International Dimensions of the Pontian Question] (Athens, 2006).
14. Doulis, *Disaster and Fiction*, 286.

15. The most notable example of censorship referred to by Doulis is the political decision of the newspaper *Ethnos* in 1932 to stop the publication of Christos Spanomanolis' book about Greek war captives in Turkey, "at the instigation of the Turkish Embassy, as a gesture to Greco-Turkish Friendship" in the wake of the Ankara pact. It was finally published after the anti-Greek riots in Istanbul in 1955, in a time of deteriorating relations between the two countries. Doulis, *Disaster and Fiction*, 269. Cf. Christos Spanomanolis, *Aichmalotoi ton Tourkon* [Prisoners of the Turks] (Athens, 1956).

16. Jeffrey C. Alexander, *Trauma: A Social Theory* (Cambridge and Malden, 2012), 6.

17. See Ron Eyerman, "Cultural Trauma: Slavery and the Formation of African American Identity," in *Cultural Trauma and Collective Identity*, ed. J.C. Alexander et al. (Berkeley, 2004), 69–78.

18. Alexander, *Trauma*, 13, 98.

19. Doulis, *Disaster and Fiction*, 272.

20. Lars Baerentzen, "The 'Paidomazoma' and the Queen's camps," in L. Baerentzen, J. Iatrides and O. Smith, *Studies in the History of the Greek Civil War* (Copenhagen, 1987), 128, cited in Loring M. Danforth and Riki Van Boeschoten, *Children of the Greek Civil War: Refugees and the Politics of Memory* (Chicago and London, 2012), 4–6. This ideologically motivated use of the genocide label was also referred to by left wing journalist Nikos Filis in an attempt to discredit the interpretation of the 1922 Catastrophe as genocide. Nikos Filis, "Alli mia 'agnosti' genoktonia eis varos Ellinon" ["Another 'Unknown' Genocide against Greeks"], *Avgi*, 18 February 2001, 25.

21. Venizelos had thus claimed at the Paris peace conference in 1919 that as many as 300,000 Ottoman Greeks had been annihilated by the Young Turks during the Great War, while another 450,000 had fled to Greece in dire circumstances. Taner Akçam, *From Empire to Republic: Turkish Nationalism and the Armenian Genocide*, trans. Paul Bassemer (London, 2004), 146.

22. V. Laourdas, "I Aioloki Gi," *Filologika Chronika* 1, no. 2 (1944): 73, quoted in Doulis, *Disaster and Fiction*, 283.

23. Doulis, *Disaster and Fiction*, 285.

24. Nikos Psyroukis, *I mikrasiatiki katastrofi: I engys Anatoli meta ton Proto Pagkosmio Polemo* [The Asia Minor Catastrophe: The Near East after World War I] (Athens, 1982); Dimitris Stamatopoulos, "I mikrasiatiki ekstrateia: I anthropogeografia tis katastrofis" ["The Asia Minor Campaign: The Human Geography of the Disaster"], in *To 1922 kai oi prosfyges: Mia nea matia* [1922 and The Refugees: A New Perspective], ed. A. Liakos (Athens, 2011), 61.

25. For a long time this was also the viewpoint of international scholarship on the subject matter. See, especially, Michael Llewellyn Smith, *Ionian Vision: Greece in Asia Minor 1919–1922*, 2nd ed. (London, 1998).

26. For an analysis of the resurgent Greek irredentism and the "national claims" activism with regard to the Cyprus issue, see Ioannis Stefanidis, *Stirring the Greek Nation: Political Culture, Irredentism and Anti-Americanism in Greece, 1945–1967* (Aldershot, 2007).

27. Takis Vezyrigiannis, cited in G.D. Malouchou, "63 chronia makria apo ti Mikrasia" ["63 Years Away from Asia Minor"], *Ethnos*, 22 September 1985.

28. Michel Bruneau, "Les monastères pontiques en Macédoine. Marqueurs territoriaux de la diaspora," in *Les Grecs pontiques: Diaspora, identité, territoires*, ed. M. Bruneau (Paris, 1998), 213–28.

29. Maria Vergeti, *Apo ton Ponto stin Ellada: Diadikasies diamorfosis mias Ethnotopikis Tautotitas* [From Pontos to Greece: Formation Processes of an Ethno-regional Identity]. 2nd ed. (Thessaloniki, 2000), 405, 408–409.

30. M. Charalambidis, "Pontioi. Dikaioma sti mnimi. I 'xechasmeni' genoktonia" ["Pontians. Right to memory. The 'forgotten' Genocide"], part 1, *Eleftherotypia*, 17 September, 1986, 12–13; M. Charalambidis, "Pontioi. Dikaioma sti mnimi. Treis fores prosfyges" ["Pontians. Right to Memory. Thrice Refugees"], part 2, *Eleftherotypia*, 18 September 1986, 12–13.

31. M. Charalambidis and K. Fotiadis, eds., *Pontioi: Dikaioma sti mnimi* [Pontians: Right to Memory], 4th ed. (Athens, 2003), 28–29.

32. M. Charalambidis and K. Fotiadis, *Pontioi: Dikaioma sti mnimi*, 15.

33. The work most frequently referred to as pioneering was the lecture by historian Polychronis K. Enepekidis, presented to the Pontian association Argonautai-Komninoi at the Archaeological Society of Athens on 26 February, 1961. Polychronis Enepekidis, "Oi diogmoi ton Ellinon tou Ponto (1908–1918)" ["The Persecutions of the Greeks of Pontos (1908–1918)"] (Athens, 1962).

34. Periklis Rodakis, "Prologos stin elliniki ekdosi" ["Preface to the Greek Edition"], in Diarkes dikastirio ton laon, *To egklima tis siopis: I genoktonia ton Armenion* [A Crime of Silence: The Armenian Genocide], trans. Gianna Kourtovik and Sifis Kassessian (Athens, 1988), 7–31.

35. Michalis Charalambidis, "To Pontiako Zitima simera: I Genoktonia aitia tis Exodou kai tis diasporas" ["The Pontian Question today: The Genocide as Cause of the Exodus and the Diaspora"], in *B' Pagkosmio Synedrio Pontiakou Ellinismou* [2nd Global Congress of Pontian Hellenism], ed. P. Kaïsidis (Thessaloniki, 1990), 189–90.

36. H. Adak, "National Myths and Self-na(rra)tions: Mustafa Kemal's *Nutuk* and Halide Edip's *Memoirs* and *The Turkish Ordeal*," *South Atlantic Quarterly* 102, no. 2/3 (Spring/Summer 2003): 509–27.

37. Charalambidis and Fotiadis, *Pontioi*, 13.

38. Stathis Eustathiadis, "To Pontiako Synedrio" ["The Pontian Congress"], *Eleftherotypia*, 13 August 1988, 26.

39. Gavriil Th. Lampsidis, "To theio pontiako peisma" ["The Sublime Pontian Pigheadedness"], *Eleftherotypia*, 24 August 1988, 26.

40. Vlasis Agtzidis, "I nea genia ton Pontion" ["The New Generation of Pontians"], *Eleftherotypia*, 30 August 1988, 35.

41. Vergeti, *Apo ton Ponto*, 339.

CHAPTER 3

NATIONALIZING GENOCIDE
THE RECOGNITION PROCESS IN GREECE

"A Day of National Pain and National Memory": The Political Recognition 1994–98

The Hellenic Parliament formally recognized the "genocide of the Pontian Greeks" on 24 February 1994, as 19 May was declared a national day of remembrance.[1] The decision was unanimous, ostensibly reflecting a unique consensus among the parties on the national significance of the issue. "After some nine years [of struggle] we achieved what had been considered unattainable and utopian[:] The recognition of the great Pontian drama and the establishment of 19 May as memorial day of the Pontian Holocaust," Michalis Charalambidis triumphantly wrote. "All peoples had a memorial day of their own holocaust, only we were denied it for eight decades."[2] Perhaps more importantly, the Pontian refugee community— once the underdogs of Greek society—had been recognized as a political force to be reckoned with. Their determination in promoting their own ethnocultural features, their own uniting historical experience and their own organizations and congresses had made them much more efficient in lobbying their interests than the various other Anatolian refugee associations. With Greeks of Pontian descent amounting to about a million in Greece alone—at least according to optimistic estimates[3]—the community made up a powerful electorate, which prompted politicians from across the spectrum to court its leading organizations. PASOK and its leader Andreas Papandreou, in office from 1981 to 1989, and again from 1993 to 1996, reached out to the Pontians by attending their congresses and religious ceremonies, as well as by allocating funds. Even serials in the Pontian dialect were aired on state television. Never before, as one journalist remarks, had Pontos been so visible in Greece.[4]

Regardless of the Pontians' clout as an electoral force, the road to recognition of the genocide claim—the issue made central to their sense of ethnocultural identity—lay in the making of the trauma into a national concern. After all, trauma dramas are constructed with a wider audience in mind than just the victims, which means that outsiders to the group that perceives itself victimized need to be convinced that the suffering of that particular community is theirs as well.[5] This had been a point in question for the critics of the new genocide interpretation within the Pontian community mentioned in the previous chapter, who had cautioned against pushing the sense of a particular Pontian identity too far. "The Pontians are part of the Greek nation," one of them had stressed in opposition to the new emphasis on shared martyrdom with the Armenians and the Kurds. "Whatever injuries they suffered are injuries against the nation."[6] Too much emphasis on the uniqueness of the Black Sea Greeks' suffering as their defining historical experience, it was feared, would result in a backlash to their interests, as other Greeks, notably the West Anatolian refugees, would feel excluded.

With the internal opposition to the genocide narrative marginalized within the Pontian community in the early 1990s, advocates for its recognition went about strengthening the national credentials of their cause. This meant attaching what was referred to as the Pontian question to the list of other "national issues" dominating public debate and foreign policy concerns at the time. These included the ongoing dispute with Turkey (which during PASOK's reign had gone from bad to worse) over territorial rights in the Aegean and the still unresolved Cyprus issue, minority rights with regard to the Muslims of Thrace and the dwindling Greek-Orthodox community in Istanbul left in place at Lausanne; and above all the conflict over Macedonia's name and heritage with the Republic of Macedonia, in the wake of Yugoslavia's collapse in 1991. Greece in the early 1990s was a country struggling to come to terms with a political and economic crisis, as PASOK was swept from power in a wave of corruption scandals and popular disillusionment (only to return in the 1993 elections, after its rival, the right wing Nea Dimokratia (ND), had failed to meet popular expectations). In the field of international relations, uncertainty was king as the collapse of the Soviet bloc and the turmoil in neighboring Yugoslavia brought the prospect of war and waves of refugees closer to Greece. The breakdown of the Cold War order in the Balkans seemed to invite Turkish expansionism, under the cloak of acting as protector for the embattled Muslim populations in the region, and in the process creating an "Islamic arc" encroaching Greece, from Albania in the west to the Aegean in the east. When the former Yugoslav Republic of Macedonia (in Greece mockingly referred to as the "Skopje republic") declared its independence in 1991, and laid claim to the name and the historical heritage of Alexander the Great's ancient kingdom perceived by most Greeks to belong to their national history, while simultaneously acting as a protector for the Slav Macedonian minority in neighboring Greek Macedonia, the ghosts of the Balkan Wars and related traumas of the twentieth century's first half were let loose in the public imagination. The mainstream media of Greece were awash with calls for national unity in view of some impending doom likely to result from an alliance between Skopje and Ankara. These fears fed into deeper concerns about the values of Greek society, which some perceived had been lost on the way to democracy after 1974. Especially with regard to history education, debaters worried that the baby of patriotism had been tossed out with the tub water of the discredited right wing state nationalism of earlier decades, thereby depriving the young generation of a sense of collective memory and purpose, with potentially dire consequences. The rallying of the nation behind the slogan "Macedonia is Greek" did thus not only serve to defend Greek soil against the claims of a foreign state; it was an effort to reclaim national identity and history itself, as a response to a crisis within the nation and its historical culture, in a time of growing uncertainty.

Scholars of the Pontian identity-political phenomenon agree that the Third Global Pontian congress, which convened in Thessaloniki in May 1992, when passions about Macedonia were at their height, mark a union between the national and the particular, as Pontian identity was subordinate to the ostensibly endangered national identity.[7] By publicly participating in the struggle for Macedonia as well as making statements on Cyprus, the Aegean and other national issues, the Pontian associations could demonstrate their patriotism and hope to gain further publicity and sympathy for their own core issues, most notably the supposed genocide, but also the integration of newly arrived migrants of Greek origins from the former Soviet Union. The glasnost reforms of the late 1980s had enabled a sizeable population of diverse origins, lumped together as Greeks in the Soviet nationalities model, to follow in the footsteps of earlier Anatolian and Black Sea Greeks and "return" to Greece. Representatives of newly formed or re-established Soviet

Greek cultural associations made their first appearance at the Second Global Pontian Congress in 1988, where they were greeted as long-lost Pontian brethren. The arrival of these newcomers—nicknamed "Russo-Pontians" in Greece—brought back memories of the refugee tragedy in the early decades of the century, which the Pontian associations were quick to grasp, as these largely forgotten kinsmen were targeted for "re-Pontianization" in addition to state-sponsored initiatives for their "re-Hellenization." The Argo group, consisting of both Pontian Greek refugee descendants and newly arrived Soviet Greeks, took the very existence of these contemporary refugees from the USSR as evidence that the refugee question thought to have been buried at Lausanne still remained open and in need to be politically revisited. The history of Pontian suffering could not be allowed to be confined to the past. The key to success was to bring it on par with contemporary problems, by posing recognition of past wrongs as a prerequisite for mending the ills of the present. Several speeches at the Third Congress addressed the issue of the new wave of "uprooted Greeks" from the former Soviet republics, turning them into emblems of the Pontians' allegedly perpetual victim-hood, while the overall statements on the "genocide"—that is, the mas-sacres and expulsion of Greeks from their ancient homelands—seemed to accentuate the current threats against Greece and the urgency of recognition. The atmosphere in which the congress convened conjured up the image of an ever diminishing Greek world, beset from all sides by the danger of a new uprooting. The trauma drama of the Pontian Greeks, despite its appeal to the international community in the name of global human rights and shared suffering with Armenians and Kurds, thus played into deeply national fears and concerns.

This strategy, whereby the demand for genocide recognition, in Vergeti's words, "was confronted as a demand of the entire Greek nation, and not only of the Pontian Greeks,"[8] seemed to have resonated with politicians eager to demonstrate their sensitivity toward grass-roots con-cerns. The address of Andreas Papandreou, the once and future prime minister, to the 1992 congress read like a blueprint of Charalambidis' and other activists' demands. "No oblivion and no silence can conceal the murder of our 353,000 fellow Greeks of Pontos during the years 1916–23. Every reference to the Pontian question is devoid of any value whatsoever, if one ignores … the significance of the Genocide against the Greeks of Pontos, and the responsibility of the Turkish state for this international crime."[9] PASOK's deputies, many of whom were of Pontian descent, played a leading role in paving the way for the genocide's offi-cial recognition through legislation, but also their right wing adversaries saw fit to pay homage to the notion of genocide as a shared national experience. In 1993, almost a year before the recognition of 19 May as a national memorial day, the right wing deputy minister of foreign affairs, Vyron Polydoras, issued an official message to the Greek diaspora organizations on the occasion of the Pontians' day of remembrance, a "day of national pain and national memory," as he called it. What is noteworthy about this statement is the way in which it, despite its sensitivity toward the group's identity politics, de-emphasizes the Pontian element and stresses the alleged genocide's character of a national, Greek tragedy. The events leading up to the annihilation of almost half the Greek population in the easternmost outskirts of the Hellenic world were said to oblige all Greeks to "determine our national conduct." The fact that the victims of this act of ethnic cleansing were Greeks, something that ostensibly made Greeks more sensitive toward similar phenomena elsewhere in the present, made it especially important to remember them as a way of confirming the nation's endangered identity.

> Our nation in the difficult times that we expect draws, without hatred, on the lessons of historical memory. We the Greeks, with our deep historical consciousness, are able to confront our historical past with dignity. And with the strength of life for the future.[10]

The audience of Polydoras' statement, with its nationalizing features, was the organizations of the million-strong Greek diaspora, which needs to be taken into consideration. The diaspora, notably the people of Greek origins living in North America, was in the 1990s viewed as an international asset with a leverage that could be used to promote Greek national interests abroad. It was therefore important that the identity of its members—especially its Pontian members—as Greeks be reaffirmed. The new narrative of the supposed Pontian genocide might, just as well as the Macedonian question, serve this end, and thus the foreign policy of the nation, while the demands of the Pontian constituency at home were simultaneously met. In 1995 the World Council of Hellenes Abroad (SAE) was established as the consulting body of the Greek state in all its contacts with the diaspora organizations, which testified to the ambition of letting these play a more active role in shaping Greek foreign policy. At least one of the individuals who wrote the Council's statutes, Vlasis Agtzidis, was a prominent lobbyist for genocide recognition, and its coming into existence opened new avenues for Pontian identity politics.[11]

However, one should not overstate this interest in the potential political leverage of the Pontian genocide issue among national policymakers. Polydoras' statement in 1993 aside, the Greek Ministry of Foreign Affairs did little if anything to pursue international recognition, paying only lip service to this cause. Despite the groundbreaking significance attributed to it in later publicity, the recognition generated scant notice at best in mainstream media at the time. In the Greece that in the mid-1990s struggled to find its place in post-Cold War Europe, few participants in public debates on history, nationalism and contemporary politics took notice of the new narrative of genocide, and its implications for national historiography, or else seemed to mind. To be certain, the Parliament's recognition was of little practical consequence. Even though it was supplemented by a decision assigning the historian Konstantinos Fotiadis, a close friend and associate of Charalambidis, with the task of authoring a volume with documentation that would prove the veracity of the Pontian claim, the decree did not commit the Greek state to introduce the topic into the national history curriculum, or otherwise raise public awareness. What may have seemed a broad political consensus on the historical importance of recognizing the Pontian drama might just as well have been a lack of interest in and opposition to Pontian identity politics among the bulk of the deputies. The notion of the genocide seemed destined to remain within the confines of the Pontian Greek community, despite being blessed with a national memorial day.

The elevation of the Pontian genocide claim into some sort of official national memory was clearly intended for domestic consumption alone. Its significance lay in the example it set for other refugee organizations. As one could expect, the recognition of the Pontian community's historical experience in a way that rivaled the significance traditionally attributed to the Asia Minor Catastrophe in 1922 ignited demands for similar acknowledgment amongst other descendants of the Anatolian refugees, notably those from the Smyrna region on the Aegean littoral. One PASOK deputy, Giannis Diamantidis, criticized the recognition of the Pontian experience as a separate case of genocide, isolated from the events that took place in Ionia. In his view, the Greeks were victims of *one* genocide that occurred in two phases; before and during the Great War, 1914–18, and then over the course of the Greco-Turkish war, 1919–23. Hence, the "genocide against the Greeks of the East" ought to be recognized in its entirety.[12] This was one of the first calls for the nationalization of the genocide, which involved an explicit critique against Pontian particularism, although, ironically, the individual experts that he suggested to the Parliament for the task of rallying international support for recognition of this Greek genocide were people known for their commitment to the Pontian cause.[13]

There was another candidate date for commemoration apart from 19 May, with a precedent in Greek legislation. Already in 1986, the

Hellenic Parliament had heeded calls from the Federation of Refugee Associations (OPSE) and recognized 14 September (a date associated with the Smyrna fire) as a national day of remembrance for the victims of the Asia Minor Catastrophe. In 1997, Diamantidis, together with fellow PASOK deputies Giannis Kapsis, known for his hawkish views on Turkey, and Giannis Charalampous, submitted a motion calling for the establishment of said date as "National Memorial Day for the Genocide of the Greeks of Asia Minor by the Turkish State." The bill was debated and unanimously endorsed during the Parliament's session on 24 September 1998, with only minor reservations expressed by deputies of the Left.[14] The text of the motion paid little attention to the Pontians; instead, it stressed similarities with the internationally better known Armenian genocide, which the Hellenic Parliament had recognized two years earlier in the wake of the Pontian decision, while conveying the image of a three millennia long Hellenic presence in Anatolia, destroyed by the Young Turks through a combination of "Asian barbarism" and "coldblooded Teutonic methods." "Through the labor battalions hundreds of thousands of Greeks were exterminated in a national genocide on a par with the Armenian, during the exact same period."[15] The stated purpose of the new memorial day was to honor the memory of the Greek victims ("our brethren") of "Turkish bestiality," so as to prevent the same thing from happening again, and salvage Greek historical memory from the abyss of oblivion.

The law that established the memory of the Asia Minor Catastrophe as genocide did however not replace its Pontian predecessor; it merely complemented it. The result of this nationalizing effort was that the Hellenic Parliament now recognized *two* genocides against the Greeks of Anatolia, with separate days of commemoration, thereby sowing the seed of much future confusion, especially among foreigners for whom the subtle distinctions of intra-Greek identity politics would make little sense. It was unclear whether the "Greeks of Asia Minor" being commemorated were the Greek-Orthodox population of Asia Minor in its entirety, or if "Asia Minor" just referred to the geographically more narrow meaning of the words—the Aegean littoral in Western Anatolia—which would not include the victims in Pontos. Though greeted by Pontian activists as a further vindication of their cause, the law about 14 September evidently set the stage for competition between different versions of the memory-political project within the Anatolian Greek refugee community interpreting their historical experience as genocide. This seems not to have been the general impression at the time among supporters of these genocide narratives, who rather were inclined to see them as mutually reinforcing calls for historical truth.

In any event, it was no grave cause of concern, since the second genocide recognition was of as little consequence as the first had been. The law passed without much notice and was referred to the president's office to be duly enforced. Somewhere along the way, it was caught in the cogwheels of bureaucracy and soon forgotten. This was, however, a state of affairs that would change dramatically in the new millennium.

The Coming of the Earthquake Diplomacy

In order to understand why the genocide narrative eventually became the object of controversy in public debate, one would need to set it into a wider context of changing foreign policy considerations toward the end of the 1990s, of internal power struggles within the two major political parties, and of the growing opposition to the Greek nationalism prevalent in the years of the Macedonian conflict. The emphasis on "national historic rights" in the country's foreign policy, and the populist appeal to nationalist sentiment, was by the mid-1990s condemned as an essentially flawed strategy by contemporary analysts, who blamed it for pushing Greece into dangerous international isolation. Greece's true national interests, they argued, lay in European integration, in which Greece would play a role in securing peace and prosperity in the Balkan region, which was bound to reflect positively on its international image.

This agenda found willing adherents in the so-called "modernizer" wings of the two leading parties, chiefly within PASOK and centered on the economics professor Kostas Simitis. As the towering but ailing figure of Andreas Papandreou vanished from politics in 1996, the "modernizers" got the upper hand in the struggle for his succession and the soul of PASOK. Simitis' moderation and commitment to the European Union stood in sharp contrast to the populism of his predecessor. In the field of Greek-Turkish relations, the Simitis government eventually abandoned the confrontational approach, which as late as 1996 had led the two countries to the brink of war. The diplomatic embarrassment following the capture of the leader of the PKK (Kurdistan Workers' Party), Abdullah Öcalan, by Turkish agents outside the Greek embassy at Nairobi in early 1999 gave Simitis, eager to cut the defense budget, the opportunity to rid himself of prominent hawks in his cabinet. Although a rapprochement with Turkey was already under way, the public catalyst for the improvement of these relations was the earthquakes that struck both countries within three weeks of each other in late summer 1999, which gave cause for mutual aid and declarations of solidarity. The symbolic significance of this gesture was great and Simitis' new minister of foreign affairs and future successor, Georgios Papandreou, seized the opportunity to open up negotiations with his Turkish counterpart, Ismail Cem, on a number of issues, including Greek support for Turkey's bid for membership in the EU.[16] In January 2000, Papandreou made the first official visit to Ankara undertaken by a Greek foreign minister since 1962, and laid a wreath on the mausoleum of Kemal Atatürk, the man that the Hellenic Parliament just a few years before had held responsible for the murder and expulsion of hundreds of thousands of Greeks. Cem reciprocated the courtesy by stating that more had been done to promote good neighbor relations in the previous six months than in the past forty years.[17] The "earthquake diplomacy," as it was dubbed, held out promising prospects of Greek-Turkish reconciliation, but for advocates of the genocide narratives, this new dawn was ill news.

The "modernizing" efforts of the Simitis government did not go unopposed. Its economic policies adapted to meet EU requirements were widely unpopular and tended to reflect badly on reforms introduced to bring Greece into line with her international partners, especially with regard to minority rights. When the government proposed in 2000 to remove information about religious affiliation from the citizens' identity cards, a practice that had been criticized for discriminating against non-Orthodox Christian minorities, the staunchly nationalist Archbishop Christodoulos and the Church organized massive protest rallies similar to those held in the days of the Macedonian conflict. Christodoulos accused the forces behind the reform of plotting to "de-Christianize" the country and of endangering Greek national identity, which struck a chord with a strong portion of the public that viewed Simitis' policies as subservient to foreign interests. The gradual loss of national independence, real or perceived, to supranational institutions and the world of global finance—often referred to in conspiratorial terms as "the New Order"—along with a steady flow of immigrants to a country that until recently had taken pride in its ethnic homogeneity set the stage for public clashes on cultural symbols and issues deemed crucial to national self-understanding. It was in this politically and emotionally charged atmosphere that the notion of the Anatolian Greek genocide and the existence of its memorial day came to the public's attention.

"A Day of National Amnesia": The Public Backlash to the Genocide Narrative

The spark that ignited controversy over the interpretation and commemoration of the Catastrophe and its prelude was developments abroad relating to the recognition of the Armenian genocide; a process that in the years around 2000 gained new momentum on both sides of the Atlantic. A bill for its recognition, which had passed in the French National Assembly in 1998, was enforced by law on 29 January 2001, in a move widely interpreted as a rebuke toward Turkey, thwarting its hopes for speedy accession talks with the EU. The French example brought the Hellenic Parliament's own recognition of the Armenian genocide to the fore, as well as its alleged Greek "twin tragedy" still waiting to be legally enforced. Within twelve days after the announcement of the French "memory law," a Greek presidential decree finally enforced 14 September as a national memorial day for the "Genocide of the Greeks of Asia Minor," signed by the deputy minister of culture, Evangelos Venizelos, one of Georgios Papandreou's chief rivals in the party. The recognition of the two Greek "genocides" had largely been the work of the "patriotic" faction of PASOK, the camp associated with nationalist causes and the populism of the 1980s and early 1990s. It is therefore plausible that the genocide issue was seized upon, once again, by those traditionalists wishing to regain lost ground from Simitis' moderniz- ers. Regardless of the motives that prompted the presidential decree, its existence was bound to cause friction in the recently improved Greek-Turkish relations.

The news of the decree was met with critical reactions in mainstream press in the week following its announcement. "It seems as if the obses- sion with History will continue to haunt us as a nation for many years after the [nationalist] rallies of 1992–93," the editors of the radical "Sunday virus" group (*Iós*) wrote in their weekly column in the daily *Eleftherotypia*, condemning the genocide recognition as blatant history revisionism.[18] The main thrust against the recent decree, and its inter- pretation of 1922, came from *Avgi*, a small-circulation yet influential daily associated with the radical, ex-communist Left. In a Sunday issue dedicated to this topic, the journalist Nikos Filis stated that the law about the "Asia Minor genocide" had been enforced without any public debate; a debate that *Avgi* now wished to open before it was too late.[19] Over the next couple of weeks, a number of journalists, scholars and pol- iticians engaged in a debate where all evidence supporting the genocide claim, ranging from number of casualties among the victimized Greeks to overall interpretative framework, was open to question.

Critics of the new memorial day focused on either one or several aspects of it. For some, the main objection against it was simply that the Asia Minor Catastrophe had never before been referred to as geno- cide, and was thus nowhere to be found in either dictionaries or text- books on modern Greek history.[20] Others were wary of 14 September as the designated date of commemoration and asked why it had been chosen instead of 27 August (9 September), when Smyrna was captured by Kemal's forces.[21] The conclusion they reached was that it coincided with the celebration of the Exaltation of the Holy Cross as well as the beginning of the school year, indicating an attempt to reinforce the bond between State and Church, and to rehabilitate the much discredited notion of the "Greece of the Christian Greeks" championed by the old junta and the present Archbishop Christodoulos. All critics seemed in agreement that the renaming of the Asia Minor Catastrophe as genocide was a politically imposed interpretation, which stood in sharp opposition to the, supposedly, genuine collective memory of the event. This was especially stressed by Angelos Elefantis, historian and editor of the left wing intellectual journal *O Politis* (The Citizen), who made what he perceived as the state-led assault on true historical knowledge his rallying point. "All of History must be an object of national, meaning collective, memory"; precisely for this reason, he argued, there was no cause for adding 14 September to already existing national anniversaries (of, for example, the national holidays commemorating the outbreak of the 1821 uprising, or the defiance against Italian aggression in 1940). Elefantis did not oppose the idea of anniversaries commemorating the glories and sorrows of national history, as long as these served to foster the nation's historical self-knowledge, which he understood as a critical engagement with Greek nationalism and the follies it had prompted in the past.

In the present case, however, the duty to remember gives rise to a new interpretation of History, by decree. The very same state comes and decides by way of raising the arms to impose a new interpretation of 1922, in disregard of its own positions for the past 80 years, in disregard of all the [different] shades of historiography, in disregard of the facts and, above all, of the real collective consciousness and memory of the modern Greeks. In collective, then, consciousness, the Asia Minor Disaster has been a *catastrophe* from 1922 until today. A strong word which says it all. It was the catastrophe of the Greek army. The Catastrophe of Asia Minor Hellenism, our cradles from time immemorial, of Greek civilization and its people, a catastrophe that came as a consequence of Greek expansionism [*megaloïdeatismos*]. It followed as a consequence of a bloody war in which Greece not only was the first to act unjust, but got entangled in a dead end for purposes of conquest rather than of liberation, as in the Balkan Wars, or of defense, as in 1940. Having adopted the chimera of 'the five seas and the three continents,' exceeding her forces as well as being indifferent to the legitimate resistance of the Turkish people and misjudging the international conjuncture at the time, she got entangled into an inexorable war in which there, besides the military disasters, were reciprocal violations and atrocities committed by both sides against the civilian populations.[22]

While Elefantis dwelled upon the meaning of the Catastrophe for national self-knowledge, others sought to knock down the wobbly pillars on which the genocide claim rested. One of these was the unduly high death tolls presented to convey the magnitude of Greek suffering; according to the historian Leonidas Kalivretakis, Giannis Kapsis, the initiator of the 14 September motion, had talked about a million dead, and some of his supporters in Parliament even about 1.5 million, while earlier authorities (notably Alexandros Pallis) had put the estimate at 640,000. Kalivretakis himself set the death toll at a considerably lower number, approximately 400,000 Anatolian Greeks, which together with some 50,000 military casualties amounted to almost half a million dead. "They are not few and there is no need to inflate their numbers."[23] Also the historian Charis Exertzoglou, a scholar on the history of the Ottoman Greeks, pointed to the problem of the unreliable population statistics from the period in question, by which he meant that all serious researchers remain skeptical of them, but dismissed the numbers issue as irrelevant. "If this number is a million, eight hundred thousand or five hundred thousand does not really matter, as we in any event are talking about appalling numbers." Exertzoglou remarked that the "so-called historians" who in Greece attempted to calculate a final death toll had their counterparts in Turkish historiography, who tried to reach similar conclusions regarding casualties among Anatolian Muslims from equally flawed census data. "If we are to believe Justin McCarthy, the number of Muslims who lost their lives in a violent way between 1915 and 1922 exceeds four million. But what is the meaning of this 'beauty contest' of victims which not only disrespects the memory of the dead but usurps it for other ends?"[24]

The heart of the matter lay elsewhere, in his and other commentators' view; namely in the question of the perpetrators' intent and how the concept of genocide was to be understood. The UN Convention's notion of systematic destruction of a national, ethnic, religious or racial group, "in whole or in part," emerged as a bone of contention, since a very large number of Anatolian Greeks had been expelled rather than exterminated. "Genocide, a non-existent word in all languages before 1944, is according to dictionaries the systematic ... annihilation of an *entire* nationality" (my emphasis), argued three researchers at the Centre for Asia Minor Studies (KMS). For them it followed that the atrocities "committed in conditions of war and at times far-reaching ... do not justify the use of the term genocide on a scholarly level."[25] Tasos Kostopoulos, one of the editors of the *Iós* group, took a similar point of view with regard to the case of the Asia Minor Greeks, but extended his critique to the very concept of genocide, the criteria of which "are neither well-defined nor universally accepted or applicable." The editor raised two main objections against the genocide concept; the first being that it had been unknown before 1944, when it was coined to describe Nazi atrocities in occupied Europe, and hence would not be applicable to events that had taken place before (thus paying no attention to Raphael Lemkin's earlier writings on the Armenian massacres). Secondly, its definition was so vague that it virtually included any gruesome situation and as a result was devoid of value. This had led to abuses of all sorts, which a simple search on the Internet gave ample evidence of. Apart from references to the Holocaust of the Jews and other groups persecuted by the Third Reich, and the "equally torrential annihilations of the Armenians, the [East] Timorese and the Tutsis of Rwanda," there were web pages that applied the genocide label to what Kostopoulos described as the recent "tragic but clearly minor histories" of the vanished in Chile and the civil war in El Salvador, Bosnia, Kosovo, Cyprus, Iraq, the Kurdish problem in Turkey, and in the case of Cambodia the "grotesque label 'auto-genocide.'" For all the good it would do, he sarcastically noted, the nationalists of Turkey might as well respond to the Greek memorial day by commemorating the "genocide" of the Muslims massacred in the Peloponnese during the 1821 uprising.[26] Their objection was thus in essence a definitional one—if not all members of a group are slated for extermination in the way the Jews were in Hitler's Europe, it is not genocide.[27]

Other commentators trod more carefully with regard to this issue. Antonis Bredimas, a professor of international law, departed from the UN Genocide Convention in his discussion of whether the Catastrophe fit with the definition or not. Unlike the three KMS researchers and the *Iós* editors, Bredimas did not dismiss the genocide interpretation out of hand, stating that there is no obstacle to the use of the term genocide, even in instances before 1948, when the Convention was signed. One would, however, be bound to observe the criteria mentioned in it. Herein lay the crucial problem of demonstrating genocidal intent. It could be demonstrated in the case of the Armenians in 1915 and Rwanda in 1994, but in the case of Asia Minor Bredimas considered it harder to prove the actual intent of the Young Turks and the Kemalists to annihilate the Greeks, in whole or in part. One could argue that genocide would follow from the goal of these movements to solve the problem of non-Turkish populations by force, which is what occurred in the case of the Armenian massacres. Bredimas, however, argued that the Kemalist government had not opted for the full or partial extermination of the Greek population, but rather expulsion, which was

largely brought about within the framework of the compulsory population exchange. What the Greeks of Asia Minor endured in 1922–23
certainly constituted human rights violations, war crimes and even
crimes against humanity, but it did not constitute genocide.[28] A similar
viewpoint was expressed by a scholar of international relations, Alexis
Heraclides (Irakleidis), who nonetheless added a disclaimer of his
own making, namely that the crime of genocide, as defined in the UN
Convention, exclusively refers to states that within their own boundaries persecute ethnic, national, religious or racial minorities with the
intent to destroy them, "physically and biologically." The 1922 expulsion of the Anatolian Greeks, though clearly a crime against humanity,
could not be considered genocide, Heraclides argued. The reason for
this was that the Catastrophe had been preceded (and caused) by a regular war between the Greek army and Kemal's nationalist forces. For
Heraclides, this war had started with the former's landing at Smyrna
in 1919; no reference was made to the complex issue of anti-Greek
persecutions during the Great War. In his account of the Asia Minor
drama, the Greek expeditionary force had brought down the doom on
their Anatolian kin by abusing its mandate from the Great Powers to
secure peace and order. "Instead of setting an example of leniency and
just government toward the Turkish population," wrote Heraclides,
the Greek troops had succumbed to the massacre of civilians and the
burning of villages. They had thus proved to be unworthy of the noble
task entrusted to them and provoked the enmity of the Turks, thereby
destroying the chances of Hellenism's survival in Asia Minor. This,
he hastened to add, did not diminish the suffering of the Anatolian
Greeks, but it did not make their tragedy genocide either. That would
only have been the case if the Turkish state after the Greek military
defeat in 1922 had annihilated the bulk of those Anatolian Greeks left
behind. Instead they had been expelled, much like all the Muslims, who
beginning in 1912 were driven eastward by the advancing armies of
Greece and other Balkan states.[29]

Heraclides' core argument was problematic, resting as it did on a
somewhat misguided assumption of war and genocide as mutually
excluding. It did, however, point to the significance of a broader context, in which the Greeks themselves were not only victims but also
perpetrators, motivated by similar concerns as the Young Turks and the
Kemalists in their nation-building efforts. Historian Charis Exertzoglou
made this point more explicitly. In his view, the emphasis on proving
genocidal intent and establishing final death tolls blurred the understanding of the larger historical processes at work during the years
1914–22.

[Was] the number of deaths among the Greeks, whatever its size, the result of an organized plan or not? In my opinion, the way the question is phrased is wrong. Given the fact that there was no central command, but also given the fact that Christian populations who lived in territories controlled by the Kemalist army, such as Cilicia for example, did not suffer persecution, one could argue that an organized plan doesn't exist. On the other hand, however, there is no doubt that military commanders and irregular forces on a local level were responsible for the annihilation of large groups of Christians, mainly during the Turkish army's phase of advance. By consequence, a 'yes' or 'no' answer simply by-passes the polymorphism of violence that developed and does not answer to the main problem that in my opinion is posed. Were the strategies adopted by the Turkish national movement, which aimed at the creation of a 'nationally pure' Turkish state, [the] sole cases of ethnic cleansing in the wider area of the Balkans and Asia Minor? The Lausanne Treaty and the population exchange certainly testify to this direction. But this treaty is simply an episode in a series of ethnic cleansings completely intertwined with the creation of nation states in the Balkans, which started in the European provinces of the Ottoman Empire and ended in those of Asia Minor and spans the entire period between 1821 and 1950. The nation states of the Balkan lands, including that of Greece, pursued the path toward national purity, through the violent incorporation of local populations, expelling or exterminating those who were not considered to be 'assimilable.'[30]

Exertzoglou pointed to the precedent set by the armies of Greece and other Christian states during the Balkan Wars, 1912–13, when large numbers of Muslims in Macedonia and Thrace were driven from their homes in the name of national self-determination for the local Christians. Also, in the Asia Minor campaign, 1919–22, large numbers of Muslim civilians were killed by Greek regular forces in retaliation for attacks by Turkish irregulars. The Greek state had, either as victor or vanquished, contributed to the state of fear that divided Christians and Muslims. "In the Ottoman Empire, the sense of imminent threat during World War I led the Young Turkish leadership to pursue a systematic policy of ethnic cleansing toward the Armenian community, just as the nationalist movement of Kemal identified the policy of survival with the creation of a 'nationally pure' state." By stressing the Greeks' role as perpetrators as well as victims, Exertzoglou stated his wish not to "normalize" the atrocities, "but to widen the confines of our memory, so as thus to confront our own ghosts as well." The real culprit in the drama was nationalism itself and the logic it introduced into the Ottoman world. "Only within this prism are we able to understand the politics of violence, of expulsion and of massacres, which may have known different versions, but always was a component in the birth of nations in general."[31]

For Angelos Elefantis, one of the most vociferous critics of genocide recognition, things were more straightforward than that. The heart of the matter, in his opinion, was neither the number of victims ("exclamations of nationalistic fermentation")[32] nor the problem of genocidal intent; it was the way in which Greek imperialism was exculpated for having caused the tragedy in Asia Minor and the suffering of the refugees.

> If the Greco-Turkish war of 1919–22 and the uprooting of the Greeks from Asia Minor are renamed, by decree, genocide of the Greeks, this conceals a more general revision of a critical phase of modern Greek history: it will expunge the meaning of the Catastrophe from historical self-knowledge. Certainly no one can deny the massacres or the persecutions of all kinds that the Greeks suffered. The label 'genocide,' however, passes the Greco-Turkish war over in silence, leaving only one protagonist in the limelight, the Turks and their infernal plans, while the Greeks are being expiated. Thus, this day of 'national remembrance' will provide great services to national amnesia and the complete ideologicization of our History.[33]

In contrast to Exertzoglou, Elefantis was less interested in establishing what had happened in Asia Minor through weighing the evidence or discussing the validity of different interpretations. For him, things boiled down to whether the decision to go to war with Turkey in 1919 had been legitimate or not. Here a dividing line was drawn between the patriotic war, fought for "just" reasons (national liberation or defense against foreign aggression), and its nationalistic counterpart; wars of conquest fought to extend one nation's rule into territories predominantly populated by a foreign nationality, in violation of the latter's right to self-determination.[34] If the Asia Minor tragedy was recast as "the Greek genocide," the "imperialist aggression" of Greece in 1919, justly resisted by the Turkish people, would retroactively transform into a whitewashed humanitarian intervention for the protection of the Anatolian Greeks; similar to the NATO campaign during the recent Kosovo crisis, much resented by Elefantis and Greek public opinion at large.[35]

If there was no "Holocaust template" in which this event in Greek history could be made sense of, there was nonetheless a "German" template. Guilt was the core issue in the articles that rejected genocide recognition; on the one hand national guilt for the atrocities done to Muslims during both the Greco-Turkish war and earlier conflicts, and on the other hand guilt for having compromised the vulnerable position of the Ottoman Greeks in the pursuit of Greater Greece, thereby causing their expulsion, in the same way as the Third Reich had brought disaster upon millions of ethnic Germans in Central and Eastern Europe, 1944–45. Elefantis made this comparison explicit when he, unlike most other Greek critics of the genocide interpretation, put it in a broader international context. He saw an analogy to the Greek case in the West German Historikerstreit (historians' clash) of the 1980s, and what he viewed as conservative historian Ernst Nolte's attempt at relativizing the history of genocides in order to whitewash Germany's past by presenting the Germans as victims too. The same "history revisionism," wrote Elefantis, had paved the way for NATO aggression in Yugoslavia under the cloak of humanitarianism, by way of demonizing the Serbs through questionable analogies with the Nazis.[36]

While the genocide interpretation of the Catastrophe in western Asia Minor was being castigated, however, few if anyone commented on the corresponding narrative on the Pontian experience or made any reference to the original "memory by decree" of 1994. A possible reason for this is that the wartime developments in the Pontos had remained, as Tasos Kostopoulos has put it, "in the margins of the Greek national narrative."[37] Therefore they were not as familiar to the Greek public and critics, such as Elefantis, as the iconic fall of Smyrna; nor could the massacres and forced marches that took place there be as easily linked to the presence of the Greek army, which had operated hundreds of miles away.[38] With no war crimes sanctioned by the Greek state, it did not seem to fit into the German template suggested by Elefantis. Some debaters even made precautionary distinctions between the Pontian case and the events further to the west, thereby thwarting the attempt to merge them into a unified "genocide memory."[39] Nevertheless, the easily made conflation of the two genocide narratives meant that criticism of one of them would eventually spill over onto the other. Not long after the revocation of the controversial decree on 14 September (see below), the Speaker of the Hellenic Parliament expressed doubts about the "scientific seriousness" of the collection of documents in support of the Pontian genocide claim that had been commissioned to Konstantinos Fotiadis in 1996.[40] Although the 19 May memorial day and its supporting Pontian narrative emerged more unscathed from the controversy than 14 September, it would eventually attract more critical attention; especially as a response to the growth of right wing extremist parties in the twenty-first century (LAOS and Golden Dawn), which sought to exploit it. The effect was that the fates of the two respective genocide narratives became more intertwined; something that will be described in the later chapters of this book.

The "Genocide against Memory": Making Sense of Rejection

The new trauma drama presented by the advocates of genocide recognition, or rather their recasting of an already existing trauma as genocide, had been firmly rejected by prominent public intellectuals. This way of writing history, argued the journalist that had spearheaded the campaign against genocide recognition, did not reflect the "consciousness" that the Greek common citizen had had about 1922 for the past eighty years. "The result is that Greek society, despite the fact that it was taken by surprise by the 'genocide' decision, perceives this history revisionism as imposed in a vulgar fashion from above."[41] Also politicians who had supported the genocide bill in Parliament, mindful of the resistance it had met, expressed second thoughts about the wisdom of the memorial day. The leader of the Coalition of the Left and Progress (SYN), a party that had endorsed the bill in 1998, now spoke of it as founded in "ahistorical and anti-scientific opinion,"[42] while a SYN deputy regretted having let "arbitrary rewriting of history" pass into law.[43] Similar views were expressed across the political spectrum as well as within the ruling PASOK. More importantly, the foreign minister Georgios Papandreou acted to defuse the newly arisen threat toward the gains of his earthquake diplomacy. On 21 February, twelve days after the signing of the disputed presidential decree and three days after *Avgi*'s critical Sunday issue, the decree was revoked "for further examination"; in other words, the enforcement of the law on the commemoration of the genocide in Asia Minor, if not the law itself, was scrapped.[44]

This decision was interpreted in two ways in Greek media. For those who had come forward as critics of the new memorial day, with its implications for modern Greek history, it represented a triumph of civil society against state-sponsored revisionism. Others saw it as purely expedient to contemporary foreign policy. After all, the need for rapprochement with Turkey had been invoked by various debaters, in ways that suggested the newfound prospect of a Greek-Turkish settlement to be the real issue at stake and not so much the shared history of violence. With this emerging prospect, "certain circles," argued a liberal politician, "caught up in interpretative frameworks of the past and bringing out disputable evidence … adopt a deeply conservative approach to matters. With their eyes fixed on the past, they move about in dead time, captives of a non-temporal historicism."[45] But this determination not to let the "shadow of history" impede the improvement of Greek-Turkish relations could as easily be (and often was) interpreted as Greek subservience to Turkey. This was the view propagated by the left wing nationalist publisher Giorgos Karabelias (who would a few years later appear as a witness of the defense in the trial against the infamous 17 November terrorist group, charged with the murder of, among others, Anglo-American and Turkish diplomats).[46] In a special feature issue of the nationalist *Ardin* magazine on the legacy of 1922, he lashed out against Elefantis and other "advocates of historical amnesia" for their failure to recognize the "true" dimensions of the issue.

> The debate about 1922, regarding the genocide—or, if you prefer, the 'ethnic cleansing'—of Asia Minor Hellenism, is not about 'history' or historical memory in the same way as [it would be in the case of] the German-Italian Occupation, even though the latter is more recent. 1922 is 'present' in contemporary reality, it continues in Cyprus and the Aegean, it threatens Thrace and the islands, it determines the orientations of our domestic and foreign policy, it seals the future of Hellenism ... Whoever wishes to forget the 'genocide' is working—due to ideological blindness and/or subservience—for its completion against Hellenism in its entirety ... by way of threat and the internalization of fear, the mutation of the Greek state, once again, after a thousand years of attempts by Turkish expansionism, into a vassal state under the 'Ankara sultanate.' And only 'non-temporal historicism,' i.e. the awareness that 1922 continues, can allow us to resist, be it for a few more years ... The bipolarity of Turkish expansionism and Greek resistance will not be obliterated unless one of the two poles that it consists of will disappear; either Turkish expansionism falls silent at one point or Hellenism's every attempt at resistance is stamped out. And this, the latter, is what the followers of historical amnesia are calling upon us to do.[47]

The doom-laden prophecies and blatant Turcophobia notwithstanding, there was a legacy of realpolitik that made Karabelias' allegations ring true. The recent political decision to scrap the memorial day seemed to echo a long tradition of silence on the Asia Minor question in service of Greek-Turkish friendship; the final stage in a long history stretching back at least to the Ankara Convention of 1930, reinforced during Metaxas' regime and the NATO partnership of the 1950s. To the original trauma cultivated by the refugee lobby was added the trauma of rejection and belittlement.[48] But this was, after all, not a new trauma. It had been a component of the trauma drama presented to the public by the Pontian activists in the 1980s and later by their counterparts in other refugee associations, who motivated their calls for recognition with the allegation that the Greek state had known about the atrocities but kept silent. As a result of the backlash in 2001, this aspect acquired new relevance. Denial in posterity is often identified as the final stage of genocide, especially in scholarship on the Armenian case and the often vicious resistance it has been met with from Turkey and its allies.[49]

The Armenian experience, ever the role model to which Greek activists looked, provided a template through which the recent backlash could be made sense of. This "Armenian" template became a standard feature in the discourse cultivated in commemorative articles published each memorial day in the early twenty-first century. Vlasis Agtzidis thus saw a clear parallel between the "denial of the Greek genocide" and the Turkish-sponsored attempts to discredit the Armenian genocide; another aspect in which the two peoples allegedly shared the same trauma. This phenomenon was in its turn related to the wider international history revisionism, which according to Agtzidis encompassed everything from neo-Nazi denial of the Holocaust to the state-directed denial of genocides against ethnic minorities and aboriginal populations all around the world. In the era of globalization, the state-imposed whitewashing of history had been replaced by acceptance of the negative past and a new appraisal of the multicultural by most countries. The main exceptions were Turkey and, in Agtzidis' opinion, Greece, "which denies her own history and conceals or questions genocide suffered by a part of its own population."[50]

This contextualization of the failure to gain acceptance—that is, the attempt to make sense of rejection in a much larger international framework, may be analyzed as a step toward the cosmopolitanization of "Greek genocide" remembrance. By being inscribed into the history of peoples that worldwide had been victimized by colonialism and state nationalism, the local trauma narrative is opened up toward identification with a wider community of suffering than just the national Greek or ethnic Pontian one.[51] However, the goal of debaters like Agtzidis and Karabelias was first and foremost to make sense of the Asia Minor Catastrophe within the context of national history. As a result, the narrative and arguments for recognition they presented reflected strongly nationalist concerns as well as tropes of writing about the nation, with a pedigree in the nineteenth century antagonism between the indigenous "Helladic" Greeks of the old kingdom and the Ottoman Greek "outsiders." According to these, the "national center" of the Greek world (Athens) had, due to a narrow perception of national interest rooted in rural backwardness, on more than one occasion betrayed the interests of the "periphery," the borderlands where the struggle for the survival of Hellenism was fought by unsung heroes. It was this alleged unwillingness of "Old Greece" to come to the unredeemed Greeks' aid that accounted for the National Schism during World War I, the refusal to join up with the Christian guerrilla in the Pontos and thus open a second front in the Greco-Turkish war, and the failure to protect the Asia Minor Greeks after the military defeat in 1922.[52] The interwar years, Agtzidis claimed, had seen sharpened tensions between the indigenous and the refugee community, which had found their expression in a form of intra-Greek "racism" that denied the latter's identity as true Hellenes.[53] The "shock of 1922" had led to the "ideological entrenchment around the interests of the state," dictated by the policy of cordial relations with Ankara, and a "new order" in which the recent history of the "genocide of the Greeks and other Christians" transformed into a direct threat that needed to be banned from official commemoration.[54] In this longer perspective, the "genocide against memory" was but the latest insult added to a long catalog of injuries.

This was the sort of resentment that once had spawned Pontian identity politics. However, the main objective for activists like Agtzidis was to incorporate the experience of genocide into national, canonical memory. Revealing the "truth" about this history was not only a matter of historiographic duty, but more so an issue of national identity. In order for the Greek nation to be complete and reconciled with its past, he argued, a synthesis of the different historical experiences of all the Greeks into a new unified identity, a new collective memory, was necessary.[55] Such a policy, argued another debater, called for the Greek state's acknowledgment of its own guilt for the wrongs done to the Anatolian Greeks as well as the recognition of the central importance of their experience in national memory. An official political apology for the greatest tragedy in modern Greek history, the losses of which dwarfed those of the civil war, would pave the way toward resolving many lesser traumas, the argument went, for how could amends be made for the lesser injustices if the greatest one was not addressed?[56] "Yes, there is no day of national memory more significant than 14 September!" Karabelias wrote in response to Elefantis' dismissal of the memorial day.[57] For him and other debaters, this date represented the passing of an alternative Greece, grander and in a sense more cosmopolitan than the "rump" nation state that came out of the Catastrophe. The territories in Ionia that would have been annexed to Greece would only have made a small addition to the national territory, argued the sociologist Neoklis Sarris, but this addition would have made the difference between Greece as a client to the Great Powers and Greece as a truly independent great power in her own right.[58] Departing from the observation that the Ottoman Greek merchant class together with its Armenian counterpart had evolved into something resembling a Western bourgeoisie, he along with Vlasis Agtzidis identified the failure of Greece to annex the prosperous and cosmopolitan cities in the Near East (Constantinople and Smyrna) as the root of the country's backwardness. It was the prism through which Greek history as well as contemporary phenomena was made sense of.

Practically all ills that ever had befallen modern Greek society, even the economic crisis from 2009 and onward, could be traced to the impact of genocide and the failure of the Great Idea, which, had it succeeded, "would have led to the restoration of a natural social structure in the Greek nation state."[59] Remembrance of "1922" thus held the putative key to the future of Greece, to national reconciliation between the descendants of the autochthons and the heterochthons. Only through its acceptance could the "maimed" national body be made whole again and find its place in the globalized world, which some of the supporters of genocide recognition feared would threaten Greek identity with extinction,[60] and which others perceived as a counterweight against small state parochialism.[61]

Writings emanating from the movement for Greek genocide recognition display a curious mix of nineteenth century irredentism and contemporary critique of the nation state in the name of multiculturalism. Globalization is on the one hand seen as a threat toward the particular, toward traditional forms of self-identification and remembrance ("I don't want to bargain away my memory nor do I want to 'modernize' it," as a contributor of *Ardin* put it).[62] On the other hand, globalization is portrayed as an opportunity to overcome an outmoded nationalism that no longer imbues past and present with meaning. Part of the trauma of uprooting, which the genocide interpretation sought to make sense of, was the mourning of the old ways of life that had been lost in Asia Minor; perceived in retrospect as a world of cosmopolitan values, a chance of modernization (spearheaded by the Europeanized Ottoman Greek bourgeoisie) destroyed by the arrival of twentieth century nationalism. Embracing cosmopolitanism was a way of reconnecting with this past as well as of making the national community whole. There was thus a tension inherent in the trauma drama between traditional nationalist elements and the new, which stressed commonality with victims of the nation state worldwide; the latter tendency becoming more palpable as a result of the (partial) failure of nationalization. Herein lay the seeds of cosmopolitanization, which sociologists Levy and Sznaider argue transform national and ethnic memories in the era of globalization, by combining the new emphasis on human rights with pre-existing elements.[63]

This is an analysis that will be further elaborated in the later chapters of this book, which deal with the attempts to promote and make sense of the trauma drama outside of a national context. For the time being, it is important to note some similarities between its advocates and opponents. Both camps (albeit the former to a somewhat lesser extent) often framed their arguments within a predominantly antinationalist, antiestablishment discourse. Both camps viewed their opponents as servants of the state and their "memory" as imposed from above, and as such the enemies of a supposedly genuine memory of the "uprooting." The controversy over the interpretation of the Catastrophe as genocide (premeditated since before 1914) or as a consequence of a war of conquest (starting with the Greek army's landing at Smyrna in 1919) can therefore be understood as a clash of different conceptualizations of the nation and the meaning of globalization. The similarities in the seemingly diametrically opposed views reflect common roots in the political camp, which in the past had embodied (at least in theory) the values of internationalism; the only force that traditionally had challenged Greek state nationalism and the silences in history for which it stood. In order to grasp the deeper causes to the resistance to genocide recognition, but also the rifts that at times have divided its supporters, it is necessary to address the history of the Greek Left and its relation with the Asia Minor question.

The Deeper Causes of the Opposition to Genocide Recognition: The Left's Relation to the Asia Minor Issue

As noted in the previous chapter, the Greek Left had held a certain appeal to the Asia Minor refugees in the interwar years. The Socialist Labor Party of Greece (SEKE)—after 1924 the Communist Party of Greece (KKE)—had from its inception in 1918 positioned itself as the only political force critical of Greek irredentism and the war in Asia Minor. As such it had emerged untainted by the political decisions that paved the way for the disaster, and as a result it could with some credibility portray itself as the true champion of the destitute refugees' rights. According to the interpretation that was to become the official truth of KKE, the Greco-Turkish war had been an imperialistic adventure in which the ruling bourgeois class of Greece had acted as a pawn for British interests. The war had not been a national struggle as much as a means for international capitalism to exploit the Greek and Turkish peoples alike, by pitting them against each other. This was basically the interpretation of the Comintern, which SEKE had joined in 1920, thereby aligning itself with the foreign policy of the new Bolshevik regime in Russia, which at the time supported the Kemalist cause. However, it was a model of explanation that would retain its appeal long after the war itself and the end of Soviet-Turkish friendship. As noted earlier, the Asia Minor disaster had offered left wing opposition in the 1950s a substitute for critical discussion about the civil war and the Greek state's subservience to foreign masters. Remembrance of this national calamity had thus served to compromise the political establishment of the country, accused of once again betraying the Greek people of Cyprus in the service of Western and Turkish interests. Even for intellectuals not aligned with the communist Left, the Catastrophe was a powerful symbol, indeed the didactic example par excellence, of the misguided character of right wing nationalism and, by default, the virtues of its socialist alternative; internationalism, as represented by worker solidarity across borders.

This class-based, anti-imperialistic perception of Greek and international history had at least initially left an imprint upon the "right to memory" discourse. As Vlasis Agtzidis would later put it, the 1980s saw the union of Pontian tradition with the politics of the non-parliamentarian Left and the third world socialism of the ruling PASOK. The early proclamations of Agtzidis' own group Argo were full of references to the Greek "bourgeois" state's sell-out of the Pontian refugees' interests to its Turkish equivalent.[64] This was also the case with Michalis Charalambidis and his "Italians," who had fled the country during the junta and joined the resistance in exile, which was later absorbed into PASOK, where he served as a member of the party's central committee for some years.[65] Inspired by the writings of world system theorists like Samir Amin, Charalambidis made sense of the Pontian question through the prism of anti-colonial struggle, in which Turkey was portrayed as the leading imperialist power in the Eastern Mediterranean. The goal of this "struggle against imperialism and its substitutes" was the dissolution of the Turkish state and the emergence of "free and independent socialist nations which will pave the way for a united socialist mankind."[66]

This perspective also had repercussions on Charalambidis' perception of the (Pontian) Greek minority's situation in the Soviet Union. In his view, the "great October Revolution" in 1917 had come as liberation for the Pontians living in Russia and the Caucasus, who under Bolshevik rule for the first time in centuries enjoyed cultural, political and national liberty. Even though Charalambidis mentioned in passing that persecutions were carried out against them, for "reasons ... that we cannot comprehend," in spite of their heroism in the "Great Patriotic War against Fascism," his belief that the Soviet Union was the one country that had solved the national question on the basis of equality, liberty and the "respect for the national identity of a people" remained unwavering in his manifesto on the "right to memory."[67] He further clarified this view by stating that the history of the Pontians in the Soviet Union must not be allowed to become the subject of anti-Soviet propaganda, in the service of "forces alien to the interests of the Pontian people."[68]

Even if the Greek state and the Soviet Union had a moral obligation to defend the rights of this victimized group, it was the "racist" Turkish state alone that was to be held accountable for the crimes committed against the Pontian Greeks.[69]

This view did not go undisputed within the Pontian community. The 1980s glasnost and subsequent decline of the Soviet Union, along with the coming of the "Russo-Pontians," brought different perspectives on the Pontian experience to the fore. These highlighted the Stalinist terror in 1937 and the later deportations of the Greek communities that in the 1940s spelled the doom of their thitherto cultural autonomy. To the story of the (allegedly) racially motivated Pontian genocide in Anatolia was added a second trauma drama of the Pontians who had fled to the Soviet Union and once again been victimized, this time in the name of socialism. Argo, which counted many Soviet Greek immigrants among its members, petitioned the global Pontian congresses for commemoration of the Stalinist purges, along with the Turkish atrocities.[70] While the "Italians" of KEPOME refused to adopt this demand, arguing that it would diminish the significance of 19 May in Pontian collective memory and thus impede the work for its recognition, Argo was eventually heeded by the 4th Global Pontian Congress, which in 1997 proclaimed 13 June as the Memorial Day for the victims of Stalinist persecution in the former Soviet Union.[71] Even if this second memorial day could never rival the supremacy given to 19 May in Pontian circles, it did raise awkward questions about the Greek Left's own ideologically motivated silence on Pontian history. By extension, it also opened the issue of whether the same Left had actively contributed to the Anatolian Greek tragedy by sabotaging the Greek war effort.[72] The end of the Cold War and the "death of ideologies" offered a welcome occasion to challenge the Left's dominant reading of the Asia Minor Catastrophe.[73]

The leading public spokesman of this new approach was Vlasis Agtzidis, the vice president of Argo, whose cue was picked up in the conservative press, eager to expose the Left as fellow travelers with the nation's enemies. The timing with the unfolding Macedonian conflict was once again crucial, as Agtzidis' indictment of the "ideological descendants of SEKE" reinforced similar allegations against the Left for having sold out national interests by heeding Comintern's call for an autonomous, Slav-dominated Macedonia.[74] In his writings, Agtzidis lamented the fact that the early socialist movement in Greece had come under the influence of the Bulgarian communist party, with its adherence to Slavic nationalism, as well as the "extreme Jewish internationalism" of the Federacion, the labor union that organized Jewish workers in Salonica and whose leader Avraam Benaroya had played a pivotal role in bringing the newly founded SEKE in line with Bolshevik foreign policy. With its pacifist propaganda, SEKE had contributed to the defeat-ist mood that enabled the military disaster in the summer of 1922.[75] Similar accusations had emerged during the Parliament's debate that had preceded the vote regarding genocide recognition, both in 1994 and 1998, which put deputies of the Left (KKE and the reformist Coalition of the Left and of Progress) on the defensive.[76] Although these parties joined PASOK and Nea Dimokratia in the vote, the stigma of national treason that some sought to stick to the Left was a cause of bad senti-ment with regard to the genocide issue.

This link between the movement for genocide recognition and what was perceived as (and often was) traditional anti-communism goes a long way toward explaining the growing opposition to the genocide nar-rative among influential debaters in the media and the academe. For them (often members or sympathizers of SYN, the Coalition of the Left and Progress; later SYRIZA), the activism did not at all represent a genuine popular demand for justice for the victims of the Asia Minor Catastrophe, but rather an attempt to legitimate the rabidly anti-communist views of the old Right that had lost its hegemonic grip on state and society after 1974. It was not coincidental that Nikos Filis put the 2001 presidential decree in the context of the civil war period's accusations (unfounded as it turned out) against the Greek communists for committing genocide in guerrilla-held territory, rather than in the context of the earlier events in Asia Minor, while adding that today's school pupils needed protection from this propaganda.[77]

Nevertheless, the political party that was the main target for accusa-tions of complicity in the Asia Minor tragedy was KKE, the unreformed wing of the larger Greek Left. Being the party with the closest ties to the old Soviet Union, KKE adopted an apologetic position with regard to the persecutions of the Pontian Greeks there, which became more pal-pable in view of its 18th Congress in 2006 that saw the rehabilitation of Stalin and condemnation of all post-1956 "revisionism."[78] If the embar-rassing anti-Greek purges during Stalinism from the KKE's perspective could be either justified (by reference to the minority's alleged wartime collaboration with the Germans) or altogether dismissed as anti-Soviet propaganda, the matter of the original crime against the Pontians pre-sented the party with a problem in which various considerations had to be taken into account. The Pontian electorate was traditionally import-ant for the communists, who maintained close relations with its leading organizations, with promises of determined support for the efforts to have Pontian history included on the school curriculum (or at least the parts that did not challenge the party's own interpretation of national history).[79] Repudiation of the genocide claim, in its Pontian version, as "anti-scientific" would certainly backfire against the KKE; yet the addresses of its leader and other party representatives at 19 May events in the twenty-first century expressed concern about the way Pontian history was being used to bolster "anti-communism," calling for "more systematic research using actual facts and objective scholarly methodology."[80] While publically declaring the communists' support for international recognition of the Pontian experience as genocide, "as we have done until today in the National Parliament as well as in the European Parliament," KKE leader Aleka Paparriga urged the Pontians not to be deceived by the upsurge of political interest, abroad and at home, in the massacres of their forebears and the Armenians. Instead, they ought to remember the "true" roots of their tragedy in class struggle and imperialistic machinations.[81]

It therefore fell on the party's Historical Section, the scholars employed to convey the Central Committee's official views on historical matters in its mouthpiece *Rizospastis*, to educate Pontian and other readers about the "correct" framework of interpretation with regard to the Asia Minor Catastrophe. An "objective approach," argued Nikos Papageorgakis and Anastasis Gikas, meant moving away from the narrow perspective that attributed the "destruction of Pontian Hellenism in Turkey to 'racial' criteria," and instead emphasize the socio-economic conditions that led to the disaster.[82] According to this historiography, the emerging Greek and Armenian middle classes were agents of Western imperialism whose wealth had come at the expense of the workers and the peasants (both Christian and Muslim), while Kemalism was presented as a revolutionary force (if only in a "bourgeois" sense) and a movement of national liberation, fighting both the old feudal order and the last sultan's new "imperialist protectors." In this struggle, Kemal's "revolutionary patriots" (the label "nationalist" was in *Rizospastis* reserved for their Christian "bourgeois" foes) not only faced the foreign invaders' and the puppet sultan's combined forces, but "also the native non-Turkish populations," who made common cause with Western imperialism and the Porte, the "tyrannical institution which for years had oppressed and annihilated them." Thus the Kurds rose up incited by the British, while the "nationalist Armenian forces of Dashnak" occupied Eastern Anatolia to create Greater Armenia, just as the Pontians took up arms at the incitement of the ruling class in Greece. "It is understandable that only with great resolve (and at the same time harshness) could the revolutionary army [of Kemal] cope with such a struggle on multiple fronts." The blame for the ordeals suffered by the Christians was thus put on the victims themselves, or to be more precise, on the Greek and Armenian bourgeoisie that had refused to view the Kemalist cause as representing the true interests of the Ottoman peoples during the Empire's transition from feudalism to capitalism, incarnated in the "national bourgeois revolution of Kemal Atatürk." As for the Pontian aspirations for national self-determination in the wake of the Ottoman collapse, the coworkers of the Historical Section had only scorn. "What still remains to be scrutinized is on what ground the expectation of Pontian Hellenism (at least parts of it) was founded, which being in minority in all the lands was in the delusion that it would found an independent state or that ... a portion on the coast of the Black Sea would be united (through magic?) with the Greek state!"[83]

The predominantly positive portrayal of Kemal's movement ("bourgeois" revolutionary for sure, but more progressive than its Ottoman "feudal" alternative) made by KKE's "historical experts" as late as in 2005 reflected the evaluation Lenin had made of it in 1920. However, as the party's support for Pontian genocide recognition became more pronounced during the twenty-first century's first decade, the communist narrative changed in some notable respects. More attention was given to the issue of Young Turkish genocidal intent with regard to the Armenians and the Greeks, while Kemalism was no longer a movement for national liberation but rather the vehicle of a rival bourgeois class. The atrocities that befell the Anatolian Greeks were to be understood as the result of competition between the Turkish and Greek middle classes, each of them aided by their respective imperialist allies in Europe. Thus Pontian scholar-activist Konstantinos Fotiadis' interpretation of Imperial Germany's involvement in the crime (on the grounds that the Ottoman Greek and Armenian middle classes were obstacles to further German economic penetration of the Empire and therefore had to be eliminated) was adopted as further evidence of how foreign economic interests had fanned the flames of hatred.[84] Given that Germans allegedly introduced the practice of mass killing in the twentieth century through their suppression of the Herero people's uprising in their southwest African colony, "it was no surprise at all that the first mass annihilation of Greeks of Asia Minor and Pontos by way of 'resettlement' took place as the result of German military planning."[85] Nevertheless, it was the Greek bourgeoisie—in Greece as well as in Pontos—that bore the brunt of the blame for the Catastrophe. The Greek occupation of Western Anatolia "had ... of course nothing to do with the protection and the right to self-determination of the peoples of the Ottoman Empire, but rather with securing the interests of international capitalism and the Greek bourgeois class."[86] The Greek elites of Pontos had ostensibly deceived the Pontians to rise up in arms for national independence, but abandoned them upon realizing that no external aid was to be expected, leaving those who did not have the economic means of escape to face the wrath of the Turks. The "Pontian workers" of today, the party's historians wrote, must realize that the interests of the bourgeois class and those of the people could never be the same, and that the nationalistic rhetoric employed to deceive them now was the same that had led to their disaster after World War I. While neither embracing nor rejecting the notion of this experience as genocide, the communist scholars dismissed the idea of "genocide memory" as having any potential to unify the nation.

> Memory cannot have the same meaning and contents for all: They did not have the same experiences, hence not even common memory, the Greek bourgeois class and the political and military figures who represented it (whose class interests led to a war of conquest against Turkey and who, therefore, carry a large part of responsibility for the massacres against the Greek populations of the region), and the Greek peasants, workers and small shopkeepers, who suffered the inhumane consequences of the clash between two bourgeois classes.[87]

The Academic Community and the "Ideological Use of History"

If the Greek communists' adoption of the genocide narrative was selective and self-serving, it nevertheless mirrored objections to it that had arisen elsewhere. The common denominator for critics was, as we have seen, the suspicion of exculpating Greek nationalism. The fact that the advocates of the new genocide narrative included political figures well known for their commitment to the "national issues" of the 1990s—such as Stelios Papathemelis, who posed as an ardent defender of "national rights" during the Macedonian controversy—only served to discredit it in the eyes of its adversaries.[88]

However, the opposition to the genocide interpretation also reflected deeper concerns about history and society that had evolved as a result of the democratic transition after 1974. The passing of the old regime had meant that a number of leftist intellectuals previously banned from state service were able to embark upon academic career paths. For the field of historical studies, the post-junta decade was marked by rejuvenation and expansion, which became intertwined with the emergence of the so-called "new history." The "new" historians that rose to prominence within the academe were often Marxists, who defined themselves in contrast to the traditional history of the old establishment and whose research interests pointed away from the history of the nation toward the history of society. In contrast to traditional historiography, "new history" focused on the modernization process of Greece, or rather its perceived failure, which often determined theoretical approaches. The "new historians" were with few exceptions people who had come of age at the time of the first great split in the Greek communist movement, following the Soviet invasion of Czechoslovakia in 1968. The break with Soviet Marxism was the context in which one of "new history's" key theoretical concepts developed: the "ideological use of history." Defined by historian Filippos Iliou as the distorted reconstruction of the past in service of contemporary political and social interests, the notion of the ideological use, or rather abuse, offered a negative example of what history ought not to be. This was a reaction to what he perceived as a double abuse of history; by the national historiography of the Right as well as the dogmatic KKE, which for decades had demanded the loyalty of Marxist historians. Through exposing ideologically motivated distortions of the historical record, Iliou and his peers hoped to free themselves and historical science from all political restrictions, while educating the common citizen toward self-knowledge. As the historian Spyros Asdrachas put it, the use of history in Greece was principally ideological, yet there was hope that his peers would one day, within the state system, be able to "make *History* and not *Ideology* [, to] speak of the facts and not to construct myths."[89]

For all their rhetoric, the "new historians" never really challenged their traditional counterparts. Rather they were able to coexist in the climate of reconciliation, often by avoiding politically controversial topics, such as the civil war, well into the 1990s. The Macedonian conflict therefore found them ill-prepared, and criticism against the way history was mobilized to serve dubious political agendas remained mute for a long time. For some of them, the "hysteria" of that period nevertheless alerted them to the danger of the ideological use of history, which this time did not emanate from the parochial politics of the communist movement but from resurgent right wing nationalism, supported by powerful forces in the mainstream media. This experience reinforced the notion of the historian as citizen, bound by duty to preserve the ethics of the profession. It was thus no coincidence that Angelos Elefantis, the historian and editor that had been a leading critic of Greece's Macedonian policy, assumed a similar role in the opposition to genocide recognition. The lens through which he viewed the national past was the discourse of the "new historians," with their emphasis on deconstructing nationalistic mythology and empowering the citizens with true historical knowledge.

But while Elefantis vehemently criticized the master narrative of Greek state nationalism, he (and many with him) seemed to assume an unquestioning position toward the corresponding master narrative of the Turkish state, with its portrayal of Kemal as his nation's liberator. What could explain this inconsistency? A plausible explanation can be found in the position he adopted during the Macedonian conflict together with fellow "new" historian Filippos Iliou, who considered the confrontation with domestic nationalism the prime responsibility of Greek intellectuals. To try to expose the nationalistic myths of other countries would be to play the game of the Greek nationalists, ever eager to condemn the chauvinism of others; in other words to succumb to the ideological use of history. However, Elefantis' own texts also illustrate the pitfalls of the "anti-nationalistic" historiography he advocated, which Iliou had warned about already in the early 1990s, namely that history-writing that comes with labels also runs the risk of turning history into the maidservant of political expediency. In a sense, Elefantis' own approach to the history of the Asia Minor Catastrophe amounted to the ideological use he had set out to combat, since it was marked more by the desire to thwart contemporary nationalist designs than by openness toward historical interpretation of the event itself.

The unwillingness of the scholarly community to acknowledge the genocide narrative as true history played a major role in its partial failure to enter the national canon of memories.[90] It is evident that the new interpretation ran counter to many people's political beliefs as well as notion of professional ethics. Advocates of that narrative tended to interpret the skepticism of the "new historians" as a betrayal of the radical quest to change society from within the state system. Recognition of the genocide, argued Karabelias, would have invalidated the "ideological constructs" of these new "regime intellectuals" regarding the nationalism of Greece and destroy the hegemony they had enjoyed in education and public debate since 1974. "Only thus can we make sense of the alarm that the issue of genocide recognition provoked within the 'anti-nationalistic Left', since the word 'Catastrophe' would have ceased to connote 'creation of Greek irredentism' and simply emphasize the genocide-ethnic cleansing of Kemalism as the cause of the Disaster."[91] Vlasis Agtzidis points out the irony in that the movement for recognition was dismissed as rightist nationalism, despite its roots in leftist radicalism, but nevertheless admits that the "nationalistic discourse which for a period prevailed in some Pontian organizations" had contributed to an unfavorable impression of their cause.[92]

Though some of the genocide narrative's leading advocates were trained as historians, they operated outside of or from marginal positions within the academic milieu. Branded as either amateurs or of dubious scholarly reputation at home, the self-styled "refugee historians" set out to acquire the necessary credentials abroad, through gaining the support of international genocide scholars. This process will be further explored in the later chapters. As for Greece, forcing a "dialogue" between the "new historians" and those of the refugee community became an important objective.[93]

The Textbook Controversy and the Retrial of the Six

The decision by Simitis and Papandreou to remove the genocide issue from the agenda of foreign policy did not put an end to the debate. Though temporarily buried through the revocation of the decree that would have turned it into a binding state commitment, the Parliament's original recognition from 1998—as well as the establishment of the Pontian memorial day, which had set the precedent—still remained a nuisance in Greek-Turkish relations as well as a half-fulfilled promise for its proponents. This was a point not lost on Nikos Filis of the newspaper *Avgi*. While confidently portraying the defeated decree as the triumph of civil society over state nationalism, he cautioned against new "surprise attacks," in the name of the "fading but for electoral purposes profitable Asia Minor irredentism."[94]

The reality of Filis' prediction would not be long in wait. As the hopes for a speedy solution to Cyprus' division and other issues that had soured Greek-Turkish relations were either thwarted or stalled, the narrative of unhealed wounds crept back into the heart of public debate. Within five years after the controversy over the presidential decree, and two years after the election that ousted Simitis' government, the "Cold War of genocides" raged again on both sides of the Aegean. Ostensibly, it was the initiative to erect a new monument for victims of the alleged Pontian genocide in Thessaloniki by its mayor in May 2006 that provoked Turkey's stern reaction. In a wider sense though, the sudden frost reflected the worsening relation between Turkey and France over Armenian genocide recognition, which prompted the former country's premier Recep Tayyip Erdoğan to show resolve in foreign policy matters. In this context, the Pontian issue became particularly sensitive; more so since it had already become entwined with the issue of minority rights for the (in many cases Turkish-speaking) Muslims of Greek Thrace, with nationalists in Turkey calling for a museum of the Greek's "genocide" against their brethren across the border.[95] While the Greek government kept a low profile, the incident illustrated how the Pontian genocide issue was becoming more entwined with its Armenian paragon at an international level; a point brought home also by the minor success of some Greek MEPs in having the Pontian massacres mentioned alongside the Armenian in a European Parliament resolution on Turkish EU membership in September 2006.[96]

Of far greater significance was the year-long controversy over textbook revision, which erupted almost simultaneously. The fall term of 2006 saw the introduction of new history textbooks as part of an overhaul of the Greek school syllabi, initiated by the previous Simitis government. Informed by pedagogical debates on the dangers of ethnocentrism as well as efforts by NGOs to revise the mutually antagonistic national school histories of the Balkan states, these textbooks were written in a language that avoided the old clichés about the heroism and suffering of Greeks, and the vilification of the nation's traditional enemies.[97] Even before the new textbooks had been used in classrooms, vociferous calls were made for their immediate withdrawal. There was nothing per se unusual about this. Since textbook production is centralized in Greece, with only one centrally approved text made available for each grade, public debates about history teaching come to focus on the contents of this material, with each sentence, each real or perceived omission, under close and often malicious scrutiny. Greece had seen several such textbook controversies in the decades following the democratic transition, as each political camp sought to impose or safeguard their truth, or as attempts were made to break the monopoly of individual authors. Often these debates were framed as efforts to protect the students' national and religious sentiment, prescribed in the curriculum, from ideological distortions of or deviations from national history.[98] This essentially meant that history as a primary and secondary education subject remained a hostage of state supervision and political manipulation. Anything that seemed to challenge the core assumptions of traditional national historiography—the schema of Hellenism's centuries-long struggle for survival under the guidance of the Orthodox Church—was bound to encounter opposition.

What did surprise observers was the magnitude of this opposition, which mainly targeted the history textbook for the sixth grade of elementary school. Archbishop Christodoulos condemned the book and its authors, headed by Professor Maria Repoussi, for severing the ties between the Church and the nation by diminishing the significance of Orthodoxy in the preservation of Greek identity under the "Turkish yoke." The ministry of education on Cyprus, where Greek textbooks are also used, issued its own complaints about the book's portrayal of the island's struggle for national liberation, while members of the far-right

Golden Dawn burnt copies of it in front of the Parliament building in Athens on the national day parade on 25 March, 2007. Also KKE joined in the demands for its withdrawal, attempting to navigate "between the black of nationalism and the 'chlorine' of bourgeois cosmopolitanism."[99] On television shows and on numerous blogs and web forums, the "rewriting of Greek history" was debated, defended or condemned, as well as in everyday conversations.

The bulk of criticism emanated from the refugee associations and the advocates of the Greek genocide narrative(s).[100] This was no coincidence, as Giannis Kapsis, who authored the motion on 14 September, had already in the Parliament debate in 1998 raged against the "persecution" of Asia Minor Greeks in history textbooks through "deliberate" omission of them. To conquer the historical narrative taught to future generations had always been a goal for these advocates. However, the only tangible inroad made into state-governed education had been the inclusion of a chapter on Pontian Hellenism (with a separate passage on the supposed genocide) written by Konstantinos Fotiadis in the textbook prepared for the senior high school's optional history course on the "national issues"; a course that few students reportedly bothered to choose.[101] Attempts were made to have the Pontian genocide narrative included in the compulsory materials prepared for the third year of secondary education, as part of the 2005–2006 overhaul, but met with fierce opposition from other authors, who threatened to withdraw their own texts.[102] Public castigation offered a venue for those who were otherwise unable to influence educators and academic views. A target was found in the dispassionate wording of a single sentence in the sixth-graders' new textbook, which described how the Greek civilians attempting to escape Smyrna in 1922 "crowded" on the waterfront to find ship passage. The word "crowded" came to stand at the center of the controversy, as critics accused the authors of glossing over the horror and pain associated with the "Smyrna holocaust." This was an allegation that would stick in popular perception, as it dovetailed with long-established views on how the Catastrophe ought to be represented and remembered, regardless of whether it was to be considered a genocide or not. The textbook authors were forced to replace the wording with "evacuation under dramatic conditions" to alleviate the wounded feelings of the Mikrasiates, while the government took pains to appease their organizations with symbolic gestures of solidarity.

Nothing would in the end slow the tide of hostility, however. When the education minister who had supported the textbook failed to win her own constituency in the 2007 election in which also the far-right Popular Orthodox Rally (LAOS) for the first time entered parliament, vowing to proscribe the book, the battle was over. The new education minister withdrew the textbook and commissioned the writing of a new one to another team of authors; a process brought full circle in 2012 with the announcement of a new textbook that would do justice to the "scenes of unspeakable pain" that took place in Smyrna. "Christ is risen, He is truly risen!" rejoiced a columnist of the daily *Kathimerini*, in the midst of crisis gloom. "The refugees of the first generation … are now able to rest. Their grandchildren and great grandchildren will have a true picture, if only in one paragraph, of the historical truth about the nightmare of the Asia Minor Catastrophe, which their new textbook will give them."[103]

The textbook controversy was without doubt a defeat for those who had hoped to reform the teaching of history in Greece toward greater tolerance and less emphasis on "national pain." What is more, it signaled the return to the preoccupation with national history and grievances long thought buried as matters of public concern. In December 2009, the Supreme Court of Greece announced its decision to re-examine the infamous Trial of the Six, at the request of a grandson of one of the royalist politicians condemned and executed in November 1922 as responsible for the military calamity in Asia Minor.[104] The posthumous rehabilitation of the Six reportedly struck a chord among rightist nationalists, notably among the supporters of the abolished monarchy, but also strong reactions of dissent from refugee associations, expressing dismay at the "insult" being made against their collective memory.[105] In the media, supporters as well as opponents of the genocide interpretation of the Catastrophe found themselves set up against a common enemy, albeit with radically diverging motives and conclusions. While Agtzidis condemned the retrial as a way of reigniting the wartime National Schism and argued that the Six had been convicted on valid grounds for their failure to win the war,[106] his critics of the *Iós* journalist group did so on the ground that these six had opted to continue an already doomed war effort, and thereby prolonged suffering. The legal grounds for their prosecution (on trumped up charges of high treason) were palpably dubious, the latter contended, but not the moral grounds; the royalist government had established a "proto-fascist regime," sent thousands of Greek soldiers to their death in the Anatolian interior, despite its original electoral promise to end the war, and then sacrificed the Ottoman Greeks to the vengeance of the Kemalists by forbidding them to enter Greece in view of the imminent humanitarian disaster. Just as the original verdict had been constructed around a legally false but morally true charge of having betrayed the war-weary Greek people, the *Iós* editors argued, so the present reversal of the judgment foreshadowed the retrospective vindication of this ill-fated war and the Great Idea that had borne it.[107]

Concluding Remarks

Although the genocide interpretation has not yet had the impact on national historical culture as its advocates would have wanted—literature on the alleged genocide(s) is still found on the bookshelves for the local history of Asia Minor rather than on the ones for national, political history in most bookstores—it is evident that it has reinforced the old, tragic narrative of national suffering, with its concomitant accusations of guilt. For all its obvious flaws and omissions, the old state narrative of the Catastrophe and the refugees' integration into their new homeland had been progressive, in the sense that it considered the horrors of the expulsion a closed chapter, and offered the survivors a forward-looking story of national assimilation. The genocide interpretation, the tragic counterpart of the "progressive" narrative, is one of trauma, which forever traps remembrance of the Ottoman Greek world in 1922, unable to move beyond the moment of destruction and pain. The response of Greek historians, aside from leaving it be altogether, has been to direct attention to other aspects of the Ottoman Greek experience than the history of violence and expulsion, as a counterweight to what Antonis Liakos has called "the ideology of the lost homelands."[108]

Nonetheless, the Catastrophe of the Ottoman Greeks has in the early twenty-first century become a "past that will not pass," as the title of the article that once ignited the German "historians' clash" (Historikerstreit) had read.[109] There are, as already noted, similarities between the German and Greek debates, as both involved the contentious relationship between national pride and national guilt. Similar controversies over the past have for the past two to three decades been a standing feature in the culture wars in Japan, Australia, the United States and Canada, where conservative efforts to restore patriotic values perceived to be lost are countered with allegations of whitewashing history by suppressing the perspectives of minorities and other national "Others." For the historian Sia Anagnostopoulou, writing on occasion of the Catastrophe's 90th anniversary, the Great Idea represented an evil legacy whose repercussions still haunted Greece; reinforced by the recent economic crisis and the rise of Golden Dawn, which fed on the perceived national humiliation at the hands of foreigners.[110] In her eyes, as in the case of many other commentators, there was and is a direct link between the Great Idea of the early twentieth century, which triggered by the forces of international capitalism had spelled national disaster, and the challenge of racism and right wing extremism in the present. The interpretation that presents the Catastrophe as an anti-nationalistic morality play has thus been infused with new relevance, as a response to the rising tide of intolerance.

However, matters are not always as straightforward as the often simplistic reading of the Greek "history war" as a contest between rightist nationalists and leftist progressives. The dividing line in this "war" often transcends the traditional schism between Left and Right; while many conservatives remain indifferent to the genocide narrative, many self-proclaimed socialists with internationalist leanings view the case for recognition as just, despite its connotations with traditional nationalism and anti-communism. Nor do the different attitudes toward it reflect the "eternal" division between indigenous Greeks and Anatolian refugees, as its advocates are prone to claim. Critics of the genocide interpretation are also found among the descendants of the latter. It is easy to dismiss the advocates of the genocide narrative by pointing to their obvious ethnocentrism and one-sided perspectives. Charis Exertzoglou has rightly observed the way the genocide narrative, as presented in the 1998 bill and countless other sources, reinforces traditional stereotypes about the Turks as the national Others, whose cruel acts of violence against "innocent" and "civilized" Christian Greeks supposedly sprung from their "barbaric," "Asiatic" nature.[111] These orientalist prejudices, common already at the beginning of the twentieth century and perpetuated by the nationalistic educational system and the mass media of Greece, contribute without doubt to cloud historical understanding of the period, as well as feeding Greco-Turkish enmity in the present. It is also easy to expose the scholarly misconduct of recognition activists by demonstrating how their figures of victims are based on wartime exaggerations, misconceptions and wishful thinking about the demographic strength of the Ottoman Greeks.[112]

There are nonetheless elements that merit closer attention. Vlasis Agtzidis and others point out that the historical analysis of their critics heavily emphasizes the atrocities of the Greek army that took place after the landing at Smyrna in 1919, but fails to take the earlier anti-Greek persecutions of 1914 into account.[113] The answer to this criticism has usually been to refer to the similar acts of violence and partial expulsion of Muslims from Macedonia and Epirus at the hands of Greek troops during the Balkan Wars 1912–13. There is much to be said in favor of this wider contextualization, but it does not convincingly explain why the Ottoman Greek Christians of Asia Minor should be held accountable for these atrocities. By overlooking this morally charged issue, the critics of the genocide interpretation tend to avoid the crucial questions over the intentions the Young Turks and their Kemalist successors might have had for the Greek-Orthodox minority, regardless of the policy choices made in Athens. In their eagerness to expose their opponents as nationalistic charlatans, they themselves run the risk of obscuring historical understanding by imbuing past events with the meanings and concerns of the present. Put differently, the people and politics they dislike in the present influence their understanding of the past, but this is not the same as a scholarly evaluation of the genocide claim—even though the case for genocide, at present, would be based on conjecture rather than hard evidence.

Ethnocentrism is at the heart of arguments made both for and against the Greek genocide narrative. It has been remarked that its advocates celebrate national bias and are indifferent to the perspectives of international scholarship, since their priorities are political rather than scholarly.[114] Yet the writings and statements of their critics reveal, with some exceptions, little in terms of familiarity with international scholarly debates on genocide. The exchange in Greece has until recently been almost exclusively premised on national debates, or the genocide narrative's relation with other, specific Greek traumas; the civil war, the legacy of dictatorship, the alienation of the 1922 refugees, and so forth. Nonetheless, the arguments of both sides point to larger international contexts. By invoking human rights and the UN Convention on genocide, the activists by definition situate their case in a nontraditional framework of references, which transcend the confines of national history. Comparison and contextualization (which, after all, are what historians consider central to their discipline) may not initially have played that significant a role in their narrative, as the Holocaust and the Armenian tragedy were merely recalled to illustrate Greek suffering. Nonetheless, these "external" points of reference would over time acquire greater significance in the debate over the "Greek genocide(s)." The reason for this is that Holocaust recognition not only served as an example to be emulated (awareness of Jewish suffering, as well as Armenian, was a precondition for the Greek genocide narrative), but increasingly the elevation of it into a unifying European memory also made it a contender for official commemoration. As Greece entered the twenty-first century, both external and domestic pressures contributed in making state and society confront this hitherto neglected trauma, as a way of reaffirming the country's European identity. Along with this heightened awareness of "non-Greek" suffering in the past, contemporary immigration and the growth of right-wing extremism brought new attention to the dangers of racism, anti-Semitism, and xenophobia. This and the lingering taint of nationalism force advocates of the Greek genocide narrative to reconsider its relation to the suffering of Others. Similarly, their opponents, who have hitherto discussed the fate of the Ottoman Greeks in isolation from the persecution suffered by Christians elsewhere in the Empire, have lately come to pay more attention to the Armenian genocide and similar tragedies, since the refutation of the Greek genocide claim presupposes comparison with what it is and what it is not. In the following chapter, this debate pertaining to historical analogies and the suffering of Others will be explored.

Notes

1. Law 2193 of 8/3 1994. Efimeris tis Kyverniseos tis Ellinikis Dimokratias [Government Gazette of the Hellenic Republic], issue 2193/94.
2. M. Charalambidis and K. Fotiadis, eds., *Pontioi: Dikaioma sti mnimi* [Pontians: Right to Memory], 4th ed. (Athens, 2003), 124.
3. Gavriil Th. Lampsidis, "Statistiki-Dimografia ton Pontion" ["Statistics-Demographics of the Pontians"], in *A' Pagkosmio Pontiako Synedrio* [1st Global Pontian Congress], ed. P.G. Efraimidis (Thessaloniki: Organotiki Epitropi A' PPS, 1986), 103, cited in Maria Vergeti, *Apo ton Ponto stin Ellada: Diadikasies diamorfosis mias Ethnotopikis Tautotitas* [From Pontos to Greece: Formation Processes of an Ethno-regional Identity]. 2nd ed. (Thessaloniki, 2000), 322–23. The total estimate of Pontian Greeks in Greece and the diaspora is given at 1.8 million. It is, however, not clear how this figure was arrived at or what criteria were used to determine Pontian Greek ethnicity.
4. Takis Kampylis, "Konstantinoupoli kai Pontos se poreies antistrofes" ["Constantinople and Pontos Set on Opposite Courses"], *Kathimerini*, 23 August 2009.
5. Jeffrey C. Alexander, *Trauma: A Social Theory* (Cambridge and Malden, 2012).
6. Stathis Eustathiadis, "To Pontiako Synedrio" ["The Pontian Congress"], *Eleftherotypia*, 13 August 1988, 26.
7. Vergeti, *Apo ton Ponto*, 343; Erik Sjöberg, *Battlefields of Memory: The Macedonian Conflict and Greek Historical Culture* (Umeå, 2011), 135–41.
8. Vergeti, *Apo ton Ponto*, 344.
9. Andreas Papandreou's address to the Third World Congress of Pontian Hellenism, reproduced in Konstantinos Fotiadis, *I Genoktonia ton Ellinon tou Pontou* [The Genocide of the Greeks of Pontos] (Athens, 2004), 16–17.
10. Vyron Polydoras, "Timi stous 353. 000 Ellines pou exontonthikan ston Ponto (1919–1923)" ["Honor the 353 000 Greeks Who Were Annihilated in Pontos (1919–1923)"], communiqué to the Greek diaspora, reproduced in *Oikonomikos Tachydromos*, 2 September 1993, 25.
11. "Anazitontas ton pagkosmio Ellinismo" ["In Search of Global Hellenism"], *Oikonomikos Tachydromos*, 27 July 1995, 62–63. See also Eleftheria Deltsou, "Pontiakes mnimes, syllogoi kai politiki: I dimosia diamorfosi kai i simasia tis mnimis ton pontion prosfygon sti Thessaloniki tou 2000" ["Pontian Memories, Associations and Politics: The Public Formation and the Importance of Memory among Pontian Refugees in 2000 Thessaloniki"], in *Prosfyges sta Valkania: Mnimi kai ensomatosi* [Refugees in the Balkans: Memory and Integration], ed. V. Gounaris

and I. Michailidis (Thessaloniki, 2004), 282–83; E. Voutira, "Post-Soviet Diaspora Politics: The Case of the Soviet Greeks," *Journal of Modern Greek Studies* 24 (2006): 382, 400.

12. Giannis Diamantidis, cited in Nikos Filis, "'Axioi tis patridos!'" ["'Worthy of the Fatherland!'"], *Avgi*, 18 Febraury 2001, 26.

13. Filis, "'Axioi tis patridos!,'" 26. The experts suggested to this parliamentary committee were historians Polychronis Enepekidis, Konstantinos Fotiadis, and Vlasis Agtzidis, and author Charis Tsirkinidis.

14. Law 2645 of 13/10 1998. Efimeris tis Kyverniseos tis Ellinikis Dimokratias [Government Gazette of the Hellenic Republic], issue 2645/98.

15. "Kathierosi tis 14is Septemvriou os Imeras Ethnikis Mnimis tis Genoktonias ton Ellinon tis Mikras Asias apo to Tourkiko Kratos" ["Establishment of September 14 as National Memorial Day for the Genocide of the Greeks of Asia Minor by the Turkish State"], motion by Giannis Kapsis, Giannis Diamantidis and Giannis Charalampous, dated 12 May 1997, adopted as Law 2645 by the Hellenic Parliament, reproduced in *Avgi*, 18 February 2001, 25.

16. Alexis Heraclides, *The Greek-Turkish Conflict in the Aegean: Imagined Enemies* (Basingstoke, 2010), 132–51.

17. Richard Clogg, *A Concise History of Greece*, 2nd ed. (Cambridge, 2002), 232–33. Cf. Erik J. Zürcher, *Turkey: A Modern History*, 3rd ed. (London, 2009), 332.

18. Iós tis Kyriakis (Kostopoulos, Trimis, Psarras), "Kathenas ki i genoktonia tou" ["To Everyone His Genocide"], *Eleftherotypia*, 17 February 2001, 61. For other reactions, see *To Vima*, 13 February 2001; Dionysis Gousetis, "Genoktonies" ["Genocides"], *Avgi*, 17 February 2001, 15.

19. "Mikrasiatiki Katastrofi í genoktonia?" ["Asia Minor Catastrophe or Genocide?"], *Avgi*, 18 February 2001, 24–27.

20. Angelos Elefantis, "'Giati apo tin 'katastrofi' sti 'genoktonia'?" ["Why from 'Catastrophe' to 'Genocide'"?], *Avgi*, 18 February 2001, 27.

21. Filis, "'Axioi tis patridos!,'" 26; Eleni Syrigou Rigou, "Imera Ethnikis Mnimis" ["National Memorial Day"], *Epochi*, 25 February 2001, reproduced in *Eleftherotypia*, 18 October 2003. The different dates given reflect in part the discrepancy between the Gregorian calendar and the Julian still in use in Greece and elsewhere in Orthodox Christendom at the time. Kemal's forces entered Smyrna on 27 August/9 September, while the fire that razed the Christian and Jewish quarters broke out in the night between 31 August and 1 September/13 and 14 September 1922.

22. Angelos Elefantis, "14 Septemvriou: Imera ethnikis amnisias" ["14 September: Day of National Amnesia"], *Ta Nea*, 24–25 February 2001, 11.

23. Panagis Galatsiatos, "Erotimatika apo aima gia Mikrasiatiki Katastrofi" ["Question Marks in Blood Regarding Asia Minor Catastrophe"], *Ta Nea*, 24–25 February 2001, 10–11.

24. Charis Exertzoglou, "Ethnikismoi kai genoktonies" ["Nationalisms and Genocides"], *Avgi*, 22 April 2001, 33.

25. Statement by Stavros Anestidis, Matoula Kouroupou, and Ioanna Petropoulou, *Avgi*, 18 February 2001, 26.

26. Iós tis Kyriakis (Kostopoulos, Trimis, Psarras), "Kathenas ki i genoktonia tou," 61.

27. The *Iós* editor Tasos Kostopoulos in a later publication moderated his views on the topic and recognized the Armenian genocide, while continuing to deny similar status to the Anatolian Greeks. Tasos Kostopoulos, *Polemos kai ethnokatharsi: I xechasmeni pleura mias dekaetous ethnikis exormisis (1912–1922)* [War and Ethnic Cleansing: The Forgotten Side of a Ten Years Long National Campaign (1912–1922)], 4th ed. (Athens, 2008), 213–24.

28. Antonis Bredimas, "Itan i Mikrasiatiki Katastrofi mia genoktonia?" ["Was the Asia Minor Catastrophe a Genocide?"], *Avgi*, 18 February 2001, 25.
29. Alexis Heraclides, "1922: Genoktonia í Katastrofi?" ["1922: Genocide or Catastrophe?"], *Ta Nea*, 8 March 2001, 6.
30. Exertzoglou, "Ethnikismoi," 33.
31. Exertzoglou, "Ethnikismoi," 33. A similar conclusion was reached by historian Antonis Liakos, who nevertheless stressed that this did not entail a condemnation of the nation state per se. Rather than meting out guilt, which would only serve to invigorate old hatreds, the collective task ought to be to understand why nation-building in the Balkans had engendered such violence in the first place. Antonis Liakos, "Apo ti mnimi-ekdikisi sti mnimi-katanoisi" ["From Memory as Vengeance to Memory as Understanding"], *To Vima*, 11 March 2001.
32. Elefantis, "Giati apo tin 'katastrofi' sti 'genoktonia'?," 27.
33. Elefantis, "14 Septemvriou," 11.
34. Ironically, Elefantis referred to the Balkan Wars 1912–13 as an example of the former, in sharp contrast to what he had done in earlier writings during the years of the Macedonian name controversy. Back then he had portrayed them essentially as wars of conquest, while questioning popular views of Greek Macedonia as having been eternally Greek. Sjöberg, *Battlefields*, 220–24.
35. For an analysis of Greek responses to the Kosovo crisis and the 1990s wars in Yugoslavia, see Takis Michas, *Unholy Alliance: Greece and Milošević's Serbia* (College Station, 2002).
36. Elefantis, "Giati apo tin 'katastrofi,'" 27.
37. Kostopoulos, *Polemos*, 224.
38. Save for the Greek navy's bombardment of Samsun, Trabzon and other Black Sea ports during summer 1921, the Greek High Command confined military operations to Western Anatolia. The presence of enemy warships was, however, perceived as the preamble to a Greek landing and seems to have played a pivotal role in the Kemalists' decision to remove potential fifth-columnists among the local Christian population from the coastal region. Kostopoulos, *Polemos*, 235, 239.
39. The former foreign minister Theodoros Pangalos thus argued that in the instance of Pontos the characterization as genocide was more appropriate, since the Greeks there had been subjected to asymmetric violence, as opposed to what was to become the case in western Asia Minor, where regular armies were involved on both sides. Nikos Filis, "To sch. P. D. gia ti 'genoktonia' anapempetai gia meleti" ["The Plan for Presidential Decree on the 'Genocide' is Referred Back for Examination], *Avgi*, 25 February 2001, 5.
40. The immediate cause of this disagreement was that Fotiadis asked for funding for fourteen volumes, instead of just one as originally decided. The refusal for additional allocations was founded in criticism of Fotiadis' scholarly qualities, but it is clear that the incident provided the Parliament speaker with an excuse to back down from a decision that had become politically inopportune. After years of accusations and negotiating proposals for partial funding, the Parliament finally published one volume, as originally agreed. Charalambidis and Fotiadis, *Pontioi*, 116–33; Fotiadis, *Genoktonia*; Kostopoulos, *Polemos*, 222 n11.
41. Filis, "To sch. P. D.," 5.
42. Filis, "To sch. P. D.," 5.
43. Spyros Danellis, "Ta peri 'genoktonias' kai i chrisimothiriki (epana)grafi tis istorias" ["Regarding 'Genocide' and the Utilitarian (Re-)writing of History"], *Ta Nea*, 7 March 2001, 10.

44. Eirini Karanasopoulou, "Anakaleitai i 'genoktonia'" ["The 'Genocide' is Revoked"], *Ta Nea* 22 February 2001, 7. "'Pagonei' i ekdosi tou P. D. gia to Mikrasiatiko" ["The Edition of the Presidential Decree is 'Put on Ice'"], *Avgi*, 23 February 2001, 7.
45. Dimitris Skalkos, cited in *Avgi*, 27 February 2001, and in Giorgos Karabelias, "Katastrofi í genoktonia" ["Catastrophe or Genocide"], *Ardin*, no. 38–39 (November 2002), http://www.ardin-rixi.gr/archives/195214. Last accessed 2 May 2016.
46. For further details, see Neni Panourgiá, *Dangerous Citizens: The Greek Left and the Terror of the State* (New York, 2009), 158–59.
47. Karabelias, "Katastrofi í genoktonia."
48. For further discussion on trauma of rejection, see Ron Eyerman, "Cultural Trauma: Slavery and the Formation of African American Identity," in *Cultural Trauma and Collective Identity*, ed. J.C. Alexander et al. (Berkeley, 2004).
49. For example, Richard Hovannisian, ed., *Remembrance and Denial: The Case of the Armenian Genocide* (Detroit, 1999).
50. Vlasis Agtzidis, "Mikra Asia kai amfisvitisi tis Istorias" ["Asia Minor and Contestation of History"], *Kathimerini*, 16 September 2001.
51. This is especially salient in another article from 2004, in which Agtzidis claims the Asia Minor Greeks to be united with "all peoples who have suffered persecutions and ethnic cleansing"; Australian aborigines, the Jews of the Holocaust, the "punished nationalities" in the Soviet Union under Stalin, the native American Indians, and the Palestinians and the Bosnians. Vlasis Agtzidis, "Ellinotourkikes scheseis kai istoriki mnimi" ["Greek-Turkish Relations and Historical Memory"], *Kathimerini*, 14 April 2004.
52. Vlasis Agtzidis, "I Smyrni kai oi neoellinikes enoches" ["Smyrna and Modern Greek Guilt"], *Kathimerini*, 17 November 2009. Vlasis Agtzidis, "Ideologikes agkyloseis kai i 'diki ton exi'" ["Ideological Dogmas and 'The Trial of the Six'"], *Kathimerini*, 23 December 2009.
53. Vlasis Agtzidis, "Mnimi, tautotita kai ideologia ston pontiako ellinismo" ["Memory, Identity and Ideology among Pontian Greeks"], in G. Kokkinos, E. Lemonidou and V. Agtzidis, *To trauma kai oi politikes tis mnimis: Endeiktikes opseis ton symvolikon polemon gia tin Istoria kai ti Mnimi* [The Trauma and the Politics of Memory: Indicative Aspects of the Symbolic Wars for History and Memory] (Athens, 2010), 223–51.
54. Vlasis Agtzidis, "To '22 kai i neoelliniki ideologia" ["1922 and Neo-Hellenic Ideology"], *Kathimerini*, 16 November, 2003.
55. Agtzidis, "Mikra Asia kai amfisvitisi."
56. Antonis Pantelis, "To 'syggnomi' gia to 1922" ["The 'Apology' for 1922"], *Kathimerini*, 24 September 2008; Agtzidis, "Mikra Asia kai amfisvitisi."
57. Karabelias, "Katastrofi í genoktonia."
58. Neoklis Sarris, "I karatomisi tis ellinikis koinonias apo to ethniko kratos" ["The Beheading of Greek Society by the Nation State"], *Ardin*, no. 38–39 (November 2002), http://www.ardin-rixi.gr/archives/4952. Last accessed 2 May 2016.
59. Vlasis Agtzidis, "Poia Ellada katarrei?" ["Which Greece is Crumbling?"], *Kathimerini*, 18 December 2011.
60. Vasos Ftochopoulos, "To chameno mythistorima" ["The Lost Novel"], *Ardin*, no. 38–39 (November 2002), http://www.ardin-rixi.gr/archives/195193.
61. Agtzidis, "Mnimi," 328–29.
62. Ftochopoulos, "To chameno mythistorima."
63. Daniel Levy and Natan Sznaider, *The Holocaust and Memory in the Global Age*, trans. Assenka Oksiloff (Philadelphia, 2006), 3–4.
64. Agtzidis, "Mnimi," 261–62; Vergeti, *Apo ton Ponto*, 371–82.

65. Michalis Charalambidis, *The Pontian Question in the United Nations,* 2nd ed. (Thessaloniki, 2009).

66. Michalis Charalambidis, *Ethnika Zitimata* [National Issues] (Athens, 1989), 108.

67. Charalambidis and Fotiadis, *Pontioi,* 31–35.

68. Charalambidis and Fotiadis, *Pontioi,* 35.

69. Charalambidis and Fotiadis, *Pontioi,* 29, 36.

70. See proclamations by *Argo* reproduced in Vergeti, *Apo ton Ponto,* 372, 376–82.

71. Agtzidis, "Mnimi," 288–91. The date was chosen in commemoration of the deportations of Greeks from Caucasus to Central Asia, which commenced on 13 June 1949. See also Vlassis Agtsidis, "Asie centrale et Sibérie, territoires de la deportation," in *Les Grecs pontiques: Diaspora, identité, territoires,* ed. M. Bruneau (Paris, 1998), 157–75.

72. Vlasis Agtzidis, "I agnosti genoktonia tou Pontiakou ellinismou" ["The Unknown Genocide against Pontian Hellenism"], *Oikonomikos Tachydromos,* 2 September 1993, 22.

73. Vlasis Agtzidis, "Aristera kai Mikra Asia" ["Left and Asia Minor"], *Ardin,* no. 38–39 (November 2002), http://www.ardin-rixi.gr/archives/195209.

74. Sjöberg, *Battlefields,* 152–53.

75. Agtzidis, "Aristera kai Mikra Asia." Citing (exaggerated) assertions by Soviet historians, Agtzidis claimed that Greek communists, in cooperation with their Turkish comrades, had succeeded in making as many as 100,000 men desert the Greek army and bring about the collapse of the front. Yet the author has elsewhere asserted that the royalists, whom he also blamed for the defeat, had 200,000 soldiers at their disposal that easily could have stopped Kemal's assault in 1922 without reflecting on how his various claims contradict each other. Cf. Agtzidis, "Ideologikes."

76. Praktika Voulis [Acts of Parliament], session of 24 February, 1994, 1120–21. Cf. "Omofonia gia tous Pontious me 'omovrontia' apo yvreis" ["Unanimity on the Pontians with a 'Volley' of Insults"], *Kathimerini,* 25 February 1994, 6; Filis, "'Axioi tis patridos!,'" 26.

77. Nikos Filis, "Alli mia 'agnosti' genoktonia eis varos Ellinon" ["Another 'Unknown' Genocide against Greeks"] and "'Axioi tis patridos!,'" 25–26. Cf. Kostopoulos, *Polemos,* 222, 269–70.

78. Anastasis Gikas, "O pontiakos ellinismos sti Sovietiki Enosi: Mythos kai pragmatikotita" ["The Pontian Greeks in the Soviet Union. Myth and Reality"], *Kommounistiki Epitheorisi,* 4–5, (July–October 2006), 173–232; Anastasis Gikas, *Oi Ellines sti diadikasia oikodomisis tou sosialismou stin ESSD* [The Greeks in the Construction Process of Socialism in the USSR] (Athens, 2007). Cf. Agtzidis, "Mnimi," 288–302.

79. "'Stirizoume ta provlimata tou pontiakou ellinismou'" ["'We Support the Issues of the Pontian Greeks'"], *Rizospastis,* 11 December 2003.

80. "I ftochologia vrethike sti dini ischyron antagonismon" ["The Downtrodden Found Themselves in the Whirlpool of Strong Rivalries"], *Rizospastis,* 20 May 2010; "Minyma tis Alekas Papariga stin pampontiaki sygkentrosi" ["Aleka Paparriga's Message to the Pan-Pontian Rally"], *Rizospastis,* 20 May 2011.

81. "I ftochologia vrethike sti dini ischyron antagonismon"; "Minyma tis Alekas Papariga stin pampontiaki sygkentrosi." Cf. "Tin politiki ton imperialiston plirosan oi Pontioi" ["The Pontians Paid the Price of the Imperialists' Policy"], *Rizospastis,* 7 July 2006; "'Oi laoi prepei na thymountai'" ["'The People Must Remember'"], *Rizospastis,* 20 May 2008.

82. Nikos Papageorgakis and Anastasis Gikas, "Metaxy istorikis amnimosynis kai anistoritis mnimis" ["Between Historical Forgetfulness and History-less Memory"], *Rizospastis,* 21 May 2006.

83. Nikos Papageorgakis, "To koinonikopolitiko plaisio tis sfagis ton Pontion" ["The Socio-political Framework of the Massacre against the Pontians"], *Rizospastis*, 20 May 2005.

84. Anastasis Gikas, "I ekstrateia sti Mikra Asia kai to vivlio Istorias tis ST' Dimotikou" ["The Campaign in Asia Minor and the History Textbook of the 6th Grade"], *Rizospastis*, 1 April 2007.

85. Papageorgakis and Gikas, "Metaxy istorikis."

86. Gikas, "I ekstrateia."

87. Papageorgakis and Gikas, "Metaxy istorikis."

88. Stelios Papathemelis, "To 'egklima ton egklimaton' kai i apatheia ton ischyron" ["The 'Crime of All Crimes' and the Apathy of the Mighty"], *Ta Nea*, 24–25 February 2001, 10. Sjöberg, *Battlefields*, 64.

89. Spyros Asdrachas, quoted in Tasos Kostopoulos, Leonidas Embeirikos and Dimitris Lithoxoou, *Ellinikos ethnikismos, Makedoniko zitima: i ideologiki chrisi tis istorias. Mia syzitisi sti Filosofiki* [Greek Nationalism, Macedonian Question: The Ideological Use of History: A Discussion at the Faculty of Humanities] (Athens: Ekdosi tis Kinisis Aristeron, Istorikou-archaiologikou tmimatos 1992), 37, cited in Sjöberg, *Battlefields*, 206.

90. Kostopoulos, *Polemos*, 223.

91. Karabelias, "Katastrofi."

92. Agtzidis, "Mnimi," 284–85.

93. Vlasis Agtzidis, "I alli istoriografia" ["The Other Historiography"], *Kathimerini*, 24 April 2008.

94. Filis, "To sch. P. D.," 5. Filis would himself become the target of attacks on account of his views on the genocide issue during his time in office as minister of education in the SYRIZA-ANEL coalition government. In a televised interview on 2 November 2015, he argued that the atrocities in Pontos during and after World War I should be understood as a case of ethnic cleansing rather than genocide. This led to a storm of accusations of genocide denial and calls for Filis' resignation from Pontian organizations and the political opposition as well as from members of the government coalition partner ANEL, which remains committed to Greek genocide recognition. "Filis: Anagnorizoume ton pono ton Pontion alla den itan genoktonia" ["Filis: We Recognize the Pain of the Pontians But it Was Not Genocide"], *To Vima*, 3 November 2015. See also Antonis Liakos, "Genoktonies kai kanonikopoiisi tis mnimis" ["Genocides and Canonization of Memory"], *To Vima*, 11 November 2015.

95. Stavros Tzimas, "Mainetai o Psychros Polemos genoktonion" ["The Cold War of Genocides Rages"], *Kathimerini*, 13 May 2006; "Tourkia, o epikindynos geitonas" ["Turkey, the Dangerous Neighbor"], *Kathimerini*, 21 May 2006; Ios tis Kyriakis (Kostopoulos, Trimis, Psarra), "Stochos i politiki eirinis kai filias me tin Tourkia" ["The Target is the Policy of Peace and Friendship with Turkey"], *Eleftherotypia*, 23 May 2006. The domestic prelude to the incident is also to be found in the decision of Georgios Papandreou to let Mrs. Gülbeyaz Karahasan run for office on a PASOK ticket, as a step toward normalizing the Muslim minority's status in Greece. Nevertheless, or rather precisely for this reason, Karahasan was confronted in public with hostile insinuations about her national loyalty as well as questions on her view of the Pontian genocide, which quickly forced her and the PASOK leader to back down from the decision. Ios tis Kyriakis (Kostopoulos, Trimis, Psarra), "To elliniko vathy kratos" ["The Greek Deep State"], *Eleftherotypia*, 20 May 2006. Umut Özkirimli and Spyros A. Sofos, *Tormented by History: Nationalism in Greece and Turkey* (London, 2008), 160.

96. Konstantinos Kallergis, "Skliro minyma tis Eurovoulis stin Tourkia" ["Stern Message from the European Parliament to Turkey"], *Kathimerini*, 28 September 2006.
97. M. Repoussi, "Politics Questions History Education: Debates on Greek History Textbooks," *International Society for History Didactics Yearbook* (2006/2007): 99–110. Cf. Anna Frangoudaki and Thalia Dragona, eds., *Ti ein' i patrida mas? Ethnokentrismos stin ekpaideusi* [What is our Fatherland? Ethnocentrism in Education] (Athens, 1997); C. Koulouri, ed., *Clio in the Balkans: The Politics of History Education in Southeast Europe* (Thessaloniki, 2002).
98. G. Kokkinos and P. Gatsotis, "The Deviation from the Norm: Greek History School Textbooks Withdrawn from Use in the Classroom since the 1980s," *International Textbook Research* 30 (2008): 535–46.
99. Gikas, "I ekstrateia."
100. Maria Delithanasi, "Apodokimazoun to vivlio Istorias. Paremvasi omospondion Pontion kai Mikrasiaton, me epistoli tous ston prothypourgo" ["They Condemn the History Textbook. Intervention of Pontian and Asia Minor Federations by Letter to the Prime Minister"], *Kathimerini*, 15 March 2007.
101. Konstantinos Fotiadis, "Pareuxeinios Ellinismos" ["Black Sea Hellenism"], in *Themata Istorias* [Issues of History], ed. M. Nystazopoulou-Pelekidou et al. (Athens, 2002), 217–61. Despina Karakatsani, "The Macedonian Question in Greek History Textbooks," in *Clio in the Balkans: The Politics of History Education*, ed. C. Koulouri (Thessaloniki, 2002), 291.
102. Kostopoulos, *Polemos*, 223. Charis Exertzoglou, "I istoria tis prosfygikis mnimis" ["The History of Refugee Memory"], in *To 1922 kai oi prosfyges: Mia nea matia* [1922 and The Refugees: A New Perspective], ed. A. Liakos (Athens, 2011), 200.
103. Eleni Bistika, "Gia na apokatastathei i istoriki alitheia stin Prokymaia tis Smyrnis 1922 xreiasthikan ypourgoi polloi" ["It Took Many Ministers to Restore the Historical Truth on the Quay of Smyrna in 1922"], *Kathimerini*, 26 March 2012.
104. Nikos Tsangas, *I athoosi ton ex kai i anatropi tis Istorias* [The Acquittal of the Six and the Reversal of History] (Athens, 2012).
105. The Supreme Court's acquittal of the Six was reported on 20 October 2010, news.in.gr/greece/article/?aid=1231064213. Last accessed 22 October 2010.
106. Agtzidis, "Ideologikes."
107. Ios tis Kyriakis (Kostopoulos, Trimis, Psarra), "I 'anapsilafisi' tis Istorias" ["The 'Re-trial' of History"], *Eleftherotypia*, 13 February 2010.
108. Antonis Liakos, "I ideologia ton 'chamenon patridon'" ["The Ideology of 'Lost Homelands'"], *To Vima*, 13 September 1998. Thus, historian Charis Exertzoglou dedicated an entire book to the study of the Ottoman Greek world "beyond the nostalgia of the lost homelands." Charis Exertzoglou, *Oi "chamenes patrides" pera apo ti nostalgia: Mia koinoniki-politismiki istoria ton Romion tis Othomanikis Autokratorias (mesi 19ou – arches 20ou aiona* [The 'Lost Homelands' beyond Nostalgia: A Socio-cultural History of the Ottoman Empire Rum (mid 19th to early 20th century)] (Athens, 2010).
109. Ernst Nolte, "Vergangenheit, die nicht vergehen will: Eine Rede, die geschrieben, aber nicht gehalten werden konnte," *Frankfurter Allgemeine Zeitung*, 6 June 1986.
110. Sia Anagnostopoulou, "Mikrasiatiki Katastrofi, 90 chronia meta: 'Ki an sou milo me paramythia kai paravoles'" ["Asia Minor Catastrophe, 90 Years Later: 'What If I Speak to You in Stories and Parables'"], *Avgi*, 30 September 2012.
111. Exertzoglou, "Ethnikismoi," 33. Exertzoglou, "I istoria," 198.
112. Kostopoulos, *Polemos*, 252–65.
113. Agtzidis, "Mnimi," 279.
114. Exertzoglou, "I istoria," 198–99.

CHAPTER 4

THE PAIN OF OTHERS

EMPATHY AND THE PROBLEMATIC COMPARISON

Nationalizing the Holocaust in Greece

The Anatolian Greek tragedy was not the only trauma that vied for attention in 1990s and early twenty-first century Greece. While the "war" over its recognition as genocide and the meaning of the Catastrophe was being fought in the mass media, another memory of man-made disaster was steadfastly becoming nationalized. In 2004, the Hellenic Parliament voted unanimously in favor of adopting the European, later UN-designated, International Holocaust Remembrance Day on 27 January as the National Remembrance Day for the Greek Jewish Martyrs and Heroes of the Holocaust.[1] It was the fourth genocide to receive such recognition from the state; the three previous being the two alleged Greek ones and the Armenian genocide of 1915, which was acknowledged in 1996.[2] Unlike these three—observed on 19 May, 14 September and 24 April respectively—which incriminate the traditional national enemy Turkey, Holocaust commemoration points to a larger transnational context, beyond the confines of national experience and remembrance. In participating in international Holocaust commemoration, the Greek state officially demonstrated its sensibility to the suffering of a community that is non-Christian, and therefore traditionally perceived as non-Greek. Government support for the educational efforts of the Jewish Museum of Greece, which since 2004 organizes Holocaust education seminars for teachers, ostensibly testifies to the commitment to teach the lessons of cosmopolitan memory. In this respect, Greece differs little from other European states. Holocaust recognition had at the dawn of the new century become the "European entry ticket."[3] By acknowledging the wartime suffering of Europe's Jews—even to the point of admitting the complicity of one's own nation in the crime that caused it—states are able to display their European credentials, their worthiness of civilized nations' company.

The Shoah was not only a memory "imported" from abroad (as one might say for the case of Sweden or Ireland),[4] but an event that had affected Greece in more profound ways; especially the country's "second capital." As one historian has pointed out, a history of the Jews of Greece is by and large a history of the Judeo-Spanish-speaking Jews of Thessaloniki, who before 1912 had no reason at all to think of themselves as Greek Jews.[5] Thessaloniki, once the "Mother of Israel," a center of Sephardic Jewry and its branch of rabbinic learning, had since 1492 been the home of one of the largest Jewish communities in the Balkans, which, in terms of percentage of the total population at the dawn of the twentieth century, made it one of the largest Jewish cities in the world. The expulsion of the Muslim element in 1923, the simultaneous mass influx of Anatolian Christian refugees and the rapid Hellenization process of the interwar period markedly altered the demographic composition of the city, but the Jews still formed a sizeable part of Thessaloniki's population when the German occupation began in 1941. Within a few years approximately 90% of the city's (and almost as much of the entire country's) Jewish population had perished.[6] After the liberation, many of the few that had survived the concentration camps and made it back to Greece, or came out of hiding, opted for Palestine or America, in order to avoid conscription into the Greek army at the eve of the civil war. At the end of the twentieth century, only 5,000 Jews still remained in Greece, roughly 1,200 of which lived in Thessaloniki.[7]

Up until the mid-1990s, few if any outside this dwindling community paid much attention to their trauma. The few testimonies and works that were written (mostly in French) by survivors and rabbis in the early postwar years did not elicit any interest from Greek publishers, and would not be translated for several decades. In this respect, the situation in Greece differed little from elsewhere in Europe in the 1950s, where Raul Hilberg's pioneering study on the destruction of European Jewry was initially met with indifference, and Primo Levi's writings lingered in obscurity. On both sides of the Iron Curtain, Jewish suffering tended to be obscured by or subsumed into self-serving official accounts of national resistance and "the struggle against Fascism," which took no note of the distinctly anti-Semitic racism of Nazi ideology. As a consequence, the annihilation of Jews was in many countries not considered a more dramatic event than the losses suffered by the majority population under Axis rule.[8] In Greece, the selective official amnesia surrounding the wartime experience of the 1940s, which until the 1980s was more or less absent from the history curriculum, no doubt contributed to keep discussion on the Jewish ordeal of those years out of the public sphere. In the nationalistic discourse of the textbooks, observes a recent chronicler of Holocaust remembrance in Greece, there was no room for the suffering of "Others," meaning non-Orthodox Christian Greeks.[9]

The result of this was that the Greek public, despite growing awareness through exposure to TV miniseries like the 1978 NBC production *Holocaust*, remained ill-informed about this chapter of recent history. When the media covered the 50th anniversary of the 1943 deportation of Thessaloniki's Jews to Auschwitz, one journalist deemed it necessary to point out to readers that the Jews had suffered the same horrors—starvation and mass executions—as the Greeks, while at the same time giving an account that suggested the unique character of the Jewish tragedy, as Greek Jews were singled out from the rest of the population and slated for extermination.[10] Still as late as 1995, the Greek government made it clear that it considered national pride and heritage more important than honoring the Jewish victims of genocide, as it decided to boycott the 50th anniversary of Auschwitz's liberation because the Republic of Macedonia would be represented at the ceremony with the contested ancient "Star of Vergina."[11] Although this decision reflected the anti-Western popular sentiment at the time rather than any particular malice toward Jews, it was a reminder of their general invisibility in national historical culture. When Thessaloniki celebrated its 2,300th anniversary in 1985, the emphasis was on the city's eternally Hellenic character, while the presence of Jews and other groups was largely passed over in silence. Against this backdrop, it seemed unlikely that the notion of Jewish suffering would ever cross the boundaries of their own community.

Nonetheless, there were signs that also the climate in Greece was changing. Starting in the 1980s, a number of Jewish survivors from the Nazi camps published their testimonies in Greek, of which one became a bestseller, while translations of foreign scholarly works during the following decade paved the way for historiographical interest in the wartime catastrophe of Greek Jewry.[12] As Thessaloniki reinvented its image in view of its year as European Capital of Culture in 1997, the city rediscovered its Jewish past. Whereas the presence of Jews for much of the century had served as an uncomfortable reminder of the Ottoman era, the publicity now highlighted their positive contribution in making the city a cosmopolitan metropolis. A part of this celebration was the inauguration of a memorial to the murdered Jews of Thessaloniki, which eight years later, in 2005, was moved to Eleftheria square at the very heart of the city.[13] The 2004 Parliament decision to observe the International Holocaust Remembrance Day was accompanied by government-sponsored efforts to educate Greek teachers, through annual workshops organized by the Jewish Museum of Greece, in cooperation with the Task Force for International Cooperation on Holocaust Education, Remembrance, and Research (ITF). In 2007, the Holocaust entered the history textbooks, and in 2010 a national memorial was finally inaugurated in Athens on a somewhat secluded lot adjacent to the synagogue. "The Greek Jews' Holocaust is an integral part of Greek history," announced the author of a 2006 report, speaking on behalf of the ministry of education.[14] Furthermore, the report rosily stated, the Greek state "did not meet with any difficulties in establishing this remembrance day in the conscience of the Greek people, since Greek Christians have coexisted peacefully and creatively with Greek Jews since the Hellenistic Era," sharing with them "all the good and bad times in Greek history" and even helping them escape their tragic fate in World War II.[15]

The truth was that until recently neither state nor society had bothered much about the history of the Jews or any of the other minorities living in Greece. One precondition for the upsurge in interest was the coming to terms with the other ideological and historiographical taboos of the 1940s—the leftist resistance, the civil war and the issue of wartime collaborators in said order—which had previously overshadowed the annihilation of the Jews. Although one ought not to belittle the efforts of local Jewish communities in breaking the silence, or the genuine sympathy felt by many individual Christian Greeks toward their plight, the main impetus for official remembrance came from abroad. The timing with the ascent of the "modernizers" in PASOK and their subsequent drive for "Europeanization" is crucial; in fact, Greek participation in international Holocaust commemoration and education was high up on foreign minister Georgios Papandreou's agenda.[16] Also the growing immigration to a country uneasy at the prospect of ethnic cohabitation enhanced the need to embrace the notion of multiculturalism and the fight against racism. With remarkable speed, the Greek state adopted the outer trappings of this cosmopolitan memory in the early twenty-first century. The public response is a whole other matter.

Historical cultures incorporate events and processes into a narrative in which they make sense. However, as Jörn Rüsen has argued with regard to the German case, some events are of such a critical nature that they can force a reconceptualization of the relationship between past, present, and future.[17] The Holocaust, regardless of whether it is understood as a specifically Jewish tragedy or a more universal concern, is one such event that often challenges the national and ethnocentric conceptualization of history and victimhood. The solution to this problem, opted for in the way Holocaust remembrance was officially communicated in Greece, was distinctly national, more often than not. The process of assimilating the new cosmopolitan memory into national experience was enhanced by the fact that the wartime destruction of the Jewish community could be presented and made sense of as a national tragedy, first and foremost. The key word was the qualifier "Greek." It was Greek Jews that had suffered at the hands of an enemy that had also victimized the country's majority population. This link between Greek and Jewish suffering was also stressed by the SYN politician Manolis Glezos, the legendary resistance veteran who in 2008 spearheaded an initiative to have Thessaloniki proclaimed a "martyr city" on account of its murdered Jews. In an address to the leftist municipal movement "Thessaloniki of the Citizens and of Ecology," in view of the upcoming remembrance day in January 2009, Glezos reportedly stated that the "holocaust against Greece" began immediately after the German invasion in 1941, with the implementation of a long since premeditated plan "aimed at the partition of Greece and the extermination of the Greek people." He also saw the occasion fit to accuse the Israeli government of applying Nazi practices in its treatment of the Palestinians, though added that he had no regrets for having saved Jews during the occupation despite Israel's present crimes against another people.[18]

Statements like these testify to the highly problematic character of the nationalized Holocaust in a society preoccupied with national victimhood, and among people that do not always care to distinguish between Israel, its policies and supporters, and Jews in general. That Greek public opinion since at least the 1980s reflected strongly anti-Israeli sentiment with regard to the Palestinian issue is not per se evidence of rampant anti-Semitism. Nonetheless, these attitudes, together with the history of close relations between Israel and Greece's arch-rival Turkey, helped to sustain various forms of anti-Semitism in mainstream debate.[19] The new sensibility toward the Holocaust may in light of this be read, at least partially, as a token of the philo-Semitism that is the flipside of anti-Semitism; since Jews purportedly govern the world, it is all the more important to befriend them.[20] This is a form of latent anti-Semitism from which a backlash readily ensues whenever Jews or the state of Israel prove to be unsupportive of Greek goals.

With this uneasiness in popular attitudes toward Jews and things Jewish, it seems as if the universal lessons of the Holocaust still have a long way to go before becoming part of a collective conscience in Greece. Even commentators with a genuine commitment to teach these lessons express a certain ambiguity about the speedy and successful "national-ization" of the Holocaust. Odette Varon-Vassard, a French-Greek historian with impeccable credentials in raising public awareness about the Jewish tragedy, viewed this process in mostly positive terms, but expressed doubts on whether the emphasis on commemorating Greek Jews really conveyed the proper lesson of a memorial day that in essence is international. The deeper meaning of the event was in her opinion not that it had happened to Jews, but that it had contemporary relevance for all victims of racism and exclusion. "I ask myself if an opportunity to connect with the more general European history and also with the wider meaning of the day is lost, when memory is entrenched around the victims of one country."[21]

Bystanders, "Similar Fate," and the Problem of Empathy

The awkward questions surrounding the Holocaust's incorporation into national historical culture point to a more general problem in popular sensibility toward the suffering of others. This problem became particularly manifest in the overall Greek public response to the wars in Yugoslavia during the 1990s. In a book about the relations between Greece and the regime of Slobodan Milošević, the Greek liberal journalist Takis Michas lashed out at the Greek political and media establishment for having turned a blind eye on the gross human rights violations carried out by Serbs.[22] Widespread public sympathy for the struggle of fellow Orthodox Christians had prompted mainstream media to avoid coverage of the plight of Muslims in Bosnia as well as in Kosovo, while political leaders entertained cordial relations with Belgrade. The result, argued Michas, was that the Greek public had remained ill-informed about the Yugoslav conflict for much of its duration, and displayed a shameful indifference to human suffering.

The root of this fault was found in the ethno-religious nationalism of Greece, in which Orthodoxy was made synonymous with "Greekness," and the consequent failure of its society to develop the civic norm of individual rights, as opposed to those of groups. The result of this was an enduring tendency to view the outside world in terms of friends or foes, "Philhellenes" or "anti-Hellenes."[23] Being a small country on the outskirts of Europe, isolated by language, a notion of Greece as a "brother-less nation," misunderstood by the West and surrounded by hostile neighbors, had evolved.[24] This notion resonated with a public frustrated at the lack of sensitivity for the Greek people's perceived interests amongst the mighty of the world, displayed at almost every critical moment in national history, from the Catastrophe of 1922 to the more recent setbacks with regard to Cyprus and the Macedonian name issue.[25] In want of close kin or fast friends to the west, many participants in public debate stressed the similar religion or fate that the Greeks supposedly shared with other "brother-less nations." In other persecuted or simply misunderstood peoples, they were able to recognize themselves. "[W]e are to the West the new Jews of the end of the 20th and the beginning of the 21st century," wrote a teacher in a letter to the editor of a national magazine in the 1990s, suggesting that the negative coverage of Greece in foreign media was a sign of a new "anti-Hellenism" that had come to replace anti-Semitism in the West's purportedly eternal quest for scapegoats.[26]

As the cited letter suggests, this sense of common destiny, or solidarity, could be extended to groups outside the pale of Orthodox Christendom. Apart from the occasional mention of Jews, reference was commonly made to the Kurds of Turkey, and the Palestinians; peoples who in PASOK's Third World rhetoric were portrayed as victims of the much resented United States' regional allies. Far more common in the 1990s was, however, the sense of identification with Orthodox "brethren" perceived to suffer at the hands of a common enemy. Just as Turkey was seen to support the cause of the besieged Muslims in Bosnia both morally and financially, it was in the eyes of many Greeks natural to extend their sympathies to the Serbs.[27] Not only Michas saw this as evidence that something was amiss in the moral condition of the country. As leading war crime suspects were brought to The Hague to stand trial in the aftermath of the Yugoslav wars, critical voices emerged in Greek debate that problematized the uncritical moral support that these suspects had enjoyed in Greece. As one journalist put it, one cannot make a difference between friends and foes among perpetrators of crimes against mankind. "In genocide there are no 'our guys.'"[28]

In the vocabulary pertaining to the Holocaust, and increasingly in human rights discourse, the bystander has come to symbolize a party of crucial importance. Unlike the suffering victim, the bystander is confronted with a moral choice; either to, as the word implies, stand idly by and watch (and, by doing nothing, aid the perpetrator), or to actively take a stand for universal justice.[29] The experience of the 1990s, of witnessing the unfolding Yugoslav drama in the present as well as rediscovering the annihilation of Greek Jewry, made this dilemma topical. To analyze Greek popular and political responses to particular mass atrocities (e.g., Cambodia, Rwanda) or human rights abuse in general would extend far beyond the scope of this study. Nonetheless, some attention is due to cases of the suffering of others where Greeks were perceived to have been more directly involved, either as witnesses, co-victims or even perpetrators, as these also informed debates about the "Greek genocide(s)." These instances were on the one hand (albeit to a lesser extent) the Jewish Holocaust, both as paradigmatic genocide and local Greek experience; on the other hand, the Armenian genocide.

The moral choice in the face of persecution of the Jewish "Other" had been addressed in one of the very few works on the subject written by a Greek historian in the early postwar decades. In 1969, Polychronis Enepekidis, a historian of the early modern era at the University of Vienna, translated and published a collection of documents relating to the wartime deportation of the Greek Jews that he had stumbled across in Austrian and German archives.[30] Enepekidis, who himself was of Pontian origins, had a few years earlier published a similarly entitled work on the persecution of the Greeks of Pontos, based on Austrian documents, which in later "refugee historiography" was hailed as a pioneering study on the presumed Pontian genocide.[31] There was thus at least one direct link between the resurgence of interest in the respective traumas of Greek Jews and Pontian refugees, albeit of little consequence at the time. As for the Greek response to the Jewish plight during the occupation, Enepekidis went to great lengths to present his fellow Greeks as benevolent helpers. In particular, he portrayed the Orthodox Church and the civil administration forced to comply with German orders as having done their utmost to save the Greek Jews, out of sheer compassion.[32]

As one would expect, this traditional understanding of the majority society's response to the Holocaust, although still echoed in official commemoration, has come increasingly into question in more recent times. The new public and scholarly attention to the 1940s and the history of anti-Semitism in Greece led some to reverse the self-ingratiating narrative favored by the Greek state. In 2005, the leftist historian (and critic of the Greek genocide claim) Giorgos Margaritis argued that widespread anti-Semitism among the Greeks themselves was the reason why almost all the country's Jews had perished.[33] The indifference toward and active collaboration of Greek officials in their destruction was interpreted as part of an overall ambition to rid the nation of unwanted minorities, as demonstrated by the ethnic cleansing carried out by rightist guerrillas against the Albanian Chams in the midst of occupation. Although Margaritis has been criticized for overstating the significance of local

anti-Semitism, as well as the ability of Greek authorities to influence
Nazi policy, he has in his provocative way brought a more problematizing
perspective into the debate on Holocaust commemoration in Greece.[34]
This tendency to shatter national myths by exposing the hypocrisy of
official attitudes toward national Others would also emerge in public
debate on the Armenian genocide, at times overlapping with and reinforcing the controversies surrounding the Greek genocide narrative.

If the Jews were Others that until recently had received scant attention at best, the Armenians were more readily accepted as a sort of kin,
united with the Greeks by religion as well as a similar experience of
victimization at the hands of a common foe. Although Greek history
textbooks made no particular reference to their fate, the Greek public
was becoming acquainted with it, as it was revisiting the Asia Minor
Catastrophe in the popular cinema and books of the 1970s and 1980s.
In the director Nikos Koundouros' 1982 movie *1922* (originally shot
in 1978, but withheld from distribution following official Turkish protests),[35] a scene depicts the massacre of Armenians as Kemalist troops
enter Smyrna. This occurs while the city's Greek inhabitants cling to the
hope that the victorious Turks will spare them from the same fate; an
illusion that shatters as the movie's main protagonists are being herded
on a death march to the Anatolian interior.[36] A notion of shared fate
with the Armenians could also be found in testimonies from aging first
generation Asia Minor Greek refugees. One of them, Eudokia Epeoglou-
Bakalaki, even made the historical analogy with the Holocaust bystanders explicit in her book about the town of her childhood, Amasya in the
western Pontos, when addressing the Ottoman Greek reactions to the
Armenian deportations of 1915. "I nowadays think that the reactions of
the Greeks of Amaseia toward the persecution of the Armenians were
more or less similar to those of the Greeks toward the annihilation of
the Jews during World War II, at least in Greece."[37] Whereas all pitied
the Armenians, some blamed them for having brought down their own
doom by plotting against the state that had sheltered them, while others
took some comfort in the riddance of their economic competition, convinced that their own association with independent Greece would keep
them from harm. Only a few, wrote Epeoglou-Bakalaki, anticipated the
annihilation of their own community. In retrospect, the Armenian genocide was thus a beacon ignored by the Greeks, a lesson not learned.

A similar point, though more exaggerated, was made in the preface
written by Periklis Rodakis, a coworker of Michalis Charalambidis, to
the Greek translation of *A Crime of Silence*, a publication of the NGO
Permanent Peoples' Tribunal, which made the case for recognition of the
Armenian genocide. Knowledge of the Armenians' fate was especially

relevant in a Greek context, argued Rodakis, not just because of the presence of a small Armenian community in Greece, but because of the continuous threat that Turkey, in his view, still posed to the existence of Kurds and Greeks alike. The Great Powers' failure to address this crime after 1918, he furthermore asserted, had led to a recurrence of the genocide; this time against the Greeks of the Aegean littoral and the Pontos, carried out by Kemal, the "little brother of Talaat and Enver."[38] Rodakis thus established a direct causal link between the events of 1915 and 1922, although at the same time suggesting that the former had been of greater magnitude and consequence, since the Armenians, unlike their later expelled Greek coreligionists, had had no country to go to. Both he and others who addressed the topic in the 1980s observed the distinction between the Armenians' more total annihilation and the Anatolian Greeks' experience as one of expulsion rather than extermination. Yet Greek media coverage of Armenian genocide commemoration tended to put emphasis on the special historical relation between the two peoples, native to Asia Minor since ancient times.[39]

However, just as the self-congratulating rhetoric on Greek-Jewish friendship came under attack, so did the notion of eternal bonds with the Armenians, from the same quarters that opposed the Greek genocide narrative. On the 90th anniversary of their genocide, the *Iós* editorial group published an article on the "forgotten 'national enemy,'" with the intent to quash the myth of shared fate, by pointing to instances in modern history where Armenians had been perceived as foes rather than friends to the Greeks.[40] The group was famed for its journalistic inquiries into the darker aspects of recent Greek history, often framed as exposure of chauvinism and state-imposed lies. This case was no exception. The editors pointed to the economic competition between Greeks and Armenians in the Ottoman Empire as well as the contacts between Dashnak and the Greeks' Bulgarian rivals in Macedonia at the dawn of the twentieth century, which ostensibly did little to endear the two peoples to each other.[41] As for Greek reactions to the Armenian genocide in 1915, they pointed to certain awkward ambiguities. On the one hand, some Anatolian Greeks had risked their lives to save Armenian children, while the Metropolitan Chrysanthos of Trebizond and other Greek-Orthodox clergymen had sought to hinder massacres. "On the other hand, these very same representatives had been informed beforehand by the authorities about the oncoming massacre, during which they symbolically stood on the side of the killers." The implication of this statement was that Greeks, by choosing to become bystanders despite prior knowledge of the fate that awaited the Armenians, became complicit in the crime of the Young Turkish perpetrators. The rest of the article highlighted the disagreements between the Pontian Greek and Armenian movements for independence after the Great War and sketched the sometimes hostile attitudes that Armenian refugees encountered in Greece up until World War II. After 1945, through what the *Iós* editors described as, "ethnic cleansing through 'repatriation,'" 18,409 people, about 60% of the Greek Armenian community, had been transferred to Soviet Armenia, while a government report as late as 1952 proposed restrictions to Armenians' right to education and settlement in Greece. Overall, readers were left with a very discomforting image of Greek-Armenian relations.

As expected, the Armenian community in Greece responded to the article with letters of outrage, which induced the *Iós* editors to remark that in fifty or a hundred years the descendants of today's immigrants would respond with similar shock at the revelation of the dominant stereotypes held at present. More attention was given to a letter from the historian Ioannis Hassiotis, the leading Greek scholar on Armenian affairs. Hassiotis criticized the editors for only having selected sources that depicted Greek-Armenian relations in a negative fashion, taken out of historical context, which made it impossible for the general reader to form a balanced opinion. Regarding the massacres (in Adana 1909) and the later genocide in 1915, the Greek population in Asia Minor was in general sympathetic toward the fate of the Armenians, even though some shortsighted people ("among them two or three consuls of Greece") expressed malevolence, failing to anticipate the disaster that would befall the Ottoman Greeks. As for the negative portrayal of Armenians in police reports during the interwar period, Hassiotis argued that it differed little from how Anatolian Greek refugees and especially Pontians were viewed by the same sources. Furthermore, the repatriation of Greek Armenians after 1945 was not an initiative of the Greek government, which rather had responded to Soviet and Armenian diaspora requests; hence no ethnic cleansing. Hassiotis concluded that *Iós'* characterization of Greek-Armenian relations as subject to conjunctures was unfounded. On the contrary, the analogies between the Greek and Armenian national experiences and movements suggested a deeper bond of friendship that had persisted for the past 170 years:

> The same also goes for the Greek participation in the manifestations at the anniversaries of the [Armenian] Genocide, which have also been stable since the time they started to take place (from 1965 and onwards). There have certainly been (and still are) persons—ignorant of history and politically myopic—who were (and are) unable to realize the significance of the phenomenon. But their cases constitute the exception, not the rule.[42]

The response of the *Iós* group was that their story had fulfilled its goal, namely to provoke a "first public debate concerning a page of History that until today has constituted a taboo." Thanks to the article and Hassiotis' response to it, the readers would be informed about this neglected history, but also able to see "how relative the invented nationalist stereotypes regarding age-old 'foes' and 'friends' are every time." The case of the Armenians was admittedly marginal but—exactly because of this—indicative of how selective the narratives of common fate really were. Hassiotis' letter to the editors was said to prove exactly this point, since it revealed circumstances that had been omitted in his "popularized" articles about Greek-Armenian relations as nothing but cordial. "It was this sort of embellishment of the past—selective and in essence misleading—that prompted us to bring the whole topic out of the closet."[43]

There was, however, and as noted earlier, a different aspect to this strategy of exposing official hypocrisy. Using the Armenian question as a sort of proxy in a domestic debate about Greek nationalism came at the risk of blurring the distinctions between these historical and contemporary phenomena. When the tragedies of Others become a mirror for national concerns, the latter also come to inform how the former are understood. This aspect of the relation between cosmopolitan and local memories will be further explored in the following.

"Real" and "False" Genocides: The Problem of Uniqueness, Comparison, and Denial

The coming of institutionalized cosmopolitan memory also carried another morally charged issue in its wake, with repercussions for domestic debates on genocide. The problem was one of the oldest in genocide scholarship, and had to with the Holocaust's standing as the paradigmatic genocide; the yardstick against which all other mass atrocities are measured (and often found wanting).[44] The question of whether the Holocaust and the Nazi evil that caused it represented something unique and unprecedented, beyond historical comparison, or something better understood in a larger context of qualitatively similar phenomena, was at the heart of the West German Historikerstreit (historians' clash), but its implications extended wider. Odette Varon-Vassard was well aware of the problematic in defending the uniqueness of the particular crime whose integration into the national canon of memories she advocated. In fact, her opposition to this claim, which threatens to make the event isolated and historically irrelevant, was the reason why she shunned the very terms "Holocaust" and "Shoah," opting instead for "the Jewish genocide" in references to the event.[45] But not all advocates of cosmopolitan memory shared her precaution in this respect. The educators involved in preparing lesson plans for Holocaust teaching in Greek high school in 2007 made clear that this event was historically unique; not because of the victims' ethnicity or religion, or the numbers killed, but because of the "programmatic, industrialized and total character of the extermination," as well as its utter irrationality.[46]

While there are many good reasons to point out the traits that distinguish the Holocaust (or for that matter any genocide) from other man-made calamities, the predictable outcome of such an approach is memory-political competition (more of which below). Another unfortunate consequence is how the emphasis on the unique features of one event blurs the historical understanding of other events. This became especially palpable in public writings commemorating anniversaries in the early twenty-first century. In a piece written in view of the 90th anniversary of the 1915 events, Antonis Karkagiannis, editor-in-chief at the prominent national daily *Kathimerini*, stressed the paradigmatic quality of the Armenian ordeal as "the first genocide of the 20th century and the model for the second one, the Nazi genocide against the Jews."[47] Drawing on Vahakn Dadrian's work, the editor pointed to the Armenian genocide's origins in both the Ottoman Empire's rapid modernization process and a much older Islamic contempt for non-Muslims, something ostensibly akin to European anti-Semitism. Although Karkagiannis set the later Greek Catastrophe in the same historical context of Turkish human rights violations, the Armenian and Jewish persecutions were presented as something qualitatively different, in a way that precluded the possibility of a third genocide aimed at the Ottoman Greeks. Karkagiannis' understanding of the genocide concept was that it made a clear distinction between politically motivated persecution and persecution as a means of annihilating an entire national or religious group. That the Armenians had been targeted for racially motivated extermination was never in doubt. "In the two genocides of the 20th century the Jews and the Armenians were annihilated because they were Jews and Armenians!"[48]

Four years later, Karkagiannis came to a different conclusion.[49] Departing from a similar analytical distinction between "genocide" aimed at the very existence of a particular group and "massacre" as a practice of political domination, he now doubted that "genocide" was an appropriate term for the Armenian case. The massacres in 1915 had, ostensibly, been the logical Ottoman response to the Armenian subjects' demands for political rights; thus being a politically motivated atrocity rather than an act of racism. The Nazi genocide against the Jews had, according to the editor, less to do with politics, since it had not been provoked by any Jewish demands for political rights. Rather it was an attack on more basic human rights, understood as the right to exist regardless of one's nationality, race, or class. The Holocaust was unique in history because its Jewish victims had been targeted simply because their killers negated their value as human beings, in an unprecedented way; hence the term "genocide" only applied to that case. In his response to the reactions of outraged, mostly Armenian-descended readers, Karkagiannis developed his critique of how Armenians and Greeks alike used the concept of genocide. In the case of the latter, this was done out of sympathy for the Armenians and/or in order to convey the magnitude of the event. Genocide, argued Karkagiannis, is however not an issue of magnitude; the annihilation of the Jews alone was genocide because it happened for different ideological reasons than what was the case with the Armenians "or any other group."[50]

Karkagiannis' attempt to diminish the significance of the Armenian genocide was precisely the sort of ethically dubious reasoning whereby some relativists have rationalized the Young Turks' actions against their Armenian subjects by explicit or implicit comparison with the Holocaust. Authors like Guenter Lewy and Michael M. Gunter have thus stressed the military threat posed by the Armenians against the Ottoman state—making no clear distinction between the armed revolutionaries of the clandestine Dashnak and the great mass of unarmed civilians targeted for persecution by the CUP. By blaming the victims for having brought the calamity down upon themselves, a distinction is made between a harsh yet rational decision to do away with a minority ostensibly threatening national security and the irrationality of racial extermination against a community (the Jews) that posed no threat to its tormentors (the Nazis).[51] The implication is thus that minorities that constitute an objective threat against the perpetrator group cannot be victims of genocide. However, it can be argued that what matters is the perception of the perpetrator. In Nazi imagination, the Jews as such represented a lethal threat, which renders the question of the victims' alleged guilt or innocence irrelevant.

A similar point was made by the Armenian National Committee of Greece in a letter protesting Karkagiannis' views. His analytical distinction between genocide as targeting the human existence of certain races and massacres as merely a political practice of the Ottoman state was refuted, as it is the very politically motivated plan to annihilate an entire people that constitutes genocide. The editor was urged to consider the definition presented in the UN convention on genocide, and recall that the Armenian massacres had been as important an inspiration for Raphael Lemkin as the more recent annihilation of the Jews. The Greek Armenian community leaders finally reminded Karkagiannis and the readers of his newspaper of the article he had written in 2005, in which he himself had pointed to the parallels between the Jewish and Armenian genocides. "What happened during the past four years that made the author of the article so radically change his opinion?"[52]

The answer to that question may very well be that Karkagiannis' newfound doubts had been born out of the Armenian genocide's growing entanglement with the Greek genocide issue, although he did not explicitly state that this was the case. It is of course possible that his insistency on the Holocaust's uniqueness was a genuine concern for its endangered status in a society marred by xenophobia. Karkagiannis, who had vivid memories of how the Jews of his native Larisa had been rounded up by German soldiers, was appalled by the widespread anti-Semitism in Greece and the hostility with which many responded to the Holocaust Remembrance Day.[53] But it is equally plausible that his re-evaluation was shaped by the Armenian genocide's increasing conflation with its Greek "twins," and a concern for the damage this did to the efforts to bind Turkey closer to Greece and the rest of Europe.[54] The Greek genocide issue's association with a nationalist agenda tended to rub off on the Armenian claim for recognition of their genocide as something akin to the Holocaust, due to the often abused notion of "similar fate."

Karkagiannis was not the only one making this distinction between the Jewish and the Armenian (and, by way of association, Ottoman Greek) tragedies. The historian Antonis Liakos, writing about the issue of whether the Turkish massacres of Armenians and Greeks really should be compared to the Holocaust, made a similar assessment. The extermination of the European Jews had had a much more disruptive impact on modernity and the faith in human progress than the more "local" Anatolian tragedy. For that reason, argued Liakos, the condemnation of the Nazis' genocide had a more universal meaning, something that did not only concern the Jewish victims and the German perpetrators.

> It concerns all of us [because it] touches upon the founding values by which modern society functions. In the case of the Balkans [and Anatolia], sacrificing the other was warranted by nation building: the purpose of the violence was the removal of the other [from the territory claimed by the perpetrator]. In the case of the Nazis, sacrificing the other was warranted by the quest for racial purity: it did not strive for his removal but rather the total annihilation of him. In the former, the violence was interspersed, primitive and done in the heat of the moment, in the latter it was programmatic, concentrated and done in cold blood. The Germans had already forged their nation state in

1940–45. They were not threatened by the Jews of Thessaloniki, whom they exterminated. In the decade 1912–22, the Turks were trying to survive as a state. [These are] events of different order and significance, from the recognition of which different political projects ensue, even though the ground for our position[s] must be common: respect for human life [and] condemnation of crimes against the population, even during circumstances of war.[55]

Liakos was well aware that assessing the meaning of these different tragedies required cautious balancing of the specific and the general of each case, and above all careful contextualization. The stated ambition was to better understand why the process of nation-building in the old Ottoman lands had so often resulted in ethnic cleansing; sometimes ending violently, as in the case of the Armenians, sometimes in an agreed upon "exchange of populations," as for the Greeks and the Turks in 1923.[56]

Liakos was not wrong about some of the specific traits of the Nazis' "final solution." Yet his understanding of the genocide concept as per definition identical with the Jewish Holocaust seemed to color his understanding also of the Armenians' murder as less programmatic and calculated than what available evidence suggests. As we have seen in the previous chapter, this tendency was shared by some of the intellectuals that had participated in the 2001 debate on the law that established the Catastrophe of 1922 as genocide, in the wake of a similar French memory law on the Armenian genocide. Some had framed their critiques of the new national "genocide memory" as a case against the very concept of genocide, suggesting that it was either too general, too novel to apply to events that had taken place before 1944 or 1948, or simply that it did not correspond to events that had not resulted in the total extermination of the victim nationality. The outcome was that a whole range of man-made disasters was being held up against an unreasonably high standard, which made the concept itself seem redundant. Others had adopted a less rigid approach to the matter. In their case, the Armenian tragedy was recognized as a rather obvious instance of genocide, just like the Rwandan Hutu extremists' more recent annihilation of the Tutsi, while the corresponding Greek claim was dismissed as unsubstantiated. The *Avgi* journalist Nikos Filis thus noted in 2001 that the Armenians had no cause to consider the promotion of the Greek memory decree a blissful event, as "their own real genocide is being discussed at an international level."[57]

One of the most elaborate attempts to distinguish between the "real" genocide of the Armenians and the "false" Pontian and Anatolian Greek ones was found in the *Iós* journalist Tasos Kostopoulos' 2007 book, entitled *War and Ethnic Cleansing*. The book, which spanned the decade 1912–22, attempted to accomplish the much needed wider contextualization of the violence against civilian populations that accompanied the disintegration of the Ottoman Empire. Its central argument was that the bulk of this violence had not been carried out "in the heat of the moment," due to any inherent brutality of warfare; rather it was a calculated means to cleanse conquered or otherwise coveted territories of undesired alien groups. This was a practice that all the warring states engaged in. A main objective of the book, according to its author, was to disprove widely held assumptions that "Hellenism" was ever the victimized party, and rarely or never the victimizer.[58] The emphasis was therefore on acts of ethnic cleansing perpetrated by the Greek army, though Kostopoulos stressed that it was inevitable to also address the similar atrocities of others, so as to counter distortions in the service of new mythical constructs. Here an analytical distinction was made between genocide and the, in the author's opinion, more analytically useful notion of "ethnic cleansing"; according to his definition "that intermediate stage between counter-insurgency warfare and genocide, which consists of the violent (and often premeditated) expulsion of an alien ethnic population from its ancestral lands without an all-encompassing bloodbath."[59]

Kostopoulos had in the 2001 debate on the presidential decree criticized the genocide concept for being too vague and thus open to abuse; a critique that to some extent was reiterated in the present book. Yet the concept was not entirely discarded. In fact, Kostopoulos briefly outlined the Armenian massacres as an authentic case of genocide, as opposed to the purported "genocide" of Asia Minor Hellenism. "The 'final solution' of the Armenian Question by the Young Turkish Committee in 1915–16," Kostopoulos wrote in a familiar allusion to the later Holocaust, "is rightly considered to be the first genocide of the twentieth century."[60] As for attempts by Turkish official historiography to disprove this claim, he made note of the perpetrators' and their apologists' frequent assertions of self-defense against a hostile minority that threatened to rise up in open rebellion in the strategically vital border provinces, at the Russian enemy's incitement. This he conceded to be a largely false post facto excuse, since the deportations were not limited to the zone of combat but extended across the Empire and targeted the entire Armenian population, not just men of military age.

The same could, in his view, not be said of the violence that befell the Ottoman Greeks, whose treatment had been "radically different."[61] Kostopoulos went to considerable lengths to demonstrate this in a chapter on the tragedy of Pontos. As opposed to what happened to the

Armenians in 1915, the deportations of Greeks in Pontos 1921–22 were characterized by greater variation. There had for sure been instances when caravans of deportees had been assaulted and massacred en route by Turkish irregulars, in a way reminiscent of the "dual track mechanism" employed against the Armenians, but more often than not lives had been spared. While some Greek Orthodox villagers from the Black Sea littoral were forcibly marched as far away as Harput and Erzurum, others were just taken a few kilometers from their homes; others still were exempted from deportation well into 1923, because they had no part in the local Greek rebellion. Kostopoulos was also under the impression that those who had money to buy their lives with had fared better, which made life and death a matter of class, and thus not a repeat of the Armenian genocide, where rich and poor had suffered alike. All of this indicated the absence of any uniform plan for their destruction. The Pontian Greeks had been subjected to a combination of repressive measures —counterinsurgency warfare and ethnic cleansing—but none of these amounted to genocide. The diversity of their experience stood in sharp contrast to the uniform totality of the Armenian "final solution," and what was ostensibly true of Pontos was also said to be true of the Greek experience elsewhere in Anatolia.

Kostopoulos' study was one of the first and by far more serious efforts to critically engage the Pontian genocide narrative's underpinning claims, from a viewpoint that accepted the Armenian genocide as true. It contained several astute observations about similarities and differences, and also demonstrated how data were manipulated to inflate the Greek death toll. Nonetheless, there were elements that compromised Kostopoulos' own version of the story. In his ambition to disprove Michalis Charalambidis' assertion that the Turkish atrocities had taken place in a non-combat zone of no military importance, he made himself somewhat of an apologist for the repression that he elsewhere condemned as "barbaric." The Pontian insurgency had constituted a "potential extension of the front," both to the Russian war theater in 1916–17 and to the Greco-Turkish war further to the west in 1919–22. It was these links to Turkey's enemies that ostensibly had led to persecution of the Greek Orthodox. Simple arithmetic, he furthermore argued, showed that armed struggle for the right of a tiny minority to secede in a region where Muslims made up 85% of the total population was a "suicidal policy irrevocably destined to end in bloodbath."[62] Undoubtedly, this sounded an awful lot like the "provocation thesis" used in the denial of the Armenian genocide, according to which the victims themselves, due to their collaboration with the state's external enemies, were responsible for the retaliation meted out against them.[63] Kostopoulos seems to have been unaware of the contradiction between his condemnation of the way apologists exculpate state violence against one minority, and his own rationalizing of such violence against another. The many important differences between the Armenian and Pontian Greek cases notwithstanding, the author's own reference to the Turkish counterinsurgency as a "war of extermination" (a notion originally used by Arnold Toynbee in 1922) seemed to work against his central argument. Also reviewers of Kostopoulos' book noted the inconsistencies in the way core concepts were defined and used. The difference between ethnic cleansing and genocide, argued the historian Petros-Iosif Stanganellis in *Avgi*, cannot consist of a difference in the amount of bloodshed. Apart from contemporary political controversies, there was a central research question that could not be determined without evidence of the—in this case Turkish—central authority's intentions and concrete orders to executive organs. Until such evidence could be presented, wrote the reviewer, the definition of the Greek experience in Anatolia as genocide would remain an open question.[64]

Other critics of the Pontian identity narrative did not care to make even the distinctions that Kostopoulos made. Needless to say, in more popular debate fora, "anti-nationalist" critiques of the Greek genocide claim sometimes spilled into unabashed denial of the Armenian genocide's historical reality. In a piece posted on the website aformi. gr and later picked up by other leftist debaters, the physician Georgios Nakratzas even suggested that the Pontians and the Armenians had themselves committed "crimes of Genocide" that justified the Turkish violence against them.[65] Such interventions only served to strengthen supporters of the Greek genocide narrative in their conviction that theirs and the Armenians' struggle against genocide deniers were one and the same.[66]

By the end of the new century's first decade, the issues seemed to have become inextricably entangled in public debate, due to the notion of similar fate as well as implicit or explicit comparison, which pushed participants even with the best intentions toward morally untenable positions. An additional reason for that was that the Greek tug-of-war concerning national suffering in relation to the pain of others was informed by a wider European debate regarding legislation against Holocaust and genocide denial as a way of combating anti-Semitism and xenophobia. Originally of little consequence to Greek society, this would become an issue of topical importance as a result of dramatic developments, which will be addressed in the following.

Tainted Association: Right wing Extremism and Genocide Remembrance

As the cosmopolitan memory of the Holocaust was gaining ground in Greece, so were the forces that opposed it. The worldwide financial crisis of 2008 exposed the hollow ground on which the past decade's "modernization" had rested. Before long, austerity measures, imposed at the request of the "Troika" of the European Commission, the European Central Bank and the IMF, were taking a heavy toll, leading to political and social unrest for years to come. As the mismanagement of successive PASOK and Nea Dimokratia governments unraveled before the public's eyes, faith in the post-1974 political establishment fell to new lows. The May 2012 national election, held six months after prime minister Georgios Papandreou's resignation in favor of a caretaker government, witnessed the implosion of the once dominant PASOK. The flight from the center occupied by the discredited reformist wing of that party meant that the Coalition of the Radical Left (SYRIZA) catapulted from political irrelevance to becoming the major opposition party, and, in a few years, the senior partner of a defiant "anti-austerity" government. More ominous was the parallel flight of voters on the other side of the political spectrum. This had begun some years before when Giorgos Karatzaferis was ousted from Nea Dimokratia and formed his own splinter party, the Popular Orthodox Rally (LAOS). Described as a radical right wing populist party,[67] it entered Parliament in 2007 but fell apart after Karatzaferis' so fatal decision for a politician of his kind to join the caretaker government bent on implementing austerity measures. LAOS' disappearance left mainly two contenders to the Right of ND; the minor splinter party of the Independent Greeks (ANEL)—which in a seemingly ironic twist joined SYRIZA in government in 2015—and the hitherto obscure Golden Dawn, which with almost 7% of the electorate entered Parliament in June 2012.

The sudden rise of right wing extremism in crisis-ridden Greece is by now a familiar story. Golden Dawn had started as a magazine in 1980 for self-proclaimed neo-Nazis and neo-pagans. Headed by Nikos Michaloliakos, with a history in movements like Kostas Plevris' 4 August Party and the junta-nostalgic EPEN, it had registered as a political party in 1993, participated in rallies for Macedonia's Greekness, and sent volunteers to the Bosnian Serb forces ("our guys") during the siege of Srebrenica.[68] In the early twenty-first century, Golden Dawn along with other fringe groups was able to exploit the growing anti-globalization mood and move into the new political space opened up when ND no longer sought to contain extremist elements opposed to "Europeanization" within the party. By 2012, the presence of Golden Dawn in the Parliament, its food handouts "for Greeks only," and violent attacks on immigrants by its members had become an acute international embarrassment.[69] Greece's European success story had in less than ten years transformed into an ominous tale about Greece as a new Weimar Republic, ready to fall into the abyss.[70]

Like LAOS and ANEL, which had adopted the cause of genocide recognition, Golden Dawn bemoaned the perceived lack of knowledge among school children about "the genocide against Hellenism in Ionia and Pontos."[71] While LAOS however had toned down its anti-Semitic views and previous Holocaust denial,[72] Golden Dawn displayed no such inhibitions. For the latter party, the history that mattered was national, and Holocaust commemoration was synonymous with the cosmopolitan, "capitalist-Marxist" and "American-Zionist" civilization it vowed to rid the nation of. Here Golden Dawn was able to exploit the resentment in Anatolian Greek circles at the preference given to Jewish suffering in public commemoration ever since 2004, while the memory of "1922" was being denied this honor. By 2010, this ill feeling was manifest on Pontian websites in view of the Holocaust Remembrance Day on 27 January. "When will the Greek state recognize with deserved 'splendour,' the millions of Greek martyrs and heroes of the Greek Genocide?" asked an anonymous contributor in a piece translated into English by the site Pontosworld.com for the benefit of the non-Greek-speaking diaspora.[73] This was a criticism that, though chiefly aimed at the Greek government, fed on the impression of memory politics as a zero-sum game, and which as a result took on anti-Semitic overtones. Why should Greeks pay their respects to the memory of perished Jews when Israel remained indifferent toward Greek genocide victims, and pursued "genocidal" policies toward the Palestinians, "whilst at the same time asking the international community to impose laws on those who deny the Jewish Holocaust"? It was remarkable, continued the above-cited author, that the world's condemnation of genocide "is limited to the Jewish Holocaust and to a small extent the Armenian Genocide, while the other genocides of the 20th century remain unnoticed."[74]

Golden Dawn's interest in the genocide issue was partially informed by its ambition to adopt the "national issues" of the past decades abandoned by the large parties, but it also responded to initiatives to criminalize the party on account of its unabashed racism. This was the immediate background to the controversy over antiracism legislation, which raged from spring 2013 through September 2014, but its roots extended further back to the years before the meteoric rise of Golden

Dawn. In the past decades, a law (927/1979) against the incitement of racially motivated violence had been enforced, though seldom evoked in court sentences, despite numerous assaults on immigrants and acts of vandalism against Jewish memorials and synagogues. The impotency of the law was highlighted by the much publicized case against the Holocaust denier Kostas Plevris, who despite previous conviction was acquitted in a court of appeal in 2009, before embarking on a counter-lawsuit against the Jewish community leaders and Greek Helsinki Monitor representatives, who had testified against him. During his trial, Plevris had been very open with his view that the Holocaust's six million dead were "a fairytale" and that he could not be prosecuted for expressing it.[75] With this defiance in fresh memory, a bill introduced in 2013 as an amendment to existing legislation made explicit reference to denial of the Holocaust and other Nazi war crimes a criminal offence. The unintended effect of this initiative, however, was that other issues of crimes against mankind came to the fore, for why, argued the critics, should a law against the denial of the Jewish genocide not also encompass the other genocides recognized by the Greek state; the Pontian, the Anatolian Greek, and the Armenian?

This debate was not new, but reflected international precedents. The legal paragon was the French Gayssot law from 1990 on Holocaust denial used to remove revisionist Robert Faurisson from his university chair.[76] The fairly broad definition in its first article on what the law prohibits led Armenian activists to sue Bernard Lewis, one of the leading scholars of Middle Eastern history, in a French civil court in 1995 for having denied the reality of the 1915 genocide in an interview with *Le Monde*.[77] From that moment onward, the campaign for the Armenian genocide's international recognition often worked in tandem with efforts to outlaw negation thereof in countries like France and Switzerland. Further to the east, the issue of cosmopolitan memory's legal status triggered off similar concerns in the new EU member states, where other "local" memories of Stalinist repression abounded.[78] Historians have been divided on this issue; some argue that the law on genocide denial only targets the right wing lunatic fringe that negates the Holocaust,[79] while others, like Pierre Nora and his Liberté pour l'Histoire association, view the Gayssot law as a Pandora's box of memory decrees, which by threat of legal prosecution impinges upon the historians' profession, turning it into the hostage of memory politics.[80] As we have seen, these were concerns that had surfaced in the Greek debate on the presidential decree enforcing the law on 14 September as memorial day. "New" historians and other critics of the Greek genocide narrative were wary of the effects that a Gayssot law might have in a national Greek context.

The turn of events in 2012–13 proved these premonitions right. Twelve years after Nikos Filis' warning that the defeated remembrance decree of 2001 might still return to haunt society, as long as the 1998 law that spawned it remained unrevoked, the workings of cosmopolitan memory and its enemies returned it to the center of public attention.[81]

The motion for an amended anti-racist law that was presented by the minister of justice Antonis Roupakiotis in early May 2013 immediately fueled the frictions in the coalition government of ND, PASOK and the small Democratic Left (DIMAR). Before long, a number of parties both inside and outside the government were promoting their own anti-racist bills, leading to a political crisis when Roupakiotis' party DIMAR withdrew from the coalition. Meanwhile, Golden Dawn made its presence felt at rallies commemorating the alleged Pontian genocide on May 19 in defense of "national memory."[82] The party's website featured articles on the "genocides" of Pontian and Anatolian Greeks; even the Armenian tragedy received due coverage as the preamble not to Nazi crimes but to those of Stalin, who ostensibly had consciously emulated the Young Turks' example[83]—an ideologically distorted version of the often-quoted statement attributed to Hitler: "Who, after all, speaks today about the annihilation of the Armenians?"[84]

For activists promoting the Greek genocide narrative, in either of its versions, the attention of Golden Dawn came as an embarrassment. It was not the first time their cause was being associated with right wing extremism. The origins of this tainted association could be traced back to the 1990s, when Pontian memory activists had found themselves on the same barricades as the ultranationalists. A significant occasion was the rally that took place in Thessaloniki on October 30 1997, during the city's year as European Capital of Culture, protesting a Greek-Turkish symposium organized by the NGO Union for Democracy in the Balkans. A rumor had been cultivated by local media that the NGO would push for the renaming of a street in honor of Kemal Atatürk, born in Salonica, which prompted Pontian associations to protest this "great insult against historical memory, the dignity of the Greeks [and] in particular the Pontians."[85] Soon the protestors were joined by members of Golden Dawn and other fringe groups, which turned the rally into a violent episode. One week after the ugliness in Thessaloniki, the *Iós* journalists ran an investigative story that suggested close ties between the right wing assailants and the various Pontian organizations in what they suggested was a "planned provocation."[86] The president of the Panhellenic Federation of Pontian Associations (POPS) cited in the article admitted that things had spiraled out of control, but chiefly blamed the supporters of Michalis Charalambidis in a rival organization (OPSVE). "For the past ten years the Charalambidis group has exerted influence on Pontians and Kurds, coexisting with the fascist and religious organizations, wishing to outflank our Federation in patriotism and anti-Turkish intransigence. They do great harm."[87] The press office of the rival OPSVE responded to the accusations in an indignant letter to the editors. "The identification of us," the group asserted, "with right wing extremist chauvinistic 'Nationally minded' groups ... constitutes [an] insult against the deeply humanistic, democratic and internationalist Pontian identity. This deep internationalism of ours explains our solidarity for the martyrdom of the Kurdish people." Those who branded them "right wing extremists, nationalists and terrorists," the group concluded, were smearing the Pontian struggle for "historical truth, the human being and life, against racism and violence."[88] The *Iós* editors, for their part, highlighted the split and mutual name-calling amongst the Pontian associations, ridiculing their "peculiar presidents, who wish to map out 'national politics' with the Golden Dawners."[89]

The rise of right wing extremism in the wake of economic crisis indeed represented a direct challenge to the image of the "deeply humanistic" and "internationalist Pontian identity" cultivated among refugee descendants. Especially in the diaspora, to which Golden Dawn sought to extend its influence after the 2012 election, concerns were raised that the annual commemoration of 19 May was in acute danger of becoming hijacked. "The organizing of rallies as well as the participation in commemorative manifestations of the representatives of an ideology [Nazism] which ... carried out one of the greatest genocides known to mankind constitutes an affront ... toward the victims of the Genocide of the Greeks of Pontos," stated a press release issued in the name of a German-based Pontian diaspora federation, in view of the remembrance day in 2013.[90] In the comment sections to related posts on various Pontian websites, commenters vented their anger at fellow Pontians who had opted to march "together with the fascists" on 19 May, oblivious of the "racist" abuse their forebears had suffered "from the Greeks."[91]

There were nonetheless other issues at stake than outward appearance. Golden Dawn was active in "refugee neighborhoods," such as the Athens suburb Kallithea, where descendants of Asia Minor refugees mixed with those of the "Russo-Pontian" newcomers of the early 1990s, and more recently, the African and Pakistani immigrants, who were now the targets of xenophobic violence. Several contributors to Pontian websites observed that younger "Russo-Pontians" had become or were in danger of becoming "Golden Dawners." As one might expect, the open forums of said sites were not immune to the rhetoric of "Greeks first" in the commemoration of genocide victims; while not openly declaring themselves supporters of Golden Dawn, some anonymous commenters expressed their sympathy for the "patriotism" of that party. Here a discomforting prospect presented itself to the advocates of the Greek genocide narrative: if the viewpoints of right wing extremism were allowed to spill into the story and affect the way it was perceived, the process of its internationalization would reverse. In recent years, some Pontian and Anatolian Greek activists had sought to establish links with their Greek Jewish counterparts in the hope that this would bring positive attention to their own cause, and had to that end encouraged participation in Holocaust commemoration. It was this work that ultranationalism threatened to undo, in which case the trauma drama of the Anatolian Greeks would be of no consequence to anyone but themselves.

One way to distance this particular "genocide memory" from the embrace of neofascism was to educate the Anatolian Greek refugee community about the ostensibly true history of its past relation with the right wing extremists. Six months before the controversy over the anti-racist law, Vlasis Agtzidis posted a text on his blog, in which he sought to demonstrate 1) the origins of Golden Dawn in Nazi ideology, and 2) the presumed origins of German National Socialism in the ideas and practices of the Young Turks, so as to prove that refugee interests were incompatible with those of Michaloliakos' movement.[92] This was not an entirely novel approach. For years Armenian scholars had sought to make sense of their genocide through the Holocaust; to some extent an understandable response to definitionalist critics that held the destruction of European Jewry to be the sole genocide. In some cases, this sense-making not only stressed the similar fate of Jewish and Armenian victims, but sought to demonstrate parallels and even lineage between their respective victimizers. For some Armenian-descended American scholars, such as Vahakn Dadrian, the CUP not only resembled the Nazis in their eliminationist racial hatred for their victims, and provided a role model for a "final solution" later emulated by Hitler; his imperial German predecessors had, according to this version, actively incited and aided the Young Turks in their deportations and killings.[93] By this logic, the Armenians and other Ottoman Christians were Germany's first victims of genocide (not counting the Herero people of Namibia). This is a highly contended interpretation of Imperial Germany's role; apart from aiding its Ottoman ally militarily and suppressing information about the killings that might have enraged German opinion, there is not much evidence suggesting active involvement in the Armenian genocide.[94] But this allegation had currency, especially among left wing Pontian activists, who had incorporated it into their own genocide narrative already in the 1980s.[95] Part of its appeal, besides creating a link between the absolute evil of Nazi crimes and their own history of suffering, was that it reinforced cherished stereotypes about international capitalism, imperialism and fascism as facets of the same phenomenon. The Armenians and the Pontians had died so that international capitalism, spearheaded by Germany, could exploit the raw materials and markets of Asia Minor; an interpretation that in 2012 was further fueled by the resurgent anti-German sentiment in the wake of the euro crisis.

It was this argument that Agtzidis elaborated on, in which economic incitement was supplemented by an analysis that stressed the common roots of Nazism and Turkish nationalism in German Romanticism and Nietzsche's musings on the superman, which in both cases had resulted in a predatory racism targeting the respective Jewish and Christian minorities. As on so many other occasions, Agtzidis linked this issue to strictly domestic grievances such as the clash between "Old Greece" and the Anatolian refugees, as well as the blame for military defeat in 1922. In his view, men like Kostas Plevris and Christos Pappas ("the Göring of Golden Dawn"), admirers of the Third Hellenic Civilization of interwar dictator Ioannis Metaxas, were the direct descendants of the Greek royalist Right, sympathetic to its German counterpart and Kemalism alike, which had abandoned the Asia Minor Greeks in 1922, and, refusing to acknowledge the refugees as fellow Greeks, submitted them to "racial" discrimination. Chiefly for this reason, went the argument, no true descendant of the Anatolian refugees could sympathize with Golden Dawn.[96]

There was nonetheless a deeply problematic aspect of this branch of "antifascism." The conflation of cosmopolitan memory with past and present grievances in Greece brought the troubled relation between the Anatolian Greek refugee community and things Jewish to the fore. Agtzidis' account of Greek right wing nationalism omitted the awkward fact that the ranks of interwar organizations such as the violently anti-Semitic EEE (banned and dissolved by Metaxas, and later resurrected by the German occupier) had comprised refugees from Asia Minor.[97] Thessaloniki, in particular, had seen rising tensions between its Jewish population and the equally marginalized newcomers in the early 1930s, which blended with recent memories of the former's pro-Ottoman sentiment. There was without doubt a history of ill feeling on this account, and this legacy of anti-Semitism sometimes surfaced in the Greek genocide narrative. The activists that held German economic imperialism responsible for the Young Turks' genocidal policies also arraigned "Jewish" capitalism in this context.[98] Also Agtzidis' own writings reflected an understanding of the Jews' role in the world, which was not too dissimilar from that of Kostas Plevris. It was thus "extreme Jewish internationalism" hostile to Greek national interest that together with the supporters of the Greek monarchy and of Bolshevism respectively had sabotaged the Greek war effort in 1920–22, thus sealing the fate of Asia Minor Hellenism.[99] Though anti-Semitism was far from prominent in these writings, slips such as the one cited above suggest an ambiguous attitude toward Jews at best. For Agtzidis, like many other Greeks, Jews were national "Others" regardless if they had lived in Greece for centuries or not. In one of his surveys of how the Anatolian newcomers had been received in interwar Greece, he bitterly noted that a deputy of the royalist Popular Party once had claimed the Jews of Thessaloniki to be more Greek than the refugees.[100] Grievances like this revealed another problematic aspect of Agtzidis' antifascism. For all the many references in his writings to a legacy of racism and the present threat of ultranationalism, it is never xenophobia in general that seems to be the real problem facing Greece; it is the "racism," past and present, affecting fellow (Christian) Greeks. Even in an article that purportedly addressed the situation destitute Muslim migrants faced in contemporary Greece, Agtzidis somehow ended up in a meditation on the role of Islam in the "genocide against the Ottoman Christians."[101] This cognitive parochialism also seemed to shape the overall understanding of the Nazis' "absolute evil"; the abhorrence at Nazism found in his writings, and echoed in the pronouncements of leading Pontian organizations, was often less concerned with its record of crimes against humanity than with its perceived links to the Anatolian Greeks' Young Turkish and Kemalist tormentors.

Yet there is another side of the issue that goes beyond mere memory-political competition between self-obsessing victim groups. The unwelcome attention of Golden Dawn could also work as an incentive for advocates of the Greek genocide narrative to engage more actively with the pain of Others; especially the Shoah. While the Pontian activists of the 1980s and 1990s had invoked Holocaust recognition in support of their own cause, they had usually not elaborated on how exactly their trauma fit into a larger international context—that is, what made their experience universal. The historian Polychronis Enepekidis, considered a pioneer for scholarly interest in the respective destructions of Pontian Greeks and Greek Jews alike, had even pointed to the same fundamental differences between these cases that critics used to discredit the veracity of Greek and Armenian genocide claims, namely that the Turkish perpetrators had lacked both the pseudoscientific racism and the industrial means of mass killing of the Nazis. Yet his description of the formers' more primitive killing methods—starvation and forced death marches—as an "Auschwitz in motion" indicated the larger context in which he made sense of the Pontian tragedy.[102] In the early twenty-first century the notion of the Ottoman genocides as caused by a Nazi-like racism had become more salient in texts produced by Greek activists, probably due, on the one hand, to the introduction of the Holocaust Remembrance Day in Greece, and on the other hand to the simultaneous rise of right wing extremism. When the 70th anniversary of the deportation of the Salonican Jews to Auschwitz approached in March 2013, the Pontian website "Pontos and Left" urged the city's Anatolian refugee descendants to join in the commemorations out of "humanistic duty" toward a persecuted people whose fate mirrored their own and in recognition of their indebtedness toward Holocaust awareness for bringing their own trauma out in the public.[103] This developed the theme of an earlier pronouncement in which the webmasters of the site had sought to imbue ethnic trauma remembrance with a more universal meaning.

[The] genocide of the Jews, which included our Jewish countrymen of Greece, is one of the great crimes of the 20th century, which affects us directly. *And this crime affects us especially!* Not only because they are our fellow citizens, nor the way that the other great genocides affect us, from [those against] the indigenous of the American continent to today's Darfur, but in a somewhat specific way.

And the reason for this is that the terrible Holocaust ... enabled the cultivation of sensibility for the oppression of peoples because of their cultural differences. Thus we reached the legal definition of the crime of Genocide by the UN in 1948. And due to this we as well, the *Greeks of the East* that is, the *Armenians*, the *Assyrians*, were able to speak openly about our own Holocaust carried out by the Young Turkish teachers of the Nazis, just 20 years before the Jewish ... The Jews, then, cleared the path. And perhaps *the most symbolic venue is found in Berlin, where the local Pontian association for many years has organized a march toward the Holocaust Memorial to honor our own Genocide's dead.* In this most revealing way they are recognizing that the collective memory of mankind must be unified, when facing the crime of genocide.[104]

A cynical reading of such pronouncements suggests that they appropriate Holocaust commemoration only because it provides a welcome excuse for Greek activists to talk about their own presumed genocide, thus reinforcing ethnocentrism. While that may have been the original intention of the authors, the outcome of such initiatives was often vivid discussions on anti-Semitism and the vices of xenophobia among the visitors of the site.[105] There was much hostility toward the idea of Jewish Holocaust commemoration in the comment section, but many responses also emphasized the need to recognize the suffering of Others as "ours" as well. Herein lay the seeds of a new direction for "Greek genocide" remembrance. By imagining the catastrophes between 1915 and 1922 as caused by racism, however grossly simplified such an interpretation may be, they acquire a new meaning more universal in nature than the nationalist notion of "our for Faith and Fatherland unjustly massacred Pontian brethren."[106] However vulnerable the notion of similar fate is to backlashes of nationalist resentment in the absence of mutual recognition, it promises to open up a venue toward cosmopolitan memory and paradoxically strengthen the sensibility toward the pain of Others.

Much of this remains to be seen. Meanwhile, the narrative of the alleged Greek genocides in Anatolia has scored its most important success. After more than a year of deliberation, an amended version of the bill on the fight against xenophobia was passed in the Hellenic Parliament on 9 September, 2014.[107] Despite the protests of many historians, the second paragraph of the bill made it a criminal offence to deny not only the Holocaust, but also the genocides—whether found in evidence or conjecture—of Armenians, Pontian and Anatolian Greeks, along with other crimes against humanity recognized by international courts or the Hellenic Parliament.[108] A new phase in the genocide narrative's way toward becoming a "national memory" has begun.

Concluding Remarks

In 2011, in a time of mounting social tensions and xenophobic violence, the historian Odette Varon-Vassard asked if an opportunity to connect with a wider European history had been lost in the process of nationalizing the Holocaust. By tying this cosmopolitan memory so closely to the notion of national suffering, the boundary separating the wartime experience of a persecuted minority from that of the nation as a whole was blurred in a way that seemed to impede the empathy of majority society from extending beyond national borders and group thinking. Given the ethnocentric nature of the Greek history curriculum, however, the choice of the Greek Jewish experience as a starting point for Holocaust education is not difficult to understand. After all, the real challenge for educators in Greece is to accustom students to the idea that the Jews who once lived in their midst were (and still are) Greeks too, albeit of a different religion. There is much research on reconciliation curricula that emphasizes the importance of site-specific material adapted to the needs of teachers across diverse regions and communities traumatized by ethnic cleansing, war, and intolerance.[109]

As elsewhere in the central and eastern parts of the continent, European Holocaust commemoration entered into already ongoing debates on national suffering and unsettled scores. In Greece, this junction of transnational and domestic history-cultural concerns was not only colored by the local legacies of World War II but also by the vexed issue of the alleged Greek genocides. The timing was crucial. The Shoah was introduced in Greek history textbooks at about the same time as the "textbook war" waged for the "defense" of national history, and the meaning of the 1922 Catastrophe as a moment of national pain raged in the media. Seen against this backdrop, the entanglement of the respective issues seemed inevitable; more so since official Holocaust commemoration was endowed with greater significance than the more "domestic" instances of genocide previously recognized by the state.

When the tragedies of Others become a mirror for national concerns, the latter also come to inform how the former are understood and vice versa. Both the Jewish and the Armenian tragedies had in a rhetorical sense mattered to the advocates of the Greek genocide narrative(s) already in the 1980s, as convenient historical analogies giving meaning to their own claims and as models to be emulated in the quest for recognition. But it was not until the early twenty-first century and the appearance of the Holocaust as an (involuntary) contender in intra-national memory-political competition that the need to more actively engage with it arose. With that the domestic controversies about the interpretation of the Asia Minor Catastrophe as genocide became more influenced by international debates on how genocide is to be understood. Was the Holocaust unique or was it part of a continuum of similar atrocities in the twentieth century? What about the Armenian genocide of 1915, which had a historical connection to the Catastrophe of the Ottoman Greeks, and therefore was readily acceptable as a shared tragedy? Had the victims posed a threat to their victimizers and thus caused their own doom? For both supporters and critics of the Greek genocide narrative, comparison with these "external" tragedies played a crucial role in their line of argument. However, these comparisons entailed their own set of ethical conundrums, as too much emphasis on the unique features of one genocide sometimes implied the diminishment or even denial of other genocides, and thus the grievable quality of the one or the other group's suffering. In this fashion, even well-intentioned debaters risked veering toward morally untenable positions. The notion of the Jewish genocide and its Armenian and Anatolian Greek counterparts as "events of different order and significance, from the recognition of which different political projects ensue" was understandable from the viewpoint that the altered demographic composition of the country required memories that encouraged social cohesion and the fight against racism. But such commemoration, based on moral condemnation, also seemed to imply a hierarchy of victims.

These debates acquired a growing urgency as Greece entered the vortex of economic collapse, social unrest, and a rising tide of xenophobia. The vehement opposition toward the new cosmopolitan emphasis on Holocaust remembrance from Golden Dawn and other rightist extremists brought the tension between the local and the global into the open, as commemoration of the professed Greek genocides was deliberately pitted against it. Efforts to criminalize denial of the Holocaust led to demands for similar legal status for the vexed Greek genocide interpretation along with fears of history's politicization. Undoubtedly, such status would spare the advocates of the Greek genocide narrative from the trouble of having to argue for their claims. However, the conflation of their agenda with that of right wing extremism posed a threat to the credibility of the former. If the Greek genocide narrative became synonymous with the parochial concerns of ultranationalism it would cease to be of any relevance outside of Greece and the Anatolian refugee community. There was a palpable danger that this would estrange activists in Greece from those of the diaspora, who were themselves second- or third-generation immigrants in multicultural societies. This, then, provided some activists with an incentive to address the issue of racism more actively than before. If the Ottoman Greeks fell prey to a Nazi-like racism, as they claimed, then their descendants could not remain indifferent toward similar acts against other people.

All this came down to the problematic that Takis Michas, among others, had identified in the overall Greek response to the suffering of Others in the recent Yugoslav wars. Appalled by the lack of moral revulsion by an overwhelming majority of Greeks despite knowledge of the atrocities done by Orthodox "brethren," he concluded that Greece remained trapped in the logic of its ethnic nationalism. In this form of nationalism, as opposed to its civic counterpart, there is virtually no room for the notion of human, individual rights, since the members of the nation do not identify with humanity at large; only with their own community and its perceived friends. Michas ends his book with a more theoretical question: "Can ethnic nationalism transform itself into a civic variant?"[110] Clues to the answer to that question, I argue, can be found in the ways activists with a strongly ethnopolitical agenda seek analogies to their own trauma and, for a variety of internal and external circumstances, are forced to engage with the pain of Others. Paradoxical as it may seem, the preoccupation with one's own group's history of suffering opens up an avenue toward cosmopolitan memory. One must of course be wary of the risk of making an overstatement, as this is a complex process, severely hampered by a number of factors, such as long-held grievances and cognitive parochialism. Nonetheless, it points to the importance of studying also other contexts than the national Greek setting in the shaping of "Greek genocide" remembrance. In the following chapters, I will therefore study its reception in the Greek American diaspora and the international scholarly community.

Notes

1. Law 3218 of 27/1 2004, http://www.holocaustremembrance.com/member-countries/holocaust-education-remembrance-and-research-greece.
2. Law 2397 of 24/4 1996.
3. Tony Judt, *Postwar: A History of Europe Since 1945*, 2nd ed. (New York, 2006), 803.
4. Nonetheless, the initiative for this institutionalized European memory originated in the Stockholm International Forum on the Holocaust, launched in 2000 by Sweden's prime minister Göran Persson. David B. MacDonald, *Identity Politics in the Age of Genocide: The Holocaust and Historical Representation* (London and New York, 2008), 3.
5. Katherine E. Fleming, *Greece: A Jewish History* (Princeton, NJ, 2008), 6–8, 51.
6. Losses range from 82.5 to 90%, or around 60,000, of the prewar Jewish population in Greece. Odette Varon-Vassard, *I anadysi mias dyskolis mnimis: Keimena gia ti genoktonia ton Evraion* [The Emergence of a Difficult Memory: Essays on the Jewish Genocide] (Athens, 2012), 131, 161.
7. Fleming, *Greece: A Jewish History*, 183–189, 205.
8. Especially in Central and Eastern Europe, where local traditions of victimhood abound, the notion of a particular Jewish tragedy has in many cases been perceived as a competing narrative, which undermines the tragic conceptualization of the national past. See Johan Dietsch, *Making Sense of Suffering: Holocaust and Holodomor in Ukrainian Historical Culture* (Lund, 2006).
9. Varon-Vassard, *I Anadysi*, 137.
10. Vasilis Thasitis, "I genoktonia ton Evraion tis Thessalonikis: 50 chronia meta to megalo foniko 50, 000 synanthropon mas" ["The Genocide against the Jews of Thessaloniki: 50 Years After the Great Murder of 50,000 of our Fellow Human Beings"], *Oikonomikos Tachydromos*, 29 July 1993, 77–80.
11. Erik Sjöberg, *Battlefields of Memory: The Macedonian Conflict and Greek Historical Culture* (Umeå, 2011), 159.
12. Varon-Vassard, *I Anadysi*, 181–86. The bestselling testimony was Berry Nahmia, *Kraugi gia to aurio* [A Cry for Tomorrow] (Athens: Kaktos, 1989).
13. Anna-Maria Droumbouki, "'I Ellada epitelous thymatai': I mnimopoiisi tis Soa stin Ellada" ["'Greece Finally Remembers': The Memorialization of the Shoah in Greece"], *Avgi*, 30 January 2011.
14. Ismini Kriari-Catranis, "Report on the Teaching of the Holocaust in Greece" (Athens: MNERA, December 2006), 15, http://www.holocaustremembrance.com/educate/education-reports/.
15. Kriari-Catranis, "Report," 12.
16. Odette Varon-Vassard, "I genoktonia ton Europaion Evraion" ["The Genocide of the European Jews"], *Avgi*, 30 January 2011. See also D.K. Mavroskoufis, "Memory,

Forgetting, and History Education in Greece: The Case of Greek Jews' History as an Example of Catastrophe Didactics," *International Journal of Humanities and Social Science* 2, no. 18 (October 2012): 55–64.

17. Jörn Rüsen, "Holocaust Memory and Identity Building: Metahistorical Considerations in the Case of (West) Germany," in *Disturbing Remains: Memory, History and Crisis in the Twentieth Century*, ed. M.S. Roth and C.G. Salas (Los Angeles, 2001), 252–70.

18. "I martyriki Thessaloniki kai o Manolis Glezos" ["The Martyr City Thessaloniki and Manolis Glezos"], *Eleftherotypia*, 22 January 2009.

19. Fleming, *Greece: A Jewish History*, 206. *Gallup* polls carried out in March 1986 nonetheless revealed the extent of anti-Jewish attitudes among a good part of the general population. According to these polls, 57% of the respondents declared that they did not trust Jews, 49% that they did not wish to see a Jew run for office, and 43% that they would not seek medical assistance from a Jewish doctor. Cited in Iós tis Kyriakís (Kostopoulos, Trimis, Psarras), "Den emeinan oute ta mnimata" ["Not Even the Graves Remained"], *Eleftherotypia* 3 May 1992, section *E*, 46–50.

20. A similar observation has been made for the case of Serbia, which during the Yugoslav conflict sought to create strong links with Israel and Jewish communities worldwide, based on "the myth of the powerful Jew." MacDonald, *Identity Politics*, 187.

21. Odette Varon-Vassard, "I genoktonia."

22. Takis Michas, *Unholy Alliance: Greece and Milošević's Serbia* (College Station, 2002).

23. Michas, *Unholy Alliance*, 10–12, 120–30.

24. The origins of this notion can be traced to the schism between the Bulgarian and Greek Orthodox churches in 1870, when Russia backed her fellow Slavs, which forced Greek nationalists to realize that language and common "race" mattered more than shared religion.

25. Cf. Ioannis Stefanidis, *Stirring the Greek Nation: Political Culture, Irredentism and Anti-Americanism in Greece, 1945–1967* (Aldershot, 2007).

26. Nikos Chatzinotas, "Anthellinismos anti antisimitismou" ["Anti-Hellenism instead of Anti-Semitism], *Oikonomikos Tachydromos*, 3 June 1993, 200.

27. The courtesy was reciprocated by Bosnian Serb leader Radovan Karadžić at a rally in Athens in June 1993: "We have with us God and the Greeks." Michas, *Unholy Alliance*, 26. See also Helena Smith, "Greece Faces Shame of Role in Serb Massacre," *The Guardian*, 4 January 2003.

28. Athanasios Ellis, "Sti genoktonia den yparchoun 'dikoi mas'" ["In Genocide There Are No 'Our Guys'"], *Kathimerini*, 3 August 2008.

29. Cf. Yair Auron, *The Banality of Denial: Israel and the Armenian Genocide* (New Brunswick and London, 2003), 11.

30. Polychronis Enepekidis, *Oi diogmoi ton Evraion en Elladi 1941–1944: Epi ti vasei ton mystikon archeion ton ES-ES* [The Persecutions of the Jews in Greece 1941–1944: Based on the Secret Archives of the SS] (Athens, 1969). The book was republished in the 1990s, with the word "persecutions" exchanged for "Holocaust" in an attempt to situate it in contemporary historiography. Polychronis Enepekidis, *To Olokautoma ton Evraion tis Ellados 1941–1944: Apo germanika kai ellinika archeia* [The Holocaust of the Jews of Greece 1941–1944: From German and Greek Archives] (Athens, 1996).

31. Enepekidis, *Oi Diogmoi*.

32. Enepekidis, *Oi Diogmoi*, 41–60. See also Varon-Vassard, *I Anadysi*, 168–69.

33. Giorgos Margaritis, *Anepithymitoi sympatriotes: Stoicheia gia tin katastrofi ton meionotiton stin Ellada* [Unwanted Countrymen: Facts about the Destruction of the Minorities in Greece] (Athens, 2005).

34. Varon-Vassard, *I Anadysi*, 187.

35. *1922*, directed by Nikos Koundouros, 1978, http://www.imdb.com/title/tt0079643/ (last accessed 2 May 2016). Although not explicitly referring to genocide, the film, to some extent an adaptation of Ilias Venezis' *To noumero 31328*, was later hailed as the first cinematic dramatization of "scenes from the Catastrophe and the Asia Minor Genocide." Konstantinos Blathras, "Mikrasiatika epikaira" ["Asia Minor Newsreels"], *Ardin*, no. 38–39 (November 2002), http://www.ardin-rixi.gr/archives/195186. Last accessed 2 May 2016.

36. The Armenian population of Smyrna had largely been spared from the deportations in 1915. This meant that when the city fell to the Turkish nationalist forces in 1922 its Greek and Armenian inhabitants indeed did share the same fate. See Marjorie Housepian Dobkin, *Smyrna 1922: The Destruction of a City*, 4th ed. (New York, 1998).

37. Eudokia Epeoglou-Bakalaki, *I Amaseia* [Amasya] (Thessaloniki, 1988), 48.

38. Periklis Rodakis, "Prologos stin elliniki ekdosi" ["Preface to the Greek Edition"], in Diarkes dikastirio ton laon, *To egklima tis siopis: I genoktonia ton Armenion* [A Crime of Silence: The Armenian Genocide], trans. Gianna Kourtovik and Sifis Kassessian (Athens, 1988), 7–9.

39. For example, Spyros Alexiou. "Apo tous Armenious os tous Kourdous" ["From the Armenians to the Kurds"], *Kathimerini*, 19 April 1992, 16; Vangelis Zorbas, "Machetai gia ti dikaiosi to armeniko ethnos" ["The Armenian Nation Fights for Vindication"], *Kathimerini*, 24 April 1992, 3; Ioannis Hassiotis, "I Genoktonia ton Armenion" ["The Armenian Genocide"], *Kathimerini*, 5 February 1995, *Epta Imeres*, 10–12.

40. Iós tis Kyriakís (Kostopoulos, Trimis, Psarra), "O xechasmenos 'ethnikos echtros'" ["The Forgotten 'National Enemy'"], *Eleftherotypia*, 24 April 2005.

41. In this context, the editors made no distinction between views held by citizens of Greece and those of Ottoman Greeks.

42. Ioannis Hassiotis, letter to the editors of Iós tis Kyriakis, *Eleftherotypia*, 22 May 2005.

43. Ios tis Kyriakis (Kostopoulos, Trimis, Psarra), "Armenioi: 'filoi' í 'echtroi'?" ["Armenians: 'friends' or 'foes'?"], *Eleftherotypia*, 22 May 2005.

44. For further discussion, see A. Dirk Moses, "Holocaust and Genocide," in *The Historiography of the Holocaust*, ed. D. Stone (Basingstoke and New York, 2004), 533–55.

45. Varon-Vassard, *I Anadysi*, 158–60.

46. Giorgos Kokkinos et al., *Proseggizontas to Olokautoma sto elliniko scholeio* [Approaching the Holocaust in Greek Schools] (Athens, 2007), 19–20.

47. Antonis Karkagiannis, "I genoktonia ton Armenion, i proto frikiastiki ethnokath-arsi tou 20ou aiona" ["The Armenian Genocide, The First Abhorrent Ethnic Cleansing of the 20th Century], *Kathimerini*, 17 April 2005.

48. Karkagiannis, "I genoktonia."

49. Antonis Karkagiannis, "'I lexi 'genoktonia'" ["The Word 'Genocide'"], *Kathimerini*, 30 April 2009.

50. Antonis Karkagiannis, "I lexi 'genoktonia' II" [The Word "Genocide" II], *Kathimerini*, 8 May 2009.

51. Guenter Lewy, *The Armenian Massacres in Ottoman Turkey: A Disputed Genocide* (Salt Lake City, 2005), 252–57; Michael M. Gunter, *Armenian History and the Question of Genocide* (New York, 2011), ix–xi, 20–21, 36–46.

52. Armeniki Ethniki Epitropi Ellados, "I genoktonia ton Armenion" ["The Armenian Genocide"], *Kathimerini*, 21 May 2009.

53. Antonis Karkagiannis, "Erpon antisimitismos" ["Creeping Anti-Semitism"], *Kathimerini*, 25 January 2005.

54. Karkagiannis' friendship with Angelos Elefantis, with whom he cofounded the magazine *O Politis*, may also have swayed him in this direction.

55. Antonis Liakos, "Eisagogi" ["Introduction"], in *To 1922 kai oi prosfyges: Mia nea matia* [1922 and The Refugees: A New Perspective], ed. A. Liakos (Athens, 2011), 16.

56. The author had developed similar arguments about the appropriateness of Holocaust analogies with regard to both the Kosovo conflict and the revoked presidential decree on the 14 September memorial day. Antonis Liakos, "Ti den didachtikame apo ton polemo" ["What We Did Not Learn From the War"], *To Vima*, 27 June 1999; Liakos, "Apo ti mnimi-ekdikisi sti mnimi-katanoisi" ["From Memory as Vengeance to Memory as Understanding"], *To Vima*, 11 March 2001.

57. Nikos Filis, "To sch. P. D. gia ti 'genoktonia' anapempetai gia meleti" ["The Plan for Presidential Decree on the 'Genocide' is Referred Back for Examination"], *Avgi*, 25 February 2001, 5.

58. Tasos Kostopoulos, *Polemos kai ethnokatharsi: I xechasmeni pleura mias dekaetous ethnikis exormisis (1912–1922)* [War and Ethnic Cleansing: The Forgotten Side of a Ten Years Long National Campaign (1912–1922)], 4th ed. (Athens, 2008), 13.

59. Kostopoulos, *Polemos*, 18–19.

60. Kostopoulos, *Polemos*, 213.

61. Kostopoulos, *Polemos*, 227.

62. Kostopoulos, *Polemos*, 248.

63. Cf. Donald Bloxham, *The Great Game of Genocide: Imperialism, Nationalism, and the Destruction of the Ottoman Armenians* (Oxford, 2005), 17. The notion of "provocation thesis" was originally advanced by Robert Melson in a polemic with Bernard Lewis, whom he accused of legitimating Turkish genocidal practices by claiming them to derive from the supposedly provocative behavior of the victims themselves. Robert F. Melson, *Revolution and Genocide: On the Origins of the Armenian Genocide and the Holocaust* (Chicago, 1992), 10–12, 152–59.

64. Petros-Iosif Stanganellis, "(Kai) ta dika mas fousata" ["(And) Our Own Hordes"], *Avgi*, 19 September 2010.

65. Georgios Nakratzas, "O thoryvos schetika me tin genoktonia ton Pontion" ["The Fuss about the Pontian Genocide"], last modified 23 February 2011, last accessed 23 August 2013, http://www.aformi.gr/. See also Nasos Theodoridis, "Mia psychraimi proseggisi tou istorikou zitimatos peri Pontion" ["A Sober Approach to the Historical Issue Concerning the Pontians"], *Avgi*, 20 May 2011.

66. Giannis Chatziantoniou, "Alitheies gia ti Genoktonia ton Pontion" ["Truths about the Pontian Genocide"], *Avgi*, 22 May 2012.

67. Vasiliki Georgiadou, "Right-Wing Populism and Extremism: The Rapid Rise of 'Golden Dawn' in Crisis-Ridden Greece," in *Right-Wing Extremism in Europe: Country-Analyses, Counter-Strategies and Labor-Market Oriented Exit Strategies*, ed. R. Melzer and S. Serafin (Berlin, 2013), 75–101.

68. Georgiadou, "Right-Wing Populism," 85–87. See also Michas, *Unholy Alliance*, 17–41.

69. See, for example, Human Rights Watch, *Hate on the Streets: Xenophobic Violence in Greece* (July, 2012).

70. Takis S. Pappas, *Populism and Crisis Politics in Greece* (Basingstoke, 2014).

71. "Chrysi Avgi: Ena ideologiko kinima" ["Golden Dawn: An Ideological Movement"], http://www.xryshaygh.com/index.php/kinima/ideologia. Last accessed 13 December 2013.

72. Georgiadou, "Right-Wing Populism," 83–84.

73. "Does Israel commemorate the Greek Genocide?," last modified 27 January 2010, accessed 18 February 2013, http://www.pontosworld.com/.

74. "Does Israel commemorate the Greek Genocide?"

75. Kostas Plevris quoted in "Archise i diki tou K. Plevri gia paravasi tou antirasistikou nomou" ["The Trial of K. Plevris For Violation of the Anti-Racist Law Has Begun"], *To Vima*, 4 December 2007.

76. P. Nora, "History, Memory and the Law in France, 1990–2010," *Historein* 11 (2011): 10, doi:10.12681/historein.136.

77. On the Bernard Lewis affair, see Auron, *Banality of Denial*, 226–30; Yves Ternon, "Freedom and Responsibility of the Historian," in *Remembrance and Denial: The Case of the Armenian Genocide*, ed. R. Hovannisian (Detroit, 1998), 237–48.

78. Judt, *Postwar*, 820–26. L. Cajani, "Criminal Laws on History: The Case of the European Union," *Historein* 11 (2011): 19–48, doi: 10.12681/historein.138.

79. For example, W. Benz, "Holocaust Denial: Anti-Semitism as a Refusal to Accept Reality," *Historein* 11 (2011): 69–79, doi: 10.12681/historein.141.

80. Nora, "History, Memory," 10–13.

81. Nikos Filis, "To sch. P. D.," 5.

82. "Ekdiloseis tis Chrysis Avgis gia tin genoktonia ton Pontion stin Voreia Ellada" ["Manifestations of Golden Dawn about the Pontian Genocide in Northern Greece"], last accessed 26 January 2014, http://www.xryshaygh.com/.

83. "24 Apriliou 1915 – Genoktonia Armenion: Den xechnoume ta egklimata ton Othomanon" ["April 24 1915 – The Armenian Genocide: We Don't Forget the Crimes of the Ottomans"], last accessed 26 January 2014, http://www.xryshaygh.com/.

84. Cited in MacDonald, *Identity Politics*, 129.

85. Statement of the Federation of Pontian associations of Northern Greece (OPSVE) in "Ta pontiaka somateia kai ta epeisodia" ["The Pontian Associations and the Incidents"], *Eleftherotypia*, 15 November 1997.

86. Ios tis Kyriakis (Kostopoulos, Trimis, Psarra), "'Provokatores' me onomateponymo" ["'Provocateurs' with a Name"], *Eleftherotypia*, 8 November 1997. This was one of the first instances in which the editors' group addressed the "Pontian question," to the lasting dismay of activists for genocide recognition. See Vlasis Agtzidis, "Mnimi, tautotita kai ideologia ston pontiako ellinismo" ["Memory, Identity and Ideology among Pontian Greeks"], in G. Kokkinos, E. Lemonidou and V. Agtzidis, *To trauma kai oi politikes tis mnimis: Endeiktikes opseis ton symvolikon polemon gia tin Istoria kai ti Mnimi* [The Trauma and the Politics of Memory: Indicative Aspects of the Symbolic Wars for History and Memory] (Athens, 2010), 268–73.

87. Stefanos Tanimanidis quoted in Ios tis Kyriakis (Kostopoulos, Trimis, Psarra), "'Provokatores.'"

88. Statement of the OPSVE in "Ta pontiaka."

89. Ios tis Kyriakis (Kostopoulos, Trimis, Psarra), "I apantisi tou 'Iou'" ["The Response of the 'Virus'"], *Eleftherotypia*, 15 November 1997.

90. Press release of the Federation of Pontian Greek Associations of Europe (OSEPE), 17 July 2013, reposted as "Pontioi vs. Chrysi Avgi" ["Pontians vs. Golden Dawn"], last accessed 23 August 2013, http://www.pontosandaristera.wordpress.com/.

91. For example, Andreas, comment on "Pontioi vs. Chrysi Avgi," posted 19 May, 2013.

92. Vlasis Agtzidis, "I 'Chrysi Avgi' kai oi prosfyges tou '22'" ["'Golden Dawn' and the Refugees of 1922"], *Und ich dachte immer* (blog), 30 November 2012, last accessed 18 February 2013, http://kars1918.wordpress.com/2012/11/30/xrisi_avgi-vs-prosfyges/.

93. Vahakn N. Dadrian, *German Responsibility in the Armenian Genocide: A Review of the Historical Evidence of German Complicity* (Cambridge, MA, 1996).

94. Klas-Göran Karlsson, *"De som är oskyldiga idag kan bli skyldiga imorgon": Det armeniska folkmordet och dess efterbörd* ["Those Who Are Innocent Today Might Become Guilty Tomorrow": The Armenian Genocide and its Aftermath] (Stockholm, 2012), 152–63.

95. For example, M. Charalambidis and K. Fotiadis, eds., *Pontioi: Dikaioma sti mnimi* [Pontians: Right to Memory], 4th ed. (Athens, 2003), 52–55; Rodakis, "Prologos," 24–26.

96. Vlasis Agtzidis, "I 'Chrysi Avgi.'"

97. Mark Mazower, *Salonica – City of Ghosts: Christians, Muslims and Jews 1430–1950* (London, 2004), 413–16, 423.

98. Rodakis, "Prologos," 25–26. Cf. *Convoy* 7 (1987), 31.

99. Vlasis Agtzidis, "Aristera kai Mikra Asia" ["Left and Asia Minor"], *Ardin*, no. 38–39 (November 2002) http://www.ardin-rixi.gr/archives/195209. Last accessed 3 May 2016. Cf. Agtzidis, "I agnosti genoktonia tou Pontiakou ellinismou" ["The Unknown Genocide against Pontian Hellenism"], *Oikonomikos Tachydromos*, 2 September 1993, 26.

100. Agtzidis, "Mnimi," 231–32.

101. Vlasis Agtzidis, "Emeis kai to Islam" ["Islam and Us"], *Kathimerini*, 6 January 2011.

102. Polychronis Enepekidis, "Aousvits en roi i pontiaki genoktonia" ["The Pontian Genocide an Auschwitz in Motion"], *Kathimerini*, 17 August 1997, 24. Sjöberg, *Battlefields*, 150.

103. "Na timisoume ti Genoktonia ton Evraion" ["Let us Honor the Jewish Genocide"], 13 March, 2013, last accessed 23 August 2013, http://pontosandaristera.wordpress.com/2013/03/13/soa/.

104. "Gia ton Abravanel" ["For Abravanel"], 7 January 2008, last accessed 23 August 2013, http://pontosandaristera.wordpress.com/2008/07/01/abravanel/. The Berlin Holocaust memorial mentioned in the text is not the famous Memorial to the murdered Jews of Europe but its more "all-inclusive" counterpart at Neue Wache, suitably dedicated to the victims of war and tyranny.

105. See, especially, the discussion thread attached to the post "'Kato ta vromochera ap' tous Ellines Evraioi" ["'Hands Off' the Greek Jews"], 17 January 2010, last accessed 23 August, 2013, http://pontosandaristera.wordpress.com/2010-01-17/17-1-2010.

106. Quoted from Charalampos Papadopoulos, "I Genoktonia ton Ellinon tou Pontou" ["The Genocide of the Greeks of Pontos"], *Kathimerini*, 26 May 2009.

107. Lambros Stavropoulos, "Yperpsifistike to arthro tou antiratsistikou gia tis genoktonies" ["The Article of the Antiracist Bill about the Genocides Passed the Vote"], *To Vima*, 9 September 2014.

108. "Istorikoi tassontai kata tou arthrou 2 tou antiratsistikou nomoschediou" ["Historians Rally against Article 2 of the Proposed Antiracist Law"], *To Vima*, 2 September 2014.

109. For example, M. Gross, "To Teach the Holocaust in Poland: Understanding Teachers' Motivations to Engage the Painful Past," *Intercultural Education* 24, no. 1–2 (2013): 103–20.

110. Michas, *Unholy Alliance*, 144.

CHAPTER 5

BECOMING COSMOPOLITAN?

THE AMERICANIZED GENOCIDE NARRATIVE IN THE DIASPORA

While the standing of "Greek genocide" remembrance in national historical culture was being bitterly contested in Greece, it was becoming part of a transnational identity abroad. In the worldwide Greek diaspora, activists in the early twenty-first century adopted the narrative of genocide, in either its Pontian or Anatolian Greek incarnation, and partook in efforts for its international recognition. Here dual (or even triple) processes were at play. On the one hand, there was—as in Greece in the 1980s and 1990s—a movement concerned with the establishment of genocide remembrance as part of a self-conscious ethnic identity, either Pontian or more broadly Greek, within the framework of host societies. On the other hand, there was also a process that aimed at the cosmopolitanization of the Ottoman Greek tragedy, undertaken by individuals not always of Greek descent, for whom this event carried larger lessons about the human condition.

This chapter explores the trajectory of the Greek genocide narrative in the United States. It does so by surveying the identity-political concerns that surfaced within the Greek American community toward the end of the twentieth century, and how the cultivation of trauma narratives became a way to emulate Zionism in its attachment to a distant "homeland." Particular attention is paid to the work of a successful Greek American author, whose discovery of family trauma set her on the path to ethnic identity politics. The content and impact of her book, which introduced the Pontian genocide narrative to an English-speaking audience, is examined as well as efforts to teach this narrative in American public schools. The chapter ends with a discussion of the prospects and pitfalls of this "Americanized" remembrance.

The Greek American Community and the Politics of Identity and Memory

The Greek diaspora had been of crucial importance in efforts to promote the cause of genocide recognition from its onset. When Michalis Charalambidis first proposed 19 May as an annual day of remembrance of the Pontian genocide in 1988, he had appealed to a perceived need to find a rallying point, a common memory for Pontians around the world. This appeal found willing ears among representatives of Pontian associations in North America, who made an unsuccessful bid to have the Third Global Congress convene in New York instead of Thessaloniki. In the following years, Charalambidis' vision materialized in 19 May rallies held by local associations in countries with a strong Greek presence; notably Germany, Canada, Australia, and the United States.

Although this phenomenon is global in scope, this chapter will for practical reasons focus on developments within the largest of the Greek diaspora communities; that of the United States. The Greek American community alone numbered some one million members in the late twentieth century, although the various estimates often rest on elusive criteria.[1] This clout (real or perceived), and the fact that its constituency could be mobilized to influence U.S. foreign policy in favor of Greek national interests, meant that developments within "Greek America" were closely monitored in Greece. The potential of this "largest and most powerful weapon which Hellenism possesses," as the Greek statesman Konstantinos Karamanlis put it, was demonstrated in 1975, when the recently founded Greek American lobby organizations in Washington DC briefly succeeded in bringing the U.S. Congress to impose an arms embargo on Turkey, in the wake of that country's invasion of Cyprus.[2] The presence of a community committed to the cause of Greece and Cyprus at the heart of the world's leading superpower, stated a later Greek government publication, fostered a view of the Greek diaspora as "a national asset and that preservation of its national [i.e., Hellenic] identity is an obligation for the Greek State."[3] It was to this end that the Greek government engaged in a process of formalizing its ties with leading expatriate associations, which in the

1990s culminated in the establishment of the World Council of Hellenes Abroad (SAE).

Preserving or promoting Hellenic identity in a country vastly unlike Greece was, however, no straightforward matter of one-way communication. The tendency to view expatriates and their descendants as simply an extension of the Greek nation on foreign soil, rather than Americans, Canadians or Australians of Greek origins, was a source of annoyance even among those sympathetic to the national interests of the "motherland." Furthermore, the anti-Americanism displayed by Andreas Papandreou's socialist government in the 1980s did much to offend the sentiments of leading Greek American lobbyists, who themselves were often politically conservative.[4] Rather than acting as spokesmen for the views of Greece in Washington, the lobby tried to sway policymakers in Athens, in what one observer has called "the reverse influence phenomenon."[5]

Meanwhile, there were broader issues confronting the Greek American community apart from diverging political goals, which also threatened to widen the chasm separating it from the distant motherland. One was the inevitable loss of Greek language proficiency among second- and third-generation immigrants, and the lack of interest in the affairs of Greece that resulted from that. This was a prospect that worried first-generation immigrants, who feared that language loss, along with mixed marriages, would also lead to the loss of Greek identity, understood as loyalty to the national homeland of the parents.[6] Greek-language newspapers in the United States were increasingly replaced by English-language Greek American periodicals, in which emphasis in the contents shifted from the motherland to domestic communal affairs. The second main issue at the end of the twentieth century was largely a consequence of the first predicament. Founded in 1987, a current within the North American branch of the Greek Orthodox Church—traditionally perceived as a bastion of Greek identity—known as the Orthodox Christian Laity movement called for the replacement of Greek language liturgy with English, as a way of establishing a new, non-ethnically defined pan-Orthodox American Church.[7]

These developments need not necessarily reflect a rejection of Greek ethnic heritage. Rather they illustrate a growing sense of autonomy toward homeland paternalism and a break with the conservatism of the elders within the Greek American community, whose political outlook was determined by the early Cold War. Nonetheless, the fear of a perceived loss of identity blended with similar concerns in Greece. This was the context in which the Macedonian conflict of the 1990s had evolved, fueled to a large extent by worries shared by forces in both the

motherland and the diaspora that the rather diffuse threat posed by
an independent Republic of Macedonia was somehow connected to the
alleged menace against Hellenic national identity and memory. Diaspora
activists were instrumental in bringing this clash between Balkan nationalisms about, thus turning it into a transnational conflict. If language
could no longer serve as a source for identification with Greek national
interests, perhaps Greek history and culture could. In this fashion, the
repudiation of Skopje's claim to Macedonia's name and history could be
construed as a defense of Greekness, which would imbue members of
the community with a sense of higher purpose. Rallies emulating those
in Greece were held in Washington DC, Toronto and Melbourne in the
early 1990s, galvanized by slogans about the exclusive Greek character
of Macedonia and notions of ethnic pride. Nevertheless, the outburst
of enthusiasm for this nationalist cause eventually backlashed. The
Greek American lobby failed to prevent the U.S. recognition of the new
state. Within short the new PASOK government in Athens quietly abandoned its policy of exclusive Greek rights in the Macedonian name issue,
which caused friction within the diaspora groups that had promoted
this cause. While most Greek American lobby organizations followed
suit, the worldwide Pan-Macedonian Federation, made up of expatriates from the Greek province of Macedonia just south of the Yugoslav
border, remained entrenched in a hard-line position, which ruled out
any compromise on the name. According to its leaders, the diaspora had
been betrayed by both the U.S. government and the Greek state, which
no longer recognized its services to the motherland. In this resentment,
there was common ground with the advocates of Greek genocide recognition, who hoped to achieve in the diaspora what they could not bring
about in Greece itself.

Despite the political and diplomatic setback, the activism of the
1990s left a legacy in the renewed emphasis on history and culture as
markers of Greek identity. Traditionally, the celebrated past had been
that of classical antiquity; the period of Hellenic history (blended with
mythology) that was also most familiar to the outside world. Greek
Americans, just like their relatives in Greece, took pride in the glorious
achievements of their presumed ancestors. But there were also more
recent historical events that shaped self-understanding among parts
of the community. The Pan-Macedonian Federation mentioned above
had been established in 1947, just after the adoption of the Truman
doctrine, which heralded the more active American involvement in the
Greek civil war that proved decisive to its outcome. The new diaspora
organization had played a crucial role in turning the Greek American
community and American public opinion in general in favor of the Greek

government. Over the following decades, the Federation continued to cultivate remembrance of "communist aggression" against the Greek Macedonian homeland, which in essence was a defense of the dominant Greek state narrative up until 1974. Many of the Greek Americans that in the 1990s rallied in support of Macedonia's Greekness did so not only as a way to demonstrate pride in a heritage harking back to the ancient kingdom of Alexander the Great. Especially in the minds of those immediately affected by the early Cold War, the Republic of Macedonia was a new incarnation of the old "Slav Communist" threat against the homeland. Social anthropologists Loring Danforth and Riki Van Boeschoten have described them as a "transnational political community of memory" composed of right wing nationalist Greek Macedonians on both sides of the Atlantic, "united by the shared political views they hold in the present and by the shared traumas they suffered in the past." [8] These people are bitter because they feel that the post-1974 Greek state no longer recognizes their sacrifice made in defense of the nation and that "their" victims' suffering at the hands of left wing enemies has been forgotten by mainstream Greek society. The disappointing outcome of the Macedonian name controversy thus added to already established grievances.

Trauma was to some extent a cornerstone of identity among parts of the heterogeneous Greek American community in the 1980s, at the time when the, as of yet unrelated, Pontian genocide narrative was taking form in Greece. The "political community of memory" to which members of the Pan-Macedonian Federation belong is also largely a "textual community," where remembrance is informed less by personal experience than on a limited number of texts, which are used as resources to imbue a common identity with meaning. The most prominent among these texts is *Eleni*, the journalist Nicholas Gage's 1983 account of his mother's ordeal and death at the hands of Greek communists during the civil war.[9] Writing the story of how his mother Eleni sacrificed herself while enabling her children to escape guerrilla-held territory in northern Greece for the freedom of America helped Gage to make sense of a trauma that had haunted him since childhood. But *Eleni* also sparked off controversy for its anti-communist bias, especially by critics in Greece, who accused its author of opening the wounds of the war anew and glossing over right wing violence. Meanwhile, the book enjoyed astounding success unrivaled by any previous Greek American author, achieving worldwide bestseller status and lauded by reviews in the American press describing it as "a Greek tragedy so overwhelming that the reader will feel as if his heart is being torn out, page by page." In 1985 it was turned into a Hollywood movie starring John Malkovich as Nicholas Gage on a quest to confront his mother's killers; a film that President Ronald Reagan cited in one of his speeches as an inspiring story.[10]

Gage's *Eleni* was a memorable example of what a powerful and convincing story could accomplish. Its success lay in the way that its author had made it not only a tale of personal tragedy, or that of a nation (Greece). It was a trauma drama that appealed to wider segments of society than just the Greek American community. At the same time, it was also a tale of success familiar to many Americans, which told the story of a child fleeing the horrors of the Old World, eventually growing up to make it in America—in Gage's case as a celebrated investigative reporter at the *Wall Street Journal* and the *New York Times*. Obviously, its anti-communist bias also resonated well with the popular mood of the 1980s, with a resurgent American right committed to the task of pushing back world communism, but this timeliness was also to become the book's undoing. With the end of the Cold War and its polarized worldview, *Eleni* seemed outdated, as the conflict it depicted no longer appeared meaningful except to those immediately affected by it. At the same time, the continued attention to victimhood in the emerging human rights paradigm ensured the relevance of trauma as an element vital to group identity. The question was which trauma.

Role Models: Ethnicity and the Americanization of the Holocaust

When studying the eventual significance of certain trauma dramas in the molding of Greek American identities, one of which would be that of the Greek genocide, attention is due to the wider ethnopolitical context in the United States, where similar dramas were long in the making. The political mobilization of the Greek American community in the 1970s in defense of Greek interests in Cyprus corresponded largely with the ongoing revival of ethnicity in the United States. The civil rights movement of the previous decade had legitimized interest in ethnocultural roots, which sometimes also manifested itself in the so-called ethnic lobby phenomenon that sought to influence policy in matters where the perceived interests of certain ethnic groups were involved. Apart from the Greek American lobby, there were organizations catering to the needs and interests of exiled Cubans, Armenian Americans and, of course, the pro-Israel Jewish American lobby. Unlike their relatives in Greece, Greek Americans were, other than being part of their ethnic community, also members of a more diverse national community in the United States. This meant that they, to a much larger extent, were exposed to other narratives of victimhood; the most visible of which was the Holocaust.

Peter Novick has argued that Holocaust remembrance became significant to American Jews from the 1960s onward, as a result of growing concerns of what it meant to be Jewish.[11] At the same time as many Jews found themselves successfully assimilated into mainstream American society, Jewish identity was increasingly perceived as endangered by secularizing forces. The rate of intermarriages rose rapidly, while attendance at synagogue steadily declined. Added to this sense of Jewish vulnerability in the United States was the predicament of Israel, which after the Six Day War acquired a status of centrality in American Jewish life and culture. Though victorious both in 1967 and 1973, Israel's wars with its Arab neighbors brought home the specter of total annihilation and fears that Jews could never feel truly secure anywhere. For many secular Jews in America, with no living interest in religion or linguistic ties to any Jewish "homeland," the lived or learned experience of the Holocaust became the most vivid aspect of their Jewishness.

The Holocaust was also the most accessible of Jewish themes to non-Jews. This was further enhanced by the process of "Americanization" that set in during the 1970s, when TV miniseries like NBC's *Holocaust* brought the drama of European Jewry to millions of viewers in the United States and Western Europe. Critics derided *Holocaust* as a simplistic morality, but its uncomplicated historical narrative did establish a framework of knowledge about the Final Solution for the viewing public. The effect of this and similar Hollywood productions, from *Sophie's Choice* (1982) to *Schindler's List* (1993), was that the genocide no longer was an exclusively Jewish trauma; it became the chosen trauma of mainstream American society. When President Jimmy Carter in 1978 launched a commission on the Holocaust, he firmly situated the event in the framework of contemporary U.S. history. Though America as a bystander had admittedly done little to prevent the genocide in Europe, U.S. troops could claim some credit for ending it. By granting asylum to many of the survivors, the United States could assume a role similar to that of Israel in a story of loss and redemption; their survival a testament to American kindness. Most importantly, the evil of the Holocaust embodied all the things that America, in the ideal sense, was not. The contrast was put in even starker words in 1993, when the United States Holocaust Memorial Museum opened its doors in Washington DC. "This museum belongs in the center of American life because ... America is the enemy of racism and its ultimate expression, genocide. An event of universal significance, the Holocaust has special

importance for Americans; in act and word the Nazis denied the deep-
est tenets of the American people." [12] The genocide of the European
Jews could thus be employed to reinforce American exceptionalism,
and restore faith in the nation after the Vietnam War and the economic
slump of the 1970s. In the longer perspective, after the end of the Cold
War, Holocaust commemoration acquired a new national significance,
providing the United States with a sense of moral stature and mission
to champion the cause of human rights.

The success of Holocaust awareness, along with the perceived influence of the "Israel lobby" in Washington DC, was a lesson to various
"ethnic" pressure groups. Although the surge of interest in Jewish victimhood was hardly caused by the activity of that lobby, it certainly created the impression that suffering carried clout, which could translate
into political gains. Scholars of memory politics have often pointed to
how the Holocaust is seen as offering "a window of opportunity" for
other groups who either have or claim to have been treated unfairly.
The Americanization of the wartime Jewish tragedy has given hope
to a number of groups that they too might achieve something similar
if they can convincingly demonstrate that similar events occurred in
their collective past. The 1990s, in particular, witnessed an upsurge in
public attention to "forgotten holocausts" and histories of ethnic victimhood, heralded by bestsellers such as *The Rape of Nanking* by Chinese
American journalist Iris Chang.[13] In similar ways, the Armenian claim
to recognition, though dating back to 1965, was further boosted by both
the upsurge of Holocaust awareness and the Cold War's end, which saw
the independence of Soviet Armenia.

This was the complex web of simultaneous developments and contemporary identity-political concerns into which the Greek genocide
narrative entered. In many ways, the fears of first-generation Greek
Americans mirrored those of their Jewish American counterparts, who
worried that assimilation would entail the reduction or loss of ethnic
identity. The strong bonds between Israel and the Jewish diaspora, epitomized in the success of the "Jewish lobby," was ever the example to
which Greek American lobbyists and other diaspora activists looked.
The stated goal of the American Hellenic Institute (AHI), one of the
leading lobby organizations in Washington DC, has for many years
been the establishment of a "special relation" between Greece and the
United States, similar to the one that Israel enjoys. But how were these
lobbyists to emulate the Zionist attachment of American Jews to their
putative national homeland when the Greek Americans were becoming
increasingly indifferent to the language, ideology and politics of Greece?
And how could such a commitment translate into political gains? The

campaign for Macedonia's Greekness in the 1990s had succeeded in rallying parts of the community in service of the national cause but failed in evincing the support of the American public. Few outsiders could relate to the Greek anxieties over the name, since the neighbor's alleged theft of identity appeared to be a victimless crime in comparison with other post-Yugoslav conflicts, notably the war in Bosnia. Anticommunism and Greece's standing as a longtime ally of the United States could sometimes be evoked by lobbyists, but it was hardly the stuff with which to forge Greek identity in America or rally widespread support in the wake of 1989.

Here remembrance of the Asia Minor Catastrophe, reinterpreted as the Pontian and/or Anatolian Greek genocide, could serve as an invigorating narrative of ethnic identity and victimhood. The Hellenic Parliament's successive recognitions between 1994 and 1998 of the Greek and Armenian genocides were mirrored in the policy documents of Greek American lobby organizations. In January 1998, the American Hellenic Institute Foundation (AHIF) announced the establishment of its Center for the Study of Turkish Genocides and Crimes Against Humanity, which promised to shed new light on the Armenian genocide, the destruction of Smyrna in 1922, and the subsequent expulsion of the Anatolian Greeks.[14] Within a year, it was relaunched as the less provocatively named AHIF Center for the Study of Human Rights and Hellenism, but its research agenda reflected the same anti-Turkish bias. The Center, stated a press release, would promote the study of "the Greek people's struggle to survive and preserve Hellenic culture," with special attention paid to the "destruction and ethnic cleansing of Anatolian Hellenism; Greece's record of courage and sacrifice against totalitarianism and fascism during the World Wars; and the Cypriot struggle for freedom and justice." It aimed to "undertake research documenting genocides against Greek and other peoples, [seeking] to identify the individuals responsible." [15] The director of the Center was Constantine Hatzidimitriou, a second-generation Greek American with a doctorate in Byzantine and Modern Greek history from Columbia University. Hatzidimitriou had established his nationalist credentials during the name conflict by defending Greece's repressive policies against its "separatist" Slav Macedonian minority.[16] In the press release he was cited as stating that a center "whose mission will be to make the American public more aware of Hellenism's long struggle to survive against invaders, hostile neighbors, and genocide is long overdue." He continued,

Most Americans, even many in high office, have no knowledge of Hellenism's modern struggles to preserve itself and to promote western values of individual human rights and political freedom in the [Balkans and Near East] region. The Center will seek to set the record straight and make this information known to a wide audience through an aggressive program of education and outreach that utilizes objective data that will conform to the highest standards of the American academic community. Particular attention will be paid to the publication of official U.S. government documents which illuminate this neglected history.[17]

The task that Hatzidimitriou set before himself was to collect and edit the various American diplomatic correspondences and press reports that testified to the Kemalists' sack of Smyrna in 1922.[18] Not only was it the defining moment of the Asia Minor Catastrophe, with a given place in Greek historical imagination; it was also an event in which America itself had faced a moral choice. U.S. warships had been present off the port as the fire raged, with strict orders not to intervene on behalf of the Christian refugees, which Turkey saw as its enemies. Here were villains, like the U.S. High Commissioner in Constantinople Mark Bristol, who sought to suppress reports on Turkish atrocities, but also courageous Americans, like Asa Jennings, whose initiative paved the way for the evacuation of the Greek and Armenian civilians from the smoldering ruins. The material lent itself to moral lessons, which emphasized America's responsibility to advance its democratic ideals in foreign policy (and the suitability of Greece as a strategic regional partner in this pursuit). Though clearly ethnocentric in outlook, Hatzidimitriou, just like AHI lobbyists in general, made efforts not to appear so, by appealing to traditional "American" values like humanitarianism and the rule of law. It thus seemed that Greek victimhood could follow the Holocaust's path to Americanization.

Ambition was one thing, impact another, however. In order to get the public's attention, something with a broader appeal was needed. Gage's success with *Eleni* had demonstrated the potential of a powerful narrative of personal courage and sacrifice. The reason why that story had worked was not just its timing with the prevailing mood of the Reagan administration, but its easily recognizable and universally appealing theme—a mother's love—that did not require intimate knowledge of the complex realities of the Greek civil war. What was needed was an *Eleni* for the twenty-first century that could bring life to the forgotten Smyrna catastrophe and the even less known tragedy of the Pontos. Such an opportunity was to offer itself when Hatzidimitriou came in contact with an aspiring author with a moving story about a mother's trauma.

"The Greek Anne Frank": Thea Halo's Ethnic Awakening and the Pontian Trauma Narrative's Breakthrough

In May 2000, the book *Not Even My Name* was published by Picador, a branch of St. Martin's Press.[19] It was written by Thea Halo, a New York-born painter of mixed ethnic heritage. Her father was an Arabic-speaking Assyrian from Mardin in southern Turkey; her mother a Greek from the Pontos, though for Thea and her siblings this had mattered little—growing up on Manhattan's Upper West Side they had sometimes told friends they were Egyptians. Thea did not know Greek nor did she partake in Greek American communal life; for most of her adult life she had remained ignorant of the large Pontian community in Queens, believing her mother Sano (born Themia) to be the only one of her kind. A journey to Turkey in 1989 in search of her mother's birthplace in the mountains south of the Black Sea became a turning point in Thea Halo's life. For the first time she learnt the story of Sano, who at the age of nine had been deported along with her family to the Diyarbakir region during the Greco-Turkish War. There she, separated from her kin, had ended up in an Assyrian household, sold into marriage and brought to America. For Thea, now middle-aged, the discovery of this traumatic heritage came like a revelation. "I felt changed in some inexplicable way. I had history. I had a people. I had love that went beyond the present ... beyond my own lifetime and my own small life."[20] Embracing her Pontian roots she also made her mother's trauma her own. The idea to write a book came to her and she started to collect information that could put her mother's story into a larger historical context. This information was found chiefly at Pontian and Assyrian websites, but guidance was also offered by Harry Psomiades, a Greek American scholar of Pontian descent at Queens College, and Constantine Hatzidimitriou at the newly established AHIF Center for the Study of Human Rights and Hellenism.

Not Even My Name is, first of all, a daughter's moving portrait of her mother; at the same time a biography, a memoir, and a novel. It tells the story of how Thea and her mother Sano, then aged seventy-nine, embark on a journey to find her native village in the mountains of Pontos. During the journey, Sano one night tells her daughter her life story, which, told in the first person, makes up the bulk of the book. The reader is presented with the lost world of pastoral life and innocence in the Pontian Greek village of Agios Antonios, before the sudden deportation of all its inhabitants in 1920; all told in vivid detail, interspersed with Thea Halo's own poems. Herded by merciless Turkish soldiers, the starving villagers are marched southwards for months, during which

Sano—then still called Themia—witness the demise, one by one, of her family and friends. Near Diyarbakir, the little girl is separated from her surviving kin and made a servant in an Assyrian household, where she, bereft of everything, is also given a new name, Sano; hence the title of the book. The later parts of the book describe her marriage to an Assyrian man thrice her age who brings her to New York, where she gives birth to ten children. Back in the present, the first-person narrative returns to Thea, who experiences what can be described as an ethnic awakening, once the two women reach their journey's end.

In a later interview, Thea Halo asserted that she had told her mother's story simply the way things happened, faithfully reproducing Sano's vivid memories of her childhood. Yet she also asserted that she had not wished "to simply tell a story"; she had wished to make readers of the book experience a sense of "being there" with Sano.[21] This literary ambition is manifest in the sense of embellishment that characterizes Halo's prose, especially in the depiction of rural life in the Pontos, but it could hypothetically also raise awkward questions about the reliability of Sano's testimony. Asked if "false" memories had ever been an issue while writing the book, Thea responded that there is an important difference between a child's vivid imagination of things past and a memory process into which a trauma enters. "Trauma always makes you remember more purely and not to forget."[22] There is no reason to doubt Sano Halo's ability to remember the details of everyday life, nor her gruesome recollections of the long march; though admittedly "a nightmare I have partially wiped from my mind so I could survive."[23] Some memories continue to haunt, but they can also change over the course of time, under the impact of powerful templates of human suffering or interpretations offered by political master narratives. There is little in Sano's story that suggests this to be the case. However, it is important to keep in mind that *Not Even My Name* is not Sano Halo's diary, as admirers, proclaiming her to be the "Greek Anne Frank," often assume. Rather it is Thea Halo's adaptation of her mother's recollections, sometimes expanded or reworked for the sake of literary effect, or as a way to feed readers with historical context as the story progresses. An example of the latter is found in the dramatized dialogues between adults in the Pontian village referring to political developments in faraway places; the Greek landing at Smyrna, the Treaty of Sèvres, and the dispatch of General Mustafa Kemal to Samsun; hardly the sort of details that a nine-year-old child is likely to remember.[24]

What is of particular interest here is not the accuracy of individual recollection but the historical context presented in the book. "In telling her mother's epic story of survival and ultimate triumph in America,

Thea Halo has written an important book about a largely unknown history: the genocide of the Pontic Greeks at the hands of the Turkish government in the years following World War I," wrote Armenian American author Peter Balakian in his endorsement ad. Its status as an unrivaled English-language account on the topic made Halo a kind of semi-official expert, as we will see in the following chapter, which is why the study of her labor as a historical author is important. Halo's claims to historical authority lie embedded in the "historical notations" that are interspersed in the narrative.[25] These vignettes are meant to do two things. The first is to introduce readers to the history of the Pontian Greeks, by which she at the time of writing understood not only as those living in Pontos but in all of Asia Minor; from time immemorial up until World War I and its aftermath. The second is to set the record straight, by exposing how histories written from the viewpoint of governments—chiefly that of Turkey but also its Western allies—have, "depending on the nationality or loyalties of the writer," obscured the facts or otherwise misrepresented the events leading to the destruction of Turkey's Christian populations.[26] It was this "slanted" historiography that her victim-centered account was intended to correct.

> Because of these systematic attempts of various governments and interested individuals to hide their country's atrocities, and to create a fictional history, survivors' testimonies, as well as eye-witness accounts from disinterested bystanders, including European and American diplomats, often provide the most authentic and legitimate sources of truth. As with the Holocaust, these firsthand accounts by survivors, such as my mother, offer us authentic ways of understanding the events, and have provided historians with their most important sources for their writing of history. My mother's story is such a firsthand account of the hell that Secretary of State, Charles Evans Hughes, attributed to 'the barbaric cruelty of the Turks.'[27]

Halo's assertion that survivors' testimonies and third-party accounts (e.g., reports by foreign diplomats or newspaper correspondents) play an important role in historical reconstructions of such events holds true; especially in circumstances where historians lack access to documents that reveal the perpetrators' intentions. It does not, however, mean that the sources or the historical interpretation of them are made by disinterested parties. It is in the book's "historical notations" that Hatzidimitriou's and Psomiades' guidance is salient, both in the choice of sources supplementing Sano's testimony and the historical data chosen to provide context. The history of the Pontian Greeks presented to the readers is essentially that of Hellenism's millennia-long struggle against foreign invaders favored by the AHIF Center. Not surprisingly, the murder of "360,000 Pontians," along with 750,000 Assyrians, was put into the larger context of the 1915 genocide of as many as 1.5 million Armenians. According to Halo, the false spring of democratic reform heralded by the Young Turks' revolution in 1908 gave way in 1909 to a plan for the extermination and expulsion of Turkey's Christians. In this way, she was ostensibly able to demonstrate "Turkey's brutal intentions long before Greece invaded" in 1919, thus exculpating the latter from the charge of having provoked the slaughter and exile of the Ottoman Greeks. The evidence of these intentions was drawn from a variety of German and Austrian diplomatic reports, citing observations and conversations with leading Young Turks scattered across a time span from 1909 to 1917.[28]

Absent from this historic account, however, was the explanatory framework surrounding the testimonies—that is, data about the varying contexts in which the statements had been made, and a more detailed chronology of events. Also absent was the more complex reality of Greece's *Megali Idea*, the Balkan Wars 1912–13, and the Muslim refugee disaster they created, which could have shed light on the Young Turkish leaders' state of mind at the time, even if this would never excuse their actions. Furthermore, by presenting the plight of Pontians, Assyrians and Armenians alike as part of the same genocide, important differences between these groups in terms of their treatment over time became blurred. This went for the Ottoman Greeks too, for while Halo noted at least three separate subcategories (Ionians, Cappadocians, and Pontians), she insisted that "the term Pontian has come to encompass the struggles and tragedies of all the Greeks of Turkey."[29] Thereby a more uniform Greek experience than the rather complex regional differences that were often the case was implied. The historical notations of the book also left out the domestic political intricacies of Greece during and after the Great War, which would have complicated the picture of unequivocal commitment to the war effort in Asia Minor. Instead, the Greek occupation in 1919 was depicted as a victorious campaign to reclaim ancient Greek lands lost centuries ago, in accordance with President Wilson's policy of the right to national self-determination. The Great Powers (Britain, France, and the United States) had accordingly been so frightened of Greece's military prowess that they abandoned their ally in favor of oil interests and trade relations with Kemal's Turkey. Blame for the ensuing Catastrophe was thus put squarely at the feet of the Western powers.

This was a history of the events that whitewashed the motives and actions of Greek political leaders. Furthermore, although Thea Halo did not seek to demonize Turks in general—in fact, she argued in public that remembrance should never be used to stir up hatred for the Turkish people[30]—the referring to the perpetrators as "the Turks" along with the absence of a broader context of the violence convey the impression of a "slanted" nationalist history, colored by the loyalties of the writer (or alternatively, the writer's faith in her historical consultants). One might of course object that Halo, who was not a trained historian, had no obligation to cover all aspects of the Anatolian drama in a memoir of her mother. Nonetheless, her claim to represent the one true account of a collective tragedy made the lack of complexity that could have deepened historical understanding all the more problematic, given the international success it would enjoy.

"Like God We Were Waiting For You": The Reception of Halo's Account

Whereas the book itself left much to be desired, Thea Halo had accomplished a rare thing in giving a voice to the fairly anonymous victims of the Pontian tragedy. Similar stories of survival had been published in Greece before; one of which, Georgios Andreadis' *Tamama – The Missing Girl of Pontos* was translated into English and eventually inspired the film *Waiting for the Clouds* (2003), by Turkish director Yeşim Ustaoğlu.[31] *Not Even My Name* had the clout of a major publishing house in the United States, which meant that its impact went beyond anything previously accomplished by Greek writers on the topic. Nicholas Gage described the book on the back cover in words once used about his own *Eleni*, as "a work of burning intensity, self-evidently powerful and true." Favorable reviews also appeared in prestigious media outlets such as the *New York Times* and the *Washington Post Book World*.[32] For many members of the Greek American community, particularly those of Anatolian descent, the success of *Not Even My Name* and its author was a source of ethnic pride and self-discovery. "Like God we were waiting for you," wrote a visitor in the online guestbook on Thea Halo's website. "It's about time someone wrote about the Greek Holocaust! Educate yourselves; this is a huge part of our history that has been tragically neglected!" exclaimed another.[33] Within months after the book's publication Sano/Themia and Thea Halo had become celebrities in the Pontian Greek community of New York and elsewhere in the United States, which welcomed them as long-lost kin.[34] Sano's story apparently struck a chord with many readers who felt that it was their story as well. Also in Greece, where a Greek edition appeared in 2001, many descendants of Pontian and other Anatolian refugees viewed it as transcending individual experience and entering the realm of collective memory. On a book tour in Greece, Thea's mother was greeted as the "grandmother of all Pontians," thus transforming her into a symbol of a community whose life she had not shared for the past eighty years of her life. The Holy Synod of the Orthodox Church of Greece's special committee on cultural identity selected chapters of the book to appear in a canon of texts about "national life." [35] In 2009, Thea and the centenarian Sano Halo swore an oath of allegiance as honorary citizens of Greece in a solemn and deeply symbolical ceremony at the Hellenic Consulate of New York.

The success of *Not Even My Name*, and with it the international breakthrough of the Pontian genocide narrative, came at about the time when the political establishment of Greece had already lost interest in its promotion. Less than a year had passed since the battle over the presidential decree, which brought the genocide interpretation of 1922 into dispute. For a government keen on reaping the political benefits of the new Greco-Turkish détente, the renewed attention to the Pontian and Asia Minor issues was something of a nuisance. Thea Halo has suggested that opposition from Simitis' government was the reason why she and her mother did not receive their honorary citizenship earlier.[36] For the supporters of genocide recognition in Greece, however, the unexpected Americanization provided new ammunition in the ideological battle for the nation's soul. One of its most outspoken advocates, the left wing nationalist publisher Giorgos Karabelias, pointed to the future of "Greek genocide" remembrance, when he set the growing American awareness of it in stark contrast with the state-sanctioned "amnesia" in Greece.[37] The failure of the "Asia Minor Holocaust's" nationalization in the homeland—that is, the making of it into a national concern—could perhaps be undone as the events of 1922 entered a global culture of remembrance. The Greek American activism for the recognition of the Anatolian tragedy as genocide in the United States could thus transform into a "reverse influence phenomenon," whereby the diaspora's lobbying organizations might persuade Athens to bring the genocide issue back on the agenda.

Not Even My Name became a central text of reference in various Greek American lobby groups' efforts to have the Pontian Greek genocide recognized by political assemblies across the United States in the early twenty-first century.[38] It was explicitly referred to in Governor George E. Pataki's proclamation that the Pontian Greek Genocide Remembrance Day on 19 May should be observed in New York State. Halo's book was praised as "an important contribution to the treasury of works that clarify our understanding of this dark chapter of history," while the "Genocide of the Greeks of Pontus and Asia Minor" it described was acknowledged as one of the events in history "that teach valuable lessons from which our greater society benefits." [39] Pataki's groundbreaking recognition in May 2002, confirmed by the state senate, was supplemented by a similarly worded proclamation later that year that acknowledged the 80th anniversary of the Smyrna Catastrophe (although in the latter case, the word genocide had been downplayed). During the following years, between 2002 and 2006, similar proclamations appeared in the legislative assemblies of New Jersey, South Carolina, Pennsylvania, Florida, Illinois, and Massachusetts; states where Greek American communities of Anatolian descent were present and active.[40] Most often it was the victims of the alleged Pontian genocide that were being commemorated rather than those of its less advertised Ionian sibling, although the figure of 353,000 casualties faithfully reproduced in nearly all these resolutions was sometimes made to include the Greeks of Asia Minor in general.

One should not make too much of these recognitions, as some Greek diaspora activists tend to do. Although the solemn proclamations of Pataki and other governors stressed the contribution of the Greek American community to the wider society and the need for their fellow American citizens and "freedom-loving people worldwide" to join in the commemoration of the Asia Minor tragedy, they were merely gestures from state assemblies without any sway over the foreign policy the AHI and other lobby organizations wished to influence. The overt condemnation of Turkish governments, past and present, ensured that a bill calling for recognition would never make it through Congress, just as several resolutions on the better publicized Armenian genocide had been defeated before. The proclamations, and their counterparts in Australia where local Greek-descended pressure groups found sympathetic ears in the state parliament of New South Wales,[41] were rather to be understood as courtesies of the kind extended by local politicians to their constituencies; symbolical rather than in any real sense political capital. Only in states where such political declarations of solidarity were accompanied by a commitment to teach the history of said "genocide" in public schools could advocates of recognition hope to achieve a broader impact. This is a process very much in its infancy, but there are cases that shed light upon such teaching endeavors in a U.S. context, or what Hatzidimitriou had referred to as "an aggressive program of education." In the following, the case of the so-called mandate for genocide teaching in the State of Illinois and its implications for the Greek genocide narrative will be the object of scrutiny.

Teaching the "Greek Genocide": Ron Levitsky and the Genocide Education Mandate of Illinois

Although most state resolutions acknowledging the Pontian tragedy as genocide stressed its potential to teach young people the value of tolerance, they never suggested any concrete measures on how to implement these lessons in their respective states' curricula. Some came a little closer toward expressing a desire to include this "shameful historical event" in the history taught at public schools. The proclamation of the State of Illinois thus boldly stated that it looked "to stories like the Greek Pontian Genocide" to help teach critical lessons meant to "instill in our youth a universal respect for other cultures, races, religions and viewpoints."[42]

The case of Illinois merits special attention, not only because of the presence of a large and active Greek American community of Pontian descent in that state, but because of its mandated genocide education. Illinois had been the first U.S. state to enact a law in 1990 requiring all public elementary and high schools to teach the Holocaust.[43] This legislated mandate was in 2005 expanded to include other genocides in the twentieth century, departing from the notion that one of the Holocaust's universal lessons is that national, ethnic, racial or religious hatred can overtake any nation or society. It was therefore deemed desirable to reinforce that lesson in the history curriculum through an additional unit of instruction, including but not limited to the Armenian genocide, the Holodomor of Ukraine, and more recent atrocities in Cambodia, Bosnia, Rwanda, and Sudan.[44] This attempt to do justice to victims of the previous century's most publicized tragedies seemed to suggest high ambition in the field of state education; a place where a more general awareness of Greek suffering could grow.

However, the reality was often different. Despite the genocide education mandate, complained an Illinois high school teacher, no funds were provided for educator training or purchasing materials. Meanwhile, federal government mandates for annual testing of students in reading and mathematics (the "No Child Left Behind" law) led many schools to cut back on funding and time allotted for social studies, the very place in the curriculum (history and geography) where genocide education was meant to be taught.[45] The resources available to educators wishing to teach in accordance with the mandate were a far cry from those attending on Holocaust curricula. Readily available teaching materials were a palpable problem. In this respect, the Greek American activists concerned with the inclusion of the Pontian Greek (later just Greek) genocide narrative on the curriculum lagged far behind their Armenian American counterparts, who at the time had enlisted the support of influential educational NGOs like Facing History and Ourselves, with a long experience in providing schools with lesson plans about the Holocaust. Therefore, the task for these advocates, like so many other cultural pressure groups, was to produce such teaching material themselves, and enlist the support of dedicated teachers.

In 2006, the year when the Governor of Illinois issued his proclamation acknowledging 19 May as Greek Pontian Genocide Remembrance Day, a Chicago-based Pontian association, "Xeniteas," presented a teaching unit adapted for use in middle and high schools (ages thirteen to eighteen).[46] "Xeniteas" is one of the Greek American organizations most dedicated to the promotion of the genocide interpretation, as sponsor of the Asia Minor and Pontos Hellenic Research Center, which in recent years has organized scholarly conferences on the subject. The teaching unit was written by Ronald Levitsky, a social studies teacher at a local high school, in cooperation with members of the association and Greek historian Theofanis Malkidis, a friend and former student of Konstantinos Fotiadis, one of the Pontian genocide narrative's "fathers." Levitsky was an enthusiast who had been awarded by the Genocide Education Project for his lesson plans about the Armenian genocide, and it was with similar enthusiasm that he pressed the case for the lesser known Greek tragedy in Anatolia. In this sense, he is an interesting link between the ethnic particularism of Pontian identity politics and more universal concerns, which illustrates a possible transition of "Greek genocide" remembrance to cosmopolitan memory. His teaching unit offers a concrete example of what an internationalized (or in this case Americanized) version of the "Greek genocide," taught in U.S. schools, looks like or might look like.

Unlike his partners at "Xeniteas," whose interest in the genocide issue mainly was a result of ethnic identity politics and family histories, Levitsky was motivated from what seems a genuine concern about genocide as a worldwide phenomenon, in the past as well as in the present. As a high school student, he wrote in a later publication, he had been deeply disturbed by the Holocaust, but sought comfort in the impression that this great evil had been an isolated aberration in mankind's history. Realizing that this "aberration" had haunted the twentieth century both before and after the Holocaust, most often without any efforts made by Western governments to stop the killing or punish the perpetrators, he saw a mission in bringing the "forgotten genocides" to his students' attention.

> It is a tragic commentary on education that because other genocides are cur-
> rently being taught, the systematic murder of one to 1, 5 million Greeks is
> not granted space in a school's curriculum. By choosing to teach about the
> Greek Genocide, as part of the greater genocide of Christians in the Ottoman
> Empire ... educators are telling their students that all those who suffered
> genocide deserve recognition.

Had the world acted against the genocides of these Christians, he
furthermore argued, all future genocides might have been avoided.[47]
This message was repeated at numerous educator workshops as well
as regional and national social studies conferences, where Levitsky
and his associates presented their lesson plans on the destruction of
Anatolia's Armenians and Greeks.

Levitsky's teaching unit on the Pontian Greek genocide—later revised
and renamed *The Genocide of the Ottoman Greeks 1914–1923* [48]—was
organized as a five-day lesson plan, complete with varying exercises and
selected historical sources. It was designed to appeal to teachers in the
subjects of history, sociology and psychology, and was presented as a
tool to make students understand the nature of genocide and current
events in places like Darfur, apart from offering a comparative study
to the Holocaust. In an introductory note to the teacher, the author
claimed that the unit would fit chronologically with the study of World
War I in a World History class as well as U.S. History, "since Americans
were leaders in relief efforts to help Armenians, Assyrians and Pontian
Greeks." [49] In this sense, the Pontian case was construed as illuminating
a forgotten aspect of America's own history, that of its role as benefac-
tor to the destitute. Levitsky pointed out that this had been the first
great international relief effort in U.S. history.[50] Through the use of
local press coverage from 1922, describing how "Chicago women and
girls" played a prominent role in aiding Asia Minor refugees with shel-
ter, food, and medicine, he was able not only to "Americanize" but also
to "localize" the foreign, by demonstrating how people from Illinois had
made history in faraway lands. The point was further brought home
in the revised edition of the unit from 2013, which added a separate
lesson called "Saving the Orphans" highlighting the American Near
East Relief's evacuation of orphaned Christian children to Greece in the
wake of the Catastrophe.[51]

The proclaimed key to the teaching unit was "the intent to engage
the student both intellectually and emotionally and to personalize this
tragedy in a way that will truly connect the past to the present."[52] The
pedagogical strategy employed to accomplish this end was the use of
narrative; not merely the textbook-styled account that briefly narrated
the history of the Pontian Greeks, but more so the vivid stories of death

and exile told in Halo's *Not Even My Name* and Andreadis' similar work *Tamama – The Missing Girl of Pontos*. The value of these accounts, written from the viewpoint of children or adolescents, was in Levitsky's opinion that they have "a powerful impact on both the cognitive and affective learning of students who not only read what happened but vicariously share these experiences."[53] Apart from sensing the victims' pain and in this way humanizing them, students were instructed to act as "mini-historians" by studying a selection of "primary sources" that were meant to illuminate the events in Pontos from multiple perspectives. In his contribution to a collective work on the "Ottoman Greek genocide," Levitsky has elaborated on his perception of the historian's method that he wished his students to emulate. Historians, he notes, examine primary sources for motivation and bias, and seek corroboration to prove a particular thesis. "Even then, they realize that as new evidence unfolds, or new interpretations are suggested, any given thesis may need to be modified." The teaching unit presents students with a lesson entitled "Why Was What Happened to the Pontian Greeks a Genocide?," along with ten documents drawn from contemporary press accounts, memoirs, and survivors' testimonies, which attest to various atrocious events between 1914 and 1922. After demonstrating a basic understanding of the sources, the students are presented with the UN definition of genocide, broken into sections with spaces left below for students to fill in with examples from the documents that fit the description ("Killing members of the group," "Causing serious bodily or mental harm to members of the group," etc.). The purpose of this exercise, Levitsky explains, is to train students to investigate and substantiate the charge of genocide. Instead of dismissing Turkish denial as propaganda, the teacher can use it as an opportunity for students to develop analytical skills. "In the ensuing class discussion, it is easier for students to understand why the Greek tragedy was, indeed, genocide, because they themselves have used documentation to prove that the UN definition applies." Armed with this insight, students can begin to compare the Greek case with other genocides, such as the Holocaust, in order to point out both the specific circumstances of each case and common patterns.[54]

The problem that Levitsky does not address is that none of the selected documents actually presents a Turkish "denier's," yet alone a perpetrator's, perspective. While several of them testify to a criminal lack of consideration for the lives of Greek POWs and civilian deportees that may be interpreted as genocidal intent, none is told from the perpetrators' or their latter-day defenders' point of view, which essentially means that students are sheltered from contradictory statements. Levitsky has noted that many students rate history as a boring subject because their textbooks create the impression of a simple cause-and-effect sequence without controversy. The worksheet on why the Pontian Greek tragedy was, indeed, genocide is meant to make the subject more engaging, by training them to think like historians. What it in fact does is push students toward a preconceived conclusion, since the exercise is designed to confirm a given thesis, rather than test or modify it. Moral certainty, not ambiguity, is the overriding goal of the lesson. These objections may sound an awful lot like the dismissive comments and accusations hurled at the Armenian genocide narrative by Turkey's defenders. My critique is not to be understood as advocacy for the inclusion of "Ankara's truth" for the sake of balance, although this could be a useful demonstration of how contentious history often is. Rather it is a concern about the lack of documents that could have shed light into the minds of Ottoman leaders instead of only Greek victims and sympathetic bystanders. Without this, students' understanding of the issue at hand is bound to be partial and misleading.

The bulk of the teaching unit is, however, geared toward emotional response rather than the cultivation of analytical skills. Here, Levitsky draws from his experience of teaching the Holocaust to high school students. What has gripped young people about this event, he notes, "are not the words of scholars in a textbook but the words of a thirteen-year old girl," Anne Frank.[55] As noted above, he wanted to make his students identify with the Pontian victims by letting them vicariously share their experiences. One way of doing this was by drawing from the multiple intelligence theory developed by educational psychologist Howard Gardner, which emphasizes students' artistic abilities. Students are in the lesson plan instructed to design a "Memorial to the Pontian Greek Genocide" as well as, in later editions, creating their own 3–5 minute documentaries to inform about the forgotten tragedy, using images, music and narration to set a suitable mood. There is also a lesson instructing students to write their own poems about the destruction of Smyrna (in a strictly geographical sense not a part of the Pontian tragedy but rich in dramatic suspense) in order to convey, in a few words, the powerful images and feelings associated with that event. According to Levitsky, this was a pedagogical strategy that worked well with many students, who were moved into empathy—"I too/Fight for my life ... /Along with the people of Smyrna," read a poem of an eighth grader.[56] Clearly, the trauma of long gone Anatolian Greeks and their descendants could also be made the trauma of American adolescents in an Illinois high school, if only vicariously.

In much of this, Levitsky was simply following established ways of teaching the Holocaust. The push behind its placement on the curriculum is the conviction that an encounter with this catastrophic event, particularly an emotional encounter, is bound to produce a moral transformation. In fact, several of the lessons in Levitsky's unit are adaptations from teaching units about the Holocaust and the Armenian genocide produced by Facing History and Ourselves and similar NGO-sponsored educational programs.[57] The purpose of some of these lessons is to teach students to become what the U.S. journalist (later American UN ambassador) Samantha Power calls "upstanders"—righteous men and women who refuse to remain idle bystanders when other human beings face persecution.[58] In the Pontian teaching unit, the upstander was represented by a Muslim Turk called Ibrahim mentioned in Andreadis' book *Tamama*, who was killed while protesting the evil done to his Christian neighbors.

Critics of Holocaust education in the United States, like Peter Novick, have argued that the extreme nature of the Jewish genocide, and generally life in Nazi-occupied Europe, makes its practical "lessons" inapplicable to everyday life in America. Young Americans are hardly likely to ever face the same choices as people who lived through the event, and moral outrage is not very helpful when trying to grasp why those people acted (or not) the way they did, the argument goes. If there is any wisdom to be acquired from contemplating an historical event, Novick contends, it derives from confronting it in all its messy complexity—not a past that has been "shaped and shaded so that inspiring lessons will emerge."[59] While Novick and like-minded critics tend to underestimate the value of lessons that may engage otherwise often apathetic students, their criticism has a point. The sort of empathy that comes from strong identification with the victimized party is not the same thing as historical understanding of the event. What is missing from many such representations of human suffering is the surrounding context. Although Levitsky briefly explained concepts like the Great Idea of Greece and mentioned in passing events like the Balkan Wars, the rest was a pretty straightforward narrative of persecution, motivated by a racist-like hatred for the Pontians and other Christian minorities. In other words, the genocide narrative presented to students was sanitized from ambiguous elements, which may have complicated the story; such as the often complex interaction between different national movements with conflicting aspirations, the differential treatment of Ottoman Greeks and Armenians over time, and changing political considerations.

Evidently this was also a concern sensed by leading advocates of the Greek genocide interpretation in America, since a significantly revised edition appeared in 2013. This time, the scholars Constantine Hatzidimitriou and the late Harry Psomiades (Thea Halo's principal historical consultants at the AHIF), along with Dan Georgakas, a noted Greek American labor historian, had assumed the writing of the historical chapter serving as background to the lesson plans, and vastly expanded it. The most significant change was the very naming of the event taught in the unit—the "Pontian Greek Genocide" had transformed into the more broadly defined "Genocide of the Ottoman Greeks" (the reasons for which will be addressed in the following chapter). The Pontian experience no longer encompassed the tragedies of all Greek-Orthodox subjects of the Ottoman Empire; rather the narrative of events in Pontos was supplemented with information of persecutions in other parts of the realm, although it was not always clear how these reflected a policy of extermination.[60]

Overall, the authors kept much of Levitsky's pedagogy in the lesson plans and simply added reading materials. Four new lessons were thus assigned to literary testimonies by George Andreadis, Thea Halo and Ilias Venezis on the horrors of the deportations and the labor battalions. Some revisions had been made to correct factual errors in the previous version.[61] Other changes did more to obscure details rather than clarify them.[62] The main changes in the unit were nonetheless to be found in the historical context into which the genocide narrative was embedded. Hatzidimitriou and his colleagues had added new historical information in an effort to make the textbook-style narrative appear more academic than Levitsky's fairly simplified account of events. They stressed to a far greater degree the international relations of the era and above all the links between the Greek case and the Armenian genocide. The section on "What caused the Ottoman Greek Genocide?" now included information about Abdul Hamid's Armenian massacres, and a more detailed account of the foreign and domestic policy repercussions of the 1908 coup. Interestingly, some attention was paid to the suffering of Muslims in the process leading up to the onslaught of the Empire's Christian populations; the expulsions of Balkan Muslims during the wars 1912–13 and the earlier refugee disaster caused by Russia's ethnic cleansing of the Circassians north of the Caucasus in the nineteenth century were mentioned as factors behind the existential fears of leading Young Turks that motivated the genocide solution, besides "racist" conceptions of nationhood. On the other hand, the authors in 2013 omitted entirely the brief mention Levitsky had made in 2006 of atrocities carried out by Greek troops in Smyrna 1919, thereby creating a more unambiguous account of the Greco-Turkish war. Instead, Greek territorial claims and military events were told in greater detail. Finally, the Ottoman Greek experience was inscribed into the Armenian and Assyrian tragedies, with a combined estimate of 2.5 million casualties, thus demonstrating that the deliberate ethnic cleansing against Christians in Anatolia should be understood as the first large-scale genocide of the twentieth century.[63]

Nevertheless, there was an element in the grim saga that the authors of the 2013 edition could not easily render intelligible to a nonspecialist readership. That was the issue of the ebb and flow of persecutions targeting Ottoman Greeks during and after the Great War. For while Levitsky had avoided going into these details, Hatzidimitriou and his associates noted that the "genocidal campaign" began in 1914 ceased during the war only to be resumed in 1917, before it was halted again in 1918 and commenced anew, with greater intensity, in 1919; though without any reference as to why this was the case (such as Greece's neutrality up until 1917 and German restraints on the CUP). The contrast with the Armenian genocide carried out within the time span of a year, 1915–16, was never addressed. This is perhaps one of the main pedagogical problems educators would have to face. The narrative of the Greek Catastrophe is much more complex, discontinuous and difficult to make sense of than the more straightforward, chronologically dense story of the 1915 Armenian genocide. Neither the 2006 nor the 2013 editions of the teaching unit went into the messiness of the National Schism in Greece or the Great Powers' conflicting interests and/or concerns about domestic opinion in electorates weary after the Great War, which complicate the moral lesson about nonintervention. Nor did any of the versions address the inherent problem that the principle of national self-determination for all the Empire's populations (including the dominant Turks) was bound to create conflict no matter how the new borders were drawn. With complexity comes ambiguity, which makes moral lessons all the harder to extract. Though the Turkish nationalists' killing of Ottoman Greek civilians and Hellenic POWs was clearly criminal, it is more difficult to demonstrate that the violence reflected a plan of extermination, or that it was wholly asymmetric or unrelated to fears that Muslim populations would be expelled from Greek-held territories once Greece held the upper hand in Anatolia. Turning the "Greek genocide" into a lesson about morality works better if the story is kept simple and decontextualized. This works as an incentive for attaching it closer to the more unambiguous (and better publicized) case of the Armenian genocide, in which the victims were not in a similar way associated with an existing state's expansionism. By blurring the distinctions between the Greek and Armenian experiences, advocates of the Greek genocide narrative stood to gain from the moral credentials enjoyed by the latter.

The main problem with the 2013 teaching unit most likely to work as an obstacle in an educational setting is its length. It seems improbable that the vastly expanded reading list would be done within the

confines of a five-day lesson plan, unless the mass of text excerpts is
intended to sell the teaching unit as a means to test students' reading
skills. However, the differences between the two editions may reflect
divergent ambitions among the authors involved. While Levitsky was an
educator, whose interest in the Pontian (and Anatolian) Greek genocide
narrative seems to have derived from a democratic ambition to recognize the suffering of all victims of genocide, Hatzidimitriou's agenda
reflected more narrowly defined concerns. For him and his associates,
the teaching unit in all probability serves a dual purpose. On the one
hand, it offers an opportunity to make the story known to an American
public unfamiliar with things Greek. On the other hand, it provides the
Greek American community with a standard account of genocide as a
defining Greek experience, along with a canon of mostly literary texts
that bear witness to its horrors. Unlike Thea Halo's book (included in
the canon), the teaching unit of 2013 does not treat the alleged genocide
as a narrowly Pontian experience. The suffering has been Hellenized to
a higher degree than before. Perhaps this Hellenization was a way to
ease the Americanization of the professed genocide, as the insistence
on a separation of Pontians from other Greeks makes no sense at all
in an American context, where audiences are ignorant of the event as
well as the subtleties of intra-Greek debates and identity politics. This
is a line of thought that, along with the attempted merging of Greek,
Armenian and Assyrian identity narratives, will be discussed in the
following chapter.

Concluding Remarks

The embattled status of the Greek genocide narrative in Greece seems
not to have worked as an obstacle for it abroad, at least not in the
United States. On the contrary, the cause for genocide recognition
gained momentum there at about the same time as opinion makers in
the motherland began to question its underlying assumptions and leading politicians expressed doubts about its wisdom. The reasons for this
are to be found in the different national contexts and the shifting audiences that were being addressed. The American reception (to the extent
that there ever was a public debate) lacked the rancor of the exchange
in Greece because it was a relatively uncontroversial topic, untainted
by associations with past and present ideological conflict. The left wing
perspective that had played such a prominent role in Greek debates on
the Asia Minor Catastrophe or the civil war was either suppressed or
wholly absent in the Greek American community. For many second- or

third-generation Americans of Greek descent, unfamiliar with the language and the politics of the distant motherland, the domestic grievances of Asia Minor Greek refugees and quarrels between different political camps were of little concern. In that sense, the notion of a Greek genocide could work better as a unifying memory for Greeks in America, or Australia, than for the divided society of the "homeland."

The growing attention to the Asia Minor Catastrophe as genocide in America is here analyzed within the context of diaspora concerns about Greek ethnicity. Seen against the backdrop of ongoing assimilation, the genocide narrative responds to a need for orientation in time and a reaffirmation of a Greek identity perceived to be in peril. The 1990s had seen a mobilization of diaspora communities in defense of Greek history and culture during the Macedonian name conflict. The end of the Cold War at the same time prompted a new approach to ideological narratives of identity, as anti-communism no longer could imbue Hellenism in America with a sense of purpose. Meanwhile, the concerns of Greek community leaders and activists were mirrored in similar debates in other diaspora groups across America, which since the 1960s had witnessed the emergence of ethnic identity politics. Often the renewed emphasis on ethnic and cultural roots went hand in hand with notions of victimhood, further fueled by the growing importance attributed to public commemoration of the Holocaust. Whether Greek American lobbyists were chiefly motivated by what John Mowitt has termed "trauma envy" [64] from contemplating the success of their Jewish and Armenian American counterparts in raising public awareness of their communities' traumatic pasts or not is hard to tell. In any event, these groups provided powerful examples. Undoubtedly, victimhood carried more awe-inspiring connotations for the collective image of Greeks in America than did the not-so-funny caricatures portrayed in films like *My Big Fat Greek Wedding*. At the turn of the millennium, a more tragic conception of Greek history was promoted by the American Hellenic Institute Foundation and other Greek American organizations; further reinforced by the success of Thea Halo's memoir of her mother. The recognition of legislative assemblies across the United States seemed to suggest a willingness to commemorate Greek victims alongside the victims of intolerance elsewhere in the world.

Did international attention mean that remembrance of the "Greek genocide" was becoming cosmopolitan, in the way that Levy and Sznaider claim the Holocaust has? Certainly, there were empathetic non-Greeks, with no vested interest in ethnic identity politics, who could be moved into moral outrage. Giles Milton, the British author of a lauded book about the destruction of "Islam's city of tolerance" Smyrna,[65] expressed regret that this event had not become a "universal lesson for the world." For him the Asia Minor Catastrophe (he never used the term "Greek genocide," despite his ambition to recognize Greek victims alongside the Armenians) was not only a watershed event in Hellenic history, but a significant yet overlooked tragedy in a wider European perspective. Its lesson was a scathing indictment of Western realpolitik. "You don't have to be Greek to sense the pain which the word Smyrna provokes but also the cynicism with which the British and American governments handled the matter is shocking," he stated in an interview with the Greek press. "[They] turned their backs on the many that were about to be massacred so that they wouldn't appear as the saviors of Turkey's enemies. I fear that this repulsive stance is still with us."[66] If the Greek tragedy in Anatolia could illustrate something universally significant, it was the human cost of nonintervention. It could also be called upon to reinforce notions of American exceptionalism and sense of mission in the world, much as the Holocaust already does. This was the preferred angle from which Constantine Hatzidimitriou presented the "forgotten genocide" at social studies workshops. The histories of the Ottoman Empire and the Soviet Union, "which discriminated against and frequently persecuted their minorities," were contrasted against the image of the United States as a nation of immigrants, which saw diversity as strength rather than a weakness (a view absent from his writing about Greece's minorities).[67]

This does not mean, however, that the Greek genocide narrative in America and elsewhere is cosmopolitan in the sense of transcending its origins in ethnic identity politics. There is a difference between those interested in the Greek case as a way to understand the phenomenon of genocide in world history and those interested in genocide merely as a way to recast national history and promote a new collective self-image. The lessons that educators hope the Greek genocide narrative will inspire work better the less national, or otherwise particular, the framework in which it is presented. The result is not always good history, or pedagogy.

There are other formidable obstacles to its Americanization too. First, Greek Americans lag far behind the Armenians in educational efforts and public visibility. Despite the fact that a leading advocate of the cause sits on the Illinois Holocaust and Genocide Commission and that the Greek genocide narrative has been taught at public schools in that state, Greek American lobbyists essentially lack the financial muscles and the right connections to promote it effectively. Lack of money was something that lobbyists kept returning to in discussions on how to proceed with efforts to inform and influence the American public, besides lack of material in English. Knowing that no funding was forthcoming from the Greek government for this purpose, they were dependent upon individual contributions by members of the Greek American community.[68]

Second, the Greek genocide narrative is but one of many ethnic and otherwise collective traumas that vie for attention on the U.S. "marketplace." Novick has made a point of how the "same sort of ethnic log-rolling that made the study of the Holocaust mandatory" in state after state also added the lessons of events such as the Armenian genocide and the Irish Potato Famine, depending on local demography and configurations of power. In the end, he argues, it did not seem to matter whether it was the lessons of the Holocaust or the Potato Famine that were being learned, because the lessons were all pretty much the same: "tolerance and diversity were good, hate was bad, the overall rubric was 'man's inhumanity to man.'"[69] Despite the condescending tone, his observation points to a problem that needs to be considered in an educational context. What is it that students are supposed to learn from the "Greek genocide" that the lessons of the Holocaust (or for that matter the Armenian genocide) have not already taught them? Arguably, the inclusion of less known events from different local settings across the world widens understanding of any historical phenomenon, but for a teacher under severe time constraints this may not be sufficiently motivating. The "Greek genocide's" continued invisibility in America, in spite of some success, in turn reflects the lack of cultural and political impact of Greek Americans in the wider society. Halo and other activists hope that a major Hollywood film could pave the way for "Greek genocide" awareness, but so far no *Schindler's List* about Anatolia is forthcoming.[70] Despite attempts to Americanize the Ottoman Greek ordeal, it does not contribute to American self-understanding or foreign policy in significant ways. Like Armenia, Greece has in geopolitical terms too little to offer the United States to make it worth risking a diplomatic confrontation with Turkey. This is the reason why Congress resolutions about the Armenian genocide have been repeatedly defeated, and a similar bill about Greek genocide recognition is unlikely to fare better at the present time.

However, there is no cause for declaring Greek genocide activism in the United States a doomed enterprise. Influencing U.S. foreign policy in favor of Greek interests is only one of the AHIF lobby's goals; another equally important objective is to strengthen a sense of Hellenic identity in the Greek American community. There is no easy way of finding out how wide an impact the genocide narrative has had upon this quite diverse community; one can only conclude that the notion of it enjoys traction among some Americans of Greek descent. The future course of it in an international setting is subject to a number of factors. The most important of these has in recent years been the scholarly arena. Only there can the "memory" of genocide acquire the status of history. This is an important aspect of the Greek genocide's internationalization that will be addressed in the following chapter.

Notes

1. For example, Charles C. Moskos, "Greek American Studies," in *Reading Greek America: Studies in the experience of Greeks in the United States*, ed. S.D. Orfanos (New York, 2002), 23–25.
2. Alexander Kitroeff, "The Limits of Political Transnationalism: The Greek American Lobby 1970s-1990s," in *Greek Diaspora and Migration since 1700*, ed. D. Tziovas (Farnham, 2009), 141–53. The quotation of Konstantinos Karamanlis is found in Nikolaos Martis, *The Falsification of Macedonian History*, trans. John Philip Smith (Athens, 1984), 118.
3. Demetri Dollis, "Greeks Abroad," in *About Greece*, ed. A. Bacaloumis (Athens, 2004), 156.
4. Kitroeff, "Greek American Lobby," 146.
5. Van Coufoudakis, "The Reverse Influence Phenomenon: The Impact of the Greek-American Lobby on the Foreign Policy of Greece," in *Diasporas in World Politics: The Greeks in Comparative Perspective*, ed. D. Constas and A. Platias (London, 1993), 51–75.
6. For example, Jordan A. Tsolakides, *Hellenism Abroad – A Continuous Struggle to Maintain Its Ethnicity: Is It Destined to Oblivion?* (Thessaloniki, 2006).
7. Victor Roudometof and Anna Karpathakis, "Greek Americans and Transnationalism: Religion, Class and Community," in *Communities across Borders: New Immigrants and Transnational Cultures*, ed. P. Kennedy and V. Roudometof (London, 2002), 41–54.
8. Loring M. Danforth and Riki Van Boeschoten, *Children of the Greek Civil War: Refugees and the Politics of Memory* (Chicago and London, 2012), 261.
9. Nicholas Gage, *Eleni* (New York, 1983).
10. Danforth and Van Boeschoten, *Children*, 270–76.
11. Peter Novick, *The Holocaust in American Life* (Boston, 1999).
12. Quoted in David B. MacDonald, *Identity Politics in the Age of Genocide: The Holocaust and Historical Representation* (London and New York, 2008), 26.
13. Iris Chang, *The Rape of Nanking: The Forgotten Holocaust of World War II* (New York, 1997). Takashi Yoshida, *The Making of the "Rape of Nanking": History and Memory in Japan, China, and the United States* (Oxford and New York, 2006), 171–79.
14. American Hellenic Institute, "The Center for the Study of Turkish Genocides and Crimes Against Humanity," press release no. 03/98, 23 January 1998, http://www.ahiworld.com/012298.html. Last accessed 15 May 2011,
15. American Hellenic Institute, "Professor Constantine Hatzidimitrou named Director of the AHIF Center for the Study of Human Rights and Hellenism," press release no. 01/99, 13 January 1999, http://www.ahiworld.com/011399.html. Last accessed 15 May 2011.

16. C.G. Hatzidimitriou, "Distorting History: Concerning a Recent Article on Ethnic Identity in Greek Macedonia," *Balkan Studies* 32, no. 2 (1993): 315–51. Erik Sjöberg, *Battlefields of Memory: The Macedonian Conflict and Greek Historical Culture* (Umeå, 2011), 245–47.

17. American Hellenic Institute, "Professor Constantine Hatzidimitrou Named Director of the AHIF Center for the Study of Human Rights and Hellenism," press release no. 01/99, 13 January 1999, http://www.ahiworld.com/011399.html. Last accessed 15 May 2011.

18. C.G. Hatzidimitriou, ed., *American Accounts Documenting the Destruction of Smyrna by the Kemalist Turkish Forces, September 1922* (New Rochelle, NY, 2005). There was also a dimension of personal involvement with trauma as Hatzidimitriou's mother and many of her family were among those rescued from the city.

19. Thea Halo, *Not Even My Name: From a Death March in Turkey to a New Home in America, a Young Girl's True Story of Genocide and Survival* (New York, 2000).

20. Halo, *Not Even My Name*, 321.

21. Thea Halo, interview by Makis Provatas, "Thea Halo – Mnimi best seller" ["Thea Halo – Memory Bestseller"], *To Vima*, 9 September 2010.

22. Thea Halo, interview by Makis Provatas.

23. Halo, *Not Even My Name*, 133.

24. For example, Halo, *Not Even My Name*, 62–63.

25. These are the "Historical Notations" on p. 39–40, 117–27, and Chapter 15, "From the beginning of time," p. 98–101.

26. Halo, *Not Even My Name*, 125.

27. Halo, *Not Even My Name*, 126.

28. Although Halo never specified which sources she used, the testimonies referred to are in all likelihood drawn from Polychronis Enepekidis' and Konstantinos Fotiadis' research in Austrian and German archives.

29. Halo, *Not Even My Name*, 126–127.

30. Thea Halo, "Report on the IAGS Greek/Assyrian Genocide Resolution: Where We Go from Here?" in *Three Genocides, One Strategy*, ed. A. Pavlidis (Thessaloniki, 2008), 115.

31. George Andreadis, *Tamama – The Missing Girl of Pontos* (Athens, 1993). Director Yeşim Ustaoğlu has described her motives for addressing the Pontos issue in a press release by Silkroad Production, last accessed 2 April 2014, http://www.silkroad production.com/pdfs/presskit.pdf.

32. In an interview with the Lebanese-Armenian *Aztag Daily*, Halo claims that UCLA used the book in the training of teachers. It was also included on reading lists in women studies and courses on the end of childhood. Thea Halo, interview by Khatchig Mouradian, "Companions in suffering," *Aztag Daily*, 3 June 2007, last accessed 28 May 2014, http://headoverhat.blogspot.com/2007/06/interview-with-thea-halo.html.

33. Dean's mom Sofia, 19 May 2000 (2:54 pm), comment on Guestbook; Sophia Kokonas, 12 May 2000 (10:03 A.M.), comment on Guestbook, last accessed 2 April 2014, http://www.notevenmyname.com/12.html.

34. Chris Hedges, "A Few Words in Greek Tell of a Homeland Lost," *New York Times*, 17 September 2000, http://www.nytimes.com/2000/09/17/nyregion/a-few-words-in-greek-tell-of-a-homeland-lost.html.

35. http://www.ecclesia.gr/greek/holysynod/commitees/identity/identity_ethniki.html.

36. Halo, "Report," 109.

37. Giorgos Karabelias, "Katastrofi í genoktonia" ["Catastrophe or Genocide"], *Ardin*, no. 38–39 (November 2002), http://www.ardin-rixi.gr/archives/195214.

38. Apart from the AHIF, these Greek American organizations were mainly the Pan-Pontian Federation of the United States of America and Canada, and the Pan-Macedonian Association.

39. Proclamation of George E. Pataki, Governor of the State of New York, reproduced in Michalis Charalambidis, *The Pontian Question in the United Nations,* 2nd ed. (Thessaloniki, 2009), 196.

40. For a list of state proclamations, see http://www.notevenmyname.com/8.html.

41. For the recognition process in Australia, see http://neoskosmos.com/news/en/a-united-commemoration-for-the-victims-of-genocide.

42. Proclamation of Rod R. Blagojevich, Governor of the State of Illinois, 2006-134, Illinois Register, Vol. 30, Issue 17, 28 April 2006, 7, 997–98.

43. http://www.ilholocaustmuseum.org/pages/for-educators/illinois-holocaust-genocide-mandate/.

44. Public Act of the State of Illinois PA 094-0478.

45. Ronald Levitsky, "Teaching the Greek Genocide," in *The Genocide of the Ottoman Greeks: Studies on the State-Sponsored Campaign of Extermination of the Christians of Asia Minor, 1912–1922 and Its Aftermath: History, Law, Memory,* ed. T. Hofmann, M. Bjørnlund and V. Meichanetsidis (New York and Athens, 2011), 342. Cf. Nicole E. Vartanian, "'No Mandate Left Behind'? Genocide Education in the Era of High-Stakes Testing", in *The Armenian Genocide: Cultural and Ethical Legacies,* ed. R. Hovannisian (New Brunswick and London, 2007), 229–38.

46. Ronald Levitsky, *The Pontian Greek Genocide: A Teaching Unit* (Chicago, 2006).

47. Levitsky, "Teaching the Greek Genocide," 349.

48. [Constantine Hatzidimitriou et al.], "The Genocide of the Ottoman Greeks 1914–1923: A Teaching Guide" (Bloomingdale, IL, 2013).

49. Levitsky, "Teaching Unit," 6.

50. Levitsky, "Teaching the Greek Genocide," 344.

51. In this lesson, students are asked to study two photographs and contemplate what feelings the depicted orphans might have experienced at the different times their pictures were taken. The first photograph shows children lined up awaiting transport out of Turkey and conveys a mood of gloomy anticipation, while the second depicts happily smiling girls from the Anatolian interior bathing at sea at their destination in Greece. Students are asked which of the two occasions is likely to evoke stronger memories. The not too subtle implication of these before-and-after snapshots is the suggestion of redemption in Greece and gratitude toward the American benefactors.

52. Levitsky, "Teaching the Greek Genocide," 343.

53. Levitsky, "Teaching the Greek Genocide," 345.

54. The comparison was, however, the least elaborated element in the teaching unit. The main example of such common patterns, which Levitsky was able to demonstrate, was how "the Turks tried to hide their Greek captives from the Red Cross, just like the Nazis tried to deceive the Red Cross about conditions in concentration camps." Levitsky, "Teaching the Greek Genocide," 346–47.

55. Levitsky, "Teaching the Greek Genocide," 344.

56. Kristine Kim, "A Hidden Hell," quoted in Levitsky, "Teaching the Greek Genocide," 347–48.

57. For example, Adam Strom, "Teaching about the Armenian Genocide," in *The Armenian Genocide: Cultural and Ethical Legacies,* ed. R. Hovannisian (New Brunswick and London, 2007), 239–44.

58. Samantha Power, *"A Problem from Hell": America and the Age of Genocide* (New York, 2002), xviii.

59. Novick, *Holocaust in American Life,* 261.

60. A telling example is found in a rather incoherent paragraph about the "similar horrors" that befell the Greek population of Ottoman Thrace. First, readers are informed that three "Albanian-Turks" killed two young Christian men in order to frighten their community in May 1919. Then follows a lengthy quotation from a British press report from 26 October 1922, which describes the evacuation of Greek troops and local civilians across the river Evros in the aftermath of the Asia Minor Catastrophe. It is unclear what this is meant to demonstrate besides that awful events also took place in Thrace.

61. The most notable change was in the caption accompanying an often-reproduced photograph in Pontian genocide publications presenting it to be an authentic image of a death march. In fact, the picture was originally published in the National Geographic November issue 1925 and depicts expelled Christians en route from the Anatolian interior to the Black Sea ports, where foreign ships were waiting to evacuate them after the end of the Greco-Turkish war in late 1922. This point had been raised within activist circles supportive of Greek genocide recognition but critical of what they viewed as Fotiadis' and other Pontian scholars' distortion of evidence. The change in the caption was probably made to reflect this criticism.

62. The most conspicuous case was one of the oral testimonies attributed to a certain Ioannis Koktzoglou about a massacre that took place in the Pontian village of Ada in the Samsun area, in May 1919 according to the 2006 edition; in the summer of 1921 according to the 2013 edition. The dates were not the only source of confusion. In the original version of the teaching unit, Koktzoglou was quoted as saying that he was extremely fortunate because he had left the village the day before the massacre to join his uncle in the mountains, and that not one of the people remaining in the village escaped (Levitsky, "Teaching Unit," 16). In the 2013 edition, however, the sentence about the informant's absence from the scene of slaughter had been omitted, creating the impression that his testimony is a firsthand account of the event. The testimony itself had been expanded to include many gruesome details from the massacre that were not present in the previous version; details that convey the impression of a genuine eyewitness account. This need not mean that Koktzoglou was never present at the scene after the massacre or could not have either witnessed or heard about similar atrocities elsewhere, but it does cast doubt on the reliability of his testimony as a primary source. By withholding that information from students, the authors of the revised edition effectively erase all traces of ambiguity.

63. [Hatzidimitriou et al.], "Genocide of the Ottoman Greeks," 34.

64. J. Mowitt, "Trauma Envy," *Cultural Critique* 46 (Autumn 2000): 272–97.

65. Giles Milton, *Paradise Lost. Smyrna 1922: The Destruction of Islam's City of Tolerance* (London, 2008).

66. Giles Milton interview by Margarita Pournara, "'I katastrofi den egine dystychos mathima'" ["The Catastrophe Did Regrettably Not Become a Lesson"], *Kathimerini* 7/12 2008.

67. "Illinois Teachers Learn about the Greek Genocide," last accessed 10 April 2015, http://www.pontiangreeks.org/.

68. Notes from the conference "The Catastrophe in Asia Minor and Pontus" (Rosemont, IL, May 9–10 2008).

69. Novick, *Holocaust in American Life*, 258–59.

70. Halo, "Report," 114–15.

CHAPTER 6

"THREE GENOCIDES, ONE RECOGNITION"
THE "CHRISTIAN HOLOCAUST"

As the story of the Pontian Greek genocide was gaining ground in the Greek diaspora, while Greece was immersed in the textbook controversy over the proper description of the Smyrna catastrophe, another important development was underway. This was the decision made in 2007 by the International Association of Genocide Scholars to include the Pontian and Anatolian Greeks alongside the Armenians and the Assyrians in a call for joint recognition of their experiences as genocide. It gave a tremendous boost to the international credibility of the Greek genocide narrative(s), which still lingered in relative obscurity. This meant that the interpretation over the fate of the Ottoman Greeks as genocide or not was no longer the exclusive domain of national or otherwise intra-Greek debates. The "memory" of genocide was quietly becoming an international concern as non-Greek scholars took an interest in the case and joined their voices to the call for recognition. But as this internationalization, or "cosmopolitanization," of Greek suffering took place, the underpinning narrative gradually changed. The strategy to place one's own group within an ever expanding circle of victims meant that circumstances in the story presented to the world that seemed too nationally or ethnically peculiar came under attack as elements that blurred the larger picture. One casualty of this approach was the Pontian narrative of separate victimhood that had started the whole process of genocide recognition in the 1980s. The transition from ethnic and/or national to cosmopolitan memory entailed its own set of problems, questions, and rivalries, which will be addressed in this chapter.

Wooing the Genocide Scholars: The Politics of Academic Recognition

As noted already, the recognition offered by state legislative assemblies in America, though it was in a symbolical sense satisfying for immigrant communities, did little to raise public awareness. The real challenge was to enlist the support of internationally acclaimed experts. The attention to the Holocaust as well as the contemporary atrocities in Bosnia and Rwanda in the 1990s had contributed to the emergence of genocide studies as an academic field, which brought together scholars from an array of disciplines, interested in comparative research, with lay activists. Two professional organizations, the International Association of Genocide Scholars (IAGS) and the International Network of Genocide Scholars (INoGS), competed with each other by regularly organizing major conferences and publishing their own respective journals. The international forum provided by their conferences was a venue that until the early twenty-first century was overlooked by Greek advocates of genocide recognition. This omission was due to the political character of their priorities up until 2001, which favored domestic agenda setting over the establishment of international academic credentials. The narrow outlook of leading activists along with the often lack of English language proficiency were obstacles in the process of making the Greek genocide(s) a universal concern, a cosmopolitan memory.

This state of affairs was about to change. The key figure in this process was Thea Halo. In the years following her publication of *Not Even My Name*, she attended the conferences of the International Association of Genocide Scholars (IAGS), giving presentations about the tragedies of her Pontian and Assyrian forebears, and using the Q&A of panels on the Armenians to draw attention to the other Ottoman Christians.[1] It was there that she made the disappointing discovery that the scholars of the Armenian genocide, whom she had thought of as natural allies to the Greeks, were in many cases every bit an obstacle as the indifference of the Greek government, the ignorance of non-Greeks, and the denial of official Turkey. In her view, the failure of these scholars and many Armenian activists to acknowledge the parallel experiences of Pontian Greek and Assyrian Christians was not a result of mere oversight, "but an actual agenda of exclusion and denial."[2]

This was indeed a grave accusation; born out of resentment at the imbalance in the relation between victimized communities. While Pontians and other descendants of Anatolian Greeks perceive themselves as sharing the trauma of the Armenians, the latter have often seemed unwilling to reciprocate the courtesy. Notions of similar fate have certainly not been absent from the discourses of commemoration in the Republic of Armenia and the Armenian diaspora; especially at grass-roots level there is the occasional manifestation of sympathy for Assyrian and Greek victims.[3] However, scholars of the Armenian genocide have rarely addressed its possible connection with the fate of other minorities in the Ottoman Empire. To the extent that it is dealt with at all, the Greek case has been discussed as a counterpoint to that of the Armenians, rather than as a parallel experience. Rouben Paul Adalian contrasts the population exchange between Greece and Turkey, which allowed for the Ottoman Greek community's survival, against the physical annihilation of the Armenians in 1915, claiming this to be "the difference that makes a genocide."[4]

The genocide scholar Hannibal Travis, taking his cue from Greek and Assyrian activists, has sought to explain the reasons behind this perceived silence. According to Travis, scholars of the Armenian genocide are "complicit in an ongoing concealment of the Assyrian and Greek genocides."[5] Since the 1960s, when the first efforts for the commemoration and recognition of the events of 1915 were made, leading Armenian activists and scholars have, supposedly consciously, excluded other groups of victims from "their" genocide. The "construction of the 'Armenian Genocide'" was thus premised on neglect of the suffering of ethnically alien coreligionists, which Travis believes was once a universally known fact: "Prior to the 1960s, it was well established in diplomatic and scholarly communities that the Armenian genocide swept Assyrians and Greeks within a general anti-Christian persecution."[6] He argues that "misguided definitionalism" has led Armenian scholars to overemphasize the similarities between their own people's near total destruction and that of the Jews during the Holocaust so as to make their case for recognition stronger; thereby concealing the experiences of groups like the Ottoman Greeks, which had a larger ratio of survivors and thus do not as easily fit into the Holocaust paradigm. In some cases, silence has been due to lack of information on massacres targeting the other Christian populations, which discourages many scholars from taking the burden of explaining how their experiences relate to the Armenian. Finally, Travis suggests pragmatism to be an important factor in what he labels the denial of the Greek and Assyrian genocides. In a highly politicized context, it would be easier for Armenian lobbyists and sympathetic scholars to secure political recognition for one genocide than it would be to win recognition for three genocides.

There are several flaws in this analysis. One is that Travis blurs the distinction between cautious assessments, due to lack of information, and outright denial.[7] Ironically, he does not state the obvious fact that virtually no one spoke in public of the Armenian genocide before 1965. The annihilation of the Armenians was thus no more spoken about than the tragedies of the other Ottoman Christians, left unattended by the international scholarly and diplomatic communities.[8] In modern Armenian identity, the trauma of 1915 has become the defining collective experience in a way unparalleled among Greeks, who are in fact latecomers to the memory politics of genocide. Why scholars of the Armenian genocide should have included the Ottoman Greeks when the Greek state and society did not is a question left unanswered.

There is, however, something to be said for the observation that pragmatism played a role in many Armenian lobbyists' lack of interest in attaching Greek victims to their own call for recognition. Whereas Greek activists would welcome such an alliance, thereby sharing the moral credentials of the Armenian cause, it is unclear what their Armenian counterparts would gain from making common cause with them. Arguably, from a purely quid pro quo perspective the Greeks have little to offer the Armenians, with their already established trauma drama, besides lobby support for international recognition. From a scholarly point of view, although much could be said in favor of comparative approaches to the study of Ottoman minority policies, there are also valid reasons for not entangling the Armenian question with the Greco-Turkish conflict. Nonetheless the sparse treatment of other Christian victims of Turkish nationalism in Armenian scholarship and activism often comes off as niggardly and mean-spirited, in the eyes of some Greek and Assyrian activists. For Thea Halo, this "exclusion" of her ancestors from the community of sufferers was doubly painful when it came from "those who should know better." In her opinion, the Armenians did themselves a great disservice by not acknowledging "the Genocides of Pontic Greeks and Assyrians" for fear of having their own tragedy somehow diminished. Following her line of argument, the Armenian cause stood to gain from a larger perspective, which would show that the Young Turks' persecution of them had not been provoked by Armenian terrorism, as claimed by official Turkey, but reflected a genocidal campaign against all Christians of the Empire.[9] To restore truth and the memory of Pontian and Assyrian suffering for Halo meant to confront the "tribalism" of the Armenians.

At the 2005 conference of IAGS, Halo presented two papers that arraigned scholars of the Armenian genocide for their alleged failure to mention the Pontian Greeks and the Assyrians. According to her own account, she found staunch supporters in genocide scholars Henry Huttenbach and Adam Jones. The latter of the two, especially, would become a close ally and a key figure in the process of winning scholarly acceptance of the Greek genocide claim. Jones was an up-and-coming scholar at the time, with an ambition to influence the ethics of the field. He envisioned a democratic ethos, which would pay due respect to the victims of genocidal experiences everywhere in the world, without any implied hierarchies between groups of sufferers. "It is my view that a kind of Hippocratic oath should prevail in our field, proclaiming the right of *all* victims and survivors of genocide to receive due consideration and concern," Jones wrote in the journal of IAGS.[10] For him genocide research was an issue of morality that extended beyond the confines of academia, or what he may have considered the privileged perspectives of certain interest groups.

This was not an isolated view among genocide scholars. Indeed their field was in many respects an offspring of Holocaust studies; premised in part on the belief that knowledge of a wide variety of genocidal events will help to prevent future genocides. Trying to break free from the powerful Holocaust paradigm, which often tends to stress the unique quality of the event, seemingly making genocide synonymous with Jewish suffering, many genocide scholars have understandably pointed to similar experiences by other victims of the Nazis (e.g., the Roma), as well as other cases that illuminate the nature of mass violence. Indignation at the realpolitik behind which atrocities receive international condemnation has played a part in this as well. Israel's refusal to acknowledge the Armenian genocide for fear of damaging diplomatic ties to an important regional ally, Turkey, has sensitized many, including Holocaust scholars, to the danger of creating "hierarchies of victims"; especially since it is believed that this denial is also motivated out of a concern for the "exclusivity" of Jewish suffering, from which the State of Israel continues to draw legitimacy.[11] Critics rightly argue that if solidarity is primordial—that is, not extending beyond the boundaries of one's own community—the universalizing moral principles of today's Holocaust remembrance are undermined. Israel W. Charny, an Israeli-American psychologist and a scholar of Holocaust education who would come out in support of Thea Halo and Adam Jones, thus argues that the unwillingness of a group that has been victimized by genocide to recognize the suffering of others may blind them to the danger of becoming perpetrators themselves.[12] That is why he in 1997 supported a resolution of the Association of Genocide Scholars, as IAGS was called then, to have the Armenian genocide recognized alongside the

Holocaust. Ironically, it was now the Armenians that faced allegations of monopolizing suffering.

There was also a more scholarly dimension of this moral issue. The years between 2004 and 2008, when supporters of the Greek genocide narrative made their bid for international academic recognition, witnessed an explosion of comparative studies on genocide. It is within this context that the interest of genocide scholars like Jones in the Greek and Assyrian cases is perhaps best understood; or rather the inclination to look favorably on their recognition as genocidal events. A part of this trend was the unearthing of little-known and under-researched atrocities, which could, for example, bring new perspectives on the links between Western colonialism and Nazi policies in Eastern Europe. Added to this trend was also the reframing of "classic" genocides into larger entities, as a way of broadening the lens through which they had been previously studied and understood. In the comprehensive textbook on genocide studies that Jones has authored, the Rwandan genocide is thus planned to be presented as part of a larger continuum of inter-ethnic strife and genocidal violence in the African Great Lakes region in the decades since independence. The other "classic" case was the Armenian genocide, which Jones wished to reconfigure as "one of a number of intertwined anti-Christian genocides," which together added up to an "Ottoman holocaust."[13]

On 19 March, 2007, in view of IAGS's upcoming biannual conference, Adam Jones and Thea Halo proposed an amendment to the organization's 1997 resolution, which recognized the Armenian genocide. Jones, who drafted the proposed revision, stated that the Ottoman wartime persecution of minority populations "is usually depicted as a genocide against Armenians alone" in a way that disregarded the "qualitatively similar genocides" against other Christian groups in the empire. He therefore proposed the following clarification: "BE IT RESOLVED that it is the conviction of the International Association of Genocide Scholars that the Ottoman campaign against the Christian minorities of the Empire between 1914 and 1923 constituted a genocide against Armenians, Assyrians, and Pontian and Anatolian Greeks." Jones' argument for this inclusive approach, developed in a later publication, is that besides accommodating the Greek and Assyrian diasporas in the present it would highlight the general anti-Christian sentiment, as opposed to narrowly anti-Armenian, of Ottoman leaders like Sultan Abdul Hamid II. The view of the events during and after World War I as "a unified campaign against all the empire's Christian minorities" would also bring to light a more staggering cumulative death toll than previously believed—to the 1.5 million Armenian deaths would be added approximately 750,000 massacred Greeks and just as many exiled, along with roughly 250,000 Assyrians; all adding up to a total of 2.5 million Christians killed. Finally, this broader framing would sensitize the world to the current predicament of Middle Eastern Christians; most notably the Assyrians of Iraq, who after the U.S. led invasion in 2003 faced a similar threat to their existence as their forebears in 1915.[14] The proposal was met with enthusiastic approval from Israel W. Charny, the outgoing president of the Association.

However, some members of the organization's various boards and the resolution committee were not as readily convinced. Far from embracing the arguments presented by Jones, several scholars raised, in Charny's view, "tedious demands for additional scholarly documentation," which he claims were "calculated to stall and derail the resolution process."[15] The opponents included Stephen Feinstein, Eric Weitz, and Taner Akçam; all three of whom worked at the University of Minnesota's Center for Holocaust and Genocide Studies. Both Feinstein and Weitz were Holocaust scholars with a long-standing commitment to comparative genocide research and the cause of Armenian genocide recognition, while Akçam had made a name for himself as one of the foremost scholars of the Young Turks' policies of extermination. Akçam was at the time researching the archive of the Ottoman Interior Ministry for traces of the CUP's decisions concerning the Empire's minorities.[16] In his estimation, there was nothing that really indicated a policy to exterminate the Greeks, comparable to the genocidal scheme that targeted the Armenians. He, along with his colleagues, therefore questioned the wisdom of rushing to recognize something that had not yet been properly studied as being genocide. What IAGS needed was not new resolutions, but rather new research. "If we call this a genocide and make a resolution, we not only preempt any scholarly study in this area, but in doing so, also discredit the organization."[17]

The critics of the resolution did not dispute that other Ottoman Christians had suffered atrocities, which may or may not have been of genocidal nature, but they did point to a lack of documentation in support of the claims made by Halo and Jones. As a result, the authors now buttressed their proposal with a list of additional references. Besides mostly contemporary English-language press reports about atrocities against Greek-Orthodox Christians, Halo supplied a list of Greek book titles, while Jones read up on the Assyrian case.[18] Nonetheless, the skeptics remained to some extent unconvinced. It was not so much the case for recognizing the Assyrians' ordeal as essentially similar to the Armenian genocide that was called into question—with regard to this case Jones also relied heavily on an article by Hannibal Travis and a recent book by Swedish historian David Gaunt.[19] It was the corresponding notion of the Greek genocide that met with resistance. Looking at the list of references in support of it, one can begin to understand why. While the Assyrian section of the list is short, consisting mainly of the two recent scholarly publications whose validity was not questioned, the list of references compiled to substantiate the case for defining the Greek experience as genocide invites certain doubts. Halo and Jones were not visibly evaluating the relevance of some of the quotations and titles listed for the study of the events, or contradictions in some of the testimonies cited, with the result that the distinction between primary and secondary sources, and between scholarship, literary work and wartime propaganda, became unclear. The fact that the Greek section to a far greater degree than the Assyrian part of the list relied on material from an activist website (www.greek-genocide.org) may have contributed to the negative impressions, as well as the often confrontational approach of its defenders. Peter Balakian, who headed the resolution committee, summarized the reservations voiced by some of the critical scholars in a memo. "Some have noted that to claim that the moral nature of a historical event can be supported by quoting scattered passages from books reveals a lack of understanding of the scholarly process." The resolution in its current form, he argued, came off as "an oversimplified statement" that was not based on a scholarly assessment of the facts. "It would seem to follow that IAGS would not want to put its name to such a statement and compromise its reputation and integrity."[20]

The exchange now turned sour. The fact that almost all opponents of immediate recognition belonged to a single institution led to insinuations that their "joint policy decision" was rooted in a desire to appease some unknown funding source, although Charny claims that he never believed this. Instead he understood their positions as "expressions of a dynamic of insistence on an exclusive victim status of a given victim people to whom they are devoted, and to whose memorial they make huge contributions."[21] Halo was more candid in her assessment. Noting their commitment to the Armenian genocide and the Armenian American community, she viewed their objections in terms of purely tribal concerns, and pointed to what she viewed as double standards.

It is interesting to note that, except for one misrepresentation of the facts, all of the objections by Board members were based on a discussion of whether or not IAGS should continue to make such resolutions, even though I believe all those who objected had voted for the two resolutions on the Armenian Genocide. To change its policy on this issue after a resolution has been presented using existing policies, would be inappropriate. It also fosters the impression that the IAGS is disproportionately invested in Armenian issues.

As I noted in one of my rebuttals, it is tantamount to saying: My horse is safely in the barn, so let's lock the door.[22]

Both Charny and Halo pointed out that people in the Republic of Armenia had no difficulty in recognizing the victimhood of Greeks, and that the Armenian National Committee of America (ANCA) had marked the Pontian genocide remembrance day in May 2007, but that it nonetheless was the Armenian diaspora communities and their advocates in Europe and the United States that had been instrumental in obscuring the suffering of fellow Christians. For Halo, an essential task was to expose the "modes of denial" used by "both Turkish officials and various Armenian/American historians and their supporters." Charny, though not as personally involved with Assyrian or Greek issues as Halo, felt obliged to stand by her and Jones, since he perceived the critique as motivated by the same unwillingness to recognize the suffering of others as he as a Jewish intellectual had experienced in Israel on the subject of the Holocaust. The heated back-and-forth discussion on the merits of the resolution waged online on the association's blog and in emails between members made him, in his own words, heartbroken.

> There may also have been some honest intellectual skepticism and caution by some of these scholars who really want a clearer intellectual record than we have amassed in our western world for some of the other genocides or some aspects of them. But I was shocked and disappointed. The unpleasant IAGS battle caused me to lose some friendships that were dear to me for years, not because of any honest questioning or differences of opinion, but because of the adamancy and political strong-arming of the opposition, and in some cases even threats of resignation from the organization ... I simply could not understand the readiness of some of the opponents to rupture longstanding personal relationships or to leave the organization we had worked so hard to build because they disagreed about this resolution.[23]

Charny's account was and is still disputed by other scholars involved in the controversy. Although initially receptive to the resolution, Peter Balakian, who had once endorsed Thea Halo's narrative of the Pontian Greek genocide, began to reconsider various aspects of its text, under the influence of the perspectives offered by Akçam, Weitz, and other scholars. In a letter posted on the organization's website, he clarified the reasons for his doubts about the resolution, whose language he found "too general and without nuance given the complexity of these histories." He also reacted strongly to the pressure exercised by Charny to pass the resolution, and the "personal attacks and inflammatory accusations" against dissenters that characterized this campaign. "To call scholars in IAGS deniers is to be blind to who such scholars are and what their work has achieved over years. Such accusations are based on false rhetoric, and such rhetoric forces one to ask what agendas lie behind such behavior and on what understanding of intellectual work they are based."[24]

In the end, the resolution was put to the vote. Halo and Jones had initially hoped to present their amendment bid at the association's conference in Sarajevo in July 2007, but now had to settle for the incoming president Gregory Stanton's promise to have the vote at some later point in time, so that the members of IAGS would have more time to study the supporting evidence. It turned out that most of the IAGS members who participated in the electronic vote on the association's mailing list voted in favor of the new resolution. On 16 December 2007, a press release from the organization stated that the International Association of Genocide Scholars had voted overwhelmingly to recognize the genocides inflicted on Assyrian and Greek populations in the Ottoman Empire.[25]

This was without doubt a victory for what Jones terms the democratic ethos of genocide research. The secure majority of over 80% of participating IAGS members who voted in favor could easily be interpreted as a rejection of the primacy of hierarchies, scholarly and others, within the politics of genocide commemoration. Halo described it as "a victory for historical accuracy and inclusion."[26] The implications arguably went beyond the historical case in question, since the principle of plebiscite seemed to challenge traditional means of building scholarly consensus. There was without question an inherent conflict within the research field between agendas aiming to create justice for all victimized peoples and a more scholarly approach to the study of genocide; often referred to among genocide scholars as an activist-scholar divide.[27] It is evident that scholarly attention to past and present mass crimes owe a lot to activism and the struggle for human rights outside academia, but critics point out that activists and scholars pursue different strategies. "Whereas scholars are bound to scientific standards and objectivity, activists want to mobilize public opinion through the spread of simple truths." Therefore, argues the genocide scholar Dominik Schaller, "categorizations should be guided by scholarly principles and contribute to analytical insights, not to politics of memory," lest genocide research become "a victim of its own success."[28] At stake is the credibility of the research field. The real or perceived contest between activists or activist scholars and their non-activist counterparts reflects a larger phenomenon, in the sociology of knowledge called boundary-work, which scholars and scientists in a wide range of disciplines engage in to defend epistemic authority against attempts to encroach upon or exploit it for nonscientific purposes.[29] The confusion surrounding the definition of genocide and its applicability to different cases of mass killing or mass death certainly invites this kind of scholarly credibility contest. In Jones' view, this confusion is to be embraced, as it leaves the research field in a constant state of evolution and exploration. The concept of genocide, contested as it may be, is "one that can spur individuals to outrage and action, [binding] together a diverse and diffuse community of knowledge and practice." According to Jones, the pluralism of definitions and the inclusiveness of genocide studies prevents the rise of dominant schools—and hence implicitly also the rise of boundary-work in the service of dangerous hierarchies.[30]

Outrage and action were key goals for Jones. The reframing of the discourse on the Armenian genocide represented in his view a kind of humanitarian intervention, not only in the realm of remembrance, but also in contemporary crises by highlighting the vulnerability of genocide victims' descendants today.[31] It was his hope that the scholarly support for the resolution would raise public awareness about the Assyrian and Greek genocides, and help draw attention to the threat of genocidal attack faced by the Assyrian population of post-2003 Iraq. If anything, the recent wave of violence against religious minorities in that region has proven Jones right in his fears on that account. Nonetheless, his passionate activism may have led him and his supporters to cut a few corners in their historical interpretation of late Ottoman policies toward the different Christian minorities. The resolution established as a fact that Pontian and Anatolian Greeks, along with the Assyrians, had been killed on "a scale equivalent in per capita terms to the catastrophe inflicted on the Armenian population of the empire—by much the same methods, including mass executions, death marches, and starvation."[32] While this may in part have been the case—no one needs to and none of the resolution's opponents did doubt that these atrocities were crimes against humanity—the focus on the equivalency of death tolls between the aforementioned victimized groups as a criterion for genocide meant that the more vexed question of the leading perpetrators' intentions for each group was simply bypassed. Some of the testimonies cited in support of the resolution, notably those of Henry Morgenthau and Arnold Toynbee, actually point to differences in the treatment of Armenians and Greeks, which hint at an alternative interpretation of Young Turkish intentions toward the latter. The reluctance of Jones and Halo to consider other explanations was at the heart of much of the criticism by scholars, who insisted on an analytical separation of genocide from other atrocities. "How one determines that question is not through an accumulation of quotes from various people," argued Eric Weitz. "It is by rigorous analysis."[33]

Looking back at the IAGS controversy, the divisive issue was not whether Greeks or Assyrians had been the victims of genocide or not, but rather how the concept of genocide was to be understood and according to which principles such interpretations were made. For Weitz and like-minded skeptics, genocidal intent was the crucial issue. As long as the intent to kill a certain group "in whole or in part" could not be demonstrated, genocide would remain a meaningless label at best and a serious historical inaccuracy at worst. It is possible that the image of the Armenians' near total annihilation in 1915 strongly influenced these scholars' understanding of what genocide in an "ideal" sense is, to the effect that experiences that did not quite fit into this powerful paradigm were seen as something different. However, it should be pointed out that none of them seems to have questioned that the Assyrians were swept along in the deportations and massacres that targeted the Armenians and thus became part of their genocide, even if they had not been explicitly targeted.[34] Some of the skeptics also seem to have been less averse to the idea of characterizing the atrocities against Pontian Greeks as genocidal in nature, as conditions in northeastern Anatolia had differed from those in western Asia Minor, during the Great War and the subsequent Greek military occupation.[35] For Jones and Halo, on the other hand, the testimony of victims or those sympathetic to them was the point of departure in all discussions about genocide, and since they made no distinction between the experiences of (Western) Anatolian Greeks and their kin in Pontos (or between Greeks and Armenians or Assyrians), the finer nuances were lost in the exchange. The significance of such distinctions would, however, be an apple of discord among activists of Greek genocide recognition.

From Ethnic Victimhood to National to Religious Holocaust: The Assault on the Pontian Genocide Narrative

The validation provided by IAGS to the claim that the Ottoman Greek ordeal was in fact genocide represented a major breakthrough in the making of the "Greek genocide" trauma, though not much publicized in either Greek or international media. More importantly, it reflected a change in the discourse about this presumed genocide among those concerned with its promotion. From 2007 and onward, the lobbyist Vlasis Agtzidis explicitly referred to a "Christian Holocaust" in articles published in the Greek national press. Construed as a parallel to the Jewish Holocaust, it was presented as encompassing Christians of all denominations and linguistic groups in the Ottoman Empire, with a total of four million dead; at least one million of which were presumably Anatolian Greeks.[36] The circle of victims (and numbers) had been significantly expanded since the 1980s, when Agtzidis and his fellow activists had made their original plea for recognizing what they assumed to be the 353,000 victims of the Pontian genocide. It was, however, a process that was fraught with inner contradictions and dispute. For while Thea Halo and her supporters sought the international recognition of Pontian victimhood by building alliances with Assyrians and combating the perceived hegemony of Armenians in the "hierarchy of victims," other activists in Greece and the diaspora sought to accomplish something similar by knocking down the perceived Pontian "exclusivity of suffering." This took the form of a general assault on the core of the past twenty-odd years of Pontian identity politics, in which even the historical reality of the alleged Pontian genocide became a target.

The roots of the new orientation can be traced to the often bitter power struggles and personal antagonisms between leading figures within the Pontian organizations from the mid-1990s and onward. More specifically, a long-standing grudge between Michalis Charalambidis, founder of KEPOME and author of the Pontian "right to memory" manifesto, and Vlasis Agtzidis, formerly of the group Argo, played a pivotal role.[37] The latter described this antagonism in a document prepared for the board of the Pan-Pontian Federation of Greece (POE) in early 2006, later published on various Pontian websites.[38] Agtzidis' document was a long list of grievances, including accusations of embezzlement, which targeted what he called the "Charalambidis-Fotiadis group." Of particular interest in this document is his assessment of the Pontian identity-political project and the repercussions of his critique on the genocide narrative. According to Agtzidis, Charalambidis and his close friend Konstantinos Fotiadis had sought to monopolize the genocide issue and use it to further their own political careers and economic interests. To this end, they had presented the genocide as their own discovery that would "deliver the Pontians from historical extinction," while marginalizing other perspectives within refugee circles as well as sabotaging independent initiatives to promote the agenda of recognition. What Agtzidis found to be the worst was the narrowness of perspective cultivated by Charalambidis and his supporters, by which the Pontian historical experience was being isolated from that of other Anatolian Greeks, and, indeed, the Greek nation itself. In this fashion, he argued, the Pontians were portrayed as a separate ethnic group, alien to the Greek nation state and to other Greeks, and set on a path of futile dreams of return to the ancient homeland, as demonstrated in the "Charalambidis-Fotiadis group's" enthusiasm for the "national liberation struggles" of Armenian and Kurdish terrorist organizations like ASALA (Armenian Secret Army for the Liberation of Armenia) and the PKK of Abdullah Öcalan.

Ironically, this was precisely the critique that elderly Pontian Greek intellectuals had directed at the zealots of the Second Global Pontian Congress in 1988, and which a young Agtzidis then had dismissed. It does not mean, however, that he had come full circle since the time he defended the *"new discourse* on Pontian history and prospects." Unlike these critics, who had also disputed the scholarly foundation of the genocide claim, Agtzidis wished to stress genocide as a defining experience shared by all Greeks of the Ottoman Empire as well as other Christian groups in Anatolia. To this end, he attacked Charalambidis and Fotiadis for not having come out in support of the recognition of the Asia Minor Greek genocide in the clash over the presidential decree in 2001, choosing instead to stress the difference between Pontos, where the Kemalists had reigned unchecked, and the parts of Western Anatolia where the Greek army had operated between 1919 and 1922. This insistency on particularistic features had, in Agtzidis' view, had a negative outcome on the efforts to win political recognition of the genocide.

> The dynamic of the claim was diminished from the outset. A part of a nation was transformed into a particular nation, because the demand for genocide recognition only applies to entire nations (Armenians, Jews, Gypsies, Assyrian-Chaldeans, Aboriginals, Native Americans, et al.). On the other hand, it distorted the real History and cultivated a false image of the Pontian population's recent past. For the genocide, which was first decided upon by the Turkish nationalists in 1911 in Ottoman Thessaloniki concerned all the Christians of the Empire and was carried out against all the Christian groups (Greeks, Armenians and Assyrian-Chaldeans). The genocide of the Greeks took different forms according to location ... In no instance, however, was the genocide to be confined only to the territory of Pontos (mainly its western part). Besides, the Turkish nationalists did not cleanse the Pontians (an unknown term at the time) but the *Romioi*, i.e. the Greek Christians.[39]

If the Pontian Greeks wished to make an impact at an international level, Agtzidis continued, they would have to stop acting in isolation as a local group, which "demands the recognition of the genocide they suffered, outside the boundaries of the nation to which it belongs." Nationalization was thus a precondition for internationalization. Although Charalambidis had stressed the shared martyrdom between Pontians and Armenians, he was blamed for the lack of efforts to cooperate with Armenians and Assyrians in a joint international information campaign. Making the case of a broader approach, overcoming all local differences, Agtzidis presented an outline of what he would later dub the Christian Holocaust.

A first condition for the success of the demand for international recognition of the genocide would be that instead of having the size of the population reduced, it would have to take the greatest possible extent and to acquire the greatest possible dynamic. That is, the first condition would be for us to refer to the genocide of the Christians and to strive to integrate into this demand the Armenians as well, who have been very successful in the documentation and promotion of their historical experience.

A second condition would be for us to partake in the struggle for the internationalization and recognition of the genocide as Greeks of the East that is ours, as is natural. Only within our own communities in Greece is it meaningful to mourn separately for our [respective community's] particular fate, which in any case was different, in Samsun, in Bafra, in Sanda, in Trebizond, or in Kars. For the fate of Western Pontos, with the armed guerilla movement and the cooperation with the Russian army during World War I, was much closer—as far as the intensity of the persecutions by Turkish nationalism is concerned—to [the fate of] Ionia than was the case with the Trebizond region or, even more, Kars.[40]

Agtzidis' line of argument, in which nationalization and cosmopolitanization were mutually reinforcing, was picked up by activists in the diaspora, for whom the existence of the (rivaling) Pontian genocide narrative was a major obstacle for a wider international awareness of Greek suffering at the hands of the Turks. The web editors of the site www.greek-genocide.org set up in 2006 with the objective of providing information in English even linked to a separate website dedicated solely to the purpose of exposing the "distortions, misconceptions and falsehoods" of the Pontian genocide.[41] "This website," declared its anonymous webmasters, "outlines the distasteful and grossly inaccurate approach to the genocide of Greeks in the Ottoman Empire by certain members of our community; in particular, re-writing history in order to elevate Pontic Greek suffering above all other Ottoman Greeks in what can only be described as an act of exclusivity of suffering." They also cited an online poll organized in 2009 at PontosWorld.com, in which, mimicking the electronic voting procedure of IAGS, the site's visitors were asked whether they felt that the term "Greek Genocide" should be used in place of "Pontian Genocide." The result of approximately 90% of an unspecified number of participants in favor was cited as sending "a clear message to all Pontian organisations worldwide, that the use of the term 'Pontian Genocide' is not only insulting towards the other Greeks who were massacred during the same period, but also wrong in that it doesn't reflect historical fact ... The use of the term 'Greek Genocide' is non-discriminatory and includes all Greeks affected."[42]

That important differences really were at stake was ostensibly demonstrated in March 2010 when the Parliament of Sweden voted to recognize the Ottoman persecution of Christians in 1915 as genocide. It was the first time that a national parliament outside Greece and Cyprus had extended recognition to Greek victims of this crime. However, what at first seemed to be a major triumph for activists concerned with recognition of the Greek genocide turned out to be only half a victory. Despite the fact that the authors of the Swedish bill made explicit reference to the IAGS resolution of 2007, which recognized the genocidal campaign against Anatolian and Pontian Greeks alike, the text adopted by the Riksdag only mentioned the latter as co-victims of the Armenians and the Assyrians/Chaldeans.[43] The reason for this omission (in all likelihood unintentional) was that the bill had been attached to earlier interpellations and motions by Swedish MPs of Pontian Greek descent, who at the time had only called for the recognition of the events in Pontos as genocide.[44] Since only the allegedly 350,000 victims in Pontos received mention in these texts, whereas Assyrian victims were estimated at half a million and Armenians as many as 1.5 million, the recognition seemed to imply that (Pontian) Greek suffering was the least significant among the Christian groups in terms of casualties. This was precisely how supporters of the wider, nationalized Greek genocide definition perceived the matter. "What happened in Sweden was a shameful act," exclaimed the Greek-Australian activist Aris Tsilfidis at the online forum PontosWorld.com. "The Pontic Greeks didn't even think of including their [dead] brothers and sisters; the Greeks from outside Pontus in this resolution."[45] Another contributor to the site rhetorically asked whether the organizations who insisted on referring to the Pontian genocide should be labeled genocide deniers, stressing that there was no excuse to persist in an erroneous assumption after the recognition by IAGS of a "unified" genocide in Anatolia.[46]

A less emotional response was provided by the activist and independent researcher Nikolaos Hlamides, who called for a more scholarly approach to the subject. He argued that the Pontians did themselves a great disservice by "failing to incorporate the broader history" in their demand for recognition. In his view, the emphasis on circumstances that were specific to the Pontos, where there had been armed resistance by the local Greek population and collaboration with the invading Russians during the Great War, made it easier for Turkish officialdom to discredit the genocide interpretation.

> Without taking into account the fate of Greeks elsewhere in the Empire, it becomes almost impossible to effectively lay down the arguments for genocide but as soon as one is prepared to broaden the context of the genocide campaign, the denialist thesis immediately disintegrates. To give but one

example, being able to point to the deportation of Greek men, women and children from, say, Konya in central Turkey completely undermines revisionist narratives which suggest that deportations were conducted on the grounds of military necessity. In light of the above, attempts to define a detached and localized genocide in the Pontus region are morally and historically untenable and all parties should be encouraged to attach precedence, first and foremost, to the historical record.[47]

Hlamides' critique also highlighted another obstacle for the recognition of the "Greek genocide" apart from the perceived Pontian hegemony in the "hierarchy of victims," which was the lack of scholarship on the subject. In his view, the organizations of the Greek diaspora had to date been more concerned with securing recognition from third parties than with building a convincing case through research and serious scholarship, which would contribute to the collective understanding of the period. "Recognition could then adopt the far more fitting role of being predicated on a vast and established body of scholarly literature."[48] This was an assessment that activists could agree upon, regardless of whether they were in favor of the "traditional" understanding of a genocide affecting mainly the Pontians or supporters of the new and more inclusive conception of the (Ottoman) Greek genocide. "History isn't fact until it is written about," stated the Greek-American scholar Theofanis Stavrou in the opening session of a conference on the Catastrophe, dedicated to strategies on how to promote awareness about the "Greek genocide(s)" among the North American public.[49] Another speaker at the same conference, George Shirinian, representing the Zoryan Institute for Armenian Genocide Studies, stressed the importance of the Pontian Greek genocide in the larger field of human rights studies, but reminded the audience that the resolution of IAGS did not mean that the academic case for recognition had been made. In his view, IAGS had only established that mass killing occurred as a favor to the activists, but that the evidence needed to build the legal case for genocide was still missing. The support of scholars in appeals to governments was one thing, but the Greeks in his opinion still lacked strong documentation and a good argument, which he believed translations of Greek scholarly works would yield.[50] Also scholar-activists like Harry Psomiades and Theofanis Stavrou agreed that the problem of what had been written on the subject so far was that most of it did not meet scholarly standards; being of a generally descriptive nature, with little in terms of analysis and synthesis.

During the years since IAGS passed its resolution, activists have attempted to achieve a more scholarly profile, with recurring conferences that sometimes have resulted in edited collective volumes. The Asia Minor and Pontos Hellenic Research Center, set up by leading members of the Chicago-based Pontian Society "Xeniteas," has in recent years spearheaded such initiatives, in the ambition to become for "Greek genocide" studies what the Zoryan Institute has been for Armenian. The advice presented by George Shirinian at the conference in 2008 was of a concrete nature, which emphasized the universal over the particular, so as to attract scholars from outside the ethnic community. The success of Armenian scholarship was based on the ability to view one's issues in a broader context, with attention both to contemporary developments elsewhere in the world and to analytical comparison with similar experiences of other nations, using the perspectives of multiple disciplines. Among the benefits of such a scholarly approach, argued Shirinian, was that the anger and emotionalism of sensitive issues would be eliminated. The Armenian-American scholar Richard Hovannisian, who had been among those who had expressed reservations about the IAGS resolution in 2007, made a similar remark in a speech addressed to the Pontian Greek community of Chicago, on account of the 19 May memorial day in 2010. Division among victims is a serious impediment to remembrance, noted Hovannisian. Armenians had often been critical of how Jews excluded them when speaking of genocide, while being blamed themselves by Greeks and Assyrians for taking the spotlight. "Everyone wants to be remembered, to be included." But before pointing fingers at others, Greeks and Assyrians would have to do their homework, and "learn to use a megaphone," instead of expecting others to speak on their behalf. For Hovannisian, this meant adopting a more professionalized and universalistic discourse.

> In the first book I edited, most of the authors were Armenian and almost all wrote descriptive chapters. They cited what [US Ambassador to the Porte Henry] Morgenthau or the *New York Times* had said but didn't dig deeper into analysis and interpretation. There was the need to draw upon the foreign sources to validate the reality of genocide. It is now a quarter century since that first book, and I am pleased that the authors of my more-recent fourth and fifth volumes have come from diverse backgrounds, including progressive Turkish scholars. Non-Armenians have made the Armenian Genocide an important object lesson in trying to understand and prevent the phenomenon of genocide. That is the direction in which the Greeks, Assyrians, and others who feel left out also need to be moving.[51]

Studying the scholarly output of Greek activists and their supporters, one is left with the impression that the professionalization and cosmopolitanization of the Ottoman Greek genocide narrative still remain

in the early stage described by Hovannisian. Contributions to edited
volumes on the subject tend to quote contemporary sources at length,
with little attention to analytical questions and methodological issues
regarding the reliability of often manipulated statistical data concerning
Ottoman demographics and heavily biased accounts of wartime atrocities issued by both parties of the Greco-Turkish conflict.[52] The Greek
scholar-activists also face economic obstacles, such as lack of funding
for their research, and the hitherto failure to attract prestigious publishers with significant distribution channels, which inevitably restrain
the much hoped-for impact.

Nonetheless, there are scattered signs of a growing interest in the experiences of other Ottoman minorities within the field of Armenian genocide studies, which might work to their advantage. Under the battle cry
"Three genocides, one strategy, one voice, one recognition, one healing,"
Greek and Assyrian diaspora activists have come together in commemorative activities, sometimes also with the support of their Armenian
counterparts, such as in the jointly organized conference "The Ottoman
Turkish Genocides of Anatolian Christians: A Common Case Study,"
held at the Illinois Holocaust and Educational Center in May 2013.[53]
Such initiatives indicate a change underway in the conceptualization
of the "Greek genocide," away from the emphasis on national experience
toward an understanding of Greek suffering as part of a greater drama
that recognizes no national or narrowly ethnic boundaries. Instead of
seeking international recognition of the "Greek genocide" as a separate
event, the future seems to lie in making sense of it as part of a Christian
Holocaust in the Ottoman lands, in which Greek victims were indistinguishable from those of the Armenian and Assyrian communities. In an
op-ed on the web-based magazine *Armenian Weekly*, posted in June
2013, the philosopher Henry Theriault argued that it would no longer
be possible to study the Armenian genocide in isolation, or approach
the Greek and Assyrian tragedies as "simply a matter of adding two
cases to a set of Ottoman-Turkish genocides." A truly comprehensive
understanding of the mass killing of Armenians required, in his view, an
approach to their catastrophe as well as those of other Christian groups
as a unified genocidal process.[54]

The idea of unity in suffering at the hands of a common perpetrator
also draws on the recent tragedy of the Middle East and a perceived continuity between that and the late Ottoman era. As we have seen, one of
Jones' intentions behind the resolution in 2007 was to bring the world's
attention to the present threat that Iraqi Christians, descendants of the
Young Turks' Assyrian victims, faced in a country torn by war and religious intolerance. In that way, knowledge of past atrocities would serve

one of the original purposes of the convention that Raphael Lemkin had drafted for the United Nations; prevention. The dramatic rise of ISIS after Syria's and Iraq's descent into chaos has served to reinforce the perception of a shared trauma with Assyrians among Greek activists eager to point out links between today's jihadists and the Young Turks' and Kemalists' hatred for things Christian. The scholarly version of these analogies is to be found in the writings of the aforementioned scholar of law Hannibal Travis, who has recently argued that the situation in 2014, in which Turkey, ever the denier of Christian victimhood, was said to have abetted a terrorist victory in Syria and benefited from it, was more or less identical to the geopolitics leading up to the "Armenian-Assyrian-Greek genocide."[55]

There are, however, also potential drawbacks from attaching one's cause too closely to that of others for those who seek to identify Greeks as victims of genocide. It is unclear from the wording of the IAGS resolution whether the mass murder of Christians is to be understood as three separate genocides or one all-encompassing. There is thus the risk that the notion of ethnicity might disappear if the three genocide narratives merge into one. Thea Halo was aware of the problem but remained optimistic:

> I do think what happened in Turkey was a Christian Genocide. But I don't think one can simply use that term without differentiating who the Christians were, because although the Assyrians, Greeks, and Armenians lived in the same land for thousands of years, their languages, cultures and histories were unique. It's important to acknowledge that there was an Armenian, Assyrian, and a Greek Genocide, but overall there was a Genocide of the Christian of Asia Minor. I even differentiate between the Asia Minor Greeks; the Ionians, Pontians, and Cappadocians, first because the Pontians had their own empire [1204–1461], and second, because I think it's important that we remember their distinctive historical names and regions in Asia Minor.[56]

Nonetheless, in the resolution that she co-authored with Adam Jones, the Chaldeans, Assyrians and Syriacs had for practical reasons been lumped together in one category as Assyrians. The ambition to do justice to the distinctive historical name (whose historicity some even doubted) and geographical provenience of each victim group was not easily reconciled with efforts to make sense of their suffering in a broader context, in which ethnic markers or complex religious denominations dating back to the schisms of the early Church seem to matter less than the things uniting these groups. The common feature of the victims was found in their religion; they had died as Christians at the hands of Muslims.

Interestingly, this point was also reflected in Agtzidis' critique of the Pontian identity politics of the "Charalambidis-Fotiadis group," despite the nationalizing nature of his argument. For Fotiadis, the existence of the so-called Crypto-Christians of Pontos—that is, converts to Islam who had covertly preserved their Christian beliefs and mores, which was the subject of his doctoral thesis—vindicated his and Charalambidis' belief that the "Pontian question" was still alive in northeastern Turkey, as these people were exempted from the population exchange in 1923. In the eyes of Pontian activists in Greece during the 1980s and 1990s, the Crypto-Christians, who in some cases preserved traits of the old Pontian Greek dialects, were every bit as "lost kin" as the Soviet Greeks, waiting to be reclaimed for Hellenism, as their hidden Christianity was thought to be a dormant Greek national consciousness. Agtzidis criticized this assumption as being misguided, since their conversion to Islam, whether forced or not, had happened centuries ago. "At the time of the final Greco-Turkish clash in Pontos, which really was a clash between Christianity and Islam, the Christians and Greek-speaking Muslims were in opposite camps," wrote Agtzidis, arguing that the only result of acting as spokesmen for these Muslims of Greek descent, arbitrarily labeled Crypto-Christians, had been to draw the suspicious attention of Turkish security services to their existence.[57]

What is significant in this reading of Pontian history is the implication it has for the interpretation of the conflict underpinning the genocide as religious rather than national. There may not have been any contradiction in Agtzidis' mind between these understandings, as the Church of Greece has traditionally been successful in making Orthodoxy synonymous with Greek national identity. However, the understanding of annihilation as an ecumenical experience, affecting not only Greek-Orthodox Christians, points to a different direction for remembrance of the "Greek genocide." A scholar of Greek religious thought has suggested that the recent economic crisis in Greece may have discredited the idea of the nation in its current form to the extent that citizens might be more ready to embrace alternative conceptions of identity, including an ecumenical understanding of Christianity.[58] A similar prognosis has surfaced in some of Agtzidis' recent writings on the crisis, which has added a new layer to his and other activists' disappointment with the Greek state's perceived indifference to genocide recognition. One should of course be cautious in making such assessments, as the notion of national belonging has so far proven more resilient to the onslaught of globalization than what some theorists expected. The turn toward religiously defined identities suggested by the concept of an Ottoman Christian holocaust can be interpreted as responding to a similar development in Turkey that has been underway ever since AKP, the Islamist party of Recep Tayyip Erdoğan, rose to power in the early twenty-first century. In the "post-Kemalist" order that has emerged after a decade of power struggles between the old establishment and the new, Turkish nationalism has veered toward a less secular understanding of nationhood, which emphasizes continuity with the Ottoman Empire and its aspirations to dominate the Muslim world. In this perception of Ottoman history, the Young Turks have been recast not as modernizers of a backward empire and heralds of a Western-style national movement, but as the defenders of Islam in an apocalyptic struggle against the encroachment of Christian states.[59]

Such fundamentalist readings of past and present realities tend to reinforce each other. For those who view the world as the battleground in an ongoing clash of civilizations, the history of a Christian holocaust or alternatively the last stand of the Ottoman Empire fits all too well into established templates. On websites dedicated to conspiracy theories about "Eurabia," the plight of Ottoman Greeks is imbued with meaning as a cautionary tale about the current "Islamic threat" against the Christian world.[60] This kind of attention may lead to unwelcome surprises, such as the awkward discovery that the Norwegian terrorist Anders Behring Breivik referred to the "genocide of Greek Christians" in Smyrna 1922 as the culmination of the "anti-Christian jihad" in his infamous manifest.[61] While this is an extreme example of how the notion of a Christian Holocaust can be abused to justify murder in the name of religious and cultural belonging, there are other examples that point to the dangers involved in overemphasizing the shared martyrdom of Christians. An illustration of this is to be found in Travis' above-mentioned piece on the lessons of the Ottoman genocides for the contemporary Middle East, in which the genocide scholar casually observes that the "Bosnian civil war, which Turkey strongly supported along with Pakistan, reduced the Serbian Christian population of Bosnia and Herzegovina by almost 300,000 persons from 1991 to 1997."[62] What is implicitly claimed here is that Muslim countries, not Serb leaders, were the instigators of the war in Bosnia, and that Serbian Christians were its chief victims, despite the fact that Serb forces held the upper hand for most of its duration. The reconfigured history of the "Armenian-Assyrian-Greek" genocide can thus be used to alter perceptions of causality in other, unrelated cases of human rights violations. The image conveyed is one of perennial Christian victimhood and Muslim aggression, regardless of local contexts. It takes little imagination to realize how dangerous the path that Travis treads on might be.

Recognition Activism, Minority Concerns, and the Issue of Greek-Turkish Reconciliation

There are, however, alternative pathways for the remembrance of the "Christian Holocaust." The recent decade has also seen the emergence of a new willingness among some Turkish intellectuals to address the history that led to the destruction of Turkey's Christian communities in earnest. For such individuals, knowledge of this hitherto repressed past holds the key to a democratic future, by exposing the lies of state authoritarianism; presenting in its stead the multicultural society that once was or might have been. The common denominator for most of them is an involvement with left wing radicalism at university campuses, which led to their persecution during the military rule of the 1980s. A window of opportunity for dissident intellectuals came in the early years of the twenty-first century, a key moment in Turkey's modern history when Kemalist hegemony was not yet completely shattered and AKP hegemony not yet fully established, which allowed for a relative openness in debates of the nation's past.[63] Milestones in this process were the groundbreaking conference on the Armenian genocide at Bilgi University in 2005 and the demonstrations following the murder of Turkish-Armenian journalist Hrant Dink in 2007. Attempts at Turkish-Armenian rapprochement, eventually stalled, led Turkish Premier Erdoğan to at least momentarily try the politics of regret, although his condolences to the Ottoman Armenians' descendants never amounted to genocide recognition or admission of national guilt.

Public discussions tend to focus on the plight of the Armenians, as they are the Christian community that has received the most coverage in Turkish and international media, but there are also some signs of interest in the fate of the Ottoman Greeks. Hidden ethnic identity among Greek-speaking Muslims in Pontos and the trauma of separation from Christian relatives in the population exchange was the subject of Turkish director Yeşim Ustaoğlu's movie *Waiting for the Clouds (Bulutlari beklerkeri)* in 2003.[64] While avoiding taking sides in the Greek-Turkish dispute regarding the Pontian Greek genocide issue, Ustaoğlu made a plea for tolerance and expressed hopes that Turkey's accession talks with the EU would further understanding for ethnic and cultural diversity.[65] Others have taken an interest in exploring local cultural identities in Pontos that allegedly transcended religious boundaries, as part of a postmodern critique of Kemalist views on national identity. As one Turkish dissident put it in an interview, it was easier to address the persecution of the Pontian Greeks in public debate than it was with the case of the Armenians, because the characterization of the formers' experience as genocide had not yet been as firmly established.[66] In his view, there was no real reason not to label the gruesome persecution of Pontian Greeks and Assyrian/Aramaic/Chaldean Christians genocide, just as the Armenians had been the victims of that crime, even if scholars argued about the differences. Other intellectuals maintain the separation between the Armenian genocide and the Greek expulsion, but hold them morally equivalent, as all Ottoman Christian groups as well as some Muslim minorities like the Alevi and the Kurds are in their own right victims of Turkish state nationalism. Naturally, Greek activists for genocide recognition view them as allies, but their agendas in many respects differ from each other. Whereas many of the former view the genocide issue in terms of irreconcilable differences between the Greek and Turkish nations, or between Christianity and Islam, the Turkish intellectuals' interest in the plight of the Ottoman Christians is mainly dictated by concerns for Turkey's present and future. Nonetheless, it is not impossible that they can make a contribution toward a more cosmopolitan reconfiguration of the Greek or Christian "holocaust," although their impact in Turkey is limited by lack of numbers and the recent nationalist backlash that came as a result of stalled negotiations with the EU and Erdoğan's increasingly authoritarian leadership.

It is ironic that the sort of liberal and leftist intellectuals that in Turkey appear supportive of Greek activism for genocide recognition, in Greece tend to oppose these demands. The reasons for this have largely been discussed in the previous chapters, but there is yet another factor to be addressed, if only briefly; the relation between the genocide issue and that of the Muslims of Greece, of which there are, in broader terms, two types of communities. The first and most diverse is the immigrants that have come to Greece over the past few decades from Albania, Pakistan and a number of other Muslim-dominated countries, with no specific legal status in Greek society. The second type is the Muslim minority in Greek Thrace, whose right to remain and freedom of worship (including the right to Islamic education in their own schools) were grudgingly recognized by the Greek state in the Treaty of Lausanne, in exchange for the exemption made for the Patriarchate and the Greek community of Constantinople, as well as those of the islands Imvros (Gökçeada) and Tenedos (Bozcaada), from the forced swap of populations. The Thracian Muslims' status as a protected community, and their absence from the quarrels that marred Greece in the decades following the Asia Minor Catastrophe, meant that they by 1950 were the only minority to remain in larger numbers inside the country. In that sense, they were the only ones standing between Greek nationalists and the fulfillment of the latter's ideal of national homogeneity. As long as Athens and Ankara remained on the friendly terms initiated by Venizelos in 1930, the existence of these over 100,000 Muslims on Greek soil was not regarded as a threat to national security; some members of the minority even started to identify themselves as Turks under the influence of secular Kemalist ideology, with little interference or objection from Greek authorities.

However, the main reason why the Greek state tolerated them was because they in essence were hostages meant to ensure Turkey's good behavior toward the Greek Christians of Istanbul. Even moderate Greeks, who pledge allegiance to liberal democracy, have tended to regret the "softness" of previous Greek regimes for allowing a pocket of Turkish nationalism in Greece, asking why their country should fulfill its end of the Lausanne bargain while Turkey has ruthlessly persecuted and expelled the Greek-Orthodox communities of Istanbul and northern Cyprus.[67] The continuously deteriorating relation between the two states led the PASOK government of the 1980s to close down public associations of Thracian Muslims that carried the word "Turkish" in their names; thereby sparking off civil unrest, which in its turn fueled Greek fears about the "Trojan horse" of Turkey and its supposed irredentist designs toward Western Thrace.[68] Only in the 1990s when Greece found itself shamed by international organizations for violating the minority's human rights were policies reversed. Under the impact of further European integration and Greece's transformation into something resembling a multicultural society, legal, economic and educational measures were introduced to combat the social exclusion of the Thracian Muslims.[69] Nonetheless, this process has not been without its setbacks, due to local suspicion of both the state and the neighboring Christian and Muslim communities.

It is to some extent also in this context of intercommunal tensions in the eastern borderlands of Greece that the genocide narrative finds resonance. The Greek state had consciously sought to populate this region, contested by Greece, Turkey, and Bulgaria alike, with the newcomers from Anatolia in order to forge a secure Greek majority. The refugees, many of which arrived from Pontos in 1924, were, understandably given the circumstances, less inclined to view their new Muslim neighbors kindly, and sought to make the most of their newfound role as the dominant community. As two scholars of Greek national and minority education have recently noted, "the coexistence of first- and second-class citizens nurtures authoritarian attitudes and drives the hegemonic group to defend its status, and maintain its socio-economic privileges."[70] This ambition was evident in one of Michalis Charalambidis' pet projects; the dream of building an entire new town, called Romania, which was supposed to become the spiritual metropolis of Pontian culture (or a "Pontian Disneyland," as some critics had it) as well as being a bulwark of Hellenism in Thrace.[71] Pontian activists as well as national-ist politicians have repeatedly drawn on the old state narrative on how the refugees "manned" the sensitive borderlands, while stressing the importance of genocide remembrance among the Pontians in keeping this corner of Greece Greek.[72] When Georgios Papandreou as foreign minister and, later, as leader of PASOK aired the possibility of giving Thracian Muslims greater freedom to call themselves Turks, and encour-aged members of the minority to engage more actively with Greek pol-itics, his initiatives were met with allegations about the Muslims' lack of national loyalty to Greece and denial of the Pontian Greek genocide. This has led left wing intellectuals and critical journalists like Tasos Kostopoulos to charge the advocates of genocide recognition with creat-ing "simulated wounds" in order to justify the repression and eventual expulsion of the country's remaining Muslims.[73]

The role of the genocide narrative in perpetuating the exclusion of this minority from Greek society is but one aspect of the still larger, many-layered issue of a possible Greek-Turkish reconciliation. There are different ways in which such a reconciliation can be conceived, and the question is of course to what extent the recognition of a Greek, or more broadly Christian, genocide helps or hinders this process. At the level of government contacts, reconciliation has usually meant mil-itary and economic cooperation, which bypasses entirely the issue of justice and compensating civilian populations for their wartime suffer-ing and loss. Only at times of hostile diplomatic relations or complex negotiations does the narrative of unhealed wounds acquire political currency, at which stage the focus is not on reconciliation but on play-ing on national pride, and vying for the international opinion. When governments cannot be reckoned with to initiate a process of mutual understanding and the coming to terms with a tormented past, civil society may take the initiative instead. In Greece and Turkey, nongov-ernmental associations of refugees and their descendants sometimes of their own accord initiate dialogue, centered on the common experience of exile and a shared cultural heritage, while taking advantage of EU funds allocated for this purpose.[74] Curiosity for and affinity with the Other is nurtured through the (re-)discovery of shared tastes in music, food, and dance, as well as the ways in which one's own customs or idiomatic expressions survive elsewhere. In Turkey, the Istanbul-based Foundation of Lausanne Treaty Emigrants (Lozan Mübadilleri Vakfı), founded in the climate of the turn of the millennium "earthquake diplo-macy," attempts to bring together the descendants of the populations "exchanged" in 1923. Among its stated aims are "to support friendship and cooperation among Turkish and Greek people, to protect the cultural and historical heritage of both sides, to conduct research on the population exchange, [and] to facilitate return visits to the place of origins of peoples on both sides."[75]

These are promising signs in the evolution of bilateral relations between Greek and Turkish civil societies, but there are also limits to how far this process can go. Several students of collective and private remembrance among refugees of the 1923 "exchange" regret that this reconciliatory agenda is not generally matched in the homeland associations of Anatolian Greeks in Greece, many of which remain committed to a nationalist agenda and a determined demand for recognition of the expulsion as the result of genocide.[76] One of the reasons for this is that private reconciliation and mutual acknowledgment of each other's pain can never give the descendants of victims the sense of justice and reimbursement for lost property that many of them want. As Nicholas Doumanis has noted, Greeks who from the 1950s onward returned to visit their places of origins in Anatolia were often received by local Turks—many of whom were themselves expellees from Greece— with all the courtesies normally extended to homecoming locals, which seemed to refute the national narratives of Greco-Turkish enmity. However, tempting as it may be to interpret such encounters in the spirit of enduring intercommunal tolerance that subverts state-imposed nationalism, these occasions are complicated by their own set of silences and unspoken conditions. For the people involved in such encounters, the catastrophic consequences of nation-building have to be reconciled with the fact that they also take pride in their national histories, meaning that the values of local community and intercommunality on the one hand and those of the nation on the other are constantly being negotiated.[77] They normally work under the assumption that intercommunal harmony was disrupted by outside agents—be that vengeful *muhacirs* (Muslim refugees) from the Balkans or Crete, the armies of Greece and other Christian states, or the interests of the European great powers and of international capital—and not forces from within the communities. Questions about guilt and local complicity are thus avoided; as are issues of rightful ownership with regard to property looted or otherwise left behind.

Renée Hirschon notes how some descendants of Asia Minor refugees have proposed a Truth and Reconciliation Commission on the Catastrophe, based on the South African model for conflict resolution, in which the issue of guilt is established but without the element of criminal justice or redress.[78] It is, however, doubtful whether such an initiative would be of much consequence, since the victims and the perpetrators are long gone. There is also a risk that such a commission becomes conflated with the dubious "reconciliation" offered as an alternative to genocide recognition by Turkish officialdom to Armenians, who are being asked to accept that both communities suffered from each other's violent acts during World War I, with the implication that both Turks and Armenians were therefore equally at fault. If everyone was guilty, so the thinking goes, no one was, meaning that the disrupted harmony can be restored as long as this does not involve an actual return of the latter group's descendants. This does not mean that the issue of Greco-Turkish reconciliation is the same as reconciliation between Turks and Armenians, or that Armenians and Greeks had identical experiences. In sum, recognition of a Christian genocide could strengthen the prospects of democracy in Turkey, as Turkish society would be encouraged to come to terms with the taboos of the national past. It does not follow from this that recognition of Christian or, more narrowly, Greek victimhood would have the same effect in Greece.

Concluding Remarks

As the centenary of the Armenian genocide approached in 2015, the idea of "three genocides, one recognition" seemed to gain traction. In March that year, the National Assembly of the Armenian Republic voted to recognize the Assyrian and Greek genocides alongside that of the Armenians, thus seemingly ending a resented "hierarchy of victims" among the peoples that had suffered death and exile at the hands of the Ottoman Turks.[79] The groundwork for this shift in the conceptualization of the Armenian genocide (albeit as of yet not adopted by the majority of scholars in that field) was laid by the resolution presented to IAGS' membership in 2007; premised on the belief that a "humanitarian intervention" in the field of historical remembrance through attention to lesser "forgotten genocides" would yield a greater awareness of similar crimes in the present.

The questions raised during the controversy caused by this resolution remain a matter of dispute in the community of genocide scholars, as they extend far beyond the issue of whether or not the Ottoman Greek Catastrophe was a genocide. For example, the historian Christian Axboe Nielsen has, in a response to scholarly criticism of the alleged failure of the UN International Criminal Tribunal for the Former Yugoslavia (ICTY) to convict Serb war criminals on the charge of genocide against the Bosnian Muslims, argued that "a myopic obsession with 'genocide' helps neither victims nor international criminal justice, and it risks obscuring rather than clarifying past historical events."[80] He notes the proliferation of narratives of genocide and ethnic victimhood that almost each of the parties involved in the Yugoslavian drama nurtured in the years leading up to the war, through the lens of which leaders of all sides read the current situation and acted accordingly to protect their own group from further victimization, thus making their historical nightmares into self-fulfilling prophecies. The specter of genocide thus brought a new and vicious cycle of atrocities into being, even if these did not per se amount to an all-encompassing genocide. Furthermore, he argues, the "maximalist" focus on seeing genocidal intent behind every occurrence of mass violence can in the worst case distract attention from other crimes against humanity, equally deserving of criminal prosecution and/or moral opprobrium. This is not genocide denial, or the dismissal of genocide as a useful analytical and legal term. Rather it is a plea for careful analysis of past injustices, based on robust evidence rather than the desire to generate prestige and publicity on charges of genocide that may prove to be unfounded, at the risk of discrediting one's legal or moral case.[81]

Here, scholars involved in the study of genocide and other mass atrocities have a great responsibility. It can well be argued that Adam Jones' democratic ethos, though well intended, unwittingly invites the devil, by bringing past events into being through labeling under-studied cases genocide as a favor to activists. This is done at the risk of inciting future violence engendered by distorted or simply misunderstood histories. Scholars may argue for less rigid interpretations of the genocide term, but the activists that sometimes are their allies, and the laymen that are their audience, are not primarily interested in scholarly debates or a more nuanced understanding of the past; rather, their motivation is identity-political. The response to a recent publication on the "Ottoman Greek genocide" illustrates this point well; a reviewer praises the volume for offering "a window into the genocidal mind of the Turks," and "an excellent introduction to the grim history of Greeks in modern times."[82]

Closely related to the danger of abetting Greek views of the Turkish Other as inherently evil, and the perpetual victimizer of one's own community, is the tendency we have seen throughout this chapter to lay claim to the dead. The demand for recognition often retroactively turns the dead into martyrs, who died for some greater collective identity that they had not themselves chosen, or a cause they most likely never identified with in life. In a vulgarly anachronistic interpretation of the Holocaust, the Jewish victims thus died so that the State of Israel would come into existence as the safe haven of Jewry. In a similar way, the victims of the deportations and mass violence in Pontos were early on made sense of through the religious notion of "neomartyres," new martyrs who had chosen death at the hands of the infidels as a way of testifying to their Christian faith. This is a highly dubious way of portraying the suffering inflicted on the nominally Christian subjects of the Ottoman Empire, who rarely sought death, and, in many cases, entrusted their children in the hands of Muslim neighbors so as to secure their survival, knowing that this would entail the children's conversion to Islam. As noted in this chapter, the recent configuration of the Christian Holocaust reinforces a perception of religion as the driving force in conflict and victimization. While this emphasis probably comes closer to the collective self-image of many contemporary Armenians and Anatolian *Rum* than latter-day notions of national belonging, it also distorts or eradicates the distinctions made by themselves and, in some cases, also the Young Turks; thereby blurring multiple and multifaceted experiences into one.

Another effect of this move away from what in lack of a better term can be called a secularized understanding of the Ottoman twilight years is that it seems to eliminate non-Christian elements from the circle of fellow victims. In the 1980s, when the Pontian genocide narrative first appeared in Greece, activists sought to establish links not only between ethnic Pontian Greek and Armenian victimhood, but also with the Kurdish victims of Turkish state nationalism. The more emphasis put on the notion of fellow Christian victimhood, the less frequent have references to Kurds and other minorities in Turkey become in the discourse of leading Greek activists for genocide recognition. While there continues to be a certain fascination with the Greek-speaking Muslims in Pontos, widely believed to harbor a concealed Christian faith that supposedly equates with a hidden Greek consciousness, few if any advocates of the genocide narrative seem willing to embrace the once Greek-speaking Muslims expelled from Greece in 1923 as lost kin. The implications of this unrealized cosmopolitanization of the Greek genocide narrative will be further addressed in the conclusion of the book.

Notes

1. Thea Halo, "Report on the IAGS Greek/Assyrian Genocide Resolution: Where We Go from Here?" in *Three Genocides, One Strategy*, ed. A. Pavlidis (Thessaloniki, 2008), 112.
2. Thea Halo, interview by Khatchig Mouradian, "Companions in suffering," *Aztag Daily*, 3 June 2007, last accessed 28 May 2014, http://headoverhat.blogspot.com/2007/06/interview-with-thea-halo.html.

3. For example, Betty Apigian-Kessel, "Forgotten Genocide: Let's Remember Perished Assyrians and Pontics, Too"; Varant Meguerditchian, "Working Together with Ancient Neighbors," last accessed 23 August 2013, http://www.armenianwekly.com.
4. R.P. Adalian, "Comparative Policy and Differential Practice in the Treatment of Minorities in Wartime: The United States Archival Evidence on the Armenians and Greeks in the Ottoman Empire," *Journal of Genocide Research* 3, no. 1 (2001): 45.
5. Hannibal Travis, "Constructing the 'Armenian Genocide': How Scholars Unremembered the Assyrian and Greek Genocides in the Ottoman Empire," in *Hidden Genocides: Power, Knowledge, Memory*, ed. A. Laban Hinton, T. La Pointe and D. Irvin-Erickson (New Brunswick and London, 2013), 172.
6. Travis, "Constructing the 'Armenian Genocide,'" 175, 180. Travis' own "impartial review of the evidence" purports to show that the Ottoman Greeks and Assyrians were actually more thoroughly destroyed than the Armenians, and that the scale of the "anti-Greek genocide" may even have exceeded the Armenian one. "The Turkish census of 1927 showed that there were more than 77,000 Armenians remaining [in the Turkish Republic], but only 71,000 Assyrians and Greeks at the most ... Although there were more Armenians than Greeks in 1927, there had been more Ottoman Greeks in 1914." In order to support this claim, one would have to assume that the Greeks that were expelled in 1922–24 were actually killed. It is noteworthy that Travis never questions the reliability of contemporary statistics or addresses the inconsistencies of the high Greek death tolls cited, between 650,000 and 900,000, which he contrasts against a likely Armenian death toll at a mere 600,000.
7. Another is that Travis exposes himself to the same allegation when he addresses the massacres against Greeks during the 1821 uprising (arguably irrelevant to a discussion about events during and after World War I), while omitting—purposefully or through lack of information—any reference to the corresponding violence against Muslim noncombatants by Greek insurgents at the time.
8. There were of course notable exceptions among public intellectuals, such as Franz Werfel, who drew attention to the Armenian massacres in his novel *The Forty Days of Musa Dagh*, first published in 1933.
9. Thea Halo, interview by Khatchig Mouradian, "Companions in suffering."
10. A. Jones, "Diffusing Genocide Studies, Defusing Genocides," *Genocide Studies and Prevention* 6, no. 3 (December 2011): 270–78, 273.
11. Yair Auron, *The Banality of Denial: Israel and the Armenian Genocide* (New Brunswick and London, 2003).
12. Israel W. Charny, "The Integrity and Courage to Recognize All the Victims of a Genocide," in *The Genocide of the Ottoman Greeks: Studies on the State-Sponsored Campaign of Extermination of the Christians of Asia Minor, 1912–1922 and Its Aftermath: History, Law, Memory*, ed. T. Hofmann, M. Bjørnlund and V. Meichanetsidis (New York and Athens, 2011), 22–25.
13. Jones, "Defusing Genocides," 273, 277n12. See also Adam Jones, *Genocide: A Comprehensive Introduction*, 2nd ed. (London, 2010).
14. Jones, *Genocide*, 150–51.
15. Charny, "Integrity and Courage," 34.
16. See Taner Akçam, *The Young Turks' Crime against Humanity: The Armenian Genocide and Ethnic Cleansing in the Ottoman Empire*, trans. Paul Bassemer (Princeton, NJ and Oxford, 2012).
17. Taner Akçam on http://www.genocidescholars.org/blog/?cat=40 (post removed), cited on http://en.wikipedia.org/wiki/Talk:Pontic_Greek_genocide/Archive_7. Last accessed 17 June 2011. Email to author, 15 April 2015. I am grateful to Taner Akçam for clarifying his views on the subject to me.

18. Thea Halo, "Report on the IAGS Conference," last accessed 8 October 2014, http://en.ado-world.org/.
19. Thea Halo and Adam Jones, "Notes on the Genocides of Christian populations of the Ottoman Empire," last accessed 8 October 2014, http://www.genocidetext.net/iags_resolution_supporting_documentation.htm; H. Travis, "Native Christians Massacred: The Ottoman Genocide of the Assyrians during World War I", *Genocide and Prevention* 1, no. 3 (2006): 327–71; David Gaunt, *Massacres, Resistance, Protectors: Muslim-Christian Relations in Eastern Anatolia during World War I* (Piscataway, NJ, 2006).
20. Memo by Peter Balakian, 2007, email message to author, 19 November 2014.
21. Charny, "Integrity and Courage," 37.
22. Thea Halo, "Report on the IAGS Conference."
23. Charny, "Integrity and Courage," 37–38.
24. Peter Balakian, letter posted on IAGS' website on 11 November 2007, email to author, 19 November 2014. I am grateful to Peter Balakian for making this letter available to me.
25. "International Genocide Scholars Association Officially Recognizes Assyrian, Greek Genocides." Press release of the International Association of Genocide Scholars (IAGS), issued 16 December 2007, last accessed 10 October 2014, http://www.notevenmyname.com/9.html.
26. Halo, "Report on the IAGS Greek/Assyrian Genocide Resolution," 112.
27. D.J. Schaller, "From Lemkin to Clooney: The Development and State of Genocide Studies," *Genocide Studies and Prevention* 6, no. 3 (December 2011): 245–56. For an opposing view, see S. Totten, "The State and Future of Genocide Studies and Prevention: An Overview and Analysis of Some Key Issues," *Genocide Studies and Prevention* 6, no. 3 (December 2011): 211–30.
28. Schaller, "From Lemkin to Clooney," 254.
29. See T.F. Gieryn, "Boundary-Work and the Demarcation of Science from Non-science: Strains and Interests in Professional Ideologies of Scientists," *American Sociological Review* 48 (1983): 781–95.
30. Jones, "Defusing Genocides," 274.
31. Jones, *Genocide*, 172.
32. "International Genocide Scholars," press release.
33. Eric Weitz on http://www.genocidescholars.org/blog/?cat=40 (post removed), cited on http://en.wikipedia.org/wiki/Talk:Pontic_Greek_genocide/Archive_7. Last accessed 17 June, 2011. Email to author, 8 March 2015.
34. I am grateful to Eric Weitz for clarifying his views on the subject to me.
35. Taner Akçam, for example, refers to the "genocidal massacres of Pontic Greeks" in 1921–22; thus placing it in the same context of exterminatory policies as the Armenians suffered during World War I, while distinguishing it from the ethnic cleansing of Greeks in Western Anatolia. Akçam, *Young Turks' Crime*, xvii.
36. Vlasis Agtzidis, "Oi Armenioi kai emeis" ["The Armenians and Us"], *Kathimerini*, 23 October 2007; Agtzidis, "I pagkosmia organosi tou pontiakou ellinismou" ["The Global Organization of Pontian Greeks"], *Kathimerini*, 6 August 2008; Agtzidis, "O tourkikos ethnikismos kai to christianiko olokautoma stin Anatoli" ["Turkish Nationalism and the Christian Holocaust in the East"], *Eleftherotypia*, 17 May 2010. The explicit notion of a Christian Holocaust as the precursor of the Jewish Holocaust was also made by Israel Charny.
37. For example, M. Charalambidis and K. Fotiadis, eds., *Pontioi: Dikaioma sti mnimi* [Pontians: Right to Memory], 4th ed. (Athens, 2003), 134–40.

38. Vlasis Agtzidis, "I omada Charalambidi-Fotiadi kai to pontiako kinima" ["The Charalambidis-Fotiadis Group and the Pontian Movement"], last accessed 7 February 2012, http://kars1918.wordpress.com/2009/10/13/italoi/.
39. Agtzidis, "I omada Charalambidi-Fotiadi."
40. Agtzidis, "I omada Charalambidi-Fotiadi."
41. "The 'Pontian Genocide': Distortions, Misconceptions and Falsehoods," last accessed 17 June 2011, http://www.pontiangenocide.com (site discontinued); www.greek-genocide.org/faq.html.
42. Cited in "The 'Pontian Genocide.'"
43. Motion 2008/09: U332 Folkmordet 1915 på armenier, assyrier/syrianer/kaldéer och pontiska greker.
44. Fråga 2005/06:1854 Sveriges erkännande av folkmordet på pontierna, by Tasso Stafilidis (v) to foreign minister Jan Eliasson (s); Motion 2008/09: U280 Erkännande av folkmordet på pontiska greker, by Nikos Papadopoulos (s), last accessed 3 May 2011, http://www.riksdagen.se/.
45. Aris Tsilfidis, "Swedish Vote: Only Pontic Greeks recognized," last accessed 13 February 2013, http://pontosworld.com/.
46. "Einai i POE arnites tis Genoktonias?" ["Are POE Deniers of the Genocide?"], last accessed 13 February 2013, http://pontosworld.com/.
47. N. Hlamides, "Pontic Greeks and the Greek Genocide," *GPN – Genocide Prevention Now* 4 (fall 2010), last accessed 23 October 2014, http://www.genocidepreventionnow.org/.
48. N. Hlamides, "Pontic Greeks."
49. Notes from the conference "The Catastrophe in Asia Minor and Pontus" (Rosemont, IL, May 9–10 2008).
50. In a later publication, however, Shirinian argues more forcefully for what he calls "the Greek Genocide." While noting the differences between the annihilation of the Armenians and the relatively few outright massacres of Ottoman Greeks in the early stages of persecution, before the Greco-Turkish war, he considers that all criteria cited in Articles 2 and 3 of the UN Genocide convention apply in the Greek case as much as in the Armenian and Assyrian cases. Despite the difficulty of proving genocidal intent, Shirinian argues that it can be inferred from "a pattern of systematic attacks on or the targeting of a group, atrocities on a large scale or repetitive destructive and discriminatory acts." George N. Shirinian, "The 'Great Catastrophe': The Genocide of the Greeks of Asia Minor, Pontos and Eastern Thrace, 1912–1923," last accessed 23 October 2014, http://www.genocidepreventionnow.org/. See also G.N. Shirinian, ed., *The Asia Minor Catastrophe and the Ottoman Greek Genocide: Essays on Asia Minor, Pontos and Eastern Thrace* (Bloomingdale, IL, 2012).
51. Address by Dr. Richard Hovannisian on 15 May 2010, last accessed 19 June 2012, http://www.xeniteas.com/.
52. For examples, see T. Hofmann, M. Bjørnlund and V. Meichanetsidis, eds., *The Genocide of the Ottoman Greeks: Studies on the State-Sponsored Campaign of Extermination of the Christians of Asia Minor, 1912–1922 and Its Aftermath: History, Law, Memory* (New York and Athens, 2011).
53. "ANC-Illinois Hosts International Conference on Ottoman Genocides," last accessed 23 August 2013, http://www.armenianweekly.com/.
54. Henry Theriault, "The Ontology of Genocide against Minorities in the Ottoman Empire," last accessed 23 August 2013, http://www.armenianweekly.com/.
55. Hannibal Travis, "The Lessons of Late Ottoman Genocides for Contemporary Iraq and Syria," last accessed 29 October 2014, http://www.armenianweekly.com/.
56. Thea Halo, interview by Khatchig Mouradian, "Companions in suffering."

57. Vlasis Agtzidis, "I omada Charalambidi-Fotiadi."
58. Trine Stauning Willert, *New Voices in Greek Orthodox Thought: Untying the Bond between Nation and Religion* (Farnham, 2014).
59. Hans-Lukas Kieser and Kerem Öktem, "Introduction: Beyond Nationalism or Beyond Kemalism? Turkey as Seen from 2006 and 2012," in *Turkey beyond Nationalism: Towards Post-National Identities*, ed. H-L. Kieser. 2nd ed. (London and New York, 2013), xii–xiii, xvi–xvii.
60. "Commemorating the Greek Genocide," last accessed 2 April 2014, http://gate sofvienna.blogspot.com/2011/03/commemorating-greek-genocide.html.
61. Alkmini Psilopoulou, "Sotires-makelarides" ["Savior Butchers"], *Avgi*, 26 July 2011.
62. Travis, "The Lessons of Late Ottoman Genocides."
63. Kieser and Öktem, "Introduction," xv.
64. The film was loosely based on Greek writer George Andreadis' book *Tamama* and Ustaoğlu's own recollections of her childhood in northeastern Turkey.
65. http://www.silkroadproduction.com/pdfs/presskit.pdf. Last accessed 2 April 2014.
66. Doğan Akanli, interview in "O ponos den tha itan mikroteros, an den milousame gia genoktonia" ["The Pain Would Not Be Lesser if We Did Not Talk of Genocide"], *Dromoi tis Istorias* (May 2011), last accessed 13 March, 2013, http://e-dromos.gr/. There are, however, signs of a harsher attitude from Turkish authorities, worried about the international attention engendered by the activism for recognition of the Greek genocide(s). See the article "Setting the Record Straight on Pontus Propaganda against Turkey" on the website of the Republic of Turkey's ministry of foreign affairs, last accessed 7 November 2014, http://www.mfa.gov.tr/. Apart from diplomatic protests, some history textbooks intended for upper secondary schools now include sections on how to counter Greek allegations of genocide, in addition to arguments against "Armenian genocide propaganda." J.M. Dixon, "Education and National Narratives: Changing Representations of the Armenian Genocide in History Textbooks in Turkey," *The International Journal for Education, Law and Policy*, Special Issue on "Legitimation and Stability of Political Systems: The Contribution of National Narratives" (2010): 103–26.
67. For a telling example, see George Th. Mavrogordatos, "The 1940s between Past and Future," in *Greece at the Crossroads: The Civil War and Its Legacy*, ed. J.O. Iatrides and L. Wrigley (University Park, 1995), 47.
68. Umut Özkirimli and Spyros A. Sofos, *Tormented by History: Nationalism in Greece and Turkey* (London, 2008), 153–60.
69. Bruce Clark, *Twice a Stranger: The Mass Expulsions that Forged Modern Greece and Turkey* (Cambridge, MA, 2006), 217–22. Thalia Dragonas and Anna Frangoudaki, "'Like a Bridge over Troubled Water': Reforming the Education of Muslim Minority Children in Greece," in *When Greeks and Turks Meet: Interdisciplinary Perspectives on the Relationship Since 1923*, ed. V. Lytra (Farnham, 2014), 289–95.
70. Dragonas and Frangoudaki, "'Like a Bridge over Troubled Water,'" 293.
71. Michalis Charalambidis, *The Pontian Question in the United Nations*, 2nd ed. (Thessaloniki, 2009), 98–105.
72. Tasos Kostopoulos, *Polemos kai ethnokatharsi: I xechasmeni pleura mias dekaetous ethnikis exormisis (1912–1922)* [War and Ethnic Cleansing: The Forgotten Side of a Ten Years Long National Campaign (1912–1922)], 4th ed. (Athens, 2008), 271–72.
73. Kostopoulos, *Polemos*, 271–73.
74. Rana Birden and Bahar Rumelili, "Rapprochement at the Grassroots: How Far Can Civil Society Engagement Go?" in *In the Long Shadow of Europe: Greeks and Turks in the Era of Postnationalism*, ed. O. Anastasakis, K. Nicolaidis and K. Öktem (Leiden and Boston, 2009), 315–30.

75. http://www.lozanmubadilleri.org/English.htm.
76. Renée Hirschon, "History, Memory and Emotion: The Long-term Significance of the 1923 Greco-Turkish Exchange of Populations," in *When Greeks and Turks Meet: Interdisciplinary Perspectives on the Relationship Since 1923*, ed. V. Lytra (Farnham, 2014), 37. See also A.S. Alpan, "But the Memory Remains: History, Memory and the 1923 Greco-Turkish Population Exchange," *The Historical Review/La Revue Historique* 9 (2012).
77. Nicholas Doumanis, *Before the Nation: Muslim-Christian Coexistence and its Destruction in Late-Ottoman Anatolia* (Oxford, 2013), xiii–xv, 170–73.
78. Hirschon, "History, Memory and Emotion," 38.
79. http://www.aina.org/news/20150324052004.htm. Last accessed 3 May 2016.
80. C.A. Nielsen, "Surmounting the Myopic Focus on Genocide: The Case of the War in Bosnia and Herzegovina," *Journal of Genocide Research* 15, no. 1 (2013): 33. The ICTY recognizes only the massacre at Srebrenica, in July 1995, as an act of genocide; not the entire campaign of ethnic cleansing against non-Serbs during the Bosnian war of 1992–95.
81. Nielsen, "Surmounting the Myopic Focus," 21–39.
82. E. Vallianatos, "Review: The Genocide of the Ottoman Greeks: Studies on the State-Sponsored Campaign of Extermination of the Christians of Asia Minor (1912–1922), and Its Aftermath; History, Law, Memory/The History of Greece," *Mediterranean Quarterly* 24, no. 4 (2013): 111–15.

CONCLUSION

Events do not exist in and of themselves in the field of collective remembrance. Rather they are made, in response to a variety of needs over the course of time. The wartime crimes of the Nazis, including the mass killing of Jews, was widely reported in the immediate aftermath of the World War II, but the event, or series of events, we today recognize as the Holocaust was long in the making. Initially viewed as a sideshow to the drama of war, one of many German atrocities, the murder of European Jewry evolved from the 1961 Eichmann trial onward into a "moral universal."[1] By the end of the twentieth century, it was the very incarnation of "absolute evil," a "chosen trauma" at the heart of a decidedly European culture of remembrance, for which the legacies of antiquity and Christianity no longer served as foundational myths. The attention given to the Holocaust in its turn informed discussions of other, some times more or less forgotten, atrocities. The once infamous Armenian massacres of 1915 re-emerged as the Armenian genocide in the public realm from the mid-1960s onward, after decades of silence. The emphasis on witness testimony underpinning narratives about these events suggested a shift of perspective in history-writing, from the history of states, political leaders and the wartime sacrifice of soldiers to the history of civilians suffering the consequences of war and nation-building.[2] These developments profoundly influence the ways in which the national past is imagined and debated.

This is the broader background that frames public discussions in Greece about the Asia Minor Catastrophe. I have argued in this book that the making of the Greek genocide offers a case through which the complex interplay between global and local history-cultural concerns, between universalism and particularism, can be understood. The quest for recognition of an historical ill reveals a dual process of nationalization and cosmopolitanization. Activists seek to convince a national audience that the event they call the (Pontian and/or Anatolian/Ottoman) Greek genocide is paramount to national or communal self-understanding, while at the same time making sense of it in a wider transnational context, using the language of human rights as opposed to narrow nationalist concerns. As a result, activists are to some extent forced to overcome national exceptionalism, as the idea of common fate with national Others belies notions of ethnic and national uniqueness.

Though the genocide labeling of the Greek Asia Minor Catastrophe is of recent vintage, the cultural trauma was long in the making. I have accounted for the history of remembrance in Greece in the aftermath of war and expulsion, and addressed some of the reasons behind the relative public silence on the topic, and also why things eventually changed. The genocide claim originated in the new identity politics of Pontian Greek refugees in the 1980s and became a dominant feature thereof; ritualized through the establishment of 19 May as a day of remembrance common to all Pontians. It was initially a purely communal affair, lobbied through the channel of the world congresses of Pontian Hellenism by activists with a background in left wing radicalism and in some cases well connected with the ruling PASOK. The purpose, besides the hope of economic benefits to come, was mainly to strengthen a sense of communal identity among Pontian Greeks, thereby establishing them as conscious historical and contemporary political subjects. From its outset, however, the new genocide narrative was accused of not being founded in historical reality and for severing the ties between the Pontian community and the larger Greek nation, thus creating an artificial ethnic identity. Activists therefore needed to convince a national audience that the Pontian trauma was the Greek nation's trauma as well, before turning to the international community. The road to internationalization of this memory lay in nationalizing it first.

Making remembrance of the alleged genocide a national concern meant situating it within a context that would make sense to Greeks in general. The story of the Pontian genocide was but one of several possible trauma dramas. Its advocates therefore needed to persuade the public that theirs mattered more or held the key toward resolving many or all of Greece's past or present ills, or "lesser traumas." This was done through the attachment of the demand for recognition to a set of other national issues dominating public debate in the 1990s, lobbied by MPs of Pontian descent and supported by other politicians willing to court an important constituency. But despite the symbolic gain made in 1994, Pontos remained in the margins of the Greek national narrative and hence was kept out of popular awareness outside the Pontian refugee community, as its relative absence from public debates on history at the time indicates. An opportunity to establish links with a better known national trauma came in 1998, when the Hellenic Parliament granted the same kind of recognition to the related drama of the Asia Minor Catastrophe, which centered on the remembrance of the conflagration of Smyrna in 1922. This event already had an established memorial day, 14 September, though this was not observed by Pontian organizations, which instead had opted for 19 May, the day of Mustafa Kemal's arrival in Samsun. Instead of a mere reference to victims of a national disaster, which did not address the reasons for and circumstances of their plight, this day was now reinterpreted and "upgraded" to signify the remembrance of a genocide against Greeks by the Turkish state, thereby eliminating all ambiguity. Just as the trauma of the Greek civil war for years seemed to conceal that of the Asia Minor Catastrophe, the memory, or notion, of an Anatolian Greek genocide can be used to obscure that of collaboration during the German occupation and the ensuing civil war in the name of national unity, by way of pointing the finger of blame for the nation's ills at the age-old foe of Turkey instead of a legacy of domestic division. This was certainly part of its appeal for politicians and governments with nationalist agendas. It was also the reason why many leftists were, and continue to be, resentful of the genocide narrative and the scapegoating of the Left that is implied in it, as communists are accused of having worked for a Turkish victory and then lying about the real causes of Anatolian Greek suffering. But there is more to the picture than settling party-political scores.

The genocide narrative thrived in a climate of national, cultural and political anxieties, in which national identity seemed threatened by the impact of globalization, European unification, cosmopolitanism, and multiculturalism. In the eyes of its critics, the genocide narrative represented a nationalist backlash; an entrenchment around old hatreds by forces hostile to change, such as the neo-Orthodox movement within the Church and its militant Archbishop Christodoulos (1998–2008), the discredited "patriotic" factions of the two mainstream parties, and, increasingly, right wing extremism. For those who identified themselves with anti-nationalism the recognition of the Catastrophe as genocide would transform the meaning of this calamity from a morality about the vices of nationalism to a retrospective endorsement of the expansionist policies that dragged the country into an unjust and unwinnable war for which the Ottoman Greeks paid dearly. If that becomes the accepted historical truth, so the argument goes, the xenophobic nationalism of the present will become vindicated.

If activists concerned with the genocide narrative were deeply influenced by an ethnocentric view of (national) history as an eternal struggle for the survival of Hellenism, the sense of rejection experienced after 2001 led some to emphasize belonging to a community that is much larger than the nation, namely "all peoples who have suffered persecutions and ethnic cleansing." These ranged from indigenous peoples victimized by Western colonialism to the victims of state repression in the name of the nation or the totalitarian ideologies of the twentieth century. While these activists continued to make sense of their trauma within a national framework, with their forebears as victims of an "intra-Greek" racism rooted in the nineteenth century's conflict between indigenous Greeks of the Hellenic Kingdom and Ottoman Greek outsiders, they also started to conceive of genocide remembrance within the bounds of a post-nationalist identity. Certainly, the post-national community they first and foremost may have had in mind was the Greek diaspora, in which activists put their hopes when the Greek state abandoned its commitment to their cause. The Greeks of the diaspora were already members of host societies in which ethnic and cultural diversity is the rule rather than the exception. From their point of view, a discourse stressing human rights and common ground with other victimized communities, which in their host countries lived alongside them, was more suitable than an exclusive focus on Greek suffering or the "national rights" used as a battle cry in the Macedonian conflict of the 1990s. However, also Greece was experiencing a rapid transformation with an ever growing immigrant share of the population, which may work as an incentive for activists concerned with the genocide narrative to adapt to the new social realities. By portraying themselves and their forebears as victims of modern state nationalism, Turkish as well as Greek activists link their story to a wider narrative of human suffering. In this way, it comes to resemble the new cosmopolitanism that Levy and Sznaider argue transforms national and ethnic memory by combining traditional elements with the language of human rights. But this also leads to an inherent tension between the various elements of this new memory that are not easily reconciled with each other.

The conflict over the "Asia Minor genocide's" recognition was at least initially mostly a debate about national history, and in that sense ethnocentric. However, by invoking the UN convention on the crime of genocide, activists pointed to a larger framework of reference that transcends the national and that their critics had to respond to. In both arguments for and against this interpretation of the Catastrophe powerful templates were at work. Apart from the way national history was understood, support or in most cases opposition was a matter of how the concept of genocide was interpreted, and how it was related to one particular event; the Holocaust of the European Jews. If the Holocaust is the "gold standard" of man's evil, it follows that those who pursue similar recognition would want "their" genocide to look like it as much as possible. Usually, this is done through stressing similarities between victim groups as well as the ideologies, methods and organizations of the respective perpetrators. The Holocaust template exerts a powerful influence on how most people understand the phenomenon of genocide, which led critics of the Greek genocide narrative to object to recognition on definitional grounds. Some argued that the concept was too novel to apply to the Ottoman Greek case, as it took place before World War II, or that not a significant enough share of the total Greek-Orthodox population in Anatolia had been annihilated, or that Young Turkish persecution thereof was motivated by a rational quest for national cohesion through expulsion of alien elements rather than by an "irrational" Nazi-like racism bent on the complete extermination of the Other. The genocide of the European Jews, in its turn, represented an event of universal significance due to its devastating impact on the founding values of modern society, unlike the more "local" Ottoman drama. This understanding of both the genocide concept and the nature and meaning of the Holocaust seemed to reject the notion of genocide in Anatolia, or the clash of nationalisms in the old empire, as a universally valid experience.

The Holocaust was by the early twenty-first century no longer a distant abstraction in Greek historical culture. Although the initiative to teach it and to honor those who fell prey to it came through the workings of cosmopolitan memory and European unification, the event had in part taken place in Greece, with Greek Jews as its victims. It could therefore also be constructed as a national trauma, and, due to the new significance given to it, not only a handy historical analogy or source of inspiration for Anatolian Greek activists, but a contender for official commemoration. I have analyzed the complexity of this relation between the cosmopolitan or European phenomenon of Holocaust remembrance and an essentially ethnocentric perception of history and victimhood in Greece. Particular attention is paid to public debate on cases of suffering by groups perceived as non-Greeks, or national Others, in which Greeks had been involved as either co-victims, bystanders, or even perpetrators, as these also influenced debates on and perceptions of the Greeks' fate in the Ottoman Empire's dying days. Apart from the Jewish Holocaust, these included another of the twentieth century's paradigmatic genocides; that of the Armenians in 1915.

The Armenian case provided Anatolian Greek activists with another powerful template through which Greek suffering could be made sense of; as a silenced crime that, unlike the Holocaust, continues to be officially denied. The fact that both communities had fallen prey to the same perpetrator suggested an even stronger link. When the tragedies of Others become a mirror for national concerns, the latter come to inform how the former are understood (and vice versa) in countries where such debates occur. The question that ultimately both activists and their critics grappled with was whether remembrance of "local" victimhood really offered lessons that were as meaningful to their contemporary society as those of the Europeanized or cosmopolitan Holocaust. This discussion became more urgent as the economic crisis along with growing immigration as well as xenophobia brought the tension between the local/national and the global/cosmopolitan to a head. Efforts to criminalize the Holocaust denial of forces hostile to the new cosmopolitan memory led to demands for similar legal status to the Pontian, Anatolian Greek, and Armenian tragedies. In some cases, commemoration of Greek victimhood (and sometimes Armenian) was deliberately pitted against Holocaust remembrance. However, Greek chauvinism also threatened to undermine the conception of the perceived genocidal experience of Greeks as universally valid. If they were the victims of extreme nationalism or even Nazi-style racism, then it would seem to follow that their descendants should be more sensitive to victims of racism in general. Paradoxical as it may seem, the preoccupation with a national or ethnic history of suffering may open an avenue toward cosmopolitan memory. When activists are forced to engage with the pain of Others, ethnic nationalism can transform itself into a civic variant, though this is a complex process vulnerable to backlashes.

Similar issues have been explored in a different national context, against the background of the identity politics of Greek Americans in the late twentieth and early twenty-first centuries. Here remembrance of the Catastrophe, reimagined as the genocide of the Pontian and/or Anatolian/Ottoman Greeks, could serve as an invigorating narrative of Greek ethnic identity in the United States (or for that matter in any country where Greeks live). For lobbyists hoping to influence American foreign policy in Greece's favor, this tragic story of loss, injustice and eventual redemption was a way of emulating the Zionist attachment of American Jews to Israel at a time when Greek Americans were losing interest in the language and politics of the old homeland. Lack of familiarity with political debates in Greece and the long absence of left wing perspectives in Greek-American communal affairs meant that the genocide narrative would have a less bumpy road toward acceptance in that community. The lived or learned experience of collective trauma became a vivid aspect of Greekness even among people who lacked interest in political affairs, leading some to a profoundly existential discovery of their heritage, whether real or imagined.

Particular attention is paid to the work of Thea Halo, *Not Even My Name*, which arguably did more to advertise the notion of the Pontian Greek genocide than any other English-language publication. The main strength of her book was its moving portrayal of a girl's survival at all odds, and her subsequent transition to motherhood and a new life in America; an easily recognizable theme, or template, which did not presuppose intimate familiarity with the historical setting of Ottoman Anatolia. Nonetheless, the representation of Halo's mother as not only an individual but the collective self of an entire people, the Pontians (Halo did not at the time identify as strongly with Greece as in later years), whose fate mirrored hers, entailed a claim to historical authority. The book's lack of complexity in its historical sections has been analyzed as problematic, given the international standing as an unrivaled expert account of events in Pontos it would acquire, making Halo a key figure in the recognition process.

This critique is also extended to other efforts to teach the history of these events in an American context, with particular attention to the lesson plans prepared for use in high school classrooms and distributed by the Chicago-based association 'Xeniteas'. It is in these lessons, largely modeled upon Holocaust and Armenian genocide teaching units, that the story of the Pontian or Ottoman Greek genocide is transformed from ethnic to cosmopolitan (or at least Americanized) memory, by way of a predominantly emotional encounter. By bringing it to bear on universal as well as typically American concerns about tolerance for other cultures, races and religions, it is demonstrated that the collective trauma of Anatolian Greeks can also be made the vicarious trauma of American high school students. But this empathy with victimized Others comes at the expense of analytical insight, as the narrative presented in these lesson plans has been sanitized from ambiguous elements that would have made it more nuanced. The morality of the story works better if it is kept simple, without too much historical context. The result is, however, neither good history nor sound pedagogy. Another question that remains unanswered in the lesson plans is what they will teach students that the Holocaust and other human rights crimes have not already taught them, if the lesson is only one of tolerance versus bigotry. This is perhaps the greatest obstacle facing the Greek genocide narrative, as in an international context it is but one of many available trauma dramas.

The tension between emotion, serving to foster empathy with victims, and analytical detachment is at the heart of the first part of Chapter 6. The bid for additional recognition of the Greek and Assyrian claims alongside the Armenian, advanced in a resolution by Thea Halo and Adam Jones to the International Association of Genocide Scholars (IAGS) in 2007, brought out the inherent conflict within a research field premised on both. The resulting controversy echoed arguments that had emerged in public debate in Greece—unfamiliar to the protagonists of the IAGS battle—regarding the confusion that surrounds the genocide concept and its applicability to the Ottoman Greek Catastrophe. The divisive issue was not whether this was a case of genocide or not, but the principles and sources according to which such an interpretation is made. For historians and other scholars, the crucial issue was the genocidal intent of the perpetrators, which none of the sources amassed in support of the resolution was able to demonstrate, at least as far as the Greeks were concerned. For activists like Halo, the testimony of victims held primacy over official histories and, presumably, the sort of state documents favored by historians. In her view, those who questioned her call for joint recognition did so out of "tribal" concerns about the "exclusivity of suffering" of those who had already obtained the status of victims. Adam Jones, her foremost supporter among the genocide scholars, advocated a less rigid interpretation of the genocide concept that would allow for the extended recognition of possible yet under-researched atrocities in the past. Emotion was for him the point of the exercise, as empathy and outrage would spur humanitarian action in the present; a goal for which the belated recognition of the presumed Greek and Assyrian genocides could be instrumental. The IAGS controversy was decided in the activists' favor, but the elevation of their claim to the status of scholarly certified "fact" also increased demands for a less emotional and more professionalized approach to the subject.

The second part of Chapter 6 deals with the question of who belonged in the (ever expanding) circle of victims. This was a question that grew urgent as a result of the internationalization process, and which changed the way the alleged genocide was presented and perhaps also perceived by the activists themselves. It seemed to make little sense to pursue separate recognition of the professed Pontian and Anatolian Greek genocides in the international arena, where Armenian activists had set an example difficult to match. Rather than trying to draw the world's attention to a parallel experience that seemed destined to dwarf by comparison, efforts would be better spent to portray Greeks, Assyrians, and Armenians as victims of one and the same genocide. The combined losses of all the Ottoman Christians would be counted in millions, approaching the sort of numbers reached in the Holocaust of the Jews, thereby creating a Christian equivalent. In this schema, the exclusively Pontian approach to the history of late Ottoman violence that had spawned the Greek movement for genocide recognition was viewed as simply too particular and ethnocentric to have any traction. The roots of the assault on Pontian identity politics were to be found in bitter personal rivalries and power struggles among the "refugee" organizations, but the quest for scholarly recognition played a role too. Setting the Greek genocide claim in a more academic context meant moving away from the particular toward the universal.

Instead of seeking recognition in isolation, the future of the Greek genocide narrative appears to lie in making it part of a greater drama, the "Christian Holocaust," in which Greek victims are indistinguishable from Assyrian and Armenian victims. Stressing unity in suffering with other Christians seems to emphasize religious belonging over ethnicity and national identity, thereby pointing to new ways of remembering a past previously conceived of in national terms. In this manner, the past becomes more cosmopolitan. Such a framing resonates with current concerns about the well-being of Christian minorities in the Middle East. There are nonetheless potential drawbacks. The most obvious is that the ethnicity of the victims, which for many is the genocide narrative's raison d'être, easily becomes diluted or disappears entirely within this ecumenical embrace. Greek victims may run the risk of remaining as anonymous within the cluster notion of the Christian Holocaust as they were outside it. A still graver danger when the history of violence is cast in religious terms lies in the way that the flames of present-day fanaticism are being fanned and in the way the history of cases unrelated to the Ottoman drama becomes distorted. Instead of demonstrating the need for universal values, it would serve to reinforce bigotry.

This brings us to a scholarly dilemma with origins in and implications for contemporary historical culture, in which historians find themselves at the receiving end of demands for useable history; not only from governments. The process of attaching canonical status to more or less unknown histories of mass atrocities and the politics surrounding these struggles reflect a broader phenomenon; the democratization of the past. Related to this are the changing priorities of historians in the Western world mentioned earlier. This interest in social history, along with the growing attention to and, resulting from that, prestige of victimhood and trauma from the 1960s onward enabled previously marginalized groups to challenge hegemonic state narratives. Often this was understood as speaking truth to power, fighting the denial and distortions of the past by authoritarian regimes. Undoubtedly, these developments have allowed for a wider range of voices to be heard in the historical culture of many societies. However, the outcome of democratizing memory politics is not always democratic history, tolerant of alternatives. Often activists themselves aspire to make their interpretation hegemonic, thus reinforcing the authoritarian tendencies of the particular historical culture they have set out to alter. The recent success of Greek activists to achieve legal protection of the genocide interpretation attest to this, as the effect of such legislation is a ban on dissenting perspectives. One of the reasons why the Greek genocide issue has become so contentious may be found in the way that Greek activists have attached their case so closely to the Armenian genocide, making the latter a template for how the former is to be understood. The battle lines of scholarship and public discourse on the Armenian genocide have for many years been defined by the persistent refusal of one state, Turkey, to restore a sense of justice to the victims and their descendants by admitting its guilt for wartime crimes and the subsequent denial thereof. Whereas Holocaust denial at least in the Western world emanates from marginal figures with no standing either in the academic community or society at large, those who deny the applicability of the genocide term with regard to the Armenian question enjoy the support of a national government and its diplomatic services. Scholars of Turkey (not only in Turkey) have in some notable cases been complicit in this state-sponsored denial, even to the point of aiding Turkish government officials with covert advice on how to combat the charge of genocide. Their critics have argued that denial in posterity is in fact the last stage of genocide, which adds insult to injury through a symbolic killing of the memory of the dead. From this follows that scholars are duty-bound by professional standards to defend historical truth and open themselves to suffering as a way of taking a stand against cruelty and killing, whatever its source.[3]

There is much to be said in favor of this ethical stand. However, the boundaries between genocide denial and legitimate scholarship are not always as clear-cut as this dichotomy suggests. One scholar of the "cultures of denial" pertaining to the Holocaust and the Armenian genocide points to the existence of "gray zones" between these poles, referring to the case of Bernard Lewis; one of the foremost scholarly authorities on Middle Eastern history, who was also sympathetic to the Kemalist project of nation-building.[4] Lewis had in his classic account from 1961, *The Emergence of Modern Turkey*, referred to the "holocaust" of 1.5 million

Armenians; a statement that in later editions was modified with language suggesting uncertainty with regard to numbers and that Turks may have suffered equally, in what was described as an Ottoman civil war between rival national movements rather than a state-controlled mass murder.[5] As mentioned earlier, the controversy that arose in 1993, following an interview in *Le Monde* where Lewis suggested that the Armenian genocide claim was but one version of the story, resulted in the conviction of the scholar in accordance with the Gayssot law banning the denial of crimes against humanity recognized by the French state. While some celebrated this as the triumph of truth, it is not evident that Lewis' opinion really reflected any malice or criminal intent toward the victims; rather, he disagreed with a growing community of scholars by remaining unconvinced by the evidence supporting the genocide interpretation. His own understanding of what caused the destruction of the Ottoman Armenians, as it appears in his writings and public statements, is deeply problematic, and certainly offensive to those identifying with the victims, but not unequivocally beyond the pale of scholarly conduct. The silence concerning the fate of the Armenians and other minorities found in many works on modern Turkey need not always be understood as active denial as much as a lack of interest and information or simply other research priorities.

The scholarly dilemma is how to address the late-Ottoman history of violence in a way that resists oversimplifying narratives serving to confirm political identities and predetermined conclusions, without inadvertently justifying the Turkish state narrative of the persecutions as legitimate self-defense against seditious minorities. By framing their case as more or less identical to that of the Armenians, Greek activists and their supporters construe critical examination of their claims as tantamount to denial also of the Armenian genocide and, by implication, all other genocides, including the Holocaust. The calls for legislation against all perspectives that do not take the accuracy of the Greek genocide narrative for granted and the lumping together of critics with deniers of better researched genocides have the effect of intimidating scholars from participation in public debate on this issue. Research on the atrocities largely becomes the preserve of activists already committed to one interpretation. The result is a chasm between a folk history of the violence in Asia Minor and its causes on the one hand, and academic historiography on less contentious aspects of the Ottoman Greek experience on the other, which remain strangers to each other.

How, then, ought the events that some choose to label the Greek genocide and others, more cautiously, the Asia Minor Catastrophe to be remembered? Is there a wise way of remembering the dead without imperiling the living? One way to begin is by getting the numbers right or by admitting the impossibility of ever getting them right, due to lack of reliable data. Before 1914, the Greek-Orthodox population of Pontos is believed to have numbered around 400,000;[6] somewhere between 260,000 and 300,000, according to conservative estimates.[7] Of these between 100,000 and 150,000 are believed to have died during the years of protracted conflict, by way of starvation, illness, massacres, and forced marches.[8] That means that either one quarter or between one third and half of the Greek-Orthodox inhabitants of that region perished before the population exchange. If the intentions and ultimate goals of the Turkish nationalist authorities remain obscure, the effects of their policies were genocidal, as Nicholas Doumanis has recently argued.[9] However, it is still a far cry from the 353,000 Pontian victims habitually claimed by activists. Numbers do matter. That is why activists tend to inflate the overall total of Ottoman Greek deaths, from the cautious assessments ranging between 300,000 and 700,000 upwards to 1.5 million or even more, out of the conviction that the more people who died the greater the significance of the demand for recognition and remembrance. When so many people were killed, their deaths must have a meaning, which can be revealed and preserved in the right sort of historical remembrance. But when meaning is found in killing, the risk is that more killing would bring more meaning. The historian Timothy Snyder warns of the danger permeating the number games of memory politics.

> By repeating exaggerated numbers [of victims], Europeans release into their culture millions of ghosts of people who never lived. Unfortunately, such specters have power. What begins as competitive martyrology can end with martyrological imperialism. The wars for Yugoslavia of the 1990s began, in part, because Serbs believed that far larger numbers of their fellows had been killed in the Second World War than was the case. When history is removed, numbers go upward and memories go inward, to all of our peril.[10]

Closely linked to this is the issue of morality. Genocide is a concept developed within the context of international law, which, though often used as a category of historical analysis, means that it cannot be separated from its original purpose, which is to indict criminals. When historians classify an event as genocide, they are assuming the role of a judge, whether they intend it or not. Those who insist upon the difference between memory, understood as a primarily emotional encounter with the past, and history, the scientific study of the past, do not usually consider this to be the historian's job. The task of scholars is to explain the past, not passing sentences. Of course, historians also remember with an eye to past and present injustice. They do not, and should not, live outside the ethical boundaries of the societies they inhabit. Historical explanation need not exclude moral condemnation, as long as we acknowledge the fundamental legal and moral principle that each adult individual is responsible for his or her own actions, regardless of circumstances and provocations, whether real or perceived. However, reducing history to morality plays does not necessarily make anyone more moral. It is easier and more inviting to identify with the victims than to understand the historical setting that they shared with their killers, let alone the bystanders, as this identification affirms a belief in our own righteousness. Yet it is unclear whether this really brings much insight or useful knowledge. Claiming victimhood does not in itself produce sound ethical choices. The Young Turks believed themselves to be the victims of Christian aggression, which forced them into a life or death struggle for national survival, in which the innocent of the day might turn into the deadly foes of tomorrow. In a similar way, the Nazis had convinced themselves that they were fighting a war in defense of the German race that the Jews had forced upon them. This was a lie perceived as truth by people who needed justification for murder. Understanding the historical context and the mindset of the perpetrators is harder than vicariously sharing trauma through identification with victims, but necessary if the dangers mentioned here are to be avoided.

The point that much of today's Holocaust remembrance simplifies a complex historical reality in order for inspiring lessons to emerge has been made by Peter Novick, who doubted its educational value. But scholarly detachment and historical analysis must not mean indifference toward the suffering of fellow human beings. Critics of Holocaust education tend to forget that historical understanding requires empathy—that is, the ability to picture oneself in someone else's position; without, of course, feeling obliged to adopt the viewpoints and ethical stance of that someone as one's own. Lessons that can bring about such insights, without falling into any of the above mentioned traps, are to be commended. The Holocaust will in all likelihood remain an event whose remembrance carries profound meaning for many people in the twenty-first century, at least in the Western world.

The question is whether the "Greek genocide" or the "Christian Holocaust" will be able to join it as a "deterritorialized" cosmopolitan memory in its own right, recognized as a universally valid historical experience, from which lessons about the human condition can be drawn. If we are to believe Jeffrey C. Alexander, every trauma claim faces the challenge of establishing what happened as well as the identities of the victims and the perpetrators respectively, if it is to be generalized as a wound to other people than those immediately affected. "Claims may be made on behalf of [a certain] group, but they must be convincingly projected to a broader collectivity." [11] However, Alexander does not sufficiently address the role that cultural factors play in the making of "trauma dramas" or "cultural traumas." An international, non-academic audience will most likely have to be able to recognize themselves in the victims; perhaps to some extent also in the perpetrators (this is the reason why Christopher Browning's "ordinary men" remains a more compelling reminder of the reader's own humanity than Daniel Goldhagen's inherently anti-Semitic nation of "willing executioners").[12] Natan Sznaider and Daniel Levy have suggested that no other catastrophe could play the same role in the memory-scape of the contemporary globalized world as the Holocaust, since Jews in the eyes of many are the personification of cosmopolitan culture. An attack on them is an attack on cosmopolitanism itself. "That is the social foundation for the historical 'uniqueness' of the Holocaust," to which a moral significance is attached "that is separate from its historical and territorial origins."[13] If they are right, their observation is bad news for activists who wish to see the Greek catastrophe, or any other atrocity that does not fit into Eurocentric preconceptions, recognized alongside the Jewish Holocaust. The reason why is that the history of the Ottoman Empire and its Christian minorities is simply too unfamiliar for most Westerners, and the contribution of those peoples to "cosmopolitan culture" too small. The story cannot escape its historical and geographical origins—and from the historian's viewpoint, it should not be separated from that context. As pointed out earlier, the Greek genocide narrative is but one of many trauma dramas that vie for attention in the international arena.

This does not mean that remembrance cannot be cosmopolitan in a local or national context. There are alternative pathways for the memory of what befell the Ottoman Christians than using it as a weapon to incite hatred. For Turkish dissident intellectuals, an open discussion of their fate is the key to the democratization of Turkey. Regardless of whether one chooses to classify the ethnic cleansing of the one Christian group or the other as genocide or not, argues Taner Akçam, the act itself constitutes a crime. The fundamental issue is not one of legal definition but moral. "I believe that regardless of how one describes it, a moral admission must be made: a recognition of the truth that a wrongful act took place, one so large and serious as to be deserving of moral opprobrium."[14] A society that shuns away from such an insight, however uncomfortable that may be for the collective self-image, will remain trapped in a climate of repression and siege mentality, where national security concerns are considered to justify any act of violence or curbing of civil liberties. The increasingly authoritarian nature of Erdoğan's reign seems to validate this observation.

The discussion of "Greek genocide" remembrance and its relation with cosmopolitan memory begins and ends in Greece. In a Greek national context it has proven to be a highly contentious issue. Critics accuse the genocide activists, with some right, of being concerned with an ethnocentric agenda that refuses to acknowledge the new social and demographic reality of the country. Instead, they point to Greece's own legacy of victimizing non-Greeks, either through wartime terror and expulsion or peacetime discrimination against minorities, in order to widen the confines of historical remembrance. Regardless of whether future research will validate or falsify the interpretation of the late Ottoman Greek experience as genocide, the ability to imagine one's own community in the role of perpetrator is the key to a truly cosmopolitan understanding of past and present national experience. The prospect of such an understanding may appear bleak, as the current economic crisis reinforces notions of national victimhood. Nonetheless, it is not impossible that the notion of Greek commonality with suffering others in the end might work against ethnocentrism, by conceiving of the Ottoman Greek tragedy as something that transcends the boundaries of the nation. If that could be the case, the dubious claims and historical distortions made by some activists would paradoxically, in their own peculiar ways, have contributed to open up Greek society and historical remembrance to the impact of cosmopolitan values. That would be no insignificant feat.

Notes

1. J.C. Alexander, "On the Social Construction of Moral Universals: The 'Holocaust' from War Crime to Trauma Drama," *European Journal of Social Theory* 5, no. 1 (February 2002), 5–85.

2. Jay Winter, *Remembering War: The Great War between Memory and History in the Twentieth Century* (New Haven and London, 2006) 6–8, 49–51. Jay Winter and Antoine Prost, *The Great War in History: Debates and Controversies, 1914 to the Present* (Cambridge, 2005), 171–72, 205.

3. R.W. Smith, E. Markusen and R.J. Lifton, "Professional Ethics and the Denial of Armenian Genocide," *Holocaust and Genocide Studies* 9, no. 3 (1995): 1–22.

4. Maria Karlsson, *Cultures of Denial: Comparing Holocaust and Armenian Genocide Denial* (Lund, 2015), 165–77.

5. Bernard Lewis, *The Emergence of Modern Turkey* (London, 1961).

6. Alexis Alexandris, "The Greek Census of Anatolia and Thrace (1910–1912): A Contribution to Ottoman Historical Demography," in *Ottoman Greeks in the Age of Nationalism: Politics, Economy, and Society in the Nineteenth Century*, ed. D. Gondicas and C. Issawi (Princeton, NJ, 1999), 66.

7. Nicholas Doumanis, *Before the Nation: Muslim-Christian Coexistence and its Destruction in Late-Ottoman Anatolia* (Oxford, 2013), 35.

8. Tasos Kostopoulos, *Polemos kai ethnokatharsi: I xechasmeni pleura mias dekaetous ethnikis exormisis (1912–1922)* [War and Ethnic Cleansing: The Forgotten Side of a Ten Years Long National Campaign (1912–1922)], 4th ed. (Athens, 2008), 263.

9. Doumanis, *Before the Nation*, 155.

10. Timothy Snyder, *Bloodlands: Europe between Hitler and Stalin*, 2nd ed. (New York, 2012), 406.

11. Jeffrey C. Alexander, *Trauma: A Social Theory* (Cambridge and Malden, 2012), 119.

12. Christopher Browning, *Ordinary Men: Reserve Police Battalion 101 and the Final Solution in Poland* (New York, 1992); Daniel J. Goldhagen, *Hitler's Willing Executioners: Ordinary Germans and the Holocaust* (New York, 1996).

13. Daniel Levy and Natan Sznaider, *The Holocaust and Memory in the Global Age*, trans. Assenka Oksiloff (Philadelphia, 2006), 199.

14. Taner Akçam, *The Young Turks' Crime against Humanity: The Armenian Genocide and Ethnic Cleansing in the Ottoman Empire*, trans. Paul Bassemer (Princeton, NJ and Oxford, 2012), 451.

REFERENCE LIST

Official Publications

Efimeris tis Kyverniseos tis Ellinikis Dimokratias [Government Gazette of the Hellenic
   Republic]
Praktika Voulis ton Ellinon [Acts of the Hellenic Parliament]
Public Acts of the State of Illinois

Newspapers and Reviews

Ardin
Armenian Weekly
Convoy
Frankfurter Allgemeine Zeitung
I Avgi
I Eleftherotypia
I Kathimerini
Kommounistiki Epitheorisi
O Oikonomikos Tachydromos
O Rizospastis
Svenska Dagbladet
Ta Nea
The Guardian
The New York Times
To Ethnos
To Vima

References

Adak, H. "National Myths and Self-na(rra)tions: Mustafa Kemal's *Nutuk* and Halide
   Edip's *Memoirs* and *The Turkish Ordeal*." *South Atlantic Quarterly* 102, no. 2/3
   (Spring/Summer 2003): 509–27.

Adalian, R.P. "Comparative Policy and Differential Practice in the Treatment of Minorities in Wartime: The United States Archival Evidence on the Armenians and Greeks in the Ottoman Empire." *Journal of Genocide Research* 3, no. 1 (2001): 31–48.

Agtsidis, Vlassis [Agtzidis, Vlasis]. "Asie centrale et Sibérie, territoires de la deportation." In *Les Grecs pontiques: Diaspora, identité, territoires*, edited by M. Bruneau, 157–75. Paris: CNRS Éditions, 1998.

———. "Mnimi, tautotita kai ideologia ston pontiako ellinismo" ["Memory, Identity and Ideology among Pontian Greeks"]. In *To trauma kai oi politikes tis mnimis: Endeiktikes opseis ton symvolikon polemon gia tin Istoria kai ti Mnimi* [The Trauma and the Politics of Memory: Indicative Aspects of the Symbolic Wars for History and Memory], edited by G. Kokkinos, E. Lemonidou and V. Agtzidis, 191–329. Athens: Taxideutis, 2010.

Ahmad, Feroz. "Unionist Relations with the Greek, Armenian, and Jewish Communities of the Ottoman Empire." In *Christians and Jews in the Ottoman Empire. The Functioning of a Plural Society. Volume 1. The Central Lands*, edited by B. Braude and B. Lewis, 401–34. London: Holmes & Meier, 1982.

Akçam, Taner. *From Empire to Republic: Turkish Nationalism and the Armenian Genocide*. Translated by Paul Bassemer. London: Zed Books, 2004.

———. *A Shameful Act: The Armenian Genocide and the Question of Turkish Responsibility*. Translated by Paul Bessemer. New York: Metropolitan Books, 2006.

———. *The Young Turks' Crime against Humanity: The Armenian Genocide and Ethnic Cleansing in the Ottoman Empire*. Translated by Paul Bassemer. Princeton, NJ and Oxford: Princeton University Press, 2012.

Akşin, Sina. *Turkey – From Empire to Revolutionary Republic: The Emergence of the Turkish Nation from 1789 to the Present*. Translated by Dexter H. Mursaloglu. New York: New York University Press, 2007.

Alexander, J.C. "On the Social Construction of Moral Universals: The 'Holocaust' from War Crime to Trauma Drama." *European Journal of Social Theory* 5, no. 1 (February 2002): 5–85.

———. *Trauma: A Social Theory*. Cambridge and Malden: Polity Press, 2012.

Alexandris, Alexis. *The Greek Minority of Istanbul and Greek-Turkish Relations 1918–1974*. Athens: Center for Asia Minor Studies, 1983.

———. "The Greek Census of Anatolia and Thrace (1910–1912): A Contribution to Ottoman Historical Demography." In *Ottoman Greeks in the Age of Nationalism: Politics, Economy, and Society in the Nineteenth Century*, edited by D. Gondicas and C. Issawi, 45–76. Princeton, NJ: The Darwin Press, 1999.

Alpan, A.S. "But the Memory Remains: History, Memory and the 1923 Greco-Turkish Population Exchange." *The Historical Review/La Revue Historique* 9 (2012): 199–232.

Andreadis, George. *Tamama – The Missing Girl of Pontos*. Athens: Gordios, 1993.

Apostolopoulos, F.D. and G. Mourelos, eds. *I Exodos* [The Exodus]. Athens: Kentro Mikrasiatikon Spoudon, 1980–82.

Atatürk, Kemal. *A Speech Delivered by Mustafa Kemal Atatürk 1927*. Istanbul: Ministry of Education Plant, 1963.

Auron, Yair. *The Banality of Denial: Israel and the Armenian Genocide*. New Brunswick and London: Transaction Publishers, 2003.

Avdela, E. "The Teaching of History in Greece." *Journal of Modern Greek Studies* 18 (2000): 239–53.

Barkan, Elazar. *The Guilt of Nations: Restitution and Negotiating Historical Injustices*. New York and London: W.W. Norton & Company, 2000.

Beaton, Roderick. *An Introduction to Modern Greek Literature*. 2nd ed. Oxford: Clarendon Press, 1999.

———. "Introduction." In *The Making of Modern Greece: Nationalism, Romanticism and the Uses of the Past (1797-1896)*, edited by R. Beaton and D. Ricks, 1–18. Farnham and London: Ashgate, 2009.

Beck, U. "The Cosmopolitan Society and its Enemies." *Theory, Culture and Society* 19, No. 1–2 (2002): 17–44.

Benz, W. "Holocaust Denial: Anti-Semitism as a Refusal to Accept Reality." *Historein* 11 (2011): 69–79, doi: 10.12681/historein.141.

Birden, Rana and Bahar Rumelili. "Rapprochement at the Grassroots: How Far Can Civil Society Engagement Go?" In *In the Long Shadow of Europe: Greeks and Turks in the Era of Postnationalism*, edited by O. Anastasakis, K. Nicolaidis and K. Öktem, 315–30. Leiden and Boston: Martinus Nijhoff Publishers, 2009.

Bjørnlund, M. "The 1914 Cleansing of Aegean Greeks as a Case of Violent Turkification." *Journal of Genocide Research* 10, no. 1 (2008): 41–57.

———. "Danish Sources on the Destruction of the Ottoman Greeks, 1914–1916." In *The Genocide of the Ottoman Greeks: Studies on the State-Sponsored Campaign of Extermination of the Christians of Asia Minor, 1912-1922 and Its Aftermath: History, Law, Memory*, edited by T. Hofmann, M. Bjørnlund and V. Meichanetsidis, 152–55. New York and Athens: Aristide D. Caratzas, 2011.

Bloxham, Donald. *The Great Game of Genocide: Imperialism, Nationalism, and the Destruction of the Ottoman Armenians*. Oxford: Oxford University Press, 2005.

Boura, Catherine. "The Greek Millet in Turkish Politics: Greeks in the Ottoman Parliament (1908-1914)." In *Ottoman Greeks in the Age of Nationalism: Politics, Economy, and Society in the Nineteenth Century*, edited by D. Gondicas and C. Issawi, 193–206. Princeton, NJ: The Darwin Press, 1999.

Browning, Christopher. *Ordinary Men: Reserve Police Battalion 101 and the Final Solution in Poland*. New York: HarperCollins, 1992.

Bruneau, Michel. "Les monastères pontiques en Macédoine. Marqueurs territoriaux de la diaspora." In *Les Grecs pontiques: Diaspora, identité, territoires*, edited by M. Bruneau, 213–228. Paris: CNRS Éditions, 1998.

Cajani, L. "Criminal Laws on History: The Case of the European Union." *Historein* 11 (2011): 19–48, doi: 10.12681/historein.138.

Chalk, Frank and Kurt Jonassohn. "Introduction." In *The History and Sociology of Genocide: Analysis and Case Studies*, edited by F. Chalk and K. Jonassohn, 3–5. New Haven, CT: Yale University Press, 1990.

Chang, Iris. *The Rape of Nanking: The Forgotten Holocaust of World War II*. New York: Basic Books, 1997.

Charalambidis, Michalis. *Ethnika Zitimata* [National Issues]. Athens: Irodotos, 1989.

———. "To Pontiako Zitima simera: I Genoktonia aitia tis Exodou kai tis diasporas" ["The Pontian Question Today: The Genocide as Cause of the Exodus and the Diaspora"]. In *B' Pagkosmio Synedrio Pontiakou Ellinismou* [2nd Global Congress of Pontian Hellenism], edited by P. Kaïsidis, 186–90. Thessaloniki: Lithografia, 1990.

———. *The Pontian Question in the United Nations*. 2nd ed. Thessaloniki: Pontian Society of Thessaloniki "Euxinos Leschi," 2009.

Charalambidis, M. and K. Fotiadis, eds. *Pontioi: Dikaioma sti mnimi* [Pontians: Right to Memory]. Athens: Gordios, 2003.

Charny, Israel W. "The Integrity and Courage to Recognize All the Victims of a Genocide." In *The Genocide of the Ottoman Greeks: Studies on the State-Sponsored Campaign of Extermination of the Christians of Asia Minor, 1912–1922 and Its Aftermath: History, Law, Memory*, edited by T. Hofmann, M. Bjørnlund and V. Meichanetsidis, 21–38. New York and Athens: Aristide D. Caratzas, 2011.

Clark, Bruce. *Twice a Stranger: The Mass Expulsions that Forged Modern Greece and Turkey*. Cambridge, MA: Harvard University Press, 2006.

Clogg, Richard. "The Greek *Millet* in the Ottoman Empire." In *Christians and Jews in the Ottoman Empire. The Functioning of a Plural Society. Volume 1. The Central Lands*, edited by B. Braude and B. Lewis, 185–207. London: Holmes & Meier, 1982.

———. *A Concise History of Greece*. 2nd ed. Cambridge: Cambridge University Press, 2002.

Conway, Martin. "The Greek Civil War: Greek Exceptionalism, or Mirror of a European Civil War?" In *The Greek Civil War: Essays on a Conflict of Exceptionalism and Silences*, edited by P. Carabott and T. Sfikas, 17–40. Aldershot: Ashgate, 2004.

Coufoudakis, Van. "The Reverse Influence Phenomenon: The Impact of the Greek-American Lobby on the Foreign Policy of Greece." In *Diasporas in World Politics: The Greeks in Comparative Perspective*, edited by D. Constas and A. Platias, 51–75. London: Macmillan, 1993.

Dadrian, V.N. "The Naim-Andonian Documents on the World War I Destruction of Ottoman Armenians: The Anatomy of a Genocide." *International Journal of Middle East Studies* 18, no. 3 (August 1986): 311–36.

Dadrian, Vahakn N. "Documentation of the Armenian Genocide in German and Austrian Sources." In *Genocide: A Critical Bibliographical Review*, vol. 2, edited by I.W. Charny and A.L. Berger, 77–125. New York: Facts on File, 1991.

———. *The History of the Armenian Genocide: Ethnic Conflict from the Balkans to Anatolia to the Caucasus*. Providence, RI: Berghahn Books, 1995.

———. *German Responsibility in the Armenian Genocide: A Review of the Historical Evidence of German Complicity*. Cambridge, MA: Blue Crane Books, 1996.

Danforth, Loring M. and Riki Van Boeschoten. *Children of the Greek Civil War: Refugees and the Politics of Memory*. Chicago and London: The University of Chicago Press, 2012.

Deltsou, Eleftheria. "Pontiakes mnimes, syllogoi kai politiki: I dimosia diamorfosi kai i simasia tis mnimis ton pontion prosfygon sti Thessaloniki tou 2000" ["Pontian Memories, Associations and Politics: The Public Formation and the Importance of Memory among Pontian Refugees in 2000 Thessaloniki"]. In *Prosfyges sta Valkania: Mnimi kai ensomatosi* [Refugees in the Balkans: Memory and Integration], edited by V. Gounaris and I. Michailidis, 253–85. Thessaloniki: Pataki, 2004.

Dietsch, Johan. *Making Sense of Suffering: Holocaust and Holodomor in Ukrainian Historical Culture*. Lund: Department of History, Lund University, 2006.

Dixon, J.M. "Education and National Narratives: Changing Representations of the Armenian Genocide in History Textbooks in Turkey." *The International Journal for Education, Law and Policy*, Special Issue on "Legitimation and Stability of Political Systems: The Contribution of National Narratives" (2010): 103–26.

Dobkin, Marjorie Housepian. *Smyrna 1922: The Destruction of a City*. 4th ed. New York: Newmark Press, 1998.

Dollis, Demetri. "Greeks Abroad." In *About Greece*, edited by A. Bacaloumis, 155–59. Athens: Hellenic Ministry of Press and Mass Media, Secretariat General of Information, 2004.

Doukas, Stratis. *Istoria enos aichmalotou* [A War Captive's Story]. 44th ed. Athens: Kedros, 2008.

Doulis, Thomas. *Disaster and Fiction: Modern Greek Fiction and the Asia Minor Disaster of 1922*. Berkeley and Los Angeles: University of California Press, 1977.

Doumanis, Nicholas. *Before the Nation: Muslim-Christian Coexistence and its Destruction in Late-Ottoman Anatolia*. Oxford: Oxford University Press, 2013.

Dragonas, Thalia and Anna Frangoudaki. "'Like a Bridge over Troubled Water': Reforming the Education of Muslim Minority Children in Greece." In *When Greeks and Turks Meet: Interdisciplinary Perspectives on the Relationship Since 1923*, edited by V. Lytra, 289–311. Farnham: Ashgate, 2014.

Dündar, Fuat. *Crime of Numbers: The Role of Statistics in the Armenian Question (1878–1918)*. New Brunswick and London: Transaction Publishers, 2010.

Enepekidis, Polychronis. "Oi diogmoi ton Ellinon tou Ponto (1908–1918)" ["The Persecutions of the Greeks of Pontos (1908-1918)"]. Athens: Syllogos Pontion "Argonautai-Komninoi," 1962.

———. *Oi diogmoi ton Evraion en Elladi 1941-1944: Epi ti vasei ton mystikon archeion ton ES-ES* [The Persecutions of the Jews in Greece 1941-1944: Based on the Secret Archives of SS]. Athens: Papazisis, 1969.

———. *To Olokautoma ton Evraion tis Ellados 1941-1944: Apo germanika kai ellinika archeia* [The Holocaust of the Jews of Greece: From German and Greek Archives]. Athens: Estia, 1996.

Epeoglou-Bakalaki, Eudokia. *I Amaseia* [Amasya]. Thessaloniki: Kyriakidi, 1988.

Exertzoglou, Ch. "Mnimi kai genoktonia: I anagnorisi tis 'Genoktonias tou Pontiakou kai Mikrasiatikou Ellinismou' apo to Elliniko Koinovoulio" ["Memory and Genocide: The Recognition of the 'Genocide of Pontian and Asia Minor Hellenism' by the Hellenic Parliament"]. *Historein* 4, 2003–2004, CD-ROM edition.

Exertzoglou, Charis. *Oi "chamenes patrides" pera apo ti nostalgia: Mia koinoniki-politismiki istoria ton Romion tis Othomanikis Autokratorias (mesi 19ou – arches 20ou aiona* [The "Lost Homelands" beyond Nostalgia: A Socio-cultural History of the Ottoman Empire Rum (mid 19th to early 20th century)"]. Athens: Nefeli, 2010.

———. "I istoria tis prosfygikis mnimis" ["The History of Refugee Memory"]. In *To 1922 kai oi prosfyges: Mia nea matia* [1922 and The Refugees: A New Perspective], edited by A. Liakos, 191–201. Athens: Nefeli, 2011.

Eyerman, Ron. "Cultural Trauma: Slavery and the Formation of African American Identity." In *Cultural Trauma and Collective Identity*, edited by J.C. Alexander, R. Eyerman, B. Giesen, N.J. Smelser and P. Sztompka, 69–78. Berkeley: University of California Press, 2004.

Fleming, Katherine E. *Greece: A Jewish History*. Princeton, NJ: Princeton University Press, 2008.

Fotiadis, Konstantinos. "Pareuxeinios Ellinismos" ["Black Sea Hellenism"]. In *Themata Istorias* [Issues of History], edited by M. Nystazopoulou-Pelekidou, E. Kofos, K. Ailianos, A. Alexandris, P. Kitromilides, P. Ioakeimidis, I. Hassiotis and K. Fotiadis, 217–61. Athens: OEDV, 2002.

———. *I Genoktonia ton Ellinon tou Pontou* [The Genocide of the Greeks of Pontos]. Athens: Idryma tis Voulis ton Ellinon gia ton Koinovouleutismo kai ti Dimokratia, 2004.

Frangoudaki, A. and T. Dragona, eds. *Ti ein' i patrida mas? Ethnokentrismos stin ekpaideusi* [What is our Fatherland? Ethnocentrism in Education]. Athens: Ekdoseis Alexandreia, 1997.

Gage, Nicholas. *Eleni*. New York: Random House, 1983.

Gallant, T. "Greek Exceptionalism and Contemporary Historiography: New Pitfalls and Old Debates." *Journal of Modern Greek Studies* 15, no. 2 (1997): 209–16.

Gaunt, David. *Massacres, Resistance, Protectors: Muslim-Christian Relations in Eastern Anatolia during World War I*. Piscataway, NJ: Gorgias Press, 2006.

Georgelin, H. "Perception of the Other's Fate: What Greek Orthodox Refugees from the Ottoman Empire Reported about the Destruction of Ottoman Armenians." *Journal of Genocide Research* 10, no. 1 (2008): 59–76.

Georgiadou, Vasiliki. "Right-Wing Populism and Extremism: The Rapid Rise of '*Golden Dawn*' in Crisis-Ridden Greece." In *Right-Wing Extremism in Europe: Country-Analyses, Counter-Strategies and Labor-Market Oriented Exit Strategies*, edited by R. Melzer and S. Serafin, 75–101. Berlin: Friedrich-Ebert-Stiftung, 2013.

Gieryn, T.F. "Boundary-Work and the Demarcation of Science from Non-science: Strains and Interests in Professional Ideologies of Scientists." *American Sociological Review* 48 (1983): 781–95.

Gikas, Anastasis. *Oi Ellines sti diadikasia oikodomisis tou sosialismou stin ESSD* [The Greeks in the Construction Process of Socialism in the USSR]. Athens: Sygchroni Epochi, 2007.

Gingeras, Ryan. *Sorrowful Shores: Violence, Ethnicity, and the End of the Ottoman Empire, 1912–1923*. Oxford: Oxford University Press, 2009.

Goldhagen, Daniel J. *Hitler's Willing Executioners: Ordinary Germans and the Holocaust*. New York: Knopf, 1996.

Gross, M. "To Teach the Holocaust in Poland: Understanding Teachers' Motivations to Engage the Painful Past." *Intercultural Education* 24, no. 1–2 (2013): 103–20.

Gunter, Michael M. *Armenian History and the Question of Genocide*. New York: Palgrave Macmillan, 2011.

Guttstadt, Corinna Görgü. "Depriving Non-Muslims of Citizenship as Part of the Turkification Policy in the Early Years of the Turkish Republic: The Case of Turkish Jews and its Consequences during the Holocaust." In *Turkey beyond Nationalism: Towards Post-National Identities*, edited by H-L. Kieser, 50–56. London and New York: I.B. Tauris, 2013.

Halbwachs, Maurice. *On Collective Memory*. Edited, translated and with an introduction by Lewis A. Coser. Chicago: University of Chicago Press, 1992.

Halo, Thea. *Not Even My Name: From a Death March in Turkey to a New Home in America, A Young Girl's True Story of Genocide and Survival*. New York: Picador, 2000.

———. "Report on the IAGS Greek/Assyrian Genocide Resolution: Where We Go From Here?" In *Three Genocides, One Strategy*, edited by A. Pavlidis, 109–15. Thessaloniki: Kyriakidi, 2008.

Hassiotis, Ioannis K. "The Armenian Genocide and the Greeks: Response and Records (1915–23)." In *The Armenian Genocide: History, Politics, Ethics*, edited by R. Hovannisian, 129–51. London: Macmillan, 1992.

Hatzidimitriou, C.G. "Distorting History: Concerning a Recent Article on Ethnic Identity in Greek Macedonia." *Balkan Studies* 32, no. 2 (1993): 315–51.

Hatzidimitriou, C.G., ed. *American Accounts Documenting the Destruction of Smyrna by the Kemalist Turkish Forces, September 1922*. New Rochelle, NY: Aristide D. Caratzas, 2005.

[Hatzidimitriou, Constantine, Harry Psomiades, Dan Georgakas and Ronald Levitsky] "The Genocide of the Ottoman Greeks 1914–1923: A Teaching Guide." Bloomingdale, IL: The Asia Minor and Pontos Hellenic Research Center, Inc., 2013.

Heraclides, Alexis. *The Greek-Turkish Conflict in the Aegean: Imagined Enemies*. Basingstoke: Palgrave Macmillan, 2010.

Hirschon, Renée. "History, Memory and Emotion: The Long-term Significance of the 1923 Greco-Turkish Exchange of Populations." In *When Greeks and Turks Meet: Interdisciplinary Perspectives on the Relationship Since 1923*, edited by V. Lytra, 23–44. Farnham: Ashgate, 2014.

Hofmann, Tessa. "Genoktonia en Roi – Cumulative Genocide: The Massacres and Deportations of the Greek Population of the Ottoman Empire (1912–1923)." In *The Genocide of the Ottoman Greeks: Studies on the State-Sponsored Campaign of Extermination of the Christians of Asia Minor, 1912-1922 and Its Aftermath: History,*

Law, Memory, edited by T. Hofmann, M. Bjørnlund and V. Meichanetsidis, 39–111. New York and Athens: Aristide D. Caratzas, 2011.

Hofmann, T., M. Bjørnlund and V. Meichanetsidis, eds. *The Genocide of the Ottoman Greeks: Studies on the State-Sponsored Campaign of Extermination of the Christians of Asia Minor, 1912-1922 and Its Aftermath: History, Law, Memory*. New York and Athens: Aristide D. Caratzas, 2011.

Hovannisian, R., ed. *Remembrance and Denial: The Case of the Armenian Genocide*. Detroit: Wayne State University Press, 1999.

Human Rights Watch. *Hate on the Streets: Xenophobic Violence in Greece*. July, 2012.

Issawi, Charles. "The Transformation of the Economic Positions of the Millets in the Nineteenth Century." In *Christians and Jews in the Ottoman Empire. The Functioning of a Plural Society. Volume 1. The Central Lands*, edited by B. Braude and B. Lewis, 261–85. London: Holmes & Meier, 1982.

———. "Introduction." In *Ottoman Greeks in the Age of Nationalism: Politics, Economy, and Society in the Nineteenth Century*, edited by D. Gondicas and C. Issawi, 1–16. Princeton, NJ: The Darwin Press, 1999.

Jones, Adam. *Genocide: A Comprehensive Introduction*. 2nd ed. London: Routledge, 2010.

Jones, A. "Diffusing Genocide Studies, Defusing Genocides." *Genocide Studies and Prevention* 6, no. 3 (December 2011): 270–78.

Judt, Tony. *Postwar: A History of Europe Since 1945*. 2nd ed. New York: Penguin Books, 2006.

Karakatsani, Despina. "The Macedonian Question in Greek History Textbooks." In *Clio in the Balkans: The Politics of History Education*, edited by C. Koulouri, 289–91. Thessaloniki: CDRSEE, 2002.

Karlsson, Klas-Göran. "The Holocaust as a Problem of Historical Culture: Theoretical and Analytical Challenges." In *Echoes of the Holocaust: Historical Cultures in Contemporary Europe*, edited by K-G Karlsson and U. Zander, 9–57. Lund: Nordic Academic Press, 2003.

———. *"De som är oskyldiga idag kan bli skyldiga imorgon": Det armeniska folkmordet och dess efterbörd* ["Those Who Are Innocent Today Might Become Guilty Tomorrow": The Armenian Genocide and its Aftermath]. Stockholm: Atlantis, 2012.

Karlsson, Maria. *Cultures of Denial: Comparing Holocaust and Armenian Genocide Denial*. Lund: Department of History, Lund University, 2015.

Karpat, Kemal. *Ottoman Population, 1830–1914: Demographic and Social Characteristics*. Madison: University of Wisconsin Press, 1985.

Kieser, Hans-Lukas and Kerem Öktem. "Introduction: Beyond Nationalism or Beyond Kemalism? Turkey as Seen From 2006 and 2012." In *Turkey beyond Nationalism: Towards Post-National Identities*, edited by H-L. Kieser, vii–xvii. 2nd ed. London and New York: I.B. Tauris, 2013.

Kitroeff, Alexander. "The Limits of Political Transnationalism: The Greek American Lobby 1970s-1990s." In *Greek Diaspora and Migration since 1700*, edited by D. Tziovas, 141–53. Farnham: Ashgate, 2009.

Kitromilides, P. and A. Alexandris. "Ethnic Survival, Nationalism and Forced Migration: The Historical Demography of the Greek Community of Asia Minor at the Close of the Ottoman Era." *Deltio Kentrou Mikrasiatikon Spoudon* 5 (1984–1985): 9–44.

Klein, K.L. "On the Emergence of Memory in Historical Discourse." *Representations* 69 (2000): 127–50.

Kokkinos, G. and P. Gatsotis. "The Deviation from the Norm: Greek History School Textbooks Withdrawn from Use in the Classroom since the 1980s." *International Textbook Research* 30 (2008): 535–46.

Kokkinos, Giorgos, Maria Vlachou, Vasiliki Sakka, Evangelia Kouneli, Angelourania Kostoglou and Stavros Papadopoulos. *Proseggizontas to Olokautoma sto elliniko scholeio* [Approaching the Holocaust in Greek schools]. Athens: Taxideutis, 2007.

Kostopoulos, Tasos. *Polemos kai ethnokatharsi: I xechasmeni pleura mias dekaetous ethnikis exormisis (1912–1922)* [War and Ethnic Cleansing: The Forgotten Side of a Ten Years Long National Campaign (1912–1922)]. 4th ed. Athens: Vivliorama, 2008.

Koulouri, C., ed. *Clio in the Balkans: The Politics of History Education in Southeast Europe*. Thessaloniki: CDRSEE, 2002.

Kuper, Leo. *Genocide: Its Political Use in the Twentieth Century*. London: Penguin Books, 1981.

Lemkin, Raphael. *Axis Rule in Occupied Europe: Laws of Occupation, Analysis of Government, Proposals for Redress*. Washington: Carnegie Endowment for International Peace, Division of international law, 1944.

Levene, M. "Creating a Modern 'Zone of Genocide': The Impact of Nation-and State-Formation on Eastern Anatolia, 1878–1923." *Holocaust and Genocide Studies* 12, no. 3 (Winter 1998): 393–433.

Levene, Mark. *Genocide in the Age of the Nation-State. Volume I: The Meaning of Genocide*. 2nd ed. London and New York: I.B. Tauris, 2008.

Levitsky, Ronald. *The Pontian Greek Genocide: A Teaching Unit*. Chicago: Pontian Society of Chicago "Xeniteas," 2006.

———. "Teaching the Greek Genocide." In *The Genocide of the Ottoman Greeks: Studies on the State-Sponsored Campaign of Extermination of the Christians of Asia Minor, 1912–1922 and Its Aftermath: History, Law, Memory*, edited by T. Hofmann, M. Bjørnlund and V. Meichanetsidis, 341–49. New York and Athens: Aristide D. Caratzas, 2011.

Levy, Daniel and Natan Sznaider. *The Holocaust and Memory in the Global Age*. Translated by Assenka Oksiloff. Philadelphia, PA: Temple University Press, 2006.

———. *Human Rights and Memory*. University Park, PA: The Pennsylvania University Press, 2010.

Lewis, Bernard. *The Emergence of Modern Turkey*. London, 1961.

Lewy, Guenter. *The Armenian Massacres in Ottoman Turkey: A Disputed Genocide*. Salt Lake City: The University of Utah Press, 2005.

Liakos, Antonis. "Eisagogi" ["Introduction"]. In *To 1922 kai oi prosfyges: Mia nea matia* [1922 and The Refugees: A New Perspective], edited by A. Liakos, 11–23. Athens: Nefeli, 2011.

MacDonald, David B. *Identity Politics in the Age of Genocide: The Holocaust and Historical Representation*. London and New York: Routledge, 2008.

Malkidis, Theofanis. *Ethnikes kai diethneis diastaseis tou Pontiakou Zitimatos* [National and International Dimensions of the Pontian Question]. Athens: Gordios, 2006.

———. *I genoktonia ton Ellinon tou Pontou: Istoria, politiki kai anagnorisi* [The Genocide of the Greeks of Pontos: History, Politics and Recognition]. Athens: Gordios, 2008.

Marantzidis, Nikos. *Yasasin Millet/Zito to Ethnos. Prosfygia, katochi kai emfylios: Ethnotiki tautotita kai politiki symperifora stous tourkofonous ellinorthodoxous tou dytikou kosmou* [Long Live the Nation. Refugeehood, Occupation and Civil War: Ethnic Identity and Political Behavior among Greek-Orthodox Turkish-Speakers of the Western World]. Iraklio: Panepistimiakes Ekdoseis Kritis, 2001.

Margaritis, Giorgos. *Anepithymitoi sympatriotes: Stoicheia gia tin katastrofi ton meionotiton stin Ellada* [Unwanted Countrymen: Facts about the Destruction of the Minorities in Greece]. Athens: Vivliorama, 2005.

Martis, Nikolaos. *The Falsification of Macedonian History*. Translated by John Philip Smith. Athens: Euroekdotiki, 1984.

Mavrogordatos, George Th. "The 1940s between Past and Future." In *Greece at the Crossroads: The Civil War and Its Legacy*, edited by J.O. Iatrides and L. Wrigley, 30–47. University Park: The Pennsylvania State University Press, 1995.

Mavroskoufis, D.K. "Memory, Forgetting, and History Education in Greece: The Case of Greek Jews' History as an Example of Catastrophe Didactics." *International Journal of Humanities and Social Science* 2, no. 18 (October 2012): 55–64.

Mazower, Mark. *Salonica – City of Ghosts: Christians, Muslims and Jews 1430–1950.* London: HarperCollins, 2004.

McCarthy, J. "Greek Statistics on the Ottoman Greek Population." *International Journal of Turkish Studies* 1, no. 2 (1980): 66–76.

McCarthy, Justin. *Muslims and Minorities: The Population of Anatolia and the End of the Empire.* New York: New York University Press, 1983.

Melson, Robert F. *Revolution and Genocide: On the Origins of the Armenian Genocide and the Holocaust.* Chicago: The University of Chicago Press, 1992.

Michas, Takis. *Unholy Alliance: Greece and Milošević's Serbia.* College Station: Texas A&M University Press, 2002.

Milton, Giles. *Paradise Lost. Smyrna 1922: The Destruction of Islam's City of Tolerance.* London: Sceptre, 2008.

Morgenthau, Henry. *Ambassador Morgenthau's Story.* Garden City, NY: Doubleday, Page & Company, 1918.

Moses, A. Dirk. "Holocaust and Genocide." In *The Historiography of the Holocaust*, edited by D. Stone, 533–55. Basingstoke and New York: Palgrave MacMillan, 2004.

Moskos, Charles C. "Greek American Studies." In *Reading Greek America: Studies in the Experience of Greeks in the United States*, edited by S.D. Orfanos, 23–62. New York: Pella, 2002.

Mourelos, J. "The 1914 Persecutions and the First Attempt at an Exchange of Minorities between Greece and Turkey." *Balkan Studies* 26, no. 2 (1986): 389–413.

Mowitt, J. "Trauma Envy." *Cultural Critique*, 46 (Autumn 2000): 272–97.

Naimark, Norman M. *Fires of Hatred: Ethnic Cleansing in Twentieth-Century Europe.* Cambridge, MA: Harvard University Press, 2001.

———. *Stalin's Genocides.* Princeton and Oxford: Princeton University Press, 2010.

Nielsen, C.A. "Surmounting the Myopic Focus on Genocide: The Case of the War in Bosnia and Herzegovina." *Journal of Genocide Research* 15, no. 1 (2013): 21–39, doi: 10.1080/14623528.2012.759397.

Nora, Pierre. "General Introduction: Between Memory and History." In *Realms of Memory: Rethinking the French Past*, vol. 1, edited by P. Nora and L.D. Kritzman, 1–20. Translated by Arthur Goldhammer. New York: Columbia University Press, 1996.

Nora, P. "History, Memory and the Law in France, 1990–2010." *Historein* 11 (2011): 10–13, doi:10.12681/historein.136.

Novick, Peter. *The Holocaust in American Life.* Boston: Houghton Mifflin, 1999.

Olick, Jeffrey K. *The Politics of Regret: On Collective Memory and Historical Responsibility.* New York: Routledge, 2007.

Özkan, Behlül. *From the Abode of Islam to the Turkish Vatan: The Making of a National Homeland in Turkey.* New Haven and London: Yale University Press, 2012.

Özkirimli, Umut and Spyros A. Sofos. *Tormented by History: Nationalism in Greece and Turkey.* London: Hurst & Company, 2008.

Panourgiá, Neni. *Dangerous Citizens: The Greek Left and the Terror of the State.* New York: Fordham University Press, 2009.

Pappas, Takis S. *Populism and Crisis Politics in Greece.* Basingstoke: Palgrave Macmillan, 2014.

Peckham, Robert Shannan. *National Histories, Natural States: Nationalism and the Politics of Place in Greece*. London and New York: I.B. Tauris, 2001.

Pentzopoulos, Dimitri. *The Balkan Exchange of Minorities and Its Impact Upon Greece*. Paris and The Hague: Mouton & Co, 1962.

Power, Samantha. *"A Problem from Hell": America and the Age of Genocide*. New York: HarperCollins, 2002.

Psyroukis, Nikos. *I mikrasiatiki katastrofi: I engys Anatoli meta ton Proto Pagkosmio Polemo* [The Asia Minor Catastrophe: The Near East after World War I]. Athens: Epikairotita, 1982.

Repoussi, M. "Politics Questions History Education: Debates on Greek History Textbooks." *International Society for History Didactics Yearbook* (2006/2007): 99–110.

Rodakis, Periklis. "Prologos stin elliniki ekdosi" ["Preface to the Greek Edition"]. In Diarkes dikastirio ton laon, *To egklima tis siopis: I genoktonia ton Armenion* [A Crime of Silence: The Armenian Genocide].Translated by Gianna Kourtovik and Sifis Kassessian, 7–31. Athens: Irodotos, 1988.

Roudometof, Victor and Anna Karpathakis. "Greek Americans and Transnationalism: Religion, Class and Community." In *Communities across Borders: New Immigrants and Transnational Cultures*, edited by P. Kennedy and V. Roudometof, 41–54. London: Routledge, 2002.

Rüsen, Jörn. "Holocaust Memory and Identity Building: Metahistorical Considerations in the Case of (West) Germany." In *Disturbing Remains: Memory, History and Crisis in the Twentieth Century*, edited by M.S. Roth and C.G. Salas, 252–70. Los Angeles: The Getty Research Institute, 2001.

Schaller, D.J. "From Lemkin to Clooney: The Development and State of Genocide Studies." *Genocide Studies and Prevention* 6, no. 3 (December 2011): 245–56.

Schaller, D.J. and J. Zimmerer. "Late Ottoman Genocides: The Dissolution of the Ottoman Empire and Young Turkish Population and Extermination Policies – Introduction." *Journal of Genocide Research* 10, no. 1 (2008): 7–14.

Shaw, Martin. *What is Genocide?* Cambridge and Malden: Polity Press, 2007.

Shirinian, G.N., ed. *The Asia Minor Catastrophe and the Ottoman Greek Genocide: Essays on Asia Minor, Pontos and Eastern Thrace*. Bloomingdale, IL: The Asia Minor and Pontos Hellenic Research Center, 2012.

Sjöberg, Erik. *Battlefields of Memory: The Macedonian Conflict and Greek Historical Culture*. Umeå: Umeå University, 2011.

Smith, Michael Llewellyn. *Ionian Vision: Greece in Asia Minor 1919–1922*. London: Hurst & Co, 1998.

Smith, R.W., E. Markusen and R.J. Lifton. "Professional Ethics and the Denial of Armenian Genocide." *Holocaust and Genocide Studies* 9, no. 3 (1995): 1–22.

Snyder, Timothy.*Bloodlands: Europe between Hitler and Stalin*. New York: Basic Books, 2012.

Sotiriou, Dido. *Farewell Anatolia*. Translated by Fred A. Reed. Athens: Kedros, 1991.

Spanomanolis, Christos. *Aichmalotoi ton Tourkon* [Prisoners of the Turks]. Athens: Estia, 1956.

Stamatopoulos, Dimitris. "I mikrasiatiki ekstrateia: I anthropogeografia tis katastrofis" ["The Asia Minor Campaign: The Human Geography of the Disaster"]. In *To 1922 kai oi prosfyges: Mia nea matia* [1922 and The Refugees: A New Perspective], edited by A. Liakos, 55–99. Athens: Nefeli, 2011.

Stefanidis, Ioannis. *Stirring the Greek Nation: Political Culture, Irredentism and Anti-Americanism in Greece, 1945–1967*. Aldershot: Ashgate, 2007.

Strom, Adam. "Teaching about the Armenian Genocide." In *The Armenian Genocide: Cultural and Ethical Legacies*, edited by R. Hovannisian, 239–44. New Brunswick and London: Transaction Publishers, 2007.

Ternon, Yves. "Freedom and Responsibility of the Historian." In *Remembrance and Denial: The Case of the Armenian Genocide*, edited by R. Hovannisian, 237–48. Detroit: Wayne State University Press, 1998.

Totten, S. "The State and Future of Genocide Studies and Prevention: An Overview and Analysis of Some Key Issues." *Genocide Studies and Prevention* 6, no. 3 (December 2011): 211–30.

Toynbee, Arnold. *The Western Question in Greece and Turkey: A Study in the Contact of Civilisations*. Boston and New York: Houghton Mifflin Company, 1922.

Travis, H. "Native Christians Massacred: The Ottoman Genocide of the Assyrians during World War I." *Genocide and Prevention* 1, no. 3 (2006): 327–71.

Travis, Hannibal. "Constructing the 'Armenian Genocide': How Scholars Unremembered the Assyrian and Greek Genocides in the Ottoman Empire." In *Hidden Genocides: Power, Knowledge, Memory*, edited by A. Laban Hinton, T. La Pointe and D. Irvin-Erickson, 170–92. New Brunswick and London: Rutgers University Press, 2013.

Tsangas, Nikos. *I athoosi ton ex kai i anatropi tis Istorias* [The Acquittal of the Six and the Reversal of History]. Athens: Govostis, 2012.

Tsolakides, Jordan A. *Hellenism Abroad – A Continuous Struggle to Maintain Its Ethnicity: Is It Destined to Oblivion?* Thessaloniki: Kyriakidi, 2006.

Tsirkinidis, Charis. *Synoptiki istoria tis genoktonias ton Ellinon tis Anatolis* [Concise History of the Genocide against the Greeks of the East]. Thessaloniki: Kyriakidi, 2009.

Üngör, Uğur Ümit. *The Making of Modern Turkey: Nation and State in Eastern Anatolia, 1913–1950*. Oxford: Oxford University Press, 2011.

———. "Paramilitary Violence in the Collapsing Ottoman Empire." In *War in Peace: Paramilitary Violence in Europe after the Great War*, edited by R. Gerwarth and J. Horne, 164–83. Oxford: Oxford University Press, 2012.

Valavanis, Georgios. *Sygchronos geniki istoria tou Pontou* [Modern General History of Pontos]. Athens: Pamprosfygiki, 1925.

Vallianatos, E. "Review: The Genocide of the Ottoman Greeks: Studies on the State-Sponsored Campaign of Extermination of the Christians of Asia Minor (1912–1922), and Its Aftermath; History, Law, Memory/The History of Greece." *Mediterranean Quarterly* 24, no. 4 (2013): 111–15.

Varon-Vassard, Odette. *I anadysi mias dyskolis mnimis: Keimena gia ti genoktonia ton Evraion* [The Emergence of a Difficult Memory: Essays on the Jewish Genocide]. Athens: Estia, 2012.

Vartanian, Nicole E. "'No Mandate Left Behind'? Genocide Education in the Era of High-Stakes Testing." In *The Armenian Genocide: Cultural and Ethical Legacies*, edited by R. Hovannisian, 229–38. New Brunswick and London: Transaction Publishers, 2007.

Venezis, Ilias. *To noumero 31328* [Number 31328]. Athens: Estia, 1931.

Veremis, Thanos. "The Hellenic Kingdom and the Ottoman Greeks: The Experiment of the 'Society of Constantinople.'" In *Ottoman Greeks in the Age of Nationalism: Politics, Economy, and Society in the Nineteenth Century*, edited by D. Gondicas and C. Issawi, 181–91. Princeton, NJ: The Darwin Press, 1999.

Vergeti, Maria. *Apo ton Ponto stin Ellada: Diadikasies diamorfosis mias Ethnotopikis Tautotitas* [From Pontos to Greece: Formation Processes of an Ethno-regional Identity]. 2nd ed. Thessaloniki: Kyriakidi, 2000.

Voutira, E. "Post-Soviet Diaspora Politics: The Case of the Soviet Greeks." *Journal of Modern Greek Studies* 24 (2006): 379–414.

Willert, Trine Stauning. *New Voices in Greek Orthodox Thought: Untying the Bond between Nation and Religion*. Farnham: Ashgate, 2014.

Winter, Jay. *Remembering War: The Great War between Memory and History in the Twentieth Century*. New Haven and London: Yale University Press, 2006.

Winter, Jay and Antoine Prost. *The Great War in History: Debates and Controversies, 1914 to the Present*. Cambridge: Cambridge University Press, 2005.

Yoshida, Takashi. *The Making of the "Rape of Nanking": History and Memory in Japan, China, and the United States*. Oxford and New York: Oxford University Press, 2006.

Zürcher, Erik J. *Turkey: A Modern History*. 3rd ed. London: I.B. Tauris, 2009.

———. *The Young Turk Legacy and Nation Building: From the Ottoman Empire to Atatürk's Turkey*. London: I.B. Tauris, 2010.

INDEX

War and Genocide

General Editors: Omer Bartov, Brown University; A. Dirk Moses, European University Institute, Florence, Italy / University of Sydney

In recent years there has been a growing interest in the study of war and genocide, not from a traditional military history perspective, but within the framework of social and cultural history. This series offers a forum for scholarly works that reflect these new approaches.

"The Berghahn series Studies on War and Genocide *has immeasurably enriched the English-language scholarship available to scholars and students of genocide and, in particular, the Holocaust."* —**Totalitarian Movements and Political Religions**

Milton Keynes UK
Ingram Content Group UK Ltd.
UKHW021835160824
447053UK00020B/252